Software Engineering with Ada

Third Edition

The Benjamin/Cummings Series in Object-Oriented Software Engineering

Grady Booch, Series Editor

Booch, *Object-Oriented Analysis and Design with Applications, Second Edition* (1994)

Booch, *Object Solutions: A Sourcebook for Developers* (1994)

Booch/Bryan, *Software Engineering with Ada, Third Edition* (1994)

Collins, *Designing Object-Oriented User Interfaces* (1995)

LaLonde, *Discovering Smalltalk* (1994)

Pohl, *Object-Oriented Programming Using C++* (1993)

Other Titles of Interest

Booch, *Software Components with Ada: Structures, Tools, and Subsystems* (1987)

Fischer/LeBlanc, *Crafting a Compiler in C* (1991)

Gonzalez, *Ada Programmer's Handbook and Language Reference Manual* (1991)

Kelley/Pohl, *A Book on C, Second Edition* (1990)

Kelley/Pohl, *C by Dissection: The Essentials of C Programming, Second Edition* (1992)

Miller/Petersen, *File Structures with Ada* (1990)

Pohl, *C++ for C Programmers* (1994)

Savitch/Petersen, *Ada: An Introduction to the Art and Science of Programming* (1992)

Sebesta, *Concepts of Programming Languages, Second Edition* (1993)

Sobell, *A Practical Guide to the Unix System, Third Edition* (1994)

Weiss, *Data Structures and Algorithm Analysis in Ada* (1992)

Software Engineering with Ada

Third Edition

Grady Booch
Rational, Santa Clara, California

Doug Bryan
Stanford University

with the collaboration of
Charles G. Petersen
Mississippi State University

The Benjamin/Cummings Publishing Company, Inc.

Redwood City, California • Menlo Park, California
Reading, Massachusetts • New York
Don Mills, Ontario • Wokingham, U.K. • Amsterdam
Bonn • Sydney • Tokyo • Madrid • San Juan

Executive Editor	*Dan Joraanstad*
Production Editor	*Wendy Earl*
Editorial Assistant	*Melissa Standen*
Text Designer	*David Granville Healy/First Image*
Cover Designer	*Yvo Riezebos Design*
Copy Editor	*Rebecca Pepper*
Illustrator	*David Granville Healy/First Image*
Proofreader	*David Rich/Edit San Jose*
Compositor	*First Image*
Indexer	*Elinor Lindheimer*

Library of Congress Cataloging-in-Publication Data

Booch, Grady
    Software engineering with Ada / Grady Booch, Doug Bryan, with the
collaboration of Charles G. Peterson. — 3rd ed.
        p. cm. — (The Benjamin/Cummings series in object-oriented
software engineering)
    Includes bibliographical references and index.
    ISBN 0-8053-0608-0
    1. Ada (Computer program language)   2. Software engineering.
I. Bryan, Douglas L.   II. Petersen, Charles G.   III. Title.
IV. Series.
QA76.73.A35B66   1994
005. 13' 3—dc20   93-5093
                                                                                   CIP

ISBN 0-8053-0608-0

1 2 3 4 5 6 7 8 9 10–AL–97 96 95 94 93

The Benjamin/Cummings Publishing Company, Inc.
390 Bridge Parkway
Redwood City, California 94065

CONTENTS

**Data
Structures**   **73**

**Algorithms
and Control**   **149**

PACKAGE 6

Systems Development   373

PREFACE

Software Engineering with Ada

Ada is a general-purpose programming language with considerable expressive power. It was developed at the initiative of the United States Department of Defense in response to the crisis in software development. Ada was designed specifically for the domain of large, real-time, embedded computer systems, although it will certainly have an impact on many other applications areas.

Unlike most other production high-order languages, such as FORTRAN, COBOL, or even Pascal, Ada not only embodies many modern software development principles but also enforces them. The greatest benefits in this common high-order language effort will thus be gained from the application of good software development methods that are facilitated by using Ada as the language of expression. As a result, the introduction of Ada represents a tremendous opportunity for improvement in the clarity, reliability, efficiency, and maintainability of software systems.

Ada is more than just another programming language, however. Along with the Ada Programming Support Environment, it represents a very powerful facility that helps us understand problems and express their solutions in a manner that directly reflects the multidimensional real world.

The Third Edition of *Software Engineering with Ada*

Ada has truly entered the mainstream of computer science. The third edition of this book was written in response to the language's growing use and to reflect the changing methods of problem solving. The third edition is, if you will excuse the pun, a repackaging of the second edition. Chapters have been combined, rewritten, and rearranged to better reflect today's way of thinking. This edition includes expanded code segments with more complete programs written in a more modern style. Most importantly, this third edition retains an emphasis on Ada's effective use in a software engineering context.

This book thus serves as a complete Ada reference that is appropriate for both the programmer who wishes to create Ada systems and the manager who needs to understand how to apply this powerful tool. The book presumes an understanding of the basic principles of programming.

Goals

This book is not just another introduction to Ada. It has been written to satisfy three specific goals:

- To provide an intensive study of Ada's features

- To motivate and provide examples of good Ada design and programming

- To introduce an object-oriented development method that exploits the power of Ada and, in addition, helps manage the complexity of large software systems

In short, this book not only describes the details of Ada programming, but also suggests ways in which to best apply the features of the language in the creation of software systems.

Content Features

Structure Many texts present the details of a programming language only from a syntactic or semantic perspective. In this book, we start with a software design approach and then introduce Ada from the top down in the context of good programming methods.

The book is divided into six packages, each of which contains three to four logically related chapters. The first package begins with a brief look at the Ada problem domain, and includes an examination of Ada's development history to provide a perspective on some of the features of the language. The primary objective of this package is to discuss the principles of software engineering as it relates to object-oriented development. Package 1 concludes with an overview of the language.

The second package contains the first two of five design problems (one of which is revisited and expanded later), as well as a discussion of abstract data types, and details of the data types provided in the Ada language.

The third through the sixth packages provide a detailed presentation of Ada built around five complete design examples. Each problem is increasingly more complex, and together they require the application of almost every Ada feature. In addition, these problems provide a vehicle for demonstrating the object-oriented development method, along with a programming style that emphasizes understandability. The chapters encompassing these five large examples present a detailed discussion of Ada's constructs. The sixth package also includes a discussion of the problems associated with very large programming systems and presents the last of the design problems.

Resources A set of exercises for students is provided at the end of most of the chapters. Difficult problems are marked with a star (*). In addition, the book concludes with six appendices that provide further technical details of Ada. The lettering of the appendices is arranged to more closely align with the LRM (Language Reference Manual). The first three describe the predefined elements of the language, and the specification for all predefined packages including those associated with all aspects of input and output. The next two appendices contain a summary style guide and comprehensive, easy-to-read, alphabetized syntax charts. The last appendix previews Ada 9X, including the major proposed changes to the language, such as:

- Full implementation of object-oriented run-time polymorphism

- Tree structure subunit library for easier management of large programming systems

- Improvements in real-time problem-solving mechanisms

- Annexes to the language for special problem areas

Course Organization This is a "generic" book in the sense that it can be used at a number of levels. Using the second edition, the material has been taught in a one-semester course (40 one-hour lessons), as a five-day seminar, and as a four-week, all-day intensive program. The following outline represents the organization of materials from this third edition with the same goals in mind.

Lesson 1	Chapter 1:	Introduction
Lessons 2–3	Chapter 2:	Software Engineering
Lessons 4–5	Chapter 3:	Object-Oriented Design
Lessons 6–8	Chapter 4:	An Overview of the Language
Lesson 9	Chapter 5:	The First Design Problem: Document Concordance
Lessons 10–12	Chapter 6:	Data Abstraction and Ada's Types
Lesson 13	Chapter 7:	The Second Design Problem: Data Base System
Lessons 14–16	Chapter 8:	Subprograms
Lessons 17–18	Chapter 9:	Expressions and Statements
Lesson 19	Chapter 10:	The Second Design Problem: Continued
Lessons 20–21	Chapter 11:	Packages
Lessons 22–23	Chapter 12:	Generic Program Units
Lesson 24	Chapter 13:	The Third Design Problem: Generic Tree Package
Lessons 25–27	Chapter 14:	Tasks
Lessons 28–29	Chapter 15:	Exception Handling
Lessons 30–31	Chapter 16:	Machine Representations
Lesson 32	Chapter 17:	The Fourth Design Problem: Environment Monitoring
Lessons 33–34	Chapter 18:	Input/Output
Lessons 35–36	Chapter 19:	The Software Life Cycle with Ada
Lessons 37–38	Chapter 20:	Programming in the Large
Lesson 39	Chapter 21:	The Fifth Design Problem: Heads-Up Display
Lesson 40	Appendix F:	Ada 9X

In addition, the following structure is appropriate as a brief introduction to the application of Ada for program managers:

Block 1	Chapter 1:	Introduction
Block 2	Chapter 2:	Software Engineering
	Chapter 19:	The Software Life Cycle with Ada
Block 3	Chapter 3:	Object-Oriented Design
	Chapter 4:	An Overview of the Language
Block 4	Chapter 21:	The Fifth Design Problem: Heads-Up Display
	Chapter 20:	Programming in the Large
	Appendix F:	Ada 9X

Reliability The *Reference Manual for the Ada Programming Language* was issued jointly by the Department of Defense as a military standard and by the American National Standards Institute as ANSI/MIL-STD-1815A, on February 17, 1983. All material in this book meets that standard. To ensure their accuracy, all of the design examples and code fragments in the book have been tested using a validated Ada compiler.

The Author Team

This edition is the result of the cooperative efforts of three people: Grady Booch, Doug Bryan, and Charles G. Petersen. The combined efforts of these three authors and teachers have influenced many thousands of programmers and managers over the past 10 years.

Grady Booch, a recognized expert in Ada, has taught at the United States Air Force Academy and has conducted seminars throughout the United States and in Europe. He has presented the technical details of the language to groups at a number of levels—undergraduates, graduate students, nonprogrammers, professional programmers, and program managers. Through this experience, he has tested various methods of presenting language features, observed their successes and failures, and heard the real needs of practicing software developers.

Doug Bryan, from Stanford University, has become a household name in the Ada community and is considered an "Ada lawyer" by many. He has gained this notoriety through the "Dear Ada" column that is a regular feature of Ada Letters, published bimonthly by the Association of Computer Machinery's Special Interest Group for Ada (SIGADA).

Charles G. Petersen, a professor at Mississippi State University with degrees in engineering and computer science, has 10 years of engineering experience and over 20 years of teaching experience at the university level. He has been involved in teaching Ada for 10 years and has published three other Ada textbooks, including *Ada: Introduction to Art and Science of Programming* with Walter J. Savitch, and *File Structures with Ada* with Nancy E. Miller.

Acknowledgments

We wish to thank a number of people who helped us during the preparation of this manuscript. Charles Petersen has played a very valuable role in bringing this project to a close and in preparing the manuscript for production, and we wish to especially acknowledge his contribution.

We also want to thank the many reviewers who provided us with guidance during this edition as well as in the earlier editions. They include Russell Abbott, Gayle Adams, Christine Ausnit, Jack Beidler, Ben Brosogol, Kenneth Bowles, Doug Bryan, Luwanna Clever, John Cupak, Larry Druffel, Michael Feldman, Gerry Fisher, John Foreman, Ray Ford, Dean Gonzalez, John Goodenough, Samuel S. Harbaugh, Hal Hart, Edward Lamie, Akhtar Lodger, Charles McKay, Mike Murphy, Elliott Organick, Carol Righini, Bryan Scharr, James Schnelker, Larry Schwartz, Sally Shepherd, Robert Shock, John Showalter, and John Warner.

PACKAGE

1

Introducing Software Engineering with Ada

And the Lord said, Behold, the people is one, and they have all one language; and this they begin to do: and now nothing will be restrained from them, which they have imagined to do.

Genesis 11:6
King James Version

CHAPTER

1

Introduction

The Software Crisis
The Ada Culture

By nature, we are tool makers and tool users. If we examine the evolution of various human endeavors, we can often point out times of revolution that were triggered by the use of a new and more powerful social or scientific tool. Clearly, the introduction of the written word, followed by the introduction of the televised word, altered the very fabric of our civilization. The tools of medicine, such as the microscope and the X-ray machine, have saved many lives, and the tools of the artist, including the guitar and the paintbrush, have enriched many more. In each situation, we created or refined a given tool to meet a particular need. Furthermore, each tool made some activities more efficient and often enabled us to do things that were once beyond our capabilities.

Compared with other fields of study, computer science is a very young discipline. It has had its revolutions, which roughly parallel what we call the *generations* of computer hardware, each made possible by the tools of the computer architect. These tools include the vacuum tube, the transistor, and now the integrated circuit. However, as Dijkstra stated in his Turing Award Lecture, the capability of our hardware tools has grown to far exceed our ability to manage them [1].

Our computers make some things more efficient and have opened areas of application that were once impossible to contemplate. Correspondingly, we have developed software tools to help us solve problems and control our machines, but many of these tools still do not help us cope with the complexity of our solutions. Thus, software development is no longer a labor-saving activity; it is labor intensive instead. We generally refer to this condition as *the software crisis.*

1.1   The Software Crisis

As we shall discuss, the symptoms of the software crisis "appear in the form of software that is nonresponsive to user needs, unreliable, excessively expensive, untimely, inflexible, difficult to maintain, and not reusable" [2]. The past several decades are littered with software-related projects that have failed or that are still just limping along (a condition we call *software rot).* Only recently have we even begun to understand the complexities of large software systems and how to manage their development. For too long, we have depended upon our software wizardry to get us through our problems. Dependence on programming to mitigate the fundamental limitations of hardware or software design is called *hacking.*

To solve the underlying problems of our crisis, we must now take a disciplined approach to software development in the form of proper software development methods. However, methods alone are not sufficient to confront the software crisis. We must also have a proper vehicle to express and execute our designs in the form of a program language.

The most popular languages, FORTRAN and COBOL, were created early in the history of computer science, long before the problems of massive software-intensive system development were understood. As a result, such languages do not reflect modern software engineering principles, and we have had to compromise them with preprocessors, extensions, and management controls to force them to fit more recent methods. In a sense, these languages constrain our way of thinking about a problem to a manner that is primarily sequential and imperative; we call this condition the *von Neumann mind-set.*

Furthermore, these language tools were created at a time when problems were simple in comparison with today's applications. FORTRAN was designed for scientific applications, COBOL for business applications, and today they are still quite suitable for their particular problem domain. However, subsequent to the development of these languages, many larger application areas have emerged, including embedded systems and real-time control systems.

Neither FORTRAN, nor COBOL, nor most other programming languages were designed for these problem domains. Yet we still see projects using COBOL for real-time processing or FORTRAN for multitasking applications involving hundreds of thousands of lines of code. No wonder the software crisis is upon us. The methods and languages we have been using are archaic and are being used for other than their intended purposes.

Developing software systems is an activity that demands much intellectual capacity. Completing an efficient, reliable, maintainable, and understandable system on time is often an even more herculean task, especially in the case of large, real-time programming projects. The professional who creates such systems must have a dual nature as a scientist/artist.

On the one hand, the programmer is a scientist in the sense that he or she works from a base of formal theory and a set of applied principles. For example, the programmer may employ software techniques such as structured analysis and object-oriented design or the mathematical concepts of queuing theory and numerical analysis. On the other hand, the programmer is also an artist who sculpts the components of a system from the raw materials of data structures and algorithms and then combines the pieces to form a whole. This dualism is perhaps what makes computer science so challenging; it also causes many problems.

Ours is a relatively new discipline, and Hoare believes we have as yet failed to develop a large body of common professional knowledge [3]. Instead, we too often rely upon our artistry to carry us through our computer problems. Often, this artistry is not sufficient in helping us cope with the complexities of our large software systems developments; we find ourselves in the software crisis.

The Nature of the Crisis

It is a cliché to say there is a software crisis [4]. For one thing, it is something we have lived with for a long time. As such, it is more of a persistent characteristic than a temporary crisis. However, the first public recognition of the existence of this "crisis" did not appear until the International Conference on Software Engineering at Garmisch, West Germany, in 1968 [5].

In a sense, the essence of the software crisis is simply that it is much more difficult to build software systems than our intuition tells us it should be. After all, aren't we just throwing together some symbols that tell our computers what to do? Experience shows us that the world is much more complex than that.

In formal computer science education, we can build systems consisting of several hundred lines of code and feel confident that we fully understand the entire project. Modifying such software is not difficult, since we can probably remember the structure of its design for several days after completing our first version. If our testing uncovers major problems, we could even easily start over.

However, designing and implementing systems consisting of tens of thousands, if not millions, of lines of code is quite a different matter. The effort required to complete such a system is clearly beyond the intellectual and physical capacity of one person. When we then add more people to the project to share the effort we introduce communication and coordination problems that multiply our woes. Modifying such a system is difficult, since usually no one person understands its complete structure; we must instead refer to that old dinosaur, external documentation, which always seems to be weeks behind the actual design work. If testing uncovers major problems, we usually do not have the luxury (or the time or money) to redesign the entire system.

Every programmer who works on massive, software-intensive systems has felt the joy of creative problem solving turn to frustration as unexpected glitches develop. If you ask that developer to tell you what the basic problem was, you may get varying answers, such as "that module had a strange side effect" or "the interface was not defined very well." As we shall see, these are really just symptoms of the underlying problems. In general, these symptoms all lead to software systems that are late, expensive, unreliable, and often in disagreement with their specifications. These, then, are the more visible effects of the software crisis.

At an intuitive level, we recognize that we have software problems, but it is difficult to grasp their full impact. As David Fisher has said, "Although there are many widely recognized symptoms, the underlying problems are not well delineated and there are few useful quantitative measures for assessing either the importance of perceived problems or the effectiveness of proposed solutions" [6]. He goes on to enumerate some of the symptoms of the software crisis [7]:

- *Responsiveness.* Computer-based systems often do not meet user needs.

- *Reliability.* Software often fails.

- *Cost.* Software costs are seldom predictable and are often perceived as excessive.

- *Modifiability.* Software maintenance is complex, costly, and error prone.

- *Timeliness.* Software is often late and frequently delivered with less-than-promised capability.

- *Transportability.* Software from one system is seldom used in another, even when similar functions are required.

- *Efficiency.* Software development efforts do not make optimal use of the resources involved (processing time and memory space).

Of course, costs are not the sole indicator of software problems; the issue of software quality remains. We need only point out the many examples of large software projects that fell behind schedule, exceeded their estimated costs, or met only part of the requirements. Two of the more publicized examples that fit this category include the IBM 05/360 and the World Wide Military Command and Control System (WWMCCS). We could mention scores of other past and present software efforts that have fallen upon hard times. This trend is expected to continue as long as software developers continue to use archaic methods, languages, and tools.

Underlying Causes of the Crisis

So far, we have mentioned only the symptoms of the software crisis. To cope with the actual problem, we must first understand the underlying reasons for its existence. Earlier, it was suggested that the software developer is often like an artist. However, when that artistry is relied upon in an engineering environment, the results are often not good. This is not to say that programming should be devoid of creativity. On the contrary, it is the creative spark that lets us see solutions in unique ways. The problem comes about when we apply undisciplined artistry. For the musician, this results in a cacophony; for the programmer, it results in costly, unreliable, and unmaintainable software systems.

Devlin observed several reasons for this ultimate reliance on undisciplined software artistry, namely [8]:

- Failure of organizations to understand the life-cycle implications of software development

- A shortage of personnel trained in software engineering

- The von Neumann architectures of most of our machines discourage the use of modern programming practices

- The tendency of organizations to become entrenched in the use of archaic programming languages and practices

He emphasized his last point by adding that "no manager would want a first generation vacuum tube computer, yet few are willing to part with first generation programming languages such as FORTRAN" [9].

We face complex application problems, but the methods, languages, and tools that currently exist fail to help us manage the complexity of our solutions. We cannot hope to reduce the complexity of our problems; as our tools become better, we continually open up a more complex—yet solvable—problem domain.

This inability to deal with the complexity of solutions is the ultimate cause of the software crisis. W. A. Wulf stated it concisely when he said, "It is our human limitations, our inability to simultaneously deal with all the relations and ramifications of a complex situation, which lies at the root of our software problems" [10]. Even as early as 1965, Dijkstra recognized the essence of the problem when he said, "I have only a very small head and must live with it" [11].

Combating the Crisis

It might seem, then, that there are fundamental human limitations that will prevent us from ever successfully creating solutions to complex software problems. Actually, this is not the case. For example, it is difficult for a person to dig a small hole bare-handed; it is impossible for that same person to dredge the Panama Canal bare-handed. Yet the canal was certainly built, and the solution to the problem was the use of powerful facilities that extended the capabilities of its builders. The same is true for software developers; we must apply methods, languages, and tools that help us manage the complexity of our software solutions.

There are a number of such software tools, including structured programming techniques, data-flow diagrams, object-oriented design methods, and integrated development environments. As we shall discuss in detail in the chapters that follow, these tools are all related to a set of underlying software principles. Furthermore, in the absence of modern programming methods, studies indicate that productivity is relatively constant (about ten lines of debugged code per day per person), irrespective of the level of programming language used [12]. This leads us to choose high-order programming languages to implement our solutions, since each statement is much more powerful than a single assembly language instruction. However, we must be careful to choose the proper language, since a given language will greatly affect how we ultimately design our solutions. This is what we referred to earlier as a mind-set that chains us to thinking in limited ways.

The ultimate solution to the problem underlying the software crisis—namely, our human limitations—lies in the application of modern software methods supported by a high-order language that encourages and enforces these principles in suitable development environments. In the next section we shall outline the development of one such high-order language.

1.2   The Ada Culture

As a reaction to the software crisis, the United States Department of Defense (DoD) sponsored the development of a very powerful programming language—Ada. Unlike most other languages, Ada was designed for a specific problem domain, namely, massive, software-intensive systems, that presented a set of specific language requirements. Ada was not designed by a committee but by a small design team. It was then refined by intensive expert and public review.

Ada represents a "major advance in programming technology, bringing together the best ideas on the subject in a coherent way designed to meet the real needs of practical programmers" [13]. Ada has not been without criticism, however. Most arguments against the language state that it is too complex and therefore not practical. We strongly disagree. Ada is based on a small set of easily understood concepts, such as data abstraction, information hiding, and strong typing. Because of this basis one can make effective use of Ada quickly by learning a subset of its features and gradually learning the entire language.

In a sense, Ada is a language that directly embodies many modern software engineering principles and is therefore an excellent vehicle with which to express programming solutions. Ada not only encourages the use of good design and programming practices but, as we shall see in succeeding chapters, it can actually enforce such practices. Like other revolutionary human tools, Ada helps us approach our solutions in new, often more efficient, ways.

Although theoretically any computation that can be expressed in a given programming language can also be expressed in any other language, the resulting solutions often vary greatly, and some of the solutions are more comprehensible than others [14]. As we shall see in the following chapter, a programming language shapes the way we think about the solutions to our problems. We need a language that leads us to systems that map directly to their problem space—a language that helps us control the complexity of programming solutions. Ada is such a language. Although Ada is not the ultimate programming language (there is no such thing), it is well suited to the creation of large, reliable, and maintainable systems. Of course, Ada was not created out of a void but is instead the product of a human process. In this section we shall trace this process and provide a rationale for the effort.

Analysis Phase

In the early 1970s, the United States Department of Defense noticed the trend of rising software costs for major defense systems. Prior to that time, hardware costs far exceeded software costs for the development of such systems. The problems of large software development were not well understood, although the effects of poor management, in terms of late deliveries, unreliable software, and cost overruns, were certainly felt. In 1973, software comprised some 46% (over $3 billion) of the estimated total DoD computer costs of $7.5 billion. Furthermore, as Figure 1.1 shows, 56% of these software costs were incurred by the embedded computer systems sector, while data processing (using mainly COBOL) took 19% and scientific applications (generally written in FORTRAN) used only 5% [15]. The remaining 20% included other indirect software costs.

From 1968 to 1973, the DoD experienced a 51% increase in the direct costs of its computer systems, even though hardware costs were decreasing dramatically [16]. Actually, these costs indicate only part of the problem the DoD was encountering. We might have been willing to say, "well, it is expensive, but our requirements justify the cost of a quality product" [17]. However, rarely did we get quality software.

In addition, there were a number of underlying shortcomings that formed a barrier to solving the basic problem, namely:

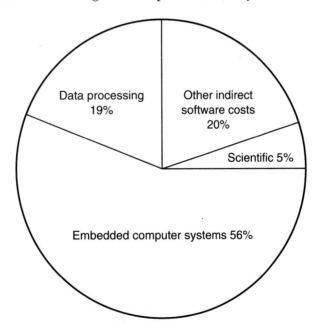

Figure 1.1 Estimated DoD software costs in 1973

- The existence of a diversity of programming languages

- The use of languages ill suited to their application

- The use of languages that did not support modern software engineering principles

- The lack of useful software development environments

At this time, there existed at least 450 general-purpose languages for DoD systems, although depending on the source cited, the actual number varied from 500 to 1500 different high-order and assembly languages [18]. Since the DoD did not then maintain a single point of control for each language, each project office was virtually free to create its own language or use an incompatible dialect of an existing one [19]. This resulted in diluted training efforts, virtually no technology transfer among projects, virtually no software reuse among projects, and a general discussion of resources [20].

There were many cases in which projects were tied to particular vendors or obsolete technologies; thus we often saw projects using COBOL for real-time applications or assembly languages for business systems. Many of the languages that were applied did not support modern software engineering principles. In the early 1970s even structured programming was neither well, understood nor generally accepted.

This proliferation of languages also diverted personnel resources from the creation of meaningful software tools. A given project would generally have only the most primitive tools available, consisting of little more than a compiler, linker, and loader. Syntax-directed editors, tools for configuration management, and incremental compilation were unheard of in most software projects; people were simply too busy fighting their software battles to deal with what they perceived as academic magic.

In January 1975, Malcolm Currie, the Director of Defense Research and Engineering (DDR&E), observed that there would be multiple benefits from the use of a single, common, high-order language, and so established a joint-service High Order Language Working Group (HOLWG). The HOLWG was chaired by Lt. Col. William Whitaker (USAF) and included representatives from each of the services, plus other DoD agencies, and a liaison from the United Kingdom, West Germany, and France. Briefly, the HOLWG was chartered to [21]:

- Identify requirements for DoD high-order languages

- Evaluate existing languages against these requirements

- Recommend the adoption or implementation of a minimal set of programming languages

Requirements Definition Phase

In April 1975, the HOLWG circulated the STRAWMAN [22] requirements document to the military departments, other federal agencies, industry, and the academic community. Comments were also solicited from selected experts in the European computing community, including Dijkstra and Hoare.

Based on the responses from the STRAWMAN review, the WOODEN-MAN [23] document was written and distributed in August 1975, again to the widest possible audience. Official responses to this review led to a complete set of requirements, called TINMAN [24], which was distributed in January 1976 and represented the desired characteristics for a DoD high-order language.

Each of these documents was written primarily by David Fisher, then of the Institute for Defense Analysis, with significant contributions by P. R. Wetherall.

The HOLWG began a formal evaluation of existing languages on the basis of the TINMAN requirements. This evaluation was continued for the remainder of 1976 by six primary contractors and a number of individuals. At the time, certain languages were selected as appropriate for any DoD organization. The list of approved languages included:

- DoD   FORTRAN

               COBOL

- Army   TACPOL

- Navy   CMS-2

               SPL/1

- Air Force   JOVIAL J3

               JOVIAL J73

In January 1977, the evaluation of existing languages against the TINMAN requirements was completed [25]. In all, the reviewers generated over 2800 pages of comments. The review team had formally examined 23 different languages: FORTRAN, COBOL, PL/1, HAL/S, TACPOL, CMS-2, CS-4, SPL/1, JOVIAL J3, JOVIAL J73, ALGOL 60, ALGOL 68, CORAL 66, Pascal, SIMULA 67, LIS, LTR, RTL/2, EUCLID, PDL2, PEARL, MORAL, and EL/l. The evaluation of this report concluded that [26]:

- No existing language was suitable for use as a common high-order language for DoD embedded computer systems.

- A single language was desired.

- A new language to meet the requirements was feasible.

- The new language should be developed from an appropriate base.

Although the evaluators felt that all of the review languages were inappropriate, they later recommended that Pascal, ALGOL, and PL/1 were appropriate as base languages.

Also in January 1977, the year-long evaluation of the TINMAN requirements was completed, and the IRONMAN [27] document, which consolidated reviewer comments, was released. Two independent economic analyses were performed from January 1977 to November 1977 to determine whether it was practical to develop a new language based on the TINMAN requirements. The results of both analyses were very positive and indicated that the adoption of a common high-order language would result in savings of hundreds of millions of dollars for the DoD every year [28].

Design Phase

The design of this new language had to be of a high quality, especially since it would become a common standard. Furthermore, it was recognized that great benefits would result from a language that was well accepted outside the defense community [29]. For these reasons, an international design competition was chosen, in which several teams would submit designs for evaluation. From this competition, a few teams would be selected to complete detailed designs for final evaluation.

In July 1977, four contractors were selected. At the same time, a revised IRONMAN requirements document was distributed [30]. The four language designs that were accepted for Phase I included proposals by:

- SofTech (Blue)

- SRI International (Yellow)

- Intermetrics (Red)

- Honeywell/Honeywell Bull (Green)

The proposals were color-coded, so that reviewers would not know their source. It is significant to note that all of these contractors used Pascal as the base language for their design of the new language.

From February 1978 to March 1978, the designs were evaluated worldwide by nearly 400 volunteers participating in 80 review teams. Based on these evaluations, two of the designs, the proposals by Intermetrics (Red) and Honeywell/Honeywell Bull (Green), were selected for further refinement.

Early in 1977, Whitaker had recognized that a programming language alone was not sufficient to ensure the desired improvements in software development, but rather the language needed to be coupled with quality tools [31]. In early 1978, HOLWG circulated a document called SANDMAN [32] that enumerated some of the technical and managerial issues in regard to programming environments; SANDMAN was later revised to form PEB-BLEMAN [33]. During the same month, HOLWG released a final language requirements document, called STEELMAN [34].

In November 1978, Defense Advance Research Projects Agency (DARPA) held a public meeting with the designers of the Red and Green languages, in which participants were permitted to ask specific questions on the technical issues of the new language.

In spring 1979, Jack Cooper of the Navy Materiel Command suggested the perfect name for this new language: Ada, in honor of Augusta Ada Byron, Countess of Lovelace and daughter of the poet Lord Byron [35].

Ada Lovelace (1815–1851) was a mathematician who worked with Charles Babbage on his difference and analytic engines. She is noted for her early observations on the potential power of the computer. In particular, Ada suggested how Babbage's machines might be programmed much like the Jacquard loom, and for this work she is considered the world's first programmer. In a formal exchange of letters between the Deputy Secretary of Defense and Lovelace's heir, the Earl of Lytton, permission was granted to use the name [36].

In May 1979 the HOLWG announced the Green language as the winner of the design competition. The primary author of the Green language was Jean Ichbiah from France. Other members of the design team included J. Heliard, 0. Roubine, and J. Abrial, also of France; P. N. Hilfinger and H. F. Ledgard of the United States; J. G. P. Barnes, B. A. Wichmann, M. Woodger, and R. Firth from the United Kingdom; and B. Krieg-Bruckner from West Germany. In addition, the *Reference Manual for the Ada Programming Language* recognizes several other individuals who provided significant contributions to the language design, namely, E. Morel and G. Ferran of France; J. B. Goodenough, M. W. Davis, L. MacLaren, I. R. Nassi, S. A. Schuman, and S. L. Vestal of the United States; and I. C. Pyle from the United Kingdom.

On December 12, 1980, during the first ACM Symposium on Ada, held in Boston, approval was granted for the creation of an Ada Joint Program Office (AJPO) to manage all Ada-related activities [37]. The HOLWG was officially dissolved and Lt. Col. Larry Druffel was named AJPO Director. On that same day, approval was granted for establishing MIL-STD 1815 as the approved DoD standard for Ada. We should add that the choice of the number

1815 was no coincidence, since December, 12, 1815 was the date of the public announcement of the birth of Augusta Ada Lovelace.

On February 17, 1983, Ada was approved as an ANSI (American National Standards Institute) standard. That same year the first interpreters and compilers were validated. In March of 1987, ISO (International Standards Organization) accepted the American and French Ada standards.

The Impact of Ada on Software Engineering

The noted psycholinguist Benjamin Whorf observed that languages "can have an important influence upon thought processes even though they do not determine all such processes" [38]. We thus expect the same from the Ada culture. Ada helps break the von Neumann mind-set and lets us deal with our solutions in terms of the actual problem space. As a result, solutions become more readable, reliable, and maintainable. In fact, Ada permits us to deal with an entirely new set of problems whose solutions were previously far too complex to manage.

Fisher has written, "Programming languages are neither the cause of nor the solution to software problems, but because of the central role they play in all software activity, they can either aggravate existing problems or simplify their solutions" [39]. In the case of Ada, we would expect the effect to be one of simplification. Although Ada alone cannot solve the software crisis, when combined with the proper software methods and tools, it provides a powerful vehicle for the creation of our software systems.

Ada has been in commercial use for more than eight years. It is appropriate that we now try to quantify its impact. There have been many published reports of productivity gains as the result of using Ada [40, 41, 42, 43, 44, 45, 46, 47]. Most of these studies compare Ada-based projects to projects with very similar requirements implemented in FORTRAN or C. All report significant productivity increases. Further, multiple studies have shown that productivity continues to increase the more a programming team works with Ada.

Productivity increases have been found to vary from 30% [44,47] to close to 100% [45,46]. A large part of these gains can be attributed to a decrease in program errors and an increase in software reuse. Reifer [40], reporting on the analysis of measurements taken from dozens of projects, has found that Ada projects generate 30% fewer errors overall and 20% fewer critical errors after product shipment. Doscher [45] compared a system implemented in C with one implemented in Ada and found 96% fewer errors after product shipment with the Ada implementation.

A study from NASA compared FORTRAN and Ada [43]. Three successive Ada projects, implemented by the same team, were examined.

They found that the team's first Ada system generated 50% fewer preshipment errors than similar FORTRAN systems. By the third project the Ada team had reduced preshipment errors by more than 66%.

Hines [46] compared a project implemented in C with one implemented in Ada. The Ada project was the first one undertaken by the programming team. It was found that the C project yielded 0% reuse, while the Ada project reused 10% of their software on their very first effort.

Reifer also found that by their third project Ada teams were able to reuse 20% of their software. NASA reported even more encouraging figures. They found that typical FORTRAN projects reuse 20% of their software. As we would expect, reuse was low on the first Ada project. In the second Ada project, reuse already exceeded that of FORTRAN projects, reaching 32%, and on the third project Ada reuse more than doubled FORTRAN reuse at 42%.

These reports of 100% increases in productivity, 100% increases in reuse, and 96% reduction in errors indicate that Ada has already made a very positive impact on the state of the practice in software engineering. As many of the above authors admit, it is not the language alone that accounts for these improvements. It is the language, combined with the new engineering methods it supports and encourages, that has the greatest impact.

Summary   ■   The *software crisis* is a reflection of the problems of developing massive, software-intensive systems that meet their requirements and that are modifiable, efficient, reliable, and understandable.

■   We can mitigate much of the difficulty of software development by engineering our systems better by applying appropriate methods, languages, and tools effectively.

■   The software crisis is characterized by problems with responsiveness, reliability, cost, modifiability, timeliness, transportability, and efficiency.

■   It is our human inability to deal with complexity that lies at the root of the software crisis.

■   Ada is a language that embodies and enforces modern software engineering principles; it can be an effective vehicle for the creation of complex systems.

■   Ada is the result of an engineering process; it is a language that was designed according to a set of well-defined requirements and was developed in a series of consciously planned phases.

- In the design phase, the DoD sponsored a competition to select a single common, high-order language that conformed to STEELMAN requirements. The winner (the Green language developed by Ichbiah) underwent intensive international public and professional review.

- Ada is now in the mainstream of the computing industry. A number of national and international policies ensure its continued existence and controlled evolution.

- Ada, when compared to similar FORTRAN and C systems, has been shown in numerous studies to significantly increase productivity by increasing software reuse while decreasing errors.

Exercises

1. Consider the largest software system that you have developed, either alone or as part of a team. Calculate the number of code lines per day per person. How close is this figure to 10 lines per day?

2. Our ability to cope with complexity is related to the capacity of our short-term memory. Name some common phenomena that illustrate the limits of our memory (e.g., the inability to remember nine-digit zip codes).

3. Determine whether the following statement is true or false: The later an error is detected during software development, the more expensive it is to correct. Defend your answer.

*4. Perhaps the most serious symptom of the software crisis is the development of low-quality software. From your own experience, what distinguishes "good" (high-quality) software from "poor" (low-quality) software?

5. We have focused on the problems associated with developing large systems, but developing a smaller system gives rise to the same concerns. Imagine that an organization must develop several 2000-line applications. What advantage is there in using common software components in all the applications?

6. What characteristics of real-time systems add to their complexity?

*7. The programming languages Pascal, Alphard, CLU, and LIS were all parents of the Ada language. To what degree did their constructs and philosophy influence the design of Ada?

8. Ada has been called "the last language" or, more accurately, the last procedural language. Do you agree? Defend your answer.

9. What are the costs of not having strongly enforced standards for a programming language?

CHAPTER 2

Software Engineering

Goals of Software Engineering
Principles of Software Engineering
Approaches to Software Development
Languages and Software Development

The fundamental cause of the software crisis is that massive, software-intensive systems have become unmanageably complex. Furthermore, we cannot expect them to become any less complex, for as we improve our tools and gain experience in designing such systems, we actually open up even more complex problem domains. As a solution to this crisis, we must therefore apply a disciplined artistry, using tools that help us manage this complexity. In a broad sense, we call this discipline *software engineering*. When we think of software engineering, what most often comes to mind are visions of structured code, PDL (Program Design Language or pseudocode), the markings of HIPO (Hierarchical Input Process Output), and data-flow diagrams. Actually, these are just some of the more visible artifacts of software engineering. Simply stated, the purpose of software engineering is to provide a consistent, life-cycle approach to the creation of software systems. In a sense, we seek to remove some of the wizardry from our work and replace it with sound engineering practice.

In this chapter, we shall further examine the goals of software engineering, then study some simple principles that can help us achieve them. Next, we shall introduce several approaches to software development that apply these principles. Finally, realizing that programming languages are the vehicles that let us express and execute our designs, we shall examine the generations of languages and study how each does or does not support the underlying principles of software engineering. As we begin to examine the technical details of Ada in this chapter, we shall see that it is indeed an embodiment of these software development principles—a fact that renders it an excellent vehicle for the creation of software systems.

2.1 Goals of Software Engineering

A most obvious goal in software development is that the solutions meet the stated requirements. However, complete or consistent requirements specifications are rarely available, especially for very large systems. The user (and implementor) often has an incomplete understanding of the problem and so usually evolves the requirements during the development of the system. Furthermore, the problem is compounded whenever we have parallel hardware and software development, as is often the case with embedded computer systems. Finally, we must accept the reality of changes in requirements over the life cycle of our software systems. As we noted in Chapter 1, more resources are spent in the maintenance phase than in any other phase of the software life cycle. Large software systems don't die; they simply get modified.

Recognizing that change is a constant factor in software development, we must have a set of goals that transcends the effects of such change. In their classic paper, O. T. Ross, J. B. Goodenough, and C. A. Irvine describe these goals: "Four properties that are sufficiently general to be accepted as goals for the entire discipline of software engineering are modifiability, efficiency, reliability, and understandability" [1].

Modifiability

Modifiability is a difficult goal to achieve and to measure. Ross, et al., state that it "implies controlled change, in which some parts or aspects remain the same while others are altered, all in such a way that a desired new result is obtained" [2]. We may have to modify a software system for one of two reasons: First, we may have to respond to a change in the requirements of the system, and second, we may have to correct an error that we introduced earlier in the development process.

Whenever we design software, we must somehow capture the architecture of the design in a manner that is clear and consistent. Traditionally, since most programming languages are not highly readable, we are forced to use external documentation to reflect this structure, but ideally we would like to capture the design in the software itself.

In order to effectively modify systems, we must honor all the explicit and implicit design decisions that are embodied in the solution. Otherwise, we are forced to patch our software independently of the original design, thus rending the logical fabric of our software. After several iterations, the original structure becomes obscure, further compounding the difficulty of modifying the system. If software systems are modifiable, it should be possible to introduce changes without increasing the complexity of the original system.

Efficiency

The goal of efficiency implies that a software system should operate using the set of available resources in an optimal manner. We can classify these resources in two groups: time resources and space resources. We can have limited time resources if a process must execute within a given period, such as sampling sensors or responding to an external interrupt. Obviously, time resources are highly dependent upon the underlying hardware, although our choice of software algorithms will certainly affect the overall execution time. Space resources, on the other hand, refer to physical aspects of the solution, such as address space or number of peripheral devices available.

Embedded computer system applications must often take both classes of resources into account. If the system must respond to real events, then an efficient use of time resources becomes critical. On the other hand, if the underlying hardware is constrained by physical size or power limitations, such as on a satellite or in an automobile, space resources are important to the solution. In many cases, the efficient use of both resources at the same time is not possible, and a compromise is required. This is the essence of engineering any real-world system.

Obviously, embedded systems are not the only systems to which developers should bring a concern for efficiency. As computers become more and more powerful, the need for effective strategies in all problem domains increases. Pattern recognition, network planning, and searching are functions that demand efficiency.

We often concern ourselves with efficiency too early in the development process, however. As a result we often focus on microefficiency instead of macroefficiency. We must note that "... insights reflecting a more unified understanding of a problem gave far more impact on efficiency than any amount of bit twiddling within a faulty structure" [3].

Reliability

Reliability is a critical goal for any computer system that must operate for long periods without human intervention. Furthermore, if that system controls a critical resource, such as a nuclear power plant or a spacecraft navigation system, the costs of failure are too high for us to allow anything less than high reliability. "Reliability must both prevent failure in conception, design, and construction, as well as recover from failure in operation or performance" [4].

As we have defined reliability, it is apparent that this goal must be present throughout the design of our software. "Reliability can only be built from the start; it cannot be added on at the end" [5]. We cannot, however, expect perfect reliability, since there will certainly be circumstances beyond our control, such as a catastrophic hardware failure that affects even backup systems. No matter what the failure mode, be it predictable or not, we would expect that a reliable system would degrade gracefully without causing any dangerous side effects, such as a reactor core melt down or a degraded satellite orbit.

Understandability

The final goal of software engineering, understandability, is perhaps the most critical in helping us manage the complexity of our software systems. Understandability is the bridge between our particular problem space and the corresponding solution. In other words, for a system to be understandable, it must be an accurate model of our view of the real world. If we are to apply our resources to a difficult problem, we must evolve a solution with an effective, discernible architecture. As was mentioned previously, capturing such a structure in the software itself is essential for our systems to be modifiable, efficient, and reliable.

A given system will be understandable because of influences from a number of levels. At the lowest level, the software solution should be readable as a result of a proper coding style. At a higher level, we should be able to easily isolate the data structures (objects) and algorithms (operations) in the solution that map to the real-world data and algorithms. As we shall see, understandability is highly dependent upon the programming language we use as the vehicle for expressing our solution.

2.2   Principles of Software Engineering

The goals we discussed in the last section are reasonable ones for any software system, large or small. However, we cannot just passively acknowledge these goals, apply an undisciplined development approach, and hope we have achieved them. Instead, as we design software, we must apply sound engineering principles to achieve these goals, including [6, 30]:

- Abstraction

- Information hiding

- Modularity

- Localization

- Uniformity

- Completeness

- Confirmability

In the following sections, we shall see how the application of these principles can lead to solutions that are modifiable, efficient, reliable, and understandable.

Abstraction and Information Hiding

We have already acknowledged that software complexity is the underlying cause of our problems. One of the fundamental principles for managing this complexity is *abstraction* [7]. Abstraction is not a new concept; we apply it in everything we do. For example, our software may interact with a disk drive, and so we can view this physical device from any of several viewpoints:

- As a collection of logical files

- As mass storage organized by tracks and sectors

- As a collection of addressable bits of storage

- As a physical device requiring control and data signals

Here, we have formed a ladder of abstraction, in which each level of abstraction is built from lower levels. In our program we can adopt the level of abstraction that is appropriate to our needs. For example, if we have a data base management system, we need to view the disk drive only as a collection of logical files. If we are writing a device driver for our operating system, we must take a different view of the same physical device, perhaps at the level of the control and data signals.

"The essence of abstraction is to extract essential properties while omitting inessential details" [8]. As we decompose our solution into its component parts, each module in the decomposition becomes a part of the abstraction at a given level. Furthermore, we can apply abstraction to both the data and the algorithms in our solutions.

Each level of an abstraction can identify abstract data types (such as `File`, `Record`, or `Disk_Sector`), each characterized by a set of values and a set of operations applicable to each object of the type. For example, the data base system may need to manipulate a set of logical files, while the operating system driver will view the disk as an addressable block of words. Obviously, if we are writing the data base system, we do not wish to concern ourselves with the physical organization of the words as they are stored on disk, nor do we care about logical files if we are writing a device driver.

There is also a parallel with algorithmic abstraction. Our data base system will need to `Open`, `Close`, `Read`, and `Write` these logical files, so we do not want to concern ourselves with the physical details of selecting a track, finding the proper sector, handling the checksum, and then delivering a segment of the desired file. Instead, we view `Open`, `Close`, `Read`, and `Write` all as abstract operations, without worrying about the details of their implementation. Of course, we eventually have to concern ourselves with such details, but we can defer the implementation to lower levels of our solution. In this way, we reduce the number of entities we have to cope with at the current level of decomposition.

In this last example, we have actually applied a second principle of software engineering, namely *information hiding*. Whereas abstractions extract the essential details of a given level, "... the purpose of hiding is to make inaccessible certain details that should not affect other parts of a system" [9]. In our data base system example, the principle of information hiding would tell us that we should not permit a programmer to access the physical details of the disk drive by, for example, writing to a given sector. To allow such an action would permit the programmer to violate our logical abstraction of a disk file.

Information hiding therefore suppresses how an object or operation is implemented, and so focuses our attention on a higher abstraction [10]. Furthermore, when we hide lower-level design decisions, such as the physical organization of files on a disk, we prevent higher-level strategies from being based on these lower-level details. Thus, in our example, if we changed disk drives to provide more storage capacity, the physical reorganization of the disk would not affect our higher-level abstraction of the logical file system.

The benefits to be gained in applying abstraction and information hiding apply to almost all goals of software engineering. Abstraction aids in the maintainability and understandability of systems by reducing the details a developer needs to know at any given level. Furthermore, we enhance the reliability of systems when, at each level of abstraction, we

permit only certain operations and prevent any operations that violate our logical view of that level.

Modularity and Localization

Another fundamental tool for helping us manage the complexity of software systems is *modularity*. "Modularity deals with how the structure of an object can make the attainment of some purpose easier. Modularity is 'purposeful structuring'" [11]. Modularity thus applies to the physical architecture of our systems.

If we apply a top-down software design method, we typically decompose each successive level into different functional modules. Generally, higher-level modules relate to our high-level abstractions, and so are relatively machine independent. Furthermore, a higher-level module will specify *what* action is to be taken, while the lower-level modules define *how* the action is to be carried out [12]. If we use a bottom-up design method, the same properties of each level apply, but instead of decomposing our system from the top down, we build the system up from low-level modules to increasingly more complex ones.

It is important to realize that production systems are rarely built in a strictly top-down or bottom-up fashion. Rather, any truly complex system will employ both approaches. A large system is usually *decomposed* from the top down. It is often *composed* of existing reusable software components—in other words, a large system is usually *composed* from the bottom up.

In a broader sense, modules can be functional (procedure-oriented) or declarative (object-oriented). If we are to build reliability into our system, we must provide a well-defined interface to each module. However, no matter how a program module is defined, it will certainly interact with other modules; we thus define "a measure of the strength of interconnection" among modules as *coupling* [13]. Ideally, we want our modules to be loosely coupled, so that we can treat each module relatively independently of the others. Another measure we can apply to modularity is *cohesion,* which defines "how tightly bound or related its internal elements are to one another" (within the module) [14]. In this case, we want modules that exhibit strong cohesion, so that the components of a given module are functionally and logically dependent.

Applying the principle of *localization* also helps us create modules that exhibit loose coupling and strong cohesion. Localization is primarily concerned with physical proximity [15]. Ideally, we want to collect logically related computational resources in one physical module, thus leading us to a module that is cohesively strong. Furthermore, localization implies that a given module is sufficiently independent, also leading us to a loosely coupled organization.

In relation to our goals of software engineering, the principles of modularity and localization directly support modifiability, reliability, and understandability. If we have a system that is well structured, we should be able to understand any given module relatively independently of other modules. Furthermore, since we have localized our design decisions in given modules, we can limit the effects of a modification to a small set of modules. In addition, if we have used purposeful modularization, we will have limited the interconnections among program modules, thus enhancing our program reliability.

Uniformity, Completeness, and Confirmability

Abstraction and modularity are perhaps the most important principles we can use to control the complexity of our software. However, they are not sufficient principles, since they do not ensure that we will end up with consistent or correct systems. We must apply the principles of uniformity, completeness, and confirmability to provide these properties.

The principle of uniformity directly supports the goal of understandability. *Uniformity* simply means that the modules use a consistent notation and are free from any unnecessary differences [16]. Uniformity generally results from a good coding style, in which we apply a consistent control structure and calling sequence for our operations and where the representation of logically related objects are the same at any given level. In later chapters and in Appendix D, we shall suggest such a coding style by example.

The principles of completeness and confirmability support the goals of reliability, efficiency, and modifiability by helping us develop solutions that are correct. Whereas abstraction extracts the essential details of a given entity, *completeness* ensures that all of the important elements are present. In a sense, abstraction and completeness help us develop modules that are necessary and sufficient. Efficiency is enhanced, since we can now tune a lower-level implementation without affecting any higher-level modules.

In conjunction with completeness, the principle of *confirmability* implies that we must decompose our system so that it can be readily tested [17], thus helping to make our systems modifiable. The principles of completeness and confirmability are not easy to apply. Some tools, such as programming languages with strong typing facilities, help provide systems that are confirmable but, as we shall see, software management tools must be applied to ensure that our systems are complete and confirmable.

2.3   Approaches to Software Development

In Chapter 1, we stated that there exists a fundamental human limitation in
our ability to manage a number of different objects or concepts at one time.
In 1954, the psychologist George Miller concluded that the limit to the
number of entities humans can process at one time is roughly seven, plus
or minus two [18]. As we see in Figure 2.1, which is derived from Miller's
work, our ability to manage the complexity of many entities falls off
sharply beyond this number [19].

Developing software systems is a problem-solving activity, and so the
limit of seven plus or minus two appears to apply. We suggest that the
principles of software engineering can help us decompose systems so that,
at each level of our solution, the number of entities we must deal with at
one time lies within this limit. In this section, we shall examine various
software design methods and management techniques that implement
these principles, and thus help us manage the complexity of our software.

Design Methods

Software engineering principles cannot be applied haphazardly; we must
construct our systems in a disciplined manner. Most importantly, as we

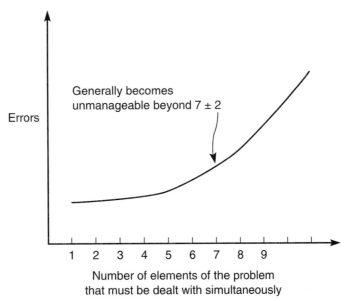

Figure 2.1 Error curve for normal problem solving. (From Edward Yourdon/Larry L.
Constantine, *Structured Design: Fundamentals of a Discipline of Computer Program and
Systems Design*, ©1979, p. 69. Reprinted by permission of Prentice-Hall, Inc., Englewood
Cliffs, N.J.)

divide our systems into modules, we must use consistent criteria for decomposing them. Such criteria are usually embodied in what we call software development *methods.* Specifically, a method is a disciplined process for producing software products. Methods are different than *methodologies,* which are cooperating collections of methods or, in a more general sense, a philosophical approach to software development [20, 31]. Methodologies provide a framework for the application of methods—a strategy to address all phases of the software development life cycle.

Methods are important for a number of reasons, foremost of which is the management of complexity. In addition, methods enhance communication among developers and couple phases of the development life cycle. Communication and smooth transitions between phases are particularly important to large software systems, which usually involve scores of developers who are separated by the time in long development life cycles and by the space between distant sites.

In Chapter 19, we shall examine the traditional phases of the software development life cycle in detail. For the moment, let us concentrate on one important category of methods: those that deal with the architectural and detailed design phases of software development.

We can divide almost every existing software design method into one of three classes [21]:

- Top-down structured design

- Data-structure design

- Object-oriented design

A full discussion of each class of methods is beyond the scope of this text, but in the next few paragraphs, we will provide the essential details of each.

Top-down structured design methods concentrate on the algorithmic abstractions of a problem. For this reason, we often call such methods *process driven.* Process-driven methods are typified by the work of Constantine, who suggests that we decompose a system by making each step in the overall process a module. Yourdon has also been a major contributor to the popularization of top-down structured design [22, 31]. Pursuing this method leads us to program modules that are highly functional. The top-down approach is strongly influenced by the topology of FORTRAN (as we will see in the next section); therefore, careful developers apply top-down design only to problems that do not involve concurrency. At the highest levels of our solution, we define the highest level of algorithmic abstraction (the "what" of the process); lower levels provide primitive operations that implement these higher-level actions. Most often, the architecture of a system is characterized in a *structure chart,* which illustrates the hierarchical dependencies among functional modules.

Data-structure design, as the name suggests, focuses on the data of a problem. D. Jackson and P. Warnier have pioneered a data-structure method that has proven very effective in COBOL-type applications [23, 32, 33]. Using this technique, we first define our data structures, then we structure the architecture of the system based on the data structures. In this manner, we attempt to clearly define the implementation of the objects in our solution space and then make their structure visible to the necessary functional units that provide the operations on the objects.

At this point, we must mention the influence of Parnas, whose work at the University of North Carolina had a great influence on design methods. Parnas suggested that we decompose our systems so that each module in the solution hides a design [24]. His approach is neither process driven nor data driven, but it serves to capture our design decisions at the lowest possible level. This is the essence of information hiding.

Parnas's work is a major influence on the third class of design methods, *object-oriented design.* We shall examine this method in detail in the next chapter. Briefly, though, the method focuses on objects as the primary agents involved in a computation; hence, the architecture of a system is organized around collections of objects—not algorithmic abstractions. In this manner, we collect each class of data and related operations into a single module. This method grew out of the work of not only Parnas, but also B. Liskov and J. Guttag of the Massachusetts Institute of Technology and Robinson and K. Leavitt of Stanford Research Institute. In addition, this method follows the object orientation encouraged by the languages Smalltalk, SIMULA 67, C++, Object Pascal, CLOS (Common Lisp Object System), and Ada 9X (see Appendix F). The particular technique we present for designing object-oriented software for Ada was pioneered to a large extent by R. Abbott of California State University, Northridge.

Management Issues

No matter what design methods we employ, we must keep in mind our human limitations in managing complexity. Since computer science has not yet progressed to the point where automatic program generation is a practical reality, we must apply management techniques to support our design methods. A full discussion of these techniques is beyond the scope of this text, so we will will provide only a brief discussion and provide references for further information.

Managing software development is no different from any other complex engineering effort, except that the project (software) is much less tangible than, say, a bridge or a ship. In most cases the software project is more complex and unique. In Chapter 19, we discuss a life-cycle approach to the development of Ada software; here we will simply point out that design methods apply to only part of the total life cycle, whereas we must apply sound management practices throughout all phases of software development.

As a first step, it is essential that we form a complete and correct model of the problem space. In this regard, we might apply a *structured analysis and design technique* (SADT) [25] to create this model. As we analyze our system, we may choose to document our design using *data-flow diagrams* [26, 34]. To arrive at the functional elements of our design, we may wish to apply *structure charts* [27]. We may embody detailed design in the form of a PDL, in which we employ a language (such as Ada) to document our detailed design decision. The *structured walk-through* is a final and powerful management tool that involves peer review of software components [28]. A walk-through provides insight into the progress of software development and a mechanism for checking the quality and completeness of the product.

2.4   Languages and Software Development

Methods alone are not sufficient to create computer solutions. We must have the proper vehicles, in the form of programming languages, to express and execute our designs. In the following list, P. Wegner has categorized some of the most popular languages into generations arranged according to the language features they introduced [29]:

- *First-generation languages* (1954–1958):

    FORTRAN I
    ALGOL 58
    Flowmatic
    IPL V
    } mathematical expressions

- *Second-generation languages* (1959–1961):

    FORTRAN II   subroutines, separate compilation
    ALGOL 60   block structure, data types
    COBOL   data description, file handling
    LISP   list processing, pointers

- *Third-generation languages* (1962-1970):

PL/1	FORTRAN + ALGOL + COBOL
ALGOL 68	rigorous successor to ALGOL 60
Pascal	simple successor to ALGOL 60
SIMULA	classes, data abstraction

- *The generation gap* (1970-1980):

  Many different languages, but none that endured

As we can see from this list, the more widely used high-order languages (namely, the variations of FORTRAN and COBOL) were created early in the history of computer science, long before we understood the problems of massive, software-intensive systems development. As a result, these languages do not reflect contemporary design methods, and so we have had to distort each language with preprocessors (such as S-FOR-TRAN) and extensions (such as FORTRAN 77) to force them to fit modern approaches. In any case, these high-order languages were developed at a time when problems were relatively simple, compared with today's application domains.

FORTRAN and COBOL are still generally suitable for their particular problem domains; however, since their development, the domain of very large computer systems has emerged. Neither FORTRAN, nor COBOL, nor most other high-order languages were designed to handle the complexities of this domain, much less deal with the difficulties of developing software consisting of thousands to millions of lines of code.

If we examine the topology of these early languages, we can begin to understand some of their inherent problems. As Figure 2.2 indicates, first and second generation languages, such as COBOL and both forms of FOR-TRAN, exhibit a relatively flat structure, consisting of global data and one level of subprograms. The arrows in the figure indicate dependencies of the subprograms' data. An error in one segment of a program can have a devastating ripple effect across the rest of the system because of the global data structures. Furthermore, when modifications are made to a large system, it is difficult if not impossible to maintain the fabric of the original design architecture. After even a short period of maintenance, a program written in one of these languages will usually contain a great deal of cross-coupling among program units. Coupling endangers the reliability of the entire system, hinders software reuse, and reduces the clarity of the solution.

With the development of languages such as ALGOL 60 in the second generation and some of the languages of the third generation, we were able

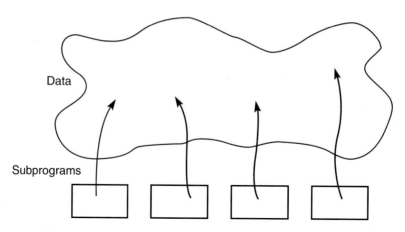

Figure 2.2 Topology of first- and second-generation languages

to provide greater nested structure to our algorithms, although there was little improvement in features for describing data structures. As shown in Figure 2.3, the topology of these languages differed only slightly from that of the previous generation and so suffered the same problems. A few languages were developed during this period that did provide greater data structuring, namely SIMULA, Alphard, CLU, and LIS, but none of them gained wide acceptance.

Since assembly languages are still commonly used for embedded computer systems, we have provided their topology in Figure 2.4. This

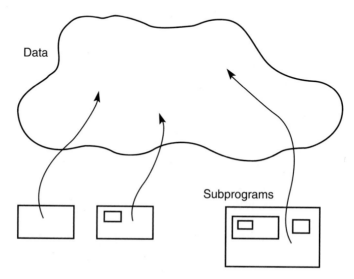

Figure 2.3 Topology of second- and third- generation languages

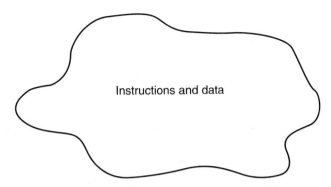

Figure 2.4 Topology of assembly languages

drawing may seem a little absurd, but it does point out the fact that assembly languages provide no inherent structure. Whatever structure exists in such a system is imposed by management and discipline among team members. It is a tribute to the competence of these developers that large assembly language systems work at all. Certainly, they provide great flexibility in creating systems, and it is possible to write structured assembly code. However, once a solution reaches even a moderate size, the nature of the assembly language complicates it.

Ada was developed at the end of the language "generation gap" and so has been influenced by contemporary software methods. In a sense, it is the first of a new generation of languages. As Figure 2.5 represents, Ada's

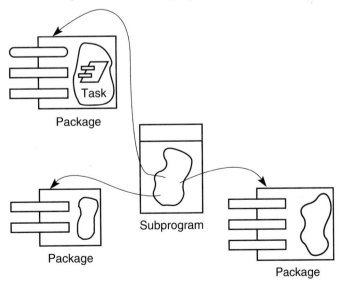

Figure 2.5 Topology of Ada

topology is not flat like those of the previous generations, but rather is three dimensional. (We will explain the meaning of the symbols in the figure in Chapter 4.) With Ada, we can describe a regular structure for our algorithms as well as our data structures. We can also control the complexity of solutions by physically hiding unnecessary details at each level. Furthermore, this topology helps us localize design decisions, and so the structure of the original design is more easily maintained as modifications are made.

In subsequent chapters, we shall further examine how Ada provides features that directly support the principles of software engineering, thereby helping us develop software solutions that are modifiable, efficient, reliable, and understandable. In the next chapter, we introduce an object-oriented development method that implements these principles and, in addition, exploits the power of Ada's topology.

Summary

- Software engineering is the application of sound engineering principles to the development of systems that are modifiable, efficient, reliable, and understandable.

- Several principles lead us to these goals, including abstraction, information hiding, modularity, localization, uniformity, completeness, and confirmability.

- The number of entities that humans seem to be able to process at one time is equal to seven plus or minus two. This limitation affects our ability to manage complexity.

- A method is a disciplined process for producing software products. A methodology is a cooperating collection of methods or a philosophical approach to software development.

- Software design methods are generally classified as top-down structured, data-structure, or object-oriented methods.

- The topology of a programming language plays an important role in the degree to which the developer can apply software engineering principles.

Exercises

1. Scan the room you are in and find a familiar object, such as a chair, a desk, or perhaps a telephone. Make a ladder of abstraction for this object, including at least ten levels.

*2. Consider each of the three classes of design methods mentioned in this chapter. What programming languages are best suited to each method? Are there any languages for which several of these methods are suitable?

3. Consider a software project of which you have been a member. What management tools did you apply during the development?

4. Choose another language, such as JOVIAL, C, or perhaps even BASIC, and draw its topology. In what generation would you place it?

*5. Consider a vending machine that dispenses candy. Using a process-driven method, characterize the major algorithmic abstractions.

*6. Consider the same vending machine. Using an object-oriented approach, characterize the major objects from the perspective of the user.

*7. Compare and contrast the approaches you outlined in questions 5 and 6 relative to the software engineering principles introduced in this chapter. Consider especially the effect of changing the price of each item.

3

Object-Oriented Design

Limitations of Functional Methods
An Object-Oriented Design Method
Ada as a Design Language

I n the previous chapter, we examined the goals of software engineering and the fundamental principles that help us achieve these goals. Throughout our discussion, one theme was clear: We must apply suitable methods, languages, and environments to manage the complexity of software systems. In this chapter, we shall introduce such a design method—a method that is directed to the creation of complex software systems. Then we shall see how our method supports and exploits the features of Ada.

3.1   Limitations of Functional Methods

No matter what the particular application, its problem space is rooted somewhere in the real world, and its solution space is implemented by a combination of software and hardware. H. Ledgard suggests a model to describe a typical programming task—the model shown in Figure 3.1 [1]. This figure illustrates that in the problem space we have a set of real-world objects, each of which has a set of appropriate operations. These objects may be as simple as a checkbook ledger or as complex as an interplanetary spacecraft. Also in the problem space we have some real-world algorithms that operate on these objects and provide transformed objects as results. For example, a real-world result may be a balanced checkbook or a course change for a spacecraft.

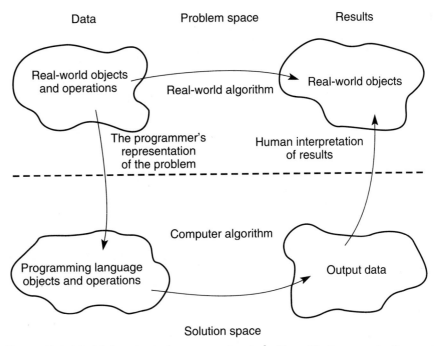

Figure 3.1 Model for a typical programming task. (From *The Programming Language Landscape* by Henry Ledgard and Michael Marcotty ©1981 Science Research Associates, Inc. Reproduced by permission of the publisher.)

Whenever we develop a software system, we either model a real-world problem entirely in software or, in the case of an embedded computer system, take real-world objects and transform them in software and hardware to produce real-world results. No matter what the implementation, our solution space must parallel the problem space. First, programming languages provide the mechanisms for a programmer to represent the real-world objects; in essence, the programmer abstracts the objects in the problem space and implements these abstractions in software. Next, computer algorithms that transform these software objects are applied. Again, the programmer must employ his or her logical abstraction of the operations in the real world. Finally, these algorithms produce some form of output that is mapped physically to some real-world action, such as the movement of a control surface, or is interpreted by humans in nonreal time.

Intuitively, it is clear that the closer the solution space maps our abstraction of the problem space, the better we can achieve our goals of modifiability, efficiency, reliability, and understandability. If our solutions are distant from the problem space, we must make a mental or physical transformation to the real-world abstractions, thus increasing the complexity of our solution.

If we examine human languages, we find that they almost all have two primary components, noun phrases and verb phrases. A parallel structure exists in programming languages, since they provide constructs for implementing objects (noun phrases) and operations (verb phrases). However, most of the languages developed prior to the introduction of Ada are primarily imperative, that is, they provide a rich set of constructs for implementing operations but are generally weak when it comes to abstracting real-world objects. Furthermore, as we have seen, the topologies of these languages indicate that they all have a relatively flat structure. However, the real world is neither flat nor sequential but is instead multidimensional and highly concurrent. Thus, the first three generations of programming languages, and especially assembly languages, widened the gap between the problem space and the solution space.

We have already discussed three software design methods:

- Top-down structured design

- Data-structure design

- Object-oriented design

Top-down design techniques are imperative in nature—that is, they force us to concentrate on the operations in the solution space with little regard for the design of the data structures. Systems that are designed with such methods tend to exhibit topologies similar to those of first- and second-generation languages. As a result, data are forced to be global, making the system less reliable because of the possibility of faulty connections between paths. The system is also less resilient because changes in data tend to ripple through the entire structure. Data-structure design is at the other end of the spectrum; this approach concentrates on objects and treats operations in a global fashion.

Using these two design methods, we may have a solution that is totally functional and thus avoids a reasonable implementation of our real-world object abstractions, or we may end up with clear data structures but with operations that are obscure. The effect is somewhat like trying to communicate in English using just verbs or just nouns. At the very least, we shall have to make a mental transformation from the solution space to the problem space, and in the worst case, we must make a physical transformation. In any case, these methods leave us with a solution that is far removed from the problem space.

3.2   An Object-Oriented Design Method

What we desire, then, is a method that lets us map our abstractions of the real world directly to the architecture of our solutions. In addition, we seek a balanced treatment between the objects and the operations in our model of reality, much as human languages offer. We call this an *object-oriented* design method to emphasize the fact that it is neither purely imperative nor purely declarative. Instead, this approach recognizes the importance of software objects as actors, each with its own set of applicable operations.

Object-oriented design is thus fundamentally different from traditional methods, for which the primary criterion for the decomposition of a system is usually that each module in the system represents a major step in the overall process. With object-oriented techniques, we apply a different criterion: *Each module in the system denotes an object or a class of objects from the problem space.* Abstraction and information hiding thus form the foundation of all object-oriented design.

Since the notion of an object plays a central role in this approach, it is reasonable that we explain what we mean by the term *object.* First, an object is an entity that has state; that is, it has some value. For example, in a cruise-control system in a car, we may treat the brake, throttle, accelerator, and engine as objects that are relevant to our model of reality. Furthermore, the behavior of a specific object is defined by the actions that it suffers. In the same cruise-control system, meaningful operations on the throttle include increasing or decreasing its value. The throttle in turn must be able to act upon the engine and so set its speed. Finally, every object is actually an instance of some class of objects. For example, a given cruise-control system interacts with one specific engine; this engine is actually one instance of a class of objects, all of which are engines. We may have six-cylinder engines or eight-cylinder engines; nonetheless, all exhibit similar behavior. The benefit of this view is that by grouping objects into sets of related objects, we factor out common properties and so localize our design decision for all instances of the class.

Keep in mind that object-oriented design is a partial life-cycle method; it focuses on the design and implementation phases of software development. (We will discuss the nature of this life cycle in more detail in Chapter 19.) As Abbott observes, "although the steps we follow in formalizing the strategy may appear mechanical... [the strategy] requires a great deal of real world knowledge and intuitive understanding of the problem" [2]. It is therefore necessary to couple object-oriented design with appropriate requirements and analysis methods in order to help create our model of reality. We have found Jackson Structured Development (JSD) to be a promising match. General data-flow techniques, such as those by Gane and Sarson, are also useful tools in building this abstraction of reality [3, 38]. A full discussion of these techniques is beyond the scope of this text, but for our purposes, it is sufficient that we work from a mental model of our abstraction of reality. The formality of JSD or data-flow approaches is essential to support the communication that must go on in massive systems where the developers are separated by time and distance.

In any approach, we recognize that we cannot expect to have perfect knowledge of the problem domain. Rather, the growth of our understanding is always iterative. As we go deeper into the design of our solution, we will most likely uncover new aspects of the problem that we did not recognize before. However, since our solution maps directly to the problem, this new-found understanding of the problem space typically does not radically affect the architecture of our solution. With an object-oriented approach, we are generally able to limit the scope of the change to those modules in the solution space that parallel objects in the problem space.

A program that implements a model of reality can thus be viewed as a set of objects that interact with one another. We can design a system in an object-oriented manner by following these steps:

- Identify the objects and their attributes.

- Identify the operations that affect each object and the operations that each object must initiate.

- Establish the visibility of each object in relation to other objects.

- Establish the interface of each object.

- Evaluate the objects.

- Implement each object.

We have evolved these steps from an approach first proposed by Abbott [4, 5, 6, 7].

Identify the Objects

The first step, *identify the objects and their attributes,* involves recognizing major actors, agents, and servers in the problem space, plus their role in our model of reality. Usually, the objects we identify in this step derive from the nouns we use in describing the problem space. We may also find several objects of interest that are similar. In such a situation, we must establish a class of objects of which there are many instances. For example, Abbott observes that in describing our model of reality, we may uncover several types of noun phrases:

- *Common nouns* name a class of entities (e.g., table, terminal, sensor).

- *Mass nouns and units of measure* name a quality, an activity, a substance, or a quantity of the same entity (e.g., water, matter, fuel).

- *Proper nouns and nouns of direct reference* name a specific instance (e.g., heat sensor, my table, abort switch).

Common nouns, mass nouns, and units of measure do not identify specific instances but rather serve to identify a class of objects, which we can characterize as abstract data types (see Chapter 6).

Identify the Operations

The identification step serves to characterize the behavior of each object or class of objects. Here we establish the semantics of the object by determining the operations that can be meaningfully performed on the object or by the object. We also at this time establish the dynamic behavior of each object by identifying the constraints on time and space that must be observed. For example, we might specify a time ordering for operations, such as that "open" is performed before "close."

Establish the Visibility

When we establish the visibility of each object in relation to other objects, we identify the static dependencies among objects and classes of objects—in other words, what objects "see" and are "seen" by a given object. The purpose of this step is to capture the topology of objects from our model of reality. In the next chapter, we will learn some symbols that we can apply to portray these relationships of visibility and scope.

Establish the Interface

To establish the interface of each object, we produce a module specification by using some suitable formal notation (in our case, Ada). This step serves to capture the static semantics of each object or class of objects that we established in the previous step. This specification also serves as a contract between the "clients" of an object and the object itself. Put another way, the interface forms the boundary between the outside view and the inside view of an object.

An interface provides an abstraction of an object or classes by defining operations. Indeed, good interfaces are often referred to simply as abstractions.

It is within interfaces that information hiding is practiced; what is not defined in an interface is often just as crucial as what is defined. The separation of the inside and outside views provides information hiding.

Evaluate the Objects

Determining which aspects of the problem space will become objects of the solution space is not an easy task. Even the most experienced designers cannot always expect to find the "right" objects on the first try. Thus, a crucial step in design is to evaluate objects (and the design as a whole) to determine if you must reiterate to identify new objects. In Chapter 10 we will introduce a number of simple heuristics that are used to evaluate objects.

Implement Each Object

The sixth and final step, implement each object, involves choosing a suitable representation for each object or class of objects and implementing the interface from the previous step. This may involve composition, further decomposition, or both. Occasionally, an object will consist of several subordinate objects. In this case, we can repeat our method to further decompose the object. More often, an object is implemented by composition, by building on top of existing lower-level objects or classes of objects. When prototyping a system, the developer may choose to defer the implementation of all objects until later. In this case the developer relies on the specification of the objects (with suitably stubbed implementations) in order to experiment with the architecture and behavior of a system. Similarly, the developer may try several alternative representations over the life of the object to experiment with the behavior of various implementations.

We will not follow a complete example of object-oriented design until Chapter 5, by which time we will have studied the necessary tools provided by our implementation language. However, even at this point we can see how our approach supports the principles of software engineering. Clearly, the object-oriented design method supports abstraction and information hiding, since the foundation of this approach is that we directly map our model of reality into the solution space. In addition, with Ada as the design language, we can physically hide the details of our operations as well as the representation of our objects.

This method also provides a purposeful strategy for decomposing a system into modules. Using this strategy, we localize our design decisions to match our view of the real world. Furthermore, we now have a uniform notation for selecting the objects and operations that are part of our design. Of course, as is the case with any development strategy, we must rely on some management tools to ensure the completeness and confirmability of our design, but because of the enforceable structure the object-oriented method provides, our task is much easier.

3.3   Ada as a Design Language

Any language, human or computer, does two things for the user: First, it provides a *range of expression*. For example, a certain Eskimo dialect has more than 30 words for snow. Similarly, an APL programmer is permitted to think in terms of vectors because of the language's rich set of vector operations. Second, a language *constrains* the user's thinking. For example, notice how rich the English language is in expressing action, while many other European languages have a richer set of nouns; think also about a FORTRAN programmer trying to solve a problem using recursion.

Within any given computer language, sufficient tools must be provided to allow us to express a problem solution. Ideally, we would like to use a language that lets us directly reflect our view of the problem space. With languages from the early generations, we too often have to fit the solution to the language, rather than adapting the language to the solution. As a result, our tools get in the way of the primary goal—solving the problem. In the case where programming from the problem space into a language directly reflects our structure of the problem space, we are presented with an implementation that is understandable and therefore helpful in managing the complexity of the larger system. Such a language must provide tools for expressing primitive objects and operations and must, in addition, be extensible, so that we can build our own abstract objects and operations. In the best case, we also need our language to enforce these abstractions.

Ada is such a language. Not only is Ada suitable as an implementation language, but it is expressive enough to serve as a vehicle for capturing our design decisions. It provides a rich set of constructs for describing primitive objects and operations and, in addition, offers a packaging construct with which we can build and enforce our own abstractions. In the next chapter, we begin an intensive examination of the technical details of the language, using it in conjunction with our object-oriented design method. Note that this method is only one model with which to apply Ada; we can apply any traditional design method with it. However, Ada provides the developer some unique features not found in most production languages, including tasking, exception handling, and packaging. As a result, the capabilities of Ada demand that we break ourselves away from the flat, sequential mind-set into which other languages force us and instead think in the broader terms of the problem space. Our object-oriented design method offers such a conceptual model.

Summary

- Functional development methods do not address abstraction and information hiding effectively. They are usually inadequate for problem domains with natural concurrency, and they are often unresponsive to changes in the problem space.

- Object-oriented design methods mitigate these problems.

- With object-oriented methods, the architecture of a system is organized around the concept of objects and classes of objects that parallel our model of reality.

- An object is an entity that has state, is characterized by the operations it undergoes and initiates, and is an instance of a class of objects.

- Object-oriented techniques map well to Ada; in this regard, Ada may serve not only as an implementation language but also as a design language.

Exercises

1. Consider an apple as an abstract data type. What are the operations applicable to objects of type apple? Consider the different users of the apple, including the farmer, the grocer, and the consumer.

2. Consider the book you are holding. What are the meaningful operations that the book might undergo?

3. Is it possible to create abstractions using assembly language? Defend your answer.

4. We can categorize the noun phrases in our sentences as direct objects, agents, sources, destinations, locations, conveyances, or cogents. Take a paragraph from any source and classify the nouns in this way.

*5. Obtain a reference manual or definition for the languages Smalltalk, CLU, and LIS, or perhaps Pascal. How do these languages permit us to create both data and functional abstractions?

*6. Consider the problem of building a cruise-control system. Using a functional approach, list the major steps in the overall process. Using an object-oriented approach, define the major objects and classes of objects in the model of reality.

*7. Consider the implementation of an automated vending machine that dispenses soft drinks. Compare and contrast a functional and an object-oriented decomposition.

CHAPTER 4

An Overview of the Language

Requirements for the Language
Ada from the Top Down
Ada from the Bottom Up
Summary of Language Characteristics

Having laid a foundation of modern software engineering principles, we are now ready to examine the Ada language itself. The goal of this gentle introduction is to give you a hint of Ada's power, while at the same time exposing you to some of its structure and terminology. Don't strive for deep understanding yet: Although several code examples are provided in this chapter, they are given only for the purpose of illustrating the Ada form. Furthermore, don't expect to comprehend the full implications of each example. A rigorous discussion of each construct will come in later chapters. For the moment, we will apply the principle of information hiding and study only the highest abstractions of the language.

4.1   Requirements for the Language

Considering the problem domain for which it was designed, it is no wonder that Ada had to be a language with considerable expressive power. In particular, consider the STEELMAN requirements, which mandated a language supporting [1]:

- Structured constructs
- Strong typing
- Relative and absolute precision specification

- Information hiding and data abstraction
- Concurrent processing
- Exception handling
- Generic definition
- Machine-dependent facilities

These requirements pushed the state of the art in some ways, but they mainly caused many design concepts found in existing programming languages to be brought together in a single, high-order language. In this sense, Ada is not a new language; rather, it represents the coherent synthesis of an engineering effort.

During the creation of any system, developers have to make design tradeoffs; the Ada project was no exception. To guide their design decisions, the Ada language team established three goals for the language, namely [2]:

- Recognition of the importance of program reliability and maintainability
- Concern for programming as a human activity
- Efficiency

It is particularly interesting to note that the goals of reliability and maintainability (modifiability) were considered first, for, as we saw in Chapter 1, these are the resource consumers in the software life cycle. The human activity of programming was considered next, with an emphasis upon helping the developer manage the complexity of software solutions. As we shall see, well-structured Ada programs are easy to read (although sometimes tedious to write). Actually, this is a reasonable tradeoff, since a programmer will write a given piece of code only once, but that code will be read many times. In many ways, the language rules can guide the programmer into using a good design and coding style. Furthermore, the use of an Ada Programming Support Environment (APSE) complements the language and can make the development of Ada systems even easier. As the third goal, the language design team considered the efficiency of implementation and execution. Any language construct whose implementation was unclear or required excessive machine resources was rejected.

4.2   Ada from the Top Down

An Ada program (or, as we prefer to call it, an Ada *system*) is composed of one or more program *units*, each of which can be separately compiled. Program units consist of subprograms, tasks, packages, and generic units. A *subprogram* is either a procedure or a function, and it expresses a sequential action. A *task*, on the other hand, defines an action that is logically executed in parallel with other tasks. A task can be implemented on a single processor, a multiprocessor, or a network of computers. A *package* is a collection of computational resources, which may encapsulate data types, data objects, subprograms, tasks, or even other packages. A package's primary purpose is to express and enforce a user's logical abstractions within the language. Finally, a *generic unit* is a template for subprograms and packages and serves as the primary mechanism for building reusable software components. Table 4.1 summarizes the characteristics of each Ada program unit and, in addition, lists the applications for each. In subsequent chapters, we shall study these applications in detail.

All Ada program units generally have a similar two-part structure, consisting of a specification and a body. The *specification* identifies the information visible to the client of that program unit (the interface), while the *body* contains the unit implementation details, which can be logically and textually hidden from the client. To aid in managing the development of large solutions, the specification part and body can also be compiled separately. Therefore, a developer can write the specification of the high-level program units, thus creating an enforceable design structure for the solution. Later in the development process, developers can add unit bodies and refine them independently to complete the implementation of the system.

Because the problem domain for which Ada was intended is complex, an Ada system may consist of hundreds if not thousands of program units.

Table 4.1 Summary of Ada Program Units

Program Unit	Characteristic	Applications
Subprogram	Sequential action	Main program units Definition of functional control Definition of type operations
Package	Collection of resources	Named collection of declarations Groups of related program units Abstract data types Abstract state machines
Task	Parallel action	Concurrent actions Routing messages Controlling resources Interrupts
Generic unit	Template	Reusable software components

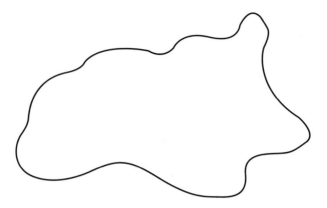

Figure 4.1 Symbol for an undefined entity

As our solution grows in size, its structure becomes increasingly difficult for us to comprehend. Recalling the notation we first introduced in Chapter 2, we can map each Ada program unit to a unique symbol [3, 4, 5]. As we describe these symbols, notice how we express the specification and body of each unit.

As Figure 4.1 indicates, we can represent an undefined or hidden entity (that is, an object) as an amorphous blob. This shape symbolizes that the structure of that entity is not relevant to us at this level and, in fact, is not even visible. In Figure 4.2, a subprogram is represented as a linear structure, implying its sequential nature. Here we emphasize the two-part

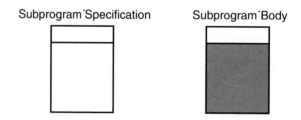

Figure 4.2 Symbols for an Ada subprogram

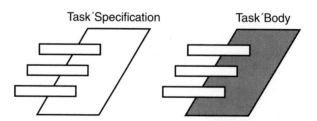

Figure 4.3 Symbols for an Ada task

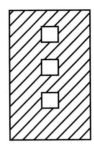

Figure 4.4 Package with visible parts

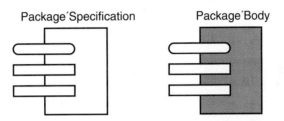

Figure 4.5 Symbols for an Ada package

structure of the unit by distinguishing its specification and its body. Figure 4.3 shows that we visualize a task as a parallelogram, implying its parallel nature. Like the subprogram symbols, the symbols separate the specification and the body.

Packages are a very important and versatile Ada structure and demand a special symbol. Ichbiah describes a package as a wall surrounding a collection of logically related entities. As shown in Figure 4.4, we conceptualize a visible portion (the specification) of a package as windows in the wall. If we rotate the wall 90 degrees on the *y* axis, we have the graphic representation for a package as viewed externally. As shown in Figure 4.5, we now see the windows as windowsills. We indicate the body as a separate figure.

Because generic units are templates, we can adopt the package and subprogram symbols. As Figure 4.6 illustrates, generic units also display a two-part structure.

We can easily represent a complex software structure using these symbols. For example, Figure 4.7 shows two communicating tasks. The line indicates that the two tasks are interdependent; the arrow points from the calling task to the subordinate (called) task. Since tasks *cannot* be compiled separately (more on this in Chapter 14), we might nest them in a package body, as we see in Figure 4.8. As Figure 4.9 illustrates, as we move up one more level, we can see more of the design. In this example, the

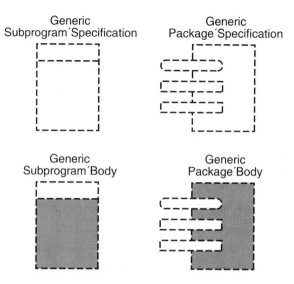

Figure 4.6 Symbols for Ada generic units

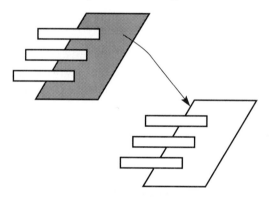

Figure 4.7 Communicating Ada tasks

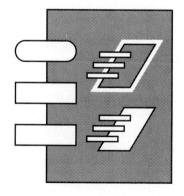

Figure 4.8 Nesting Ada program units

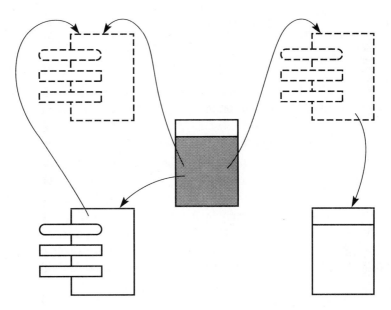

Figure 4.9 An Ada system from the top down

arrows indicate that the subprogram body uses the services of the package (its specification) as well as those of two generic packages. Notice that the topology of Ada systems is *not* strictly hierarchical. Furthermore, packages and generic units tend to be the primary units of decomposition.

4.3   Ada from the Bottom Up

We can write every Ada construct with a basic graphic character set, including:

- *Uppercase letters:*
  A B C D E F G H I J K L M N O P Q R S T U V W X Y Z
- *Digits:*
  0 1 2 3 4 5 6 7 8 9
- *Special characters:*
  " # ´ ( ) * + , - . / : ; < = > _ | &
- *The space character*

STEELMAN required such a character set to facilitate the transportability of program units at the source level. Ada permits us to extend this character set to include the rest of the 95-character ASCII (American Standard Code for Information Interchange) graphic set, including:

- *Lowercase letters:*
  a b c d e f g h i j k l m n o p q r s t u v w x y z
- *Special characters:*
  ! $? @ [\ ] ` { } ~ ^ %

Programs written with the extended character set can be converted to an equivalent program written in the basic character set.

Lexical Units

The basic tokens of the language, called *lexical units,* are built from the Ada character sets. Lexical units consist of identifiers, numeric literals, character literals, strings, delimiters, and comments. *Identifiers* are formed of a letter followed by a series of letters, digits, and/or embedded under-scores (to increase readability). Identifiers can also be reserved words; Ada has 63 of these, as indicated in Table 4.2. Ada imposes no limitation upon the length of user-defined identifier names, as long as they fit on a single line. The following are legal Ada identifiers:

```
Colors_of_rainbow

temperature_sensor_37

Page_Count

POLL_TERMINALS
```

Table 4.2   Ada Reserved Words

abort	declare	generic	of	select
abs	delay	goto	or	separate
accept	delta		others	subtype
access	digits	if	out	
all	do	in		task
and		is	package	terminate
array			pragma	then
at	else		private	type
	elsif	limited	procedure	
	end	loop		
begin	entry		raise	use
body	exception		range	
	exit	mod	record	when
			rem	while
		new	renames	with
case	for	not	return	
constant	function	null	reverse	xor

Ada makes no distinction between names using different cases. Thus, the identifiers PAGE_COUNT, Page_Count, and page_count are equivalent, but PAGECOUNT is not, since the underscore is significant. In later examples in this book, user-defined identifiers are written in mixed-case, as in Page_Count.

Numeric literals represent exact integer or real values. Numbers can be expressed in any base from two to sixteen. In addition, underscores are permitted between the digits of a number, although they serve only to enhance readability and are virtually ignored by the compiler. The following are legal integer numeric literals:

    7

    1_000_000   — the same as 1000000

    1_00_00_00   — the same value

    1e6   — the same value, read as 1×10^6

    2#1100#   — base 2 equivalent of 12_{10}

    16#C#   — base 16 equivalent of 12_{10}

The following are legal real numeric literals:

    0.125

    3.141_592_65   — the value of π

    2.78e-3   — equivalent to 0.00278

    1.0e6   — the same value as 1000000.0

    16#F.0#   — the same value as 15.0_{10}

Real numbers require at least one digit on each side of the decimal point.

A *character literal* consists of any one of the 95 graphic ASCII characters enclosed between single quotes. A *string*, on the other hand, is a sequence of zero or more characters enclosed between double quotes. For example:

    'A'   -- a character literal

    '*'   -- another character literal

    ''''   -- a character literal whose value is '

    ""   -- a null string

    "Time of day"   -- a string of length 11

    """"   -- a string whose value is "

Delimiters constitute the next class of lexical units and consist of the simple symbols:

```
´ ( ) * + , -- . / : ; < = > | &
```

To these, add the compound symbols:

```
=> .. ** := /= >= <= << >> < >
```

Delimiters have special meaning, depending upon their context.

Any number of spaces can separate adjacent lexical units. Each lexical unit must fit on one line, but can be placed anywhere on a line, since Ada is a free-field language. Lines also affect the layout of *comments*, the last formal class of lexical units. Comments start with a double hyphen (--) and terminate with the end of a line.

Although not considered a lexical unit, one other category of constructs is defined at the lowest level of the language. A *pragma*, from the Latin *pragmaticus (to order)* is simply a directive to the Ada compiler. A description of the predefined Ada pragmas is provided in Appendix B.

Type Definitions and Object Declarations

Every programming language consists of:

- Rules for expressing the language itself

- Objects and a mechanism for defining them

- Operations and a mechanism for constructing them

In the previous section, we described some of the rules for expressing the language (its tokens), and so we now turn to the second element on the list, which consists of data types and objects. An abstract *data type* characterizes:

- A set of values

- A set of operations applicable to objects of the type

In the previous chapter, we learned of classes of objects. For historical reasons, most programming languages—including Ada—use the term *type* as an equivalent expression. For example, we may consider `Waiting_Line` to be a type. Clearly, a waiting line has a set of values (the entities that can wait) and a set of operations (add to the line, remove from the line). Note that a type such as `Waiting_Line` defines only a template. If we refer to the "third checkout line at our neighborhood grocery store," then we are referencing an object whose type is `Waiting_Line`. This object may denote a particular value, such as "three people are in the line."

In Ada, several classes of types are available, including:

- *Scalar data types:*

  integer

  real

  enumeration
- *Access data types*
- *Private data types*
- *Subtype and derived types*
- *Composite data types:*

  array

  record

We consider the first class of types (integer, real, and enumeration) to be scalar types since they have no component parts and thus define one-dimensional values. *Integer types* define collections of whole numbers (numbers without fractional parts). *Real types* define collections of numbers with fractional parts (floating-point or fixed-point numbers). *Enumeration types* permit a user to define his or her own set of values. The following are integer types:

```
Integer                    -- a predefined type
Natural                    -- a predefined type, >= 0
type Index is range 1..50; -- a user-defined type
```

The following are real types:

```
Float                      -- a predefined type
type Mass      is digits 10;   -- a floating-point type
type Voltage   is delta 0.01   -- a fixed-point type
  range -12.0..+24.0;
```

The following are enumeration types:

```
Boolean                    -- a predefined type (False, True)
Character                  -- another predefined type
type Color is (Black, Red, Green, Blue, Cyan, Magenta, Orange, White);
                           -- a user-defined type
```

Collectively, integer types and enumeration types are called *discrete types.*

Ada also defines two structured types, arrays and records. *Arrays* are collections of the same types of elements, while *records* are collections of the same or different elements. For example, the following are valid array type definitions:

```
type Chess_Board is array (1..8, 1..8) of Color;
    -- a two-dimensional array type

type Pixel is array (Color) of Float;
    -- an eight-element array type

type Sensor is array (Index range 5..10) of Voltage;
    -- a six-element array type

type Vector is array (Positive range <>) of Integer;
    -- an unconstrained array type
```

The following are valid record type definitions:

```
type Date is
  record
    Day   : Integer range 1..31;
    Month : Integer range 1..12;
    Year  : Natural;
  end record;

type Valve is
  record
    Name      : String(1..20);
    Location  : String(1..30);
    Open      : Boolean;
    Flow_Rate : Float range 0.0..30.0;
    Inspected : Date;
  end record;

type Value (Defined : Boolean := False) is
  record
    case Defined is
      when False => null;
      when True  => Quantity : Integer;
    end case;
  end record;
```

So far, we have introduced types for static objects, that is, objects that are known at compilation time. However, there may be cases where data objects must be created dynamically (during execution time). For example, consider a data acquisition system that changes its sampling rate depending upon the values of the input. In this case, it is impossible to know in advance the volume of data to be buffered. In Ada, access values point to other objects and so permit us to dynamically create objects and refer to them with access objects. For example:

```
type Buffer_Pointer is access Buffer; -- pointers to Buffer objects
```

As we shall see in Chapter 14, we can name tasks as types so that we can create new tasks at execution time.

As another class of data types, Ada permits *private types,* which are used only in packages. Just like the other types, private types define a set of values and a collection of applicable operations. Unlike the other types, however, the structures of private types are not visible to a client. Furthermore, an implementor can define certain operations for private types, and these then become the only operations a user can employ. Private types thus provide a mechanism for enforcing information hiding and creating new abstract data types. For example, the following defines an abstract stack:

```
package Stacks is  -- package encapsulating a private type
   type Stack is private;
   procedure Push (Element : in  Integer; On   : in out Stack);
   procedure Pop  (Element : out Integer; From : in out Stack);
private
   Maximum_Elements : constant Integer := 100;
   type List is array (1..Maximum_Elements) of Integer;
   type Stack is
     record
       Structure : List;
       Top       : Integer range 0..Maximum_Elements := 0;
     end record;
end Stacks;
```

Generally, every package specification must have a body, but for this example, we will omit the body implementation. The only operations a client may perform on objects of type `Stack` are `Push` and `Pop`. The rules of the language prohibit clients from accessing the components of `Stack` objects directly.

Ada also has a mechanism to help us factor properties of parent types, namely, *subtypes* and *derived types.* We shall examine how these two classes of types support abstraction in Chapter 6.

Data types provide a mechanism only for describing the structure of data. *Declarations,* on the other hand, create instances (objects) of a given type. In Ada, object declarations permit the creation of variables and constants. For example, the following are variable declarations:

```
Counter   : Integer;        -- using a predefined type
Birth_Day : Date;           -- using a user-defined type
My_Buffer : Stacks.Stack;   -- another user-defined type
```

The following are examples of object constants:

```
Pi           : constant          := 3.141_592_65;
Port_Address : constant Integer := 8#777_776#;
```

Ada is strongly typed, which means that we may not directly combine objects having different types. This is another case in which the language can enforce the user's abstractions.

Names and Expressions

In any language, names are used to denote declared entities. In large problems, the name space may contain hundreds if not thousands of names. As a result, the programmer may have a difficult time avoiding using names already defined, while at the same time trying to create meaningful ones for new entities. One of the mechanisms Ada employs to avoid this problem is *overloading*. Overloading permits a programmer to use the same name for different entities, as long as the use of the name is not ambiguous. For example, it would be reasonable to overload enumeration literals:

```
type Sensor_Type is (Temperature, Humidity, Pressure);
    -- an enumeration type

type Alarm      is (Normal, Temperature, Intrusion);
    -- overloading the literal Temperature
```

Of course, the unrestricted use of overloading can be confusing, and so must be applied with care.

As we shall discuss in detail in Chapter 9, names and constants can be used in expressions to calculate a value. Ada has the usual collection of operators, including (from highest to lowest precedence):

```
**        not    abs                    -- highest precedence operator
*         /      mod     rem            -- multiplying operator
+         -                             -- unary adding operator
+         -      &                      -- binary adding operator
=         /=     <       <=   >   >= -- relational operator
and       or     xor                    -- logical operator
and then  or else                       -- short-circuit operator
```

Using these operators, one can form expressions. For example:

```
Pi                         -- a simple expression
(B ** 2) - (4.0 * A * C)   -- a more complex expression
Char in 'A'..'Z'           -- a Boolean expression
(2.789 ** 4) + 36.0        -- a static expression
```

As we shall see in Chapter 8, we can redefine some (overload) *operator symbols* so that they apply to abstract data types.

Statements

Not only does Ada have a rich set of constructs for describing data, but it also contains a powerful collection of statements for creating algorithms. Since Ada is a structured language, statements for sequential, iterative, and conditional control are provided (in addition to special statements, such as those related to tasks and exceptions). Ada's statements include:

- *Sequential control:*
  assignment
  block
  null
  return
  procedure call

- *Conditional control:*
  case
  if

- *Iterative control:*
  exit
  loop

- *Other statements:*
  abort
  accept
  code
  delay
  entry call
  goto
  raise
  select

Each statement will be studied in detail in Chapters 8, 9, 14, and 15.

The assignment statement and subprogram call form the primary sequential control structures. The *assignment statement* gives a newly calculated value to a variable:

```
Counter := Counter + 1;   -- a simple assignment
Birth_Day.Year := 1955;   -- a record component assignment
```

Subprograms permit us to invoke named algorithms. As we shall study in Chapter 8, we can match actual and formal parameters, using positional or named notation. For example:

```
Start_Filling_Tank;                  -- a procedure call
Value := Math_Functions.Tan(Angle);  -- a function call
Rotate(Points, 30.0);                -- a procedure call using
                                     -- positional notation
Rotate(Points, Angle => 17.6);       -- a procedure call using
                                     -- named parameter
                                     -- associations
```

There are several other sequential statements, but we defer a discussion of them until Chapter 9.

Ada uses the **if** and **case** statements for conditional control. The **case** statement selects for execution one of several alternatives based on a discrete expression, while the **if** statement selects for execution none or one of several alternatives based on a boolean expression. For example:

```
if Buffer_Size = Maximum_Buffer_Size then  -- an if statement
   Process_Overflow;
end if;

if Valve_Status = Open then          -- an if-then-else
   Read_Flow(Rate);                  -- structure
else
   Read_Pressure(Value);
end if;

case Buffer_Size is                          -- selection from multiple paths
   when Maximum_Buffer_Size / 2 => Send_Overflow_Warning;
                                   Get_New_Value;
   when Maximum_Buffer_Size     => Process_Overflow;
   when others                  => Get_New_Value;
end case;

case Pixel_Color is                          -- selection from multiple paths
   when Red | Green | Blue      => Increase_Saturation;
   when Cyan..White             => Make_Black;
   when others                  => null;
end case;
```

Iteration is provided in Ada with one of the forms of the **loop** statement. Ada permits a basic loop, a counting loop, and a **while** loop. We can apply an **exit** statement within a loop to quit the iteration. For example:

```
loop                          -- a basic loop
  Read_Modem(Symbol);
  exit when End_Of_Transmission;
  Displays(Symbol);
end loop;

for Item in List'range        -- a counting loop
  loop
    Sum := Sum + List(Item);
  end loop;

while Data_Available          -- a while loop
  loop
    Read(My_File, Input_Buffer);
    Process(Input_Buffer);
  end loop;
```

The remainder of Ada's statements apply mainly to tasks and exception handling; we will delay their discussion until later.

Subprograms

As we have already seen, Ada contains a number of primitive types, plus a mechanism for creating abstract data types (using private types). In terms of specifying algorithms, the Ada subprogram parallels this concept by providing a mechanism for creating abstract operations. Subprograms are the basic unit of execution in an Ada system and can be of one of two classes:

- Procedures

- Functions

Subprograms, like the other Ada program units (packages and tasks), have two parts, a specification and a body. The specification identifies the name of the subprogram along with any formal parameters and return types (for functions); this represents the client's interface to the unit. The body, on the other hand, encapsulates a sequence of statements that define the algorithm itself. For example:

```
procedure Rotate (Points : in out Coordinate; Angle  : in Radians) is
begin
    -- sequence of statements
end Rotate;
```

```
function Hash (Key : in Elements) return Hash_Value is
begin

   -- sequence of statements
end Hash;

function "*" (Left, Right : Matrix) return Matrix is
begin

   -- sequence of statements
end "*";
```

The terms in, out, and in out specify the mode, or direction, of the data flow relative to the subprogram; functions may have in parameters only. Also, note in the last example how we redefined an operator symbol to apply to matrices, an abstract data type. We shall examine the structure and applications of Ada's subprograms in detail in Chapter 8.

Packages

Packages are another of Ada's fundamental program units. Packages permit a user to encapsulate a group of logically related entities (a set of computational resources). As such, packages directly support the software principles of data abstraction and information hiding. As we shall see throughout the remaining chapters (particularly Chapter 11), there are several ways to use packages properly. Like subprograms, packages consist of a specification and a body. The specification forms the programmer's contract with the package client. A client never need see the package body, for it hides the implementation of the specification. For example, a client does not need to know how the functions work in a package with the following specification:

```
package Graphics is
   type Turtle is private;
   procedure Set_Origin (A_Turtle     : in out Turtle;
                          X_Coordinate : in      Integer;
                          Y_Coordinate : in      Integer);
   procedure Turn (A_Turtle : in out Turtle);
   procedure Move (A_Turtle : in out Turtle);
   function X_Location (A_Turtle : in Turtle) return Integer;
   function Y_Location (A_Turtle : in Turtle) return Integer;
private
   type Turtle is ...  -- completed type declaration
end Graphics;
```

The body of this package takes the form:

```
package body Graphics is
    procedure Set_Origin (A_Turtle     : in out Turtle;
                          X_Coordinate : in      Integer;
                          Y_Coordinate : in      Integer) is
    begin
       -- sequence of statements
    end Set_Origin;
    procedure Turn (A_Turtle : in out Turtle) is
    begin
       -- sequence of statements
    end Turn;
    procedure Move (A_Turtle : in out Turtle) is
    begin
       -- sequence of statements
    end Move;
    function X_Location (A_Turtle : in Turtle) return Integer is
    begin
       -- sequence of statements including a return
    end X_Location;
    function Y_Location (A_Turtle : in Turtle) return Integer is
    begin
       -- sequence of statements including a return
    end Y_Location;
end Graphics;
```

In this manner, we can separate the specifications of an abstraction from its implementation.

Tasks

Tasks form another class of Ada program units. Up to this point, we have introduced structures that are sequential in nature. In real systems, however, a number of different activities may have to progress concurrently. For example, in a process control situation, a system might have to monitor dozens of different sensors and report on them immediately if an out-of-limits condition occurs. Polling forces a timed order on reading the sensors; therefore, some transient conditions might be missed. An implementor most likely would see the process as containing several concurrent tasks; Ada permits such an abstraction directly within the language.

The Ada tasking model is based on the concept of communicating sequential processes. In other words, we can view tasks as independent, concurrent operations that communicate with one another by passing messages. When two tasks pass messages to each other, they are said to *rendezvous.* The basic mechanism for communication is through the `entry` and `accept` statements. For example, suppose we have a task that samples a line voltage, and then passes a message to another task after several samples have been made. The calling task (`Sampler`) is said to *enter* the other task (`Server`):

```
task body Sampler is  -- body of the sampling task
begin
  loop
     -- statements to get voltage samples
     Server.Report_On(Samples);
  end loop;
end Sampler;
```

The called task must accept the entry call:

```
task body Server is  -- body of the receiving task
begin
  loop
     -- sequence of statements
     accept Report_On (Samples : in Voltages) do
        -- sequence of statements
     end Report_On;
     -- sequence of statements
  end loop;
end Server;
```

In general, the way in which the called task processes the samples will be hidden from the calling task. The only visible portions of the called tasks will be found in the task specification, such as:

```
task Server is   -- the task specification
  entry Report_On (Samples : in Voltages);
end Server;
```

In any case, if one task gets to the entry point before the other, the former task will suspend itself *(put itself to sleep)* until the other task arrives at the rendezvous point. In the event that a designer desires that a task not wait, Ada has alternative constructs, including:

- Delay
- Selective entry
- Selective wait
- Timed entry

We defer the presentation of these constructs to Chapter 14.

Exception Handling

In many operations, it is critical that a system be able to recover quickly and gracefully from error conditions. In most programming languages, an input format error, or perhaps a divide by zero, would cause the program to crash and pass control back to the operating system. For an embedded system that is running independently of any human intervention, such a condition would be unacceptable. However, Ada permits a block-structured exception-handling capability. Exceptions, which are typically (but not necessarily) error conditions, can be predefined (such as a numeric error for a divide by zero) or user-defined (such as an overflowing buffer condition). Predefined exceptions are raised implicitly. For example, the following assignment statements would raise `Constraint_Error` at run-time:

```
type Index is range 1..10;
Index_I  : Index;
A_String : String (1..10);

Index_I     := 0;    -- violation of type constraint
A_String(11) := 'x';  -- violation of index constraint
```

User-defined exceptions are raised explicitly, as in the following:

```
procedure Pop (Element : out Integer; From : in out Stack) is
begin
  if Stack.Top = 0 then
    raise Stack_Empty;
  else
    -- statements
  end if;
end Pop;
```

If an exception occurs, normal processing will be abandoned and control will pass to the exception handler. If a handler is not present, then control will continue passing up to the next lexical (invoking) level until either a handler is found or the operating system (environment) is reached. We shall study the form and application of Ada's exception facility in Chapter 15.

Generic Program Units

The designers of Ada recognized that it would be applied to large programming projects. As a result, features were required to help manage the complexity of such systems. We have already mentioned one of these facilities, that of separate compilation units. In addition, Ada allows generic units as a mechanism for building reusable software components. For example, in a telemetry processing system, we may need to buffer several kinds of objects. The algorithm to process such buffers would be the same; only the data types would be different. A programmer may take this common algorithm and parameterize it with the data items, thus creating a generic unit. Note that this parameterization is performed at compilation time. For example, if we take the Stacks package introduced earlier in the chapter and add a generic part, we have:

```
generic  -- the generic part
  Limit : Natural;
  type Data is private;
package Stacks is
  type Stack is private;
  procedure Push (Element : in Data;  On   : in out Stack);
  procedure Pop  (Element : out Data; From : in out Stack);
private
  type List is array (1..Limit) of Data;
  type Stack is
    record
      Structure : List;
      Top       : Integer range 0..Limit := 0;
    end record;
end Stacks;
```

A generic definition does not create any code; it only defines a template for the algorithm. A user must *instantiate* (create an instance of) a generic unit to create a local copy. Thus, we can create several kinds of stacks:

```
package Integer_Stack is new Stacks (100, Integer);
package Float_Stack is new Stacks (Limit => 300, Data => Float);
```

In the first example, the declaration creates a package logically equivalent to the one presented earlier in the chapter. In the second example, named parameter association is used to improve readability. We shall study generics in detail in Chapter 12.

Representation Specification

Even when programming with a high-order language, it is sometimes necessary to exploit underlying hardware features. In most languages, a programmer would have to create a separate assembly language routine and then link it to the high-order language. Ada, however, includes features to specify implementation-dependent features and data representation. In particular, Ada permits the specification of:

- Address
- Enumeration type representation
- Length
- Record type representation

For example:

```
for Printer_Status   use at 16#177_776#;              -- address specification
for Alarm            use (Normal        => 0,  -- enumeration type
                          Temperature    => 5,  -- representation
                          Intrusion      => 57);
for Degrees'Size     use 3*Bytes;                     -- length specification
```

We shall examine these and other low-level programming features in Chapter 16.

Input/Output

Embedded computer systems do not usually interface to classical input/output (I/O) devices such as printers or terminals. Instead, unique "black box" interfaces are more common. To handle such a wide variety of devices, Ada I/O is achieved through several packages. In particular, Ada has predefined packages (see Appendix C) for:

- *High_level I/O:*
  - nontext I/O   -- Sequential_ I/O and Direct_I/O
  - text I/O   -- Text I/O
- *Low_level I/O*   -- Low_level I/O

Of course, a programmer is permitted to create his or her own I/O packages. Since we have not yet studied the nature of Ada's packages in detail, we shall delay a full examination of I/O until Chapter 18.

4.4   Summary of Language Characteristics

This brief overview shows that Ada is a complete, general-purpose, high-order language. It emphasizes the importance of program reliability and maintainability and is applicable for use in large, frequently modified software systems. Perhaps the most important feature of Ada is that it embodies the concepts of modern software methodologies, thus providing an effective tool for helping manage the complexity of software solutions. In the chapters that follow, we shall examine the form and use of each Ada facility in detail. Before we leave this chapter, let us study the structure of a complete Ada system as well as the steps we must follow to put it together. For example, consider an application that must manipulate complex numbers. Ada does not provide such a type directly, but through the use of packages such as abstract data types, we can extend the language to make a suitable abstraction available.

We must first ask ourselves: What operations might a complex number undergo? Certainly, we must provide a way to set and retrieve the real and imaginary parts of the value of a complex number. In addition, it would be useful to provide mathematical operations, such as addition and subtraction. Thus, we might enumerate these operations as:

- Set   `-- set the value of the complex number`
- +   `-- add two complex numbers`
- -   `-- subtract two complex numbers`
- Real_Part   `-- return the real part of the number`
- Imaginary_Part `-- return the imaginary part of the number`

Ada encourages our use of abstraction by giving us a mechanism to capture our design decisions about complex numbers. Thus, we can express our view of complex numbers in the package specification:

```
package Complex is
  type Number is private;
  procedure Set (A_Number      : out Number;
                 Real_Part      : in  Float;
                 Imaginary_Part : in  Float);
  function "+" (Left, Right : in Number) return Number;
  function "-" (Left, Right : in Number) return Number;
  function Real_Part      (A_Number : in Number) return Float;
  function Imaginary_Part (A_Number : in Number) return Float;
```

```
private
  type Number is
    record
      Real_Part      : Float;
      Imaginary_Part : Float;
    end record;
end Complex;
```

As we discussed earlier in this chapter, packages have two parts to them. The visible part of a package (extending from the first line down through the upper declarations to the reserved word `private`) denotes everything that is visible to a client of the package; the private part of a package (including the body) encompasses everything else. In this manner, the type `Number` appears to the outside as a complex number with a restricted set of meaningful operations. However, its actual representation is hidden from all clients in the private part of the package. As we will study in a later chapter, Ada's rules are such that clients of this package cannot exploit any knowledge about the representation of the type `Number`. In this way, clients cannot violate our abstraction—a simple concept, yet an extremely important one when dealing with complex systems.

Having written this package specification, we can submit it for compilation. Recall that, since Ada units can be compiled separately, it is possible for us to develop parts of a system incrementally rather than all at once.

Next, we might write a procedure that uses the resources of this package. Since the package `Complex` has been compiled separately, we can gain visibility to it simply by naming it in what is called a *context specification*. In addition to the package `Complex`, we will also import the predefined package `Text_IO`, which gives us input and output facilities. Thus, the skeleton of this procedure appears as:

```
with Complex, Text_IO;  -- context specification
procedure Calculate is
  -- declarative part
begin
  -- sequence of statements
end Calculate;
```

Let us fill in the body of this procedure. Suppose that we want to manipulate two complex numbers and then display the value of one of them. Since Ada requires that we declare all objects before we use them, we must include several declarations in the body of the procedure:

```
with Complex, Text_IO;
procedure Calculate is
     First, Second : Complex.Number;
begin
  -- sequence of statements
end Calculate;
```

Notice how we name the type of First and Second. This is known as a fully qualified name, since we must qualify the name of the type, Number, with the name of the package that exported it, Complex. Thus, the full name of the type is Complex.Number.

Next, we need some way to write numbers of type Float. As we will study in greater detail later, Ada's predefined package Text_IO doesn't directly permit I/O on floating-point types, but it does provide a generic capability. Thus, we might add the instantiation:

```
with Complex, Text_IO;
procedure Calculate is
  First, Second : Complex.Number;
  package Complex_IO is new Text_IO.Float_IO(Float);
begin
  -- sequence of statements
end Calculate;
```

Among other things, this instantiation gives us a way to Put numbers of type Float.

We can complete the body of the procedure by adding a sequence of statements that first sets the value of First and Second, then evaluates an expression that alters the value of First, and finally, displays the value of Second:

```
with Complex, Text_IO;
procedure Calculate is
  First, Second : Complex.Number;
  package Complex_IO is new Text_IO.Float_IO(Float);
begin
  Complex.Set(First,
              Real_Part      => 5.7,
              Imaginary_Part => -5.8);
  Complex.Set(Second,
              Real_Part      => 25.7,
              Imaginary_Part => 18.35);
```

```
    First := Complex."-"(First, Second);
    Text_IO.Put('The real part of First is ');
    Complex_IO.Put(Complex.Real_Part(First), Aft => 2, Exp => 0);
    Text.IO.New_Line;
    Text_IO.Put('The imaginary part of First is ');
    Complex_IO.Put(Complex.Imaginary_Part(First), Aft => 2, Exp => 0);
    Text_IO.New_Line;
end Calculate;
```

Notice that our call to the procedure `Complex_IO.Put` includes a parameter for the number of digits after the radix point (`Aft`) as well as the size of the exponent to be displayed (`Exp`). The careful reader will also observe that our subtraction of `First` and `Second` looks strange. As we will learn in a later chapter, this is a result of Ada's visibility rules. We can simplify this expression by making the subtraction operation directly visible. If we add the following line in the declarative part:

```
use Complex;
```

We may then write the assignment statement as:

```
First := First - Second;
```

We can now take this procedure body and compile it. As we see in Figure 4.10, our Ada system currently consists of three separately compiled units. However, we are not yet ready to execute the system. Although we can build on top of existing abstractions immediately (as we did for the procedure `Calculate,` which depends upon the resources of `Complex` and `Text_IO`), we must complete the body of the package `Complex` before we can run

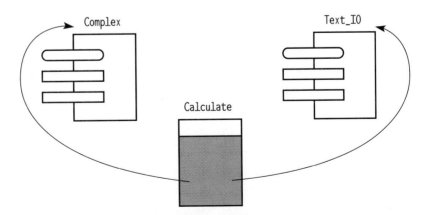

Figure 4.10 Topology of complex number system

Calculate. As we will study in greater detail later, the body of a package must complete the items introduced in the specification. Thus, the body of Complex must provide an implementation for each procedure and function introduced in the specification. The skeleton of Complex appears as:

```
package body Complex is
   procedure Set (Left            : in out Number;
                  Real_Part       : in      Float;
                  Imaginary_Part : in      Float) is ...
      function "+" (First, Second : in Number) return Number is ...
      function "-" (First, Second : in Number) return Number is ...
      function Real_Part (Left : in Number) return Float is ...
      function Imaginary_Part (Left : in Number) return Float is ...
   end Complex;
```

We can complete the body of each subprogram with a few simple statements. Recall that the body of Complex is logically hidden from view of any clients. Thus, independent of the specification of Complex as well as of its clients, we have the freedom to choose any implementation as long as it provides the behavior we expect of our abstraction. In fact, it is possible for us to alter the body of Complex without affecting the specification of any clients. Practically, this means that we can develop a large system by first building the interfaces of each module, integrating all these pieces, and only then begin to deal with the implementation of each abstraction. Furthermore, we can try new implementations without recompiling the clients of our abstraction.

To show the closure on this example, let us include a complete body for the package Complex:

```
package body Complex is
   procedure Set (Left            : in out Number;
                  Real_Part       : in      Float;
                  Imaginary_Part : in      Float) is
   begin
     Left := (Real_Part, Imaginary_Part);
   end Set;

   function "+" (First, Second : in Number) return Number is
   begin
     return (First.Real_Part + Second.Real_Part;
             Second.Imaginary_Part + Second.Imaginary_Part);
   end "+";
```

```
    function "-" (First, Second : in Number) return Number is
    begin
      return (First.Real_Part - Second.Real_Part;
              Second.Imaginary_Part - Second.Imaginary_Part);
    end "-";

    function Real_Part (Left : in Number) return Float is
    begin
      return Left.Real_Part;
    end Real_Part;

    function Imaginary_Part (Left : in Number) return Float is
    begin
      return Left.Imaginary_Part;
    end Real_Part;
  end Complex;
```

We can now compile this unit to complete our system. After we link and load our system (as required by our particular implementation), we can execute the system by invoking the procedure `Calculate`, which acts at the root, or main program, of the system. Execution of this system results in the output:

```
The real part of First is -20.00
The imaginary part of First is -24.15
```

Summary

- Ada is a general-purpose language, but it has a number of facilities that make it well suited for the creation of massive, software-intensive systems.

- Ada systems are composed of one or more program units, consisting of subprograms, tasks, packages, and generic units.

- In general, each of these units has a two-part structure formed by the specification and the body. Each part can be compiled separately to support the incremental creation of large systems.

- Ada is a strongly typed language with facilities for the creation of primitive and user-defined abstractions.

- Ada provides sequential, conditional, and iterative statements. The statements serve as the primitive vocabulary of algorithmic abstractions.

- Subprograms include procedures and functions. They indicate sequential action.

- Packages are perhaps the most important facility in Ada; they serve as collections of logically related resources; hence, they are the fundamental building block of any Ada system.

- Tasks provide a mechanism for expressing concurrent actions.

- Generic units are templates of packages or subprograms. They are the key to the creation of reusable software components.

- Exceptions provide a mechanism for detecting and reacting to errors encountered during program execution.

- Ada provides representation specifications that give access to machine-dependent facilities.

- Existing language facilities (mainly packages) provide Ada's I/O capabilities; a number of predefined I/O packages exist for every validated implementation.

- Well-structured Ada systems have a topology that is quite different from that of earlier generations of languages; the topology of Ada systems is designed to parallel our abstractions of the real world.

Exercises   1.   It is unfair to directly compare specific facilities of two different languages, since the two were probably created to meet different requirements. However, at a high level (such as the level of this chapter), comparing Ada to FORTRAN, COBOL, Pascal, or any number of other languages is a reasonable exercise. Take your favorite language and compare and contrast the scope of its facilities against Ada.

2.   What Ada features directly support the principles of abstraction and information hiding? Modularity and localization? Uniformity, completeness, and confirmability? Reusability?

3.   Ada is an extensible language, which means that we have the capability of creating our own objects and operations. From what you know at this point, which of Ada's features support extensibility?

4.   Ada was designed for readability; what language features directly support this goal?

*5.   In what ways does the topology of Ada systems differ from that of other languages?

*6.   Why is this difference important?

PACKAGE

2

Data Structures

In the development of our understanding of complex phenomena, the most powerful tool available to the human intellect is abstraction.

Abstraction arises from a recognition of similarities between certain objects, situations, or processes in the real world, and the decision to concentrate on these similarities, and to ignore for the time being the differences.

C.A.R. Hoare
Notes on Data Structuring [4]

CHAPTER 5

The First Design Problem: Document Concordance

Define the Problem
Identify the Objects
Identify the Operations
Establish the Visibility
Establish the Interface
Implement Each Object

W e have traced the evolution of Ada and have seen a glimpse of its power and form. At this point, you should not expect yourself to have an intimate understanding of the language, but you should have developed a general model of its structure and range of expression. In the next 15 chapters, we shall examine Ada in detail from the perspective of the software engineering principles and object-oriented method discussed in Chapters 2 and 3. Our study of Ada's characteristics will be driven by the solution of five problems that cover a wide range of applications, including:

- Document concordance   Chapter 5

- Album data base   Chapters 7 and 10

- Tree generic unit   Chapter 13

- Environment monitor   Chapter 17

- Heads-up display   Chapter 21

We shall take each problem through the analysis and design stages that lead to an implementation in Ada; this approach will bring us through the entire language from the top down. As we complete a solution to each problem, we shall discover the need for certain facilities within the language. At that point we will step back and study those facilities in detail. The text will offer more than a grab bag of language syntax and semantics. Rather, we shall concentrate on the effective use of Ada and suggest a programming style that emphasizes clarity and understandability and that enforces and encourages abstraction, information hiding, modularity, and locality.

Along the way, you may find several additional references useful: Appendix E provides syntax charts for the entire language and Appendix D offers a programming style guide.

5.1   Define the Problem

Recall the steps of our object-oriented method from Chapter 3:

- Identify the objects
- Identify the operations
- Establish the visibility
- Establish the interface
- Implement each object

We are now ready to apply this method to the problem of designing a system that generates a concordance from a document. A *concordance* is an alphabetical index that shows the places in a document where each word may be found. For example, a concordance for this paragraph might appear as:

Word	Line Number
a	1 2 3 4
alphabetical	3
an	3
apply	1
might	4

Concordances are typically used as an aid in the study of massive works, such as the Bible or the collected works of Shakespeare. In a slightly different form, a system that creates a concordance might be used to provide the functionality of a cross-reference generator for programs or to create an index.

Let us state our problem: We want to develop a system that, given the name of a file containing a document, produces an exhaustive concordance of the document. (An exhaustive concordance lists all words—including the articles *the* and *a*—not just principal words.) Our system will be used on short documents, such as programs; therefore, we want it to include the number of the line in which each word appears, not the page number, as is the typical style for larger works. As we will see, this problem is slightly complex but simple enough to serve as a gentle first venture into an application of Ada.

5.2   Identify the Objects

How might we proceed in creating a software solution to our problem? With a functional approach, we would start by identifying the major steps in the overall process: reading all the words, sorting the words, then producing a report. However, as we learned in the previous chapters, the limitations of this approach become apparent as we tackle problems that are more and more complex.

Instead, we will apply an object-oriented method and begin by identifying the major objects that constitute our model of the problem space. Recall from Chapter 3 that an object is an entity that has state and can be characterized by the operations that it undergoes and initiates. From our discussion of the problem, we identify four objects or classes of objects:

- Words
- Line_Numbers
- Document
- Concordance

What magic did we use to derive these objects? None, really. If we think back to our description of the problem, these are the objects we used in describing the problem space. Indeed, we can identify the objects in the problem domain in an informal manner simply by isolating the nouns and noun phrases we use to describe the problem. (However, as we have discussed, more formal approaches are necessary for complex systems.)

Each of these four items meets the criteria we established for an object. First, each represents an entity that has state. For example, a word has a value that we can view, and a document consists of a collection of words that we can extract one at a time. However, take note of a subtle point: Our description of the problem speaks of one document and one concordance but multiple words and lines. Because we want to reflect our model of reality as closely as possible, we will allow only one document and concordance in our solution; at the same time, we will allow an arbitrary number of words and lines. As we will discuss in Chapter 11, making this distinction does more than preserve our model of the problem space, it also has an impact on how we structure our system. Specifically, we will model single objects by what we call *abstract-state machines;* we will treat multiple objects as instances of an *abstract data type.* In other words, abstract-state machines denote single objects, whereas abstract data types denote classes of objects.

Are there any other objects of interest? *At this level,* our answer is no. Remember the discussion in Chapter 2, however: We view the world in levels of abstraction. Each level is understandable by itself, but it is constructed of abstractions from lower levels. Thus, at the highest level in our model of reality, we observe only these four objects. As we will see, some of these objects are built on top of lower-level abstractions. However, we will employ the principle of information hiding at this point. Since no implementation detail should affect our current model of the problem space, we will defer such details until it is necessary to implement a lower level.

5.3   Identify the Operations

We have identified the major objects of interest, but that is not sufficient to establish the architecture of our solution. Next, it is necessary to identify the behavior of each object. In this manner, we give meaning to each abstraction; in formal terms, we must establish the semantics of each object.

Our notions of an object orientation serve us especially well in this regard. What we want to do is characterize the external behavior of each object. Recall that objects can be viewed in two ways: from the outside or from the inside. The outside view captures the behavior of an object from the perspective of its clients, and the inside view reflects the implementation of the object itself. At this point in the problem-solving process, we must concentrate on the outside view. Following the principle of information hiding, we defer worrying about the details of the inside view.

In general, we can characterize the behavior of an object best by identifying the operations that it undergoes. We will discuss this point more thoroughly in the next chapter, but for the moment we will consider each object in turn.

A word is perhaps the most elementary abstraction in the problem space. From the perspective of a client, we can perform two operations on a word:

- `Create`   -- give a value to the word
- `Value_Of`   -- return the value of the word

This step may seem trivial, but it is very important. Notice that we have not concerned ourselves with how a word is represented; rather, we are concerned only with its abstract behavior. In this manner, by separating the behavior of the object from its implementation, we have applied the principles of abstraction and information hiding.

We will have more to say on this point, but for now, notice that these two operations are slightly different. The first operation (`Create`) alters the state of a word. The second operation (`Value_Of`) does not alter the state; it returns a value of the state. This difference will be important to the architecture of our solution, and so we will categorize each operation as either a *constructor* (an operation that alters the state of an object) or a *selector* (an operation that returns a value of the state of an object).

A line number is also a simple abstraction. Basically, we can view a line number as an object with an integer value. Thinking back to our problem definition, however, we realize that a more precise abstraction is possible (and desirable). Indeed, it does not make sense to permit line numbers with negative values or a value of zero. Hence, we will abstract a line number as an object that may take on only positive (> 0) values.

What operations might a line number undergo? In this case, we want to allow the full range of expression of any integer. That is to say, we want the usual mathematical operations of addition, subtraction, and comparison. Enumeration of these operations is not necessary here, but the nature of our abstraction should be sufficiently clear. Again, why all the effort? The answer is that it is important for us to build a discipline of abstraction so that as we tackle massive problems, we will have the skills necessary to manage the complexity of more-difficult problem domains.

The document requires more-difficult abstraction. We can characterize the behavior of a document by the following operations:

- `Open`   -- open a document with the given name

- `Close`   -- close the document

- `Get`   -- get the next word and its line from the document

- `Is_End_Of_File` -- return True if there are no more words to be read

We have defined three constructors and one selector. Again, by what sleight of hand did we identify these operations? Essentially, we examined our model of the problem and considered the actions that a document could undergo in that context. The careful reader will wonder why we listed the constructor `Get` with the document instead of with the word. Our rationale is that `Get` alters the state of the document; it does not alter the state of the word. We associate an operation with the object that it affects, not with the object that is simply a passive participant in the action.

Since the document is a more complicated abstraction, it is reasonable for us to ask what might go wrong in our use of it. One basic principle that we will apply is that all properties of an object should be inviolate. In other words, we want to create abstractions that are robust. For example, what if we tried to `Get` a word from a document that was not yet open? Clearly, we would desire some sort of reasonable response from the document itself. Ideally, we want to make certain that it is impossible for a client (either innocently or maliciously) to place an object in an inconsistent state.

For this reason, as part of this step we will also consider the exceptional conditions that might be associated with each object. In terms of the document, we can identify the following possible conditions:

- `Open_Error`   -- a document is already open

- `Close_Error`   -- the document is already closed

- `Word_Too_Long`   -- Get cannot process the next word

- `End_Of_File`   -- Get is called when the file is already empty

To be complete, we should add that there are no exceptional conditions for the word (it is a trivial abstraction). In the case of the line number, a client might try to assign a value outside the range we established in our characterization of the abstraction. For reasons that will become clear later, we will call this exceptional condition a `Constraint_Error`.

The concordance itself is the last object we need to consider. We find that there are only three significant operations:

- `Start`   -- initialize the concordance

- `Add`   -- add a new word with its line number to the concordance

- `Make_Report`   -- display the value of the concordance

We derive this characterization from our model of reality as well. In manipulating a concordance, we first `Start` a report, then we repeatedly add words and their corresponding line numbers to the concordance, and—when we are done—we call `Make_Report` to display its state. Notice that we have not concerned ourselves with how the concordance is organized. Rather, we simply require that the semantics of this object be such that adding new words places them in an appropriate order (along with their corresponding line numbers). When we produce a report, we get output in the form that captures the information we need. Again, we have applied the principle of separation of interface and implementation.

For the concordance, we expect there to be only one exceptional condition:

- `Overflow`   `-- no more words can be added`

We have intentionally not included an exception to describe the condition of adding words to a concordance we have not yet started. Why? We want to view the concordance from the outside as a sequential entity; that is, we want to be able to add words and make reports at any time. Indeed, we may want to make a report before we have added all of the words from a particular document. The effect of initialization is simply to clear the concordance and place it in some stable state so that we can obtain a fresh report. As we will discuss further in Chapter 11, this kind of initialization is common in packages as abstract-state machines.

5.4   Establish the Visibility

Now that we have characterized the behavior of each object and class of objects, we must consider how these objects relate to one another. As we discussed in Chapter 2, one of the problems associated with functional decomposition methods is that they tend to force data abstractions to be global; that is, data is made visible at any lower level of the system. With an object-oriented approach, we strive to do exactly the opposite. Specifically, we try to restrict the visibility of objects as much as possible. Not only does this result in modules that are more loosely coupled (which is a desirable trait in complex systems), but we can also feel more confident that there are no pathological connections in our system.

So the simple question we must answer in this step is this; Given object X, what objects must it depend on, and what objects depend on it? The dependency we are speaking of is one of simple visibility among abstractions. For example, our abstraction of a document requires that it consist of words and lines. Hence, we say that the document depends on the classes of objects for words and line numbers. However—and this is a very important point—the reverse is not true. Words and line numbers do not depend on the document. As a result, we conclude that the relationships among objects and classes of objects are unidirectional. Indeed, as we will study later, the structure of Ada discourages circularity among modules.

At this level of abstraction, we observe that the following dependencies exist;

- `Document` depends on `Words` and `Line_Numbers`.

- `Concordance` depends on `Words` and `Line_Numbers`.

Still, we need one more piece to tie all of our objects together. Ada requires that the root of every system be a subprogram. Since this root represents an algorithmic abstraction, we will name it with an active verb phrase, `Make_Concordance`. This root is not exactly an object; rather, it serves as the agent that coordinates the activities of all the other objects at this level. For reasons that will become clear in the next section, the remaining relationship exists:

- `Make_Concordance` depends on `Words`, `Line_Numbers`, `Document`, and `Concordance`.

In Chapter 4, we presented a number of symbols to represent Ada units. If we map the objects `Words`, `Line_Numbers`, `Document`, and `Concordance` to packages and the unit `Make_Concordance` to a subprogram, we can represent the architecture of our solution as in Figure 5.1. Here, we see the symbol for a procedure body as `Make_Concordance`, a main program. All the other units are displayed as unit specifications. The reason is that, at this level, only the interfaces to `Words`, `Line_Numbers`, `Document`, and `Concordance` are relevant. In

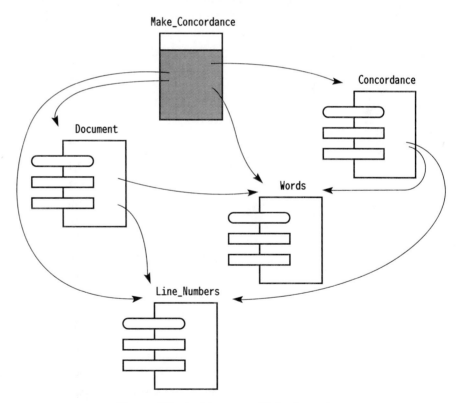

Figure 5.1 Architecture of `Make_Concordance`

a later section, we will see that other views exist at lower levels of abstraction. Thus, this figure represents the architecture of our solution at only one level of abstraction. As we move into the implementation of each unit, we may uncover other objects or classes of objects that we need in order to implement one of these higher-level objects.

We can use Figure 5.1 to analyze the impact of change on our solution. For example, if we decide to alter the actual report produced by the object Concordance, the figure shows that no other unit will be affected—no unit depends on the body of Concordance. On the other hand, if we alter the interface to the package Line_Numbers by not permitting line numbers with negative values, for example, we know that Document, Concordance, and Make_Concordance will be affected, since they depend on the outside view Line_Numbers.

We can see that these modules are coupled loosely. Because the relationships among modules are unidirectional, we can see that Words and Line_Numbers are fully independent abstractions; the same applies to Document and Concordance. This separation is essential as we move to more and more complex systems, for it gives us a higher level of confidence that changes in one part of a system will not affect another part.

5.5   Establish the Interface

Now that we have created the high-level design of our solution, we can capture all the design decisions we have made to this point in the form of Ada compilation units. In general, we seek one-to-one mapping of objects (classes of objects) to Ada units, to produce modules that are loosely coupled and highly cohesive. In this manner, we apply Ada as a design language to capture many of our design decisions about the behavior of modules in our system. Just as we learned in the previous chapter, we can compile these interfaces independently to build up our system incrementally. We will consider each module in the order in which it can legally be compiled. (Remember, a unit specification must be compiled before it is referenced.)

Line_Numbers, which denotes a class of objects, can be represented by the simple Ada package specification:

```
package Line_Numbers is
   type Number is range 1..Integer'Last;
end Line_Numbers;
```

This package exports a single type, Number, whose values may lie only in the range from 1 to some large integer value. Thus, the package Line_Numbers represents a class of objects. As we will see in the next section, we can declare objects of the type Number. Implicit with this kind of declaration is the declaration of all the usual mathematical operations, which is exactly what we desired of our object.

Notice how the package textually encapsulates the declaration of Number. This property is even more evident in the specification of the package Words:

```
package Words is
   type Word is private;

   procedure Create (The_Word       : out Word;
                     With_The_Value : in  String);
   function Value_Of (The_Word : in Word) return String;

private
   type Word is ...
end Words;
```

Here we also have an abstract data type, but the declaration of the type Word is quite different from that of the type Number. The meaning of the private type is that:

- The representation of the type is hidden from outside view.

- The only operations applicable to objects of the type are those listed in the package specification, along with assignment and test for equality.

In this manner, we have built a new abstraction according to the needs of our problem space. Ada's rules encourage our abstraction by giving us a mechanism to capture our design decisions; it enforces our abstraction by preventing violations of it. Indeed, because the type Word is private, a client is permitted to apply only the operations we have explicitly made visible, as well as assignment and test for equality.

For practical implementation reasons, the real representation of a private type must be completed in the private part. We will defer completing this part until we have learned more about the nature of Ada's types in the next chapter. (In order to compile this unit, it is necessary to complete the private part.)

Notice how we declare the interface to each explicit operation. The rules of Ada permit us to write only the specifications of these subprograms here in the package specification. Their implementation is deferred to the body of the package. In this package specification, we have one procedure with two parameters that acts as a constructor; this operation produces a word with the given string value. The function, which returns a value of the type String, acts as a selector. The reserved words out and in are called parameter modes—they indicate the direction of data flow. For example, the parameter The_Word in the procedure Create contains the mode out. This means that the procedure does not use the initial value of the parameter; rather, a produced value flows out from the procedure. Ada's rules require that parameters for functions must always be of mode in. Finally, note that we must state the type of each parameter explicitly. In the case of the selector, each parameter has a different type—one of type Word, the other of type String.

Consider the interface to Document. Document represents a single object, and so we will implement it as an abstract-state machine. Practically, this means that the package denoting Document does not export a type; it exports only the operations on the object. In this manner, the package itself serves as the object—we can guarantee that our solution has exactly one object of this kind.

Since the package Document depends on the abstractions of Words and Line_Numbers, we must state this relationship explicitly. Ada provides a mechanism to do this, the *context clause*. As we saw in the previous chapter, we can indicate a dependency among units by naming the dependent unit as part of a with clause at the beginning of the module. Thus, we may write the interface to Document as:

```
with Words, Line_Numbers;
package Document is
  procedure Open (The_Name : in String);
  procedure Close;
  procedure Get (The_Word   : out Words.Word;
                 The_Number : out Line_Numbers.Number);
  function Is_End_Of_File return Boolean;
  Open_Error    : exception;
  Close_Error   : exception;
  Word_Too_Long : exception;
  End_Of_File   : exception;
end Document;
```

Notice how we must name the types Word and Number. The rules for packages are such that we must treat package specifications as "skins" around a collection of declarations. We gain access to a separately compiled package through a context clause, but that does not automatically make the declarations inside the package interface visible. Rather, to name an entity declared in a package specification, we must qualify its name with the name of the package. Thus, the full name of the type Word is really Words.Word; the same applies to the type Line_Numbers.Number.

Also notice how we express the exceptional conditions we defined for the package Document—we simply name them as exceptions. Thus, for example, if we try to close a document that is not yet open, the exception Close_Error will become active. In a later chapter, we will discuss how to detect and react to such conditions programmatically.

Finally, consider the meaning of the type Boolean. This is a predefined type with the values True or False. It is quite suitable to operations such as Is_End_Of_File where we want to know about some binary condition.

The last object interface we must consider is that of the Concordance. It too represents a state machine. Since Concordance depends on the units Words and Line_Numbers, we must also supply an appropriate context clause:

```
with Words, Line_Numbers;
package Concordance is
  procedure Start;
  procedure Add (The_Word   : in Words.Word;
                 The_Number : in Line_Numbers.Number);
  procedure Make_Report;
  Overflow : exception;
end Concordance;
```

Since neither Document nor Concordance exports a private type, it is not appropriate for us to include a private part in the package specification. Thus, even the representation of each object is hidden from clients.

This interface completes the process of capturing our design decisions about each module. If we have compiled each unit interface along the way, we now have a high level of confidence that, at this level of abstraction, our abstractions fit together coherently.

5.6   Implement Each Object

As a final step, we must implement each object. Actually, if we are concerned only with the design of our system, we can stop right here. For purposes of discussion, however, let us go a little deeper.

We noted earlier that Ada requires that the root of each system be a subprogram; that is exactly the role played by the procedure Make_Concordance. We have not yet studied the details of Ada's statements, but let us examine the body of this unit.

As the root of our system, Make_Concordance must orchestrate the activities of all the objects at the highest level of abstraction. We have already mentioned the algorithm we must use here: Given the name of a document and after starting the report, we extract single words and their corresponding line numbers from the document and insert them in the concordance. When all the words in the document have been read, we make a report.

The algorithm is simple, but Ada requires a bit more glue to hold all the parts of the procedure together. As we did with Document and Concordance, we must supply a context clause to import all the units the procedure depends on directly. Furthermore, we must supply some declarations for objects of the type Words.Word and Line_Numbers.Number. Since Document and Concordance are state machines and do not export a type, we need not include any other declarations. Finally, we need to add two declarations and two statements that read in the name of a document from a user. This activity requires that we make the predefined package Text_IO visible by naming it in another context clause. Thus, we can express the body of Make_Concordance as:

```
with Text_IO, Words, Line_Numbers, Document, Concordance;
procedure Make_Concordance is
   The_Name        : String(1 .. 80);
   Last_Character  : Natural; -- values 0 .. Integer'Last
   The_Word        : Words.Word;
   The_Number      : Line_Numbers.Number;
begin
   Text_IO.Put("Enter a document name: ");
   Text_IO.Get_Line(The_Name, Last_Character);
   Document.Open(The_Name(1..Last_Character));
   Concordance.Start;
   loop
      exit when Document.Is_End_Of_File;
      Document.Get(The_Word, The_Number);
      Concordance.Add(The_Word, The_Number);
   end loop;
   Concordance.Make_Report;
   Document.Close;
end Make_Concordance;
```

Because of the naming conventions we have used, our algorithm appears quite readable, and it definitely parallels our model of the problem space.

If we want to make our procedure a bit more robust, we might add some code to deal with possible exceptions. For example, in the event the exception Open_Error becomes active, we might want to display an error message to the user. To do this, we would add what is called an exception handler. We will also use the predefined unit Text_IO, which accesses some facilities that provide readable output. Thus, the skeleton of our procedure now appears as:

```
with Text_IO, Words, Line_Numbers, Document, Concordance;
procedure Make_Concordance is
  The_Name : String(1..80);

  ...
begin
  Text_IO.Put("Enter a document name: ");

  ...
  Document.Close;
exception
  when Document.Open_Error => Text_IO.Put_Line("Unable to open the file.");
end Make_Concordance;
```

We might apply a similar approach for all the other exceptional conditions.

Our system is not yet ready to execute, since we must complete the implementation of each package. Happily, the rules of Ada are such that we can build and compile these unit bodies independently of their specifications. By working in this manner, we can even try alternative body implementations without ever having to recompile any of the interfaces (specifications). This is an important facility as we move to more and more complex systems.

It is in this step that our object-oriented method becomes recursive. As we implement each object from a higher level of abstraction, we can again apply an object-oriented approach to consider the objects from which it is composed. For example, as we begin to implement the package Concordance, we may choose to store individual words in order on a binary

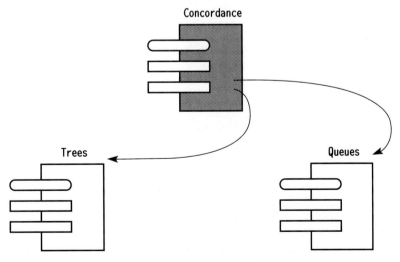

Figure 5.2 Architecture of Concordance

tree. At each node of the tree, we store the word itself as well as a collection of lines (specifically, a queue of lines). Thus, skipping ahead a few steps, we have created the level of abstraction shown by Figure 5.2 on page 87. Here we see the body of Concordance, but at this level, it is dependent on two new objects: Trees and Queues.

We will not complete the implementation of each body here; we must gain additional skills in the use of Ada's types and statements first. Throughout the next few chapters, we will consider these implementation issues. By Chapter 17, we will have provided the bodies of this program.

Exercises

1. If we make a change in the interface of the package Concordance, what other units might be affected?

2. Is it really necessary for us to supply a body for the package Line_Numbers?

3. How might we alter the procedure Make_Concordance to import the document name as a parameter rather than reading it in from the user?

4. What are the advantages of compiling individual units of a system separately?

5. What changes would be necessary to make Concordance an abstract data type rather than an abstract-state machine?

6. Modify the body of Make_Concordance to include handlers for all possible exceptional conditions.

7. Suppose we wanted the concordance to list Page_Numbers rather than Line_Numbers. How would this change affect the rest of the program?

CHAPTER 6

Data Abstraction and Ada's Types

Data Abstraction
Types
Object Declarations

Most human languages revolve around two basic structures: nouns and verbs. Other language features, such as adjectives and adverbs, serve only to amplify or constrain and are therefore subordinate to noun/verb constructs. It is the combination of all these elements that gives us a vehicle for communication and a medium in which to think.

We would expect, then, that programming languages would reflect a similar structure of objects (nouns) and operations (verbs). Actually, most high-order programming languages are primarily imperative; that is, they are filled with action. Thus, we Get our data, Push things on a stack, and loop to repeat a process. As was noted in Chapter 1, first- and second-generation languages were concerned primarily with expressions and control, both of which are action-oriented constructs. With the third generation, however, we began to recognize the importance of describing the structure of our data. In fact, the mapping of real-world objects *and* operations into computer solutions may be the most important contribution of any language. In this chapter, we shall further examine the concept of abstraction and see how Ada supports data abstraction with its typing mechanisms.

6.1   Data Abstraction

The idea of abstraction is nothing new. In fact, we can confidently state that all the things we know in the real world are abstractions. For example,

89

the chair you are sitting in is an abstraction; at a lower level, it consists simply of atoms. *Chair* is just a name we give to this collection so that we can talk about its properties. Similarly, if we have some metal, plastic, and glass organized in a special way, we name that structure *car*. As an abstraction, however, a car has properties unlike its individual metal, plastic, and glass components.

Our abstractions of the world are not monolithic but are divided into levels. As we move to higher levels of abstraction, we take a broader view while hiding details of lower levels—a process we know as getting the big picture. We can illustrate this ladder of abstraction with the following example, which presents a sequence of perspectives about a cat:

- Essence   (a very high level of abstraction)

- Living organism   (more of the lower details are left out)

- Animal   (grouping of all mobile, nonfood producers)

- Cat   (a larger class of which Sam is an instance)

- Sam   (the name of a specific collection of organs)

- Organs   (a biologically meaningful collection of atoms)

- Atoms   (a very primitive view of the world)

Each step in this ladder represents a different view of the same object. The ladder can be extended in both directions; in addition, there are other levels between the ones listed.

From this example, we observe two important characteristics of abstractions. First, there is no "correct" level from which to state our view of the world. Our current level of abstraction depends upon our needs at the moment: A veterinarian would be most concerned with the level of the organs, while a philosopher might be concerned with the essence of the object. Each view is correct for the particular application. Second, each level is implemented at a lower level. Thus, the abstraction of organs is actually implemented at a lower level as atoms; our abstraction of the cat is defined at a lower level as a specific entity named Sam.

Abstractions are more than just ways of describing single objects. In particular, they make it possible to talk about the characteristics of a class of objects. Furthermore, a given level will have unique properties that cannot simply be constructed from the properties of the lower levels. For example, a computer is an abstraction of a collection of atoms, but it would not make sense to describe the operation of a virtual-memory system at the molecular level. Similarly, consider the use of **Integer** data. Integers are implemented at a lower level in our computers as binary 1's and 0's, but we rarely think at this level. Rather, we consider the numeric properties of this special collection of bits. This allows us to speak of addition, subtraction, multiplication, and division, as opposed to thinking about the underlying algorithms that involve shift, and, or, and not operations.

Finally, abstractions help us focus on important characteristics while ignoring inessential details. When driving a car, you don't typically concern yourself with the chemical reactions going on in the cylinders—that is an implementation detail.

We solve real-world problems by employing software and hardware tools; our solutions should therefore model our abstractions of the world. For example, in the document concordance of Chapter 5, the major objects in the solution included lines, words, a document, and a concordance. We were able to manipulate them without regard for their underlying representation; the only thing important about these objects was their logical properties. At some lower level, these objects would be implemented as more primitive data structures, such as arrays or pointers. At any given level, however, we treat each object as if it were an elementary (that is, primitive) one.

First- and second-generation languages had few tools available for abstracting data in solutions. We could perhaps construct a buffer from an array and some pointers, but we would continuously have to make the mental transformation from the lower physical representation of the data structure to a higher logical representation of the buffer. Furthermore, the language would not prevent us from violating any of the buffer's logical properties. For example, if we were abstracting a first-in-first-out buffer (such as a waiting line at a checkout counter), there would be nothing in a language such as FORTRAN or COBOL that would prevent us from violating our abstraction of the buffer by, for example, assigning a value directly to the fifth element. Languages like Pascal do not do much more; compared with first-generation languages such as FORTRAN, Pascal does give us better ways to describe data, but the language still cannot enforce many logical properties.

Ideally, then, we would like our programming languages to:

- Provide tools to describe the structure of our abstract data

- Enforce the logical properties of our abstraction

In the previous chapter, we observed how the package mechanism can be used to define new abstractions and how packages can enforce their logical properties. However, any such high-level abstraction must be implemented from more primitive types of data, such as Integers or Characters. In

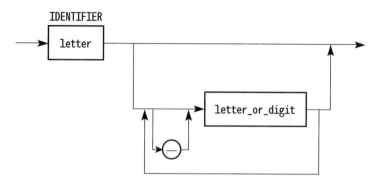

Figure 6.1 Syntax chart for IDENTIFIER

the remainder of this chapter, we shall examine the facilities Ada provides for the description of primitive data.

First, however, we need to examine a tool that will assist you in understanding the details of the Ada form, namely, *syntax charts*. As Figure 6.1 illustrates, a syntax chart gives us a road map for the correct form of a particular language construct. In this figure, the syntax chart describes an Ada identifier. To use the chart, start at the left-hand side and trace the arrows until you exit from the right-hand side of the diagram. A circle or an ellipse (such as the one containing the underscore "_") means that the string inside appears in the Ada construct exactly as shown. A rectangle (such as the one marked Letter) means that the construct in the box has a further definition, and so you must refer to its own syntax chart. Given these rules, the following are well-formed Ada identifiers, formed by tracing the identifier syntax chart:

```
X                              -- legal identifier
Acceleration                   -- legal identifier
Center_Of_Gravity              -- legal identifier
Node_77                        -- legal identifier
V003                           -- legal identifier
```

The following are not well-formed Ada identifiers—if we try to trace their construction through the syntax chart, we will leave our tracks:

```
4314                           -- illegal identifier
Distance__From__Destination    -- illegal identifier
Miles-Per-Gallon               -- illegal identifier
Number_Of_#                    -- illegal identifier
X_                             -- illegal identifier
_X                             -- illegal identifier
```

Appendix E contains syntax charts for every Ada language construct. Refer to the charts often to reinforce your knowledge of the details of Ada structure. Note, however, that a syntax chart cannot tell us everything about the meaning (the *semantics*) of a particular construct. For example, the identifier syntax chart cannot express the rule that an identifier must fit on one source line. To compensate for the limitations of syntax charts, our discussions will emphasize the effective use and the semantics of each language facility—not just the syntax.

6.2   Types

In human languages, the things that we manipulate are called *nouns;* in Ada, we call them *objects.* Formally, each object has a set of properties (which we call its *type* and its *subtype* that denote the values that the object can carry and the operations that we can apply to that object. In Ada systems, objects do not exist implicitly (as they can in FORTRAN); instead we must explicitly declare them, as in the following:

```
Coefficient      : Float;
Count            : Integer;
Name             : String (1..80);
The_Tree         : Tree;
Water_Storage    : Tank;
```

Ada requires us to declare an entity before it is used. When declaring an object in Ada, we first write its name (such as `Coefficient`, `Count`, `Name`, `The_Tree`, and `Water_Storage`) and then we associate the form of object declarations later, but for the moment, we can say that a declaration creates a named instance of a particular type. For example, the type `Integer` is a class of objects that denotes a set of values and operations; `Count` is the name of an object that has the characteristics of an `Integer` type.

Typing thus provides a mechanism for imposing structure on objects. Explicit typing is an essential feature of Ada, particularly in light of the software principles presented in Chapter 2. Typing meets several needs, including [1]:

- *Maintainability:* the need to describe objects with a factorization of properties

- *Readability:* the need to say something about the properties of objects

- *Reliability:* the need to guarantee that properties of objects are not violated

- *Reduction of complexity:* the need to hide implementation details

Formally, a type characterizes:

- A set of values

- A set of operations applicable to objects of the given type

Ada is a *strongly typed* language. This means that objects of a given type can take on *only* those values that are appropriate to the type and, in addition, that the *only* operations that can be applied to an object are those that are defined for *its type.* It is important to realize that the type of an object is static; that is, its characteristics are fixed during compilation. In contrast, the characteristics of a subtype are known only when the object is created. (The process of defining nonstatic characteristics in this way is called elaboration, which we shall discuss later.)

The emphasis that Ada places on types provides a margin of safety—as we said, a given type will assume only those values that are appropriate. Strong typing allows us to detect more errors during compilation and, as a result, allows the program developer greater confidence that a program is correct during execution. Indeed, as we shall study in detail, even if we violate our abstraction during execution, Ada provides exceptions to detect such errors programmatically.

The concept of strong typing is similar to the logical progression in the ladder of abstraction. Each level denotes specific values plus a collection of operations that are appropriate for that level. For example, the name `Apple` refers to a type of fruit. To a gardener, the operations appropriate to objects of the type `Apple` would include planting, fertilizing, picking, and fermenting, among others. It would make no sense to subtract `Apple` objects or to raise an `Apple` object to a power (in the mathematical sense).

As we mentioned, types permit us to describe the form of objects. Obviously, no language could contain facilities for directly describing every type. Rather, computer languages should provide facilities for constructing new types from more elementary types. In Ada, there are four classes of primitive types. These primitive types form the building blocks of data with which we abstract the *higher-level* objects in the problem space. Specifically, Ada's classes of types include the following:

- *Scalar values* have no components.

- *Composite values* consist of component objects.

- *Access values* provide access to other objects.

- *Private values* are not known to a user.

In addition, Ada's typing mechanism includes subtypes and derived types, both of which provide further factorization of the properties of objects. In Chapter 14, we will discuss *task types,* which have properties similar to private types.

Before discussing specific types in detail, we must make two points regarding Ada's treatment of types. First, Ada provides a number of predefined types, including `Integer, Float, Boolean,` and `Character`. These types and their operations are defined in an implementation-specific package called `Standard`, which is included in Appendix C. Whenever an Ada program unit is compiled, it is compiled inside package `Standard`, and so these types are automatically visible (available) to the unit. However, as we shall discuss later, it is generally a better practice to define our own types rather than use the predefined Ada types.

Second, when writing programs, we sometimes need to speak about the characteristics of the types themselves, such as the number of `Digits` in a numeric type, the `Length` of an array, or whether or not our target computer rounds for numeric calculations. In Ada, these characteristics are known as *attributes.* Actually, every entity, including types and objects, has certain attributes. Attributes are named in a consistent fashion, using the following notation:

```
Integer'First     -- the first Integer value
Character'Size    -- the number of bits for Character objects
Name'Address      -- the memory address of the Name object
```

We read these attributes as, for example, "Integer tick First." Appendix A describes all of Ada's predefined language attributes. In addition, the following sections present the attributes appropriate to each of Ada's classes of types.

Scalar Types

A *scalar type* defines a set of values without components. In Figure 6.2, the blob represents the fact that a type simply defines a class of objects, while the bucket indicates that an object of a scalar type can contain only one value. Ada's scalar types can be further divided into the following categories:

- Integer types
- Real types
- Enumeration types

Formally, the integer and real types are called *numeric types.* Furthermore, we call the integer and enumeration types *discrete* types, since they

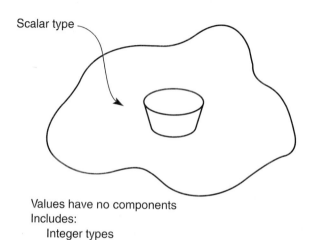

Scalar type

Values have no components
Includes:
    Integer types
    Real types
    Enumeration types

Figure 6.2 Scalar types

have discrete values (as opposed to continuous values), which can be used for indexing and iteration over loops. The values of all scalar types are ordered.

Integer Types   An *integer type* definition introduces a set of consecutive integers as values of the type. These values are exactly representable on an underlying machine; real types are only approximations. All integer literals are simply values of an unbounded anonymous type, called *universal integer*, which we can think of as representing all the integers in the mathematical world. By *anonymous,* we mean that we cannot refer directly to the universal integer type within our programs because it has no known name. A given implementation will define integer types in terms of a subtype of universal integer.

A programmer can declare objects using predefined integer types from the package Standard, such as:

```
Count      : Integer;
Population : Long_Integer;
Index      : Short_Integer;
```

The predefined Integer type (not to be confused with the broader class of Ada integer types) has a range of values dependent upon the underlying implementation. For example, on a 16-bit machine, Integer may have a range from -32_768 to 32_767. A given Ada implementation must define at least the Integer data type and may or may not define longer (Long_Integer) or shorter (Short_Integer) ranges of integers. Actually, use of the predefined integer types is not recommended practice, since the range of represented values will vary among implementations, thus hindering program portability. For example, a single-precision `Integer` value for an 8-bit machine will have quite a different range of values from that for a 32-bit machine.

Instead, it is better practice for a programmer to declare an integer type with an explicit range of values. The compiler then chooses the appropriate underlying representation, thus making the source declaration more portable. This declaration is formed by the reserved word `range`, followed by the lower bound and then the upper bound value of the integer range. Such a declaration of the limits of the values is known as a *range constraint*. The following are examples of integer type definitions:

```
type Line_Count is range 0..66;
type Index is range 55..77;
type Fathom is range -5_000..0;
```

The two periods (called double dot) are a required part of the syntax; they imply the values between the lower and upper bounds. Either one or both of the bounds may be negative. Finally, as a result of the rules defining strong typing, the range bounds must be static values, that is, their values must be known at compilation time.

This structure can support abstraction of objects in the real world. For example, we could declare objects of type `Line_Count` as `Integer` types, but that would probably not accurately reflect our view of the real world—lines on a page do not have negative values. Instead, we should declare the type with a range of values that models the objects in the problem space (e.g., 0..66). Not only does this construct let us describe such logical properties, but Ada's typing mechanism enforces the abstraction. For example, consider an object called `Lines`:

```
Lines : Line_Count;
```

If `Lines` was ever assigned a value outside the range of 0..66, the exception `Constraint_Error` would be raised during execution time, signaling that the explicit range of `Lines` had been violated. This exception-handling facility will be discussed further in Chapter 15.

The expressions that define the range of values of an integer type need not be simple literal values but instead can be more-complex static expressions. For example, if we previously named a constant `Rows` (with an integer value of 24) and a constant `Columns` (with an integer value of 80), we might write:

```
type Total_Elements is range 1..Rows * Columns;
```

At compilation time, we now know that objects of type `Total_Elements` may have values in the range 1 to 1920 inclusive.

All integer types have a number of predefined operations that are appropriate to the type, as indicated in Table 6.1. This table also summarizes the attributes for this type and objects of the type. Appendix A describes each attribute in detail.

Real Types   A *real type* defines a set of values that are approximations to the real numbers. Because a given implementation can provide only a finite number of bits for numeric data, it is impossible to provide an exact representation for all real values. For example, the real value 0.1 cannot be represented exactly on a binary machine, since it has a repeating binary fractional part. Instead, *elaboration* (the process through which a declaration takes

Table 6.1   Summary of Integer Types

Set of values	A set of consecutive integers					
Structure	range L . . U	Where L and U are static integer expressions representing the lower and upper bounds, respectively				
Set of operations	Adding	+	–			
	Assignment	:	=			
	Explicit conversion					
	Exponentiating	**				
	Membership	in	not in			
	Multiplying	*	/	mod	rem	
	Qualification					
	Relational	=	/=	<	<=	>	>=
	Unary	+	–	abs		
Attributes	Address	Pred				
	Base	Size				
	First	Succ				
	Image	Val				
	Last	Value				
	Pos	Width				
Predefined types	Integer					
	Long_Integer					
	Natural					
	Positive					
	Short_Integer					

effect) of a real type defines a set of model numbers. These numbers are generally powers of two and can be represented exactly. All other real values are defined in terms of such numbers, using an explicit error bound. A real literal is considered to be of the type *universal real,* which has unbounded precision. Such literal values are converted to model numbers having an accuracy dependent upon their use.

As is the case with the integer types, a programmer can declare objects from any of the predefined real types, such as:

```
Coefficient : Float;
Distance    : Long_Float;
Resistance  : Short_Float;
```

An implementation is not required to implement either Short_Float or Long_Float. If they are implemented however, just as is true with the integer types, the accuracy of the predefined real types may vary among implementations. Thus, a machine that uses a 32-bit word with a 24-bit fractional part (called the *significand*) for real values will have an accuracy of approximately 7 decimal digits; a 64-bit representation will have approximately 16 digits of accuracy.

Instead of using the predefined real types, it is generally a better practice to define explicitly the error bounds of a real type, and then let the compiler choose the proper implementation. This will result in source code that is more portable. Furthermore, such a practice lets us bring our abstractions of the problem space directly into our Ada solution space. For example, if we are developing a satellite guidance system, requirements may dictate that distances be measured with an accuracy of 15 significant digits (relative accuracy). On the other hand, an automatic board tester may measure voltages to within 0.001 volts (absolute accuracy). Ideally, we would like to be able to describe the accuracy of our values either way; Ada provides constructs for both cases. We need only choose a representation appropriate to the abstraction, and the Ada compiler will choose an underlying representation with equal or greater accuracy to ensure the minimal mathematical properties of such real types.

We can use *floating-point types* in Ada to describe values with relative accuracy. A floating-point definition consists of the reserved word digits, followed by a static integer expression that defines the number of decimal digits of significance. For example:

```
type Planetary_Measurement is digits 15;
type Mass_Reading          is digits 7 range 0.0..3.0;
```

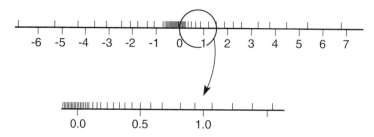

Figure 6.3 Floating-point model numbers

Notice that we can optionally combine a range constraint with an accuracy constraint. Just as it must with integer types, the range constraint for real types must be static; unlike integer types, however, the range bounds of real types must evaluate to real values. If we declare an object of type `Mass_Reading` and then attempt to assign it a value outside its declared range, the exception `Constraint_Error` will be raised.

As shown in Figure 6.3, the declaration of a floating-point type defines a set of model numbers. These model numbers are all powers of two, that is, they are numbers that can be represented exactly on the underlying machine. Of course, compared to a floating-point type with only a few digits of significance, a declaration that specifies a large number of digits will require a significand with a greater number of bits. In any case, the model numbers for a floating-point type are not evenly spaced; as we move further from zero, the model numbers are greater distances from each other.

If we make a declaration of the form:

`type F is digits N;`

an implementation must then provide a representation with at least B number of bits in the fractional part, where B is the first integer value greater than:

`N * log(10)/log(2)+1`

For example, for N = 6, B evaluates to 21 bits. In general, each digit of significance takes 3.32 bits. If we ask for an accuracy that the target machine cannot handle (perhaps `digits 100`), the compiler must reject the declaration.

Whenever we declare a floating-point type with D digits of accuracy, Ada also defines the minimum range of exponent values a representation must provide, namely, the range:

`-4 * B .. 4 * B`

Thus, for 6 digits of accuracy, the exponent must cover the range -84 to 84. As is the case with the number of fractional bits, a representation can provide a larger range of exponent values. Numbers that lie beyond the minimum range are called safe numbers (that is, they are *safe* for the particular implementation), but their use is nonportable.

A given calculation may result in a value that is not a model number (not an exact multiple of a power of two), but is instead bounded by at least two model numbers, called the *model interval*. An implementation is free to choose a value that lies within this interval (inclusive), and so guarantees the properties of the stated accuracy. For example, consider:

```
Mass : Mass_Reading;
...
Mass := 2.314_587_936;
```

Mass is an object with 7 digits of significance, but the value 2.314_587_936 lies between two model numbers for Mass. Upon assignment, an implementation will convert the numeric literal to a model number that maintains at least the 7-digit accuracy of Mass. As we see, the rules of the language support our abstraction of the properties of Mass.

A numeric type can be declared to have an absolute accuracy, as a *fixed-point* type. The form of such a declaration is the reserved word delta, followed by a static real expression defining the delta of the type. As is the case with floating-point types, an implementation may give us an actual delta value that is more accurate than asked for (due to hardware considerations), but we shall at least be guaranteed the mathematical properties of the type definition. For example:

```
type Current_Measurement    is delta 0.025 range 0.0..100.0;
type Voltage                is delta 0.1 range -12.0..24.0;
```

Unlike the example for floating-point types, a static range constraint (with real bounds) must be included for every fixed-point type definition.

Fixed-point data defines a set of evenly spaced model numbers, as Figure 6.4 illustrates. The spacing indicates the "coarseness" of values of the given type. As for floating-point numbers, the model numbers are represented

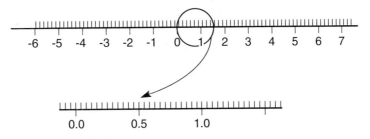

Figure 6.4 Fixed-point model numbers

exactly, and an implementation will guarantee the minimal properties of a given type by representing a real value as one of these model numbers.

Table 6.2 summarizes the operations and attributes of Ada's real types. Note that exponentiation is defined only for integer powers; thus, 9**(0.5) is illegal in Ada using the predefined operator (see Chapter 9 for further comments).

There is a reason for the many attributes that Ada defines for real types: In applications that demand strict precision, where we must concern ourselves with the limitations of the finite representation of real numbers on machines, these attributes provide a means for referring to the characteristics of the particular underlying implementation so that we can fine-tune our algorithms.

As was mentioned previously, the strong typing rules of the language generally prohibit implicit operations among objects of different numeric types. Thus, trying to directly add a real value and an integer value violates our abstraction and is an error detectable at compilation time. Instead of

Table 6.2   Summary of Real Types

Set of values	Approximations of the real numbers	
Structure	`digits N range L..U` (floating point)	Specifies relative accuracy where N is a static integer value representing the number of digits of significance, and (optionally) L and U are static real values representing the lower and upper bounds, respectively
	`delta D range L..U` (fixed point)	Specifies absolute accuracy where D is a static real value representing the delta, and L and U are static integer values representing the lower and upper bounds, respectively
Set of operations	Adding	`+` `-`
	Assignment	`:=`
	Explicit conversion	
	Exponentiating	`**`
	Membership	`in` `not in`
	Multiplying	`*` `/`
	Qualification	
	Relational	`=` `/=` `<` `<=` `>` `>=`
	Unary	`+` `-` `abs`

▶

Table 6.2   Summary of Real Types (continued)

Attributes	Fixed point:	
	Address	Last
	Aft	Machine_Overflows
	Base	Machine_Rounds
	Delta	Mantissa
	First	Size
	Fore	Safe_Large
	Large	Safe_Small
		Small
	Floating point:	
	Address	Machine_Mantissa
	Base	Machine_Overflows
	Digits	Machine_Radix
	Emax	Machine_Rounds
	Epsilon	Mantissa
	First	Safe_Emax
	Large	Safe_Large
	Last	Safe_Small
	Machine_Emax	Size
	Machine_Emin	Small
Predefined types	Float	Duration
	Long_Float	
	Short_Float	

implicit conversion, which can be nonportable and hence dangerous, the programmer must use an explicit type conversion in Ada in order to mix types. For example:

```
Integer (Mass);    -- convert to an Integer value
Mass_Reading(2);   -- convert to a floating-point value
```

Conversion is permitted among all numeric types and is accomplished by prefixing the expression with the name of the numeric type (called the *type mark*).

Enumeration Types In abstracting objects from the problem space, we find that numeric representations are not always sufficient. For example, the suits in a deck of cards are not numbers but are the values Clubs, Diamonds, Hearts, and Spades. Similarly, the position of landing gear is not the value one or zero but instead is Up or Down. In a language like FORTRAN, we could declare an object representing the suits in a deck of cards or the position of the landing gear, but we would have to represent the possible values as numbers and then make a mental transformation from the representation to the real world. This method is often not very readable; recall from Chapter 2 that the clarity of the program text will greatly affect its modifiability/maintainability.

Because a type characterizes a set of values, a better way would be to let the programmer explicitly declare the possible values. In Ada, this is done with an *enumeration type,* which takes the form of an ordered list of values. For example:

```
type Card_Suit     is (Clubs, Diamonds, Hearts, Spades);

type Gear_Position is (Down, Up);

type Motor_State   is (Off, Forward, Back);

type Hex_Digit     is ('A', 'B', 'C', 'D', 'E', 'F');
```

Notice in the last example that character literals can also be used as enumeration literals. In fact, an enumeration type can define a set of values that include both character and noncharacter literals, as in:

```
type Mix is (Left, 'L', Right, 'R');
```

We can then declare objects of these types and use the enumerated values:

```
My_Card      : Card_Suit;
Landing_Gear : Gear_Position;
Hoist        : Motor_State;
...
My_Card := Card_Suit'First;     -- yields the value Clubs
Landing_Gear := Up;
Hoist := Back;
```

Since we have listed the set of possible values for each of these types, we may use no others—to do so is illegal in Ada and would violate the logical properties of our declared data. It is important for the programmer to think of these values as elementary. The underlying representation may be integer values, but at this level, the enumeration literals are just values. Ada treats enumeration values as ordered data, going from the first literal to the last literal in the list.

Table 6.3 summarizes the operations and attributes appropriate to enumeration types. There are no mathematical operators, such as addition

Table 6.3   Summary of Enumeration Types

Set of values	An ordered set of distinct values	
Structure	(E0, E1,..., En)	Where E$_i$ is an ordered enumeration literal
Set of operations	Assignment	:=
	Membership	in not in
	Qualification	
	Relational	= /= < <= > >=
Attributes	Address Pred	
	Base Size	
	First Succ	
	Image Val	
	Last Value	
	Pos Width	
Predefined types	Boolean	
	Character	

or subtraction, but mainly ordering operations. Note also that the attributes let us obtain new enumerated values in the list, such as:

```
Card_Suit'Succ(Hearts) -- Spades is the successor to Hearts
Gear_Position'Last     -- the value Up
```

In all cases, if we generate a value outside the enumerated range, the exception Constraint_Error will be raised (if, for example, we take the predecessor of Clubs).

Ada provides two predefined enumeration types, Boolean and Character. As described in Appendix C, in package Standard the Boolean type has the values False and True (in that order), and the Character type includes the standard ASCII character set. Values of type Character are all considered character literals (a single quoted character, such as 'B'). This is in contrast to a string type. In particular, do not confuse 'B' with "B"; the first value is a character literal, and the second value is a string literal.

Composite Types

In the problem space, some objects such as Voltage or Flow_Rate do not have components and can hence be represented as scalar types. On the other hand, we often deal with objects that logically consist of several components. For example, a Personnel_Record may have several different components, such as Name, Social_Security_Number, Date_Of_Birth, and Address, while a

`Matrix` can be viewed as having several components of the same type. As Figure 6.5 illustrates, Ada provides *composite types* to help describe such data. We can further divide composite types into two categories:

- Array types

- Record types

Formally, an *array* is an indexed collection of similar (homogeneous) objects, while a *record* is a collection of potentially different (heterogeneous) objects.

Array Types   The name of an array denotes a group of components, where each component is of the same type. A particular component of an array object is selected by using one or more discrete index values. The number of indices indicates the dimensionality of the array (i.e., one index indicates a one-dimensional array, two indices denote a two-dimensional array, and so on). Ada does not place any limitation on the maximum dimensionality of arrays. It is important to note that an array whose components are themselves arrays is not the same as a two-dimensional array.

An *array type* is defined by naming the type of the indices and the type of the components, such as:

```
type Game_Board is array (1..8, 1..8) of Chess_Pieces;
type List       is array (Line_Count) of Float;
type Vector     is array (Integer range 1..Maximum_Index) of Float;
```

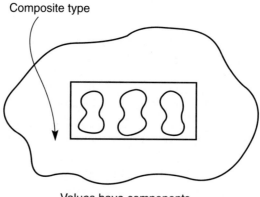

Composite type

Values have components
Includes:
    Array types
    Record types

Figure 6.5 Composite types

We can then declare objects of the type:

```
Chess_Board  : Game_Board;     -- a two-dimensional array

Sorted_List  : List;           -- a one-dimensional array

State_Vector : Vector;         -- a one-dimensional array
```

As we shall discuss more fully in Chapter 9, we can refer to individual elements of the array objects, such as `Chess_Board(1,5)`, using what is called an *indexed component.*

These examples illustrate several important points. In the declaration of `Game_Board`, note that the type of the indices is not indicated, as it is with `List` and `Vector`. When simply using literal numeric range bounds, the index type is the predefined type `Integer`. The `List` declaration illustrates the preferred style, in which we state the type of the index explicitly. In the declaration of `Vector`, note that we can include a range constraint; the index bounds need not be simple numeric literals but can be discrete static expressions instead.

We do not always have to use the predefined `Integer` type to define the type of our array indices; we can use any integer type. For example:

```
type Extended_Index is range 0..1_000;

type Long_Array     is array (Extended_Index) of Float;

type Short_Array    is array (Extended_Index range 10..49) of Float;
```

In this case, `Long_Array` defines an array type with 1001 elements, while `Short_Array` defines an array type with 40 elements. As a general style rule, a programmer should explicitly declare a type like `Extended_Index` for each array, and then declare arrays using the form shown above, rather than using the predefined `Integer` type. Since the set of values of the predefined type can vary between compilers, declaring an explicit type is a superior abstraction.

The array declarations just given are rather simple; we have used values of some integer type to index the array. However, in Ada we can index an array with any discrete type, including enumeration values. For example:

```
type Day           is (Monday, Tuesday, Wednesday, Thursday, Friday,
                          Saturday, Sunday);

type Hours         is delta 0.1 range 0.0..24.0;

type Record_Of_Work is array (Day range Monday..Friday) of Hours;

type Overtime      is array (Day range Saturday..Sunday) of Hours;

type Full_Week     is array (Day) of Hours;

Time_Card : Record_Of_Work;
```

We can then refer to elements of the object, such as Time_Card (Monday). As another style issue, notice how we used complete names instead of abbreviations to describe our Day abstraction. In addition, rather than using Float to describe the hours in a day, we instead chose to create our own Hours type that more closely matches the real world.

So far, we have discussed the declaration of array types that are constrained, that is, the bounds of the array type are known when we elaborate the array type definition. Indeed, whenever we declare an array object, we must know its array bounds. However, with constrained arrays, every object declared will, by definition, be the same size. If Ada permitted only constrained arrays, there could never be two array objects of the same type but with different array bounds. This has been recognized as a shortcoming of Pascal, since there are several applications where such a facility is needed. For example, in a message-passing system, packets of data may be of variable length. Ada solves this problem by permitting the declaration of unconstrained array types whose range of indices is not defined until an array object is declared. Furthermore, these bounds (called the *index constraint*) need not be static but can be determined at run-time.

Unconstrained arrays are described using what is called *box notation* (consisting of a type mark followed by the compound symbol). For example:

```
type Index     is range 1..64;
type Bit_Vector is array (Index range <>) of Boolean;
type Matrix    is array (Index range <>, Index range <>) of Float;
```

Unconstrained and constrained notation may not be mixed in the same type definition. Since Ada requires that the bounds of an array object be known at the time the object comes into existence (a concept called elaboration), we must provide an index constraint for objects of an unconstrained array type. For example:

```
Filter    : Bit_Vector(1..31);
Transform : Matrix(1..4, 1..3);
Inverse   : Matrix(1..N, 1..N);
```

In a sense, this feature permits us to parameterize our array types. In the first example, we have constrained the array as a one-dimensional array with 31 components. Notice in the last example that an index constraint need not be a static expression but can depend upon results computed at run-time. The range of an index constraint can be provided in several ways. For example, as shown above, the index bounds of an object are obtained from its declaration. If we use an unconstrained array type as the formal parameter of a subprogram, the array object is constrained by the index bounds of the corresponding actual parameter (see Chapter 8).

In package `Standard`, Ada provides a predefined array type called `String`, which is an unconstrained, one-dimensional array whose components are of type `Character`:

```
type String is array (Positive range <>) of Character;
```

(`Positive` is a predefined subtype of `Integer` that contains the values greater than zero.) We can declare objects of this type such as:

```
Name   : String(1..18);
Prompt : constant String := "Enter your data: ";
```

In the latter case, the length of the constant string object is determined by its value (`Prompt'Length = 16`).

For objects of type `String` (actually, for any one-dimensional array), Ada provides the catenation operator. For example:

```
Name := "Fuel cell" & " number 7";
```

This example results in a string of length 18.

Table 6.4 summarizes the characteristics of Ada's arrays. We shall study the details of applicable array operations in Chapter 9.

Record Types   Array types are useful when we abstract objects that are simple collections of the same class of objects. However, objects from the problem space often denote groups of different classes of objects. A medical history may contain different elements for men and women, and a telemetry record may exhibit a structure dependent upon the frame number. In these

Table 6.4   Summary of Array Types

Set of values	An indexed collection of similar types	
Structure	array (index{,index}) of component (unconstrained array)	Where index{,index} is a series of unconstrained discrete types; the component denotes the type of values the array can hold
	array index_constraint of component (constrained array)	Where index constraint is a list of discrete types; the component denotes the types of values the array can hold

▶

Table 6.4   Summary of Array Types (continued)

Set of operations	Adding (one-dimensional array)	`&`	
	Aggregate		
	Assignment	`:=`	
	Explicit conversion		
	Indexing		
	Logical (boolean components)	`and or xor not`	
	Membership	`in not in`	
	Qualification		
	Relational	`= /=`	
	Relational (discrete components)	`< <= > >=`	
	Unary (boolean components)	`not`	

Attributes	`Address`
	`Base`
	`First`
	`First(N)`
	`Last`
		`Last(N)`
		`Length`
		`Length(N)`
		`Range`
		`Range(N)`
		`Size`
			Where `N` is the `Nth`
			index range

Predefined types	`String`		

cases, we can use the Ada record construct to describe such data. To construct a record type definition, we use the reserved words `record...end record` to enclose the declarations of the record components.

The record components have a syntax similar to that of regular object declarations. Every object of that record type thus carries a composite value consisting of those components. For example, we can declare records such as:

```
type Day_Of_Year is
   record
      Day   : Integer range 1..31;
      Month : Month_Name;
      Year  : Natural;
   end record;
```

```
type Cpu_Flags is
  record
    Carry     : Boolean;
    Interrupt : Boolean;
    Negative  : Boolean;
    Zero      : Boolean;
  end record;

type Cpu_State is
  record
    Priority : Positive;
    Flag     : Cpu_Flags;
  end record;

Date : Day_Of_Year;
PSW  : Cpu_State;
```

Note that in the case of the object PSW, we have declared a nested record structure. As will be enlarged upon in Chapter 9, parts of a record object can be referred to by using what is called *selected component notation*. Thus, the following all name elements of the record objects:

```
Date.Year
PSW.Priority
PSW.Flag.Zero
```

Table 6.5 summarizes the characteristics of the record type. Very few operations are defined for objects of record (or array) types. Actually, this is to be expected, since the primary feature of records and arrays is to impose a physical structure upon data. Of course, we can select components of an array or record and apply any operations applicable to its type.

The record structures presented thus far contain components that are relatively independent in nature; clearly, the PSW.Priority and the PSW.Flag.Zero components do not depend upon one another. However, there are cases of composite objects where the record structure, or the value of one component, depends upon the value of another component. In the first case, for example, we may have an aircraft record that has different components depending upon the type of aircraft. In the second case, we may have a graphics package that manipulates only square transformation matrices; we would need to ensure that such matrices have equal numbers of rows and columns. To state explicitly such dependencies within our type declarations, we used a *record discriminant* (so called because its value discriminates between one form of a record and another).

Table 6.5   Summary of Record Types

Set of values	A collection of (potentially) differently named components	
Structure	record component_list end record	Where component_list declares the elements of the record
Set of operations	Aggregate Assignment Explicit conversion Membership Qualification Relational Selection	:= in not in = /=
Attributes	*Record type:* Address Base Constrained Size *Record component:* First_Bit Last_Bit Position	
Predefined types	None	

In the case of the matrix example, when we use discriminant values to indicate the interdependency of components, the discriminant is named in the type definition and can then be directly used inside the record as a bound in an index constraint, as a default value for a component, or as a value for another discriminant. By *directly,* we mean that the discriminant must stand by itself and not be part of a larger expression. For example, consider the following:

```
type Simple_Array is array (Positive range <>, Positive range <>) of Float;
```

We could declare objects as follows:

```
First_Matrix : Simple_Array(1..4, 1..5);
```

Notice how we can violate our original abstraction and declare an array object with nonsquare bounds. A better way to represent our abstraction is as follows:

```
type Square(Side : Positive := 4) is
  record
    Matrix : Simple_Array(1..Side, 1..Side);
  end record;

type Two_Squares(Length : Integer) is
  record
    First  : Square(Length);
    Second : Square(Length);
  end record;

Transform_3d : Square;            -- Square is unconstrained
Transform_2d : Square(3);         -- Square is constrained
Transform    : Square(Side => 3); -- Square is constrained
```

In the first declaration using `Square`, we defined the structure of a square matrix, with the length of a side given as the discriminant value `Side`. Note that language rules prohibit the use of anonymous array types within a record, and so the declaration of `Simple_Array` is required. Notice also the use of the default value for `Side`; we can thus declare the `Transform_3d` matrix using the default value of 4. We can now refer to elements of the matrix object, such as:

`Transform_3d.Matrix(2, 3)`

Notice how this construct uses both selected and indexed component notation. The record is said to be *unconstrained* since we did not provide a discriminant value when we declared the object `Transform_3d`; its discriminant can be changed (but only with an assignment to the whole record). We can also explicitly give the size of a side, using either positional notation (in the case of `Transform_2d`) or named parameter association (in the case of `Transform`). If we had not provided a default value for the discriminant in the type declaration, we would have had to supply a value when we declared an object. In that case, the records are considered constrained, and so their discriminant values could not be changed during execution. Notice in the second example (`Two_Squares`) that discriminant values can be passed on to nested records.

Discriminants can be used not only to indicate dependencies among record components, but also to define alternative structures, called *variant records*. For example, for an aircraft record in a command and control system, we can abstract the data as:

```
type Aircraft_Id is (Civilian, Military, Foe, Unknown);
type Aircraft_Record(Kind : Aircraft_Id := Unknown) is
  record
    Airspeed  : Speed;
    Heading   : Direction;
    Latitude  : Coordinate;
    Longitude : Coordinate;
    case Kind is
      when Civilian      => null;
      when Military      => Classification : Military_Type;
                            Source         : Country;
      when Foe | Unknown => Threat : Threat_Level;
    end case;
  end record;
Aircraft : Aircraft_Record;
```

Although we have not indicated them, all the other data types, such as Coordinate, would have had to be defined before this record type declaration.

In the above example, we have defined four record components (Airspeed, Heading, Latitude, and Longitude) that are common to every Kind of Aircraft. The case statement defines the variant part and must appear as the final component of a record; following each when are values of the discriminant indicating choices of record structure. There are several forms of the choice clause, as we have indicated. In the first case, if the Kind is Civilian, we have explicitly indicated through the null clause that there are no further components, unlike the Military choice, where two components are defined. If the structure of a record is identical for two or more discriminant values, the values can be separated with a vertical bar (read as "when Foe or Unknown then").

Although not shown in this example, one of the possible choices for any variant record is others, representing all other values (if any) that have not yet been given a record component. When we add an others clause, it can appear only after the last choice. The set of choices indicated in the case must be exhaustive for the set of values of the discriminant. When it is inconvenient to list all of the values (for example, with an Integer discriminant), the others choice provides a convenient way to list all the other choices that were not previously accounted for.

As defined above, Aircraft is unconstrained, and therefore its Kind can be altered with a full record assignment. For example, the following assignment is legal in Ada, using what is called an *aggregate value* (which will be more fully discussed in Chapter 9):

```
Aircraft := (Kind              => Military,
             Airspeed          => 150.0,
             Heading           => 97.3,
             Latitude          => 147.6,
             Longitude         => 27.1,
             Classification    => Transport,
             Source            => France);
```

Notice that we first list the value of the discriminant, followed by values for each component. Named parameter association has been used to increase the readability of the assignment.

We can also declare constrained types, such as:

```
Civilian_Aircraft : Aircraft_Record(Kind => Civilian);
Unknown_Aircraft  : Aircraft_Record(Unknown);
```

Thus, in the first case, we could refer to the components Civilian_Aircraft.Heading (or Airspeed, Latitude, or Longitude); and, in the latter case, we could reference components of the variant part, such as Unknown_Aircraft.Threat (but not Classification or Source). Because these are constrained records, their Kinds may not be changed during execution.

Access Types

One of the design concepts behind Ada is that the semantics of a given program should be static to the largest degree practical. Reliability is thereby enhanced because much of the analysis of a program can be done at compilation time. Thus, in Ada, we see that the type of any object is designed to be static and that the number, scope, and visibility of entities are known prior to execution. When we abstract objects in the problem space, however, we find that the world is not so nicely static. In particular [2]:

- Objects may be created and destroyed unpredictably (e.g., buffers in a message-passing system).

- Several names may refer to the same object (e.g., segments in a graphic scene may be known by several logical names).

- The relationships among objects may change over time (e.g., genealogical records in a database).

Ada provides the **access** *type* to permit the handling of such dynamic situations. As Figure 6.6 on page 116 indicates, objects of this type are called access objects because they take on values that provide access to other objects. We can access different objects simply by reassigning the access

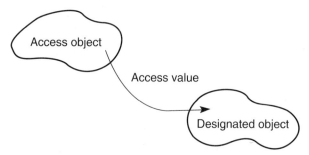

Values provide access to other objects

Figure 6.6 Access types

values; furthermore, as will be examined later in this section, we can create new objects through the use of allocators. This is in contrast to other Ada objects that are known by their name and are hence static by nature.

An access type declaration takes the form of the reserved word `access`, followed by the type name of the objects to be designated. For example:

```
type Buffer is
  record
    Message  : String(1..10);
    Priority : Positive;
  end record;
type Buffer_Pointer is access Buffer;
My_Packet, Your_Packet, Their_Packet : Buffer_Pointer;
```

`Buffer_Pointer` is the access type, and `Buffer` is the type of the designated object. Initially, `My_Packet`, `Your_Packet`, and `Their_Packet` will have the value `null`, representing the fact that they currently point to nothing. Note that this is the *only* case in which Ada defines an implicit default value; for other than access objects, we may not assume any initial value (such as a zero value for integer objects) unless we provide such a value.

We can create new objects of the type `Buffer` through the use of an allocator, which is invoked by using the reserved word `new`. For example:

```
My_Packet    := new Buffer;
Your_Packet  := new Buffer'(Message => "**********", Priority => 1);
Their_Packet := new Buffer'("----------", 10);
```

These statements each create a new object of the type `Buffer`, and the values returned by the allocators are assigned to `My_Packet`, `Your_Packet`, and `Their_Packet`, respectively, so that we can gain access to the `Buffer` objects. In the last two cases, we can explicitly initialize the `Buffer` objects, using what is called an *aggregate* (the construct delimited by the parentheses in the example). Aggregates will be studied further in Chapter 9.

Objects designated by access values need not be automatically "reclaimed" after they are no longer needed. For example, we can create an object and then remove all references to it, as in:

```
My_Packet := new Buffer;  -- a Buffer object is created
My_Packet := null;        -- the original object is unreachable
```

Ada does not require an implementation to "garbage-collect" and reuse the created object. If enough objects are created and not reclaimed, the underlying machine will eventually run out of memory. In this case the predefined exception Storage_Error will be raised when an attempt is made to allocate more objects. In these cases, it is common practice to write additional code that reclaims and reuses objects. Indeed, the abstraction and information hiding capabilities of Ada facilitate such implementations of data types.

Once we have explicitly created an object with the use of an allocator, Ada permits us to refer to either the access object or the designated object. We can refer to the access object by name, such as My_Packet, or we can refer to the designated object using dot notation, such as:

```
My_Packet.all          -- refers to the entire object
My_Packet.Priority     -- refers to the Priority component
My_Packet.Message(1)   -- refers to the first character of Message
```

When we manipulate access values, it is important that we distinguish between the access values and the objects they designate. For example, consider:

```
My_Packet   := new Buffer'(Message => "++++++++++", Priority => 1);
  --create a Buffer object
Your_Packet := new Buffer'(Message => "++++++++++", Priority => 10);
  --create another Buffer object
Their_Packet := Your_Packet;
  --point to the same object
```

The following relationships, (illustrated in Figure 6.7 on page 118) are true:

```
Your_Packet /= My_Packet
  -- they point to different objects
Your_Packet = Their_Packet
  -- they point to the same object
Your_Packet.all /= My_Packet.all
  -- the objects are not equal
Your_Packet.Message = My_Packet.Message
  -- components have equal values
```

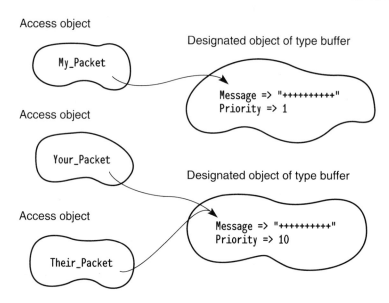

Access object

My_Packet

Designated object of type buffer

Message => "++++++++++"
Priority => 1

Access object

Your_Packet

Designated object of type buffer

Message => "++++++++++"
Priority => 10

Access object

Their_Packet

Figure 6.7 Relationship of access values and objects

So far, we have indicated how access types are used to create objects dynamically and how we can use several names to refer to the same object. As was mentioned earlier, we can also use access values to describe the relationships among objects, especially if they change over time; this is typical of data structures such as linked lists or binary trees. For example, we might implement the binary tree type mentioned in Chapter 5 (and completely implemented in Chapter 13) as:

```
type Node;
type Tree is access Node;
type Node is
  record
    Left  : Tree;
    Value : String(1..5);
    Right : Tree;
  end record;
Top_Node  : Tree;
Temp_Node : Tree;
Pointer   : Tree;
```

The first statement may look a bit strange; it is known as an *incomplete type declaration* and is required for recursive or mutually dependent access types. This incomplete type definition is similar in one respect to the private and limited private types to be discussed later in this chapter: All of these types introduce a type name but provide no other information

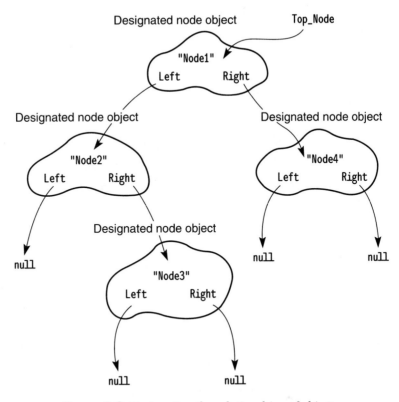

Figure 6.8 Designating the relationships of objects

about the type values and operations. The incomplete type declaration must be completed before we can further use the type name.

As Figure 6.8 illustrates, we can build a binary tree using these access objects. The Ada code used to build this tree is:

```
Top_Node         := new Node;        -- create the first node
Top_Node.Value   := "Node1";         -- give it a value
Temp_Node        := new Node;         -- create another node
Temp_Node.Value  := "Node2";         -- give it a value
Top_Node.Left    := Temp_Node;       -- link the nodes
Temp_Node        := new Node;         -- create a third node
Temp_Node.Value  := "Node3";         -- give it a value
Pointer          := Top_Node.Left;   -- point to Node2
Pointer.Right    := Temp_Node;       -- link the nodes
Temp_Node        := new Node;         -- create a fourth node
Temp_Node.Value  := "Node4";         -- give it a value
Top_Node.Right   := Temp_Node;       -- link the nodes
```

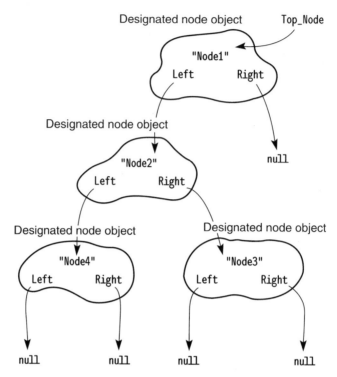

Figure 6.9 Changing the relationships of objects

We can then change the explicit relationships of these objects. For example:

```
Pointer        := Top_Node.Left;    -- point to Node2
Pointer.Left   := Top_Node.Right;   -- access Node4
Top_Node.Right := null;             -- break the duplicate link
```

Figure 6.9 illustrates the final state of the binary tree.

The above 12 assignment statements create the same tree as the following single statement. Although the 12 statements may be more readable than the single statement, the following shows the capability of Ada expressions.

```
Top_Node := new Node´(Value => "Node1",
                 Left  => new Node´(null,
                                    "Node2",
                                    new Node´(null, "Node3", null)),
                 Right => new Node´(null, "Node4", null));
```

There is an important interaction between access types and the unconstrained types we have studied so far. In particular, whenever we allocate an object, that object must be constrained, and it will remain constrained. For example, consider the package Words from Chapter 5. From the outside, this package exports the type Word: actually, Word is implemented as a pointer to the predefined type String. Thus, we can complete the specification of this package as:

```
package Words is
  type Word is private;
  procedure Create (The_Word : out Word;
                    With_The_Value : in String);
  function Value_Of (The_Word : in Word) return String;
private
  type Word is access String;
end Words;
```

Words in a document will have varying lengths. We can therefore declare objects of type Word without knowing the length of the actual word, and indeed, we bind this length only when we give the object a value. For example, in the body of Create we must allocate a new string and give it the value With_The_Value:

```
The_Word : new String'(With_The_Value);
```

Thus, the qualified expression provides the constraint required by the language rules.

Finally, in the body of the function Value_Of, we dereference the pointer Value and return the designated string by writing:

```
return The_Word.all;
```

Table 6.6 on page 122 summarizes the characteristics of access types.

Private Types

The data types discussed in detail so far (scalar, composite, and access) provide tools for describing the primitive objects in programs. Furthermore, objects of each of these types have predefined operations. However, such data types are not sufficient for describing all abstractions of the problem space. Ada does not have a Complex.Number type or a Stack type, for example. Instead, Ada provides the *private type declaration* to enable us to explicitly describe our higher-level real-world abstractions. In addition, private types directly support the principle of information hiding, in which the details of an implementation are suppressed in order to focus on the abstraction.

Table 6.6   Summary of Access Types

Set of values	Access values to designated objects	
Structure	access subtype_indication	Where subtype_indication is the type of the designated object
Set of operations	Allocation	
	Assignment	:=
	Explicit conversion	
	Indexing	
	(array-designated objects)	
	Membership	in not in
	Selection	
	(record-designated	
	objects)	
	Qualification	
	Relational	= /=
Attributes	*Access type:*	
	Address	
	Base	
	Size	
	Storage_Size	
	Array-designated objects:	
	First	
	First(N)	Where N is the Nth
	Last	index range
	Last(N)	
	Length	
	Length (N)	*Task-designated objects:*
	Range	Callable
	Range(N)	Terminated
Predefined types	None	

As we have said before, a type characterizes a set of values and a set of applicable operations. For objects of a private type, the structure and values are hidden from the user, and only explicitly named operations are visible. Private data types are declared in a package specification, taking the form of the type name followed by the reserved words `private` or `limited private`. Following the type name are the subprograms that explicitly define the operations on objects of the private type. For example:

```
package Password is
  type Value is limited private;
  function Is_Valid(Code : in Value) return Boolean;
  procedure Set(Code : out Value; Authorization_Level : in Natural);
private
  type Value is range 0..1_000_000;
end Password;
```

The package user can then declare objects of type Value as:

```
User_Authority : Password.Value;
```

This package defines a private type named Password.Value. The only operations available to this type are Is_Valid and Set; even assignment and tests for equality and inequality are disallowed (which is the effect of the limited private type). Notice that the underlying representation of the Value is an integer type, as defined in the private part of the package. However, a user of this package cannot apply any integer operations to the Password.Value (the private part of the specification is included in the Ada syntax to support the separate compilation of a package specification and body). Thus, by restricting accessibility to data, a package using a private or limited private type is said to *encapsulate* the data type; furthermore, the abstraction of the type is enforced since only the explicitly declared operations can be applied to objects of the type.

The use of limited private types requires that all operations be explicitly declared. However, we can also use simple private types, which implicitly permit assignment and tests for equality and inequality. For example:

```
package Random is
  type Number is private;
  procedure Set(Seed : in Integer; Value : in out Number);
  function Uniform_Random return Number;
private
  type Number is
    record
      Seed_Value : Integer;
      Value      : Float;
    end record;
end Random;
...
Event : Random.Number;
```

Notice how our naming conventions make the declaration of Event quite readable by directly reflecting the nature of its type. In this example,

Table 6.7	Summary of Private Types

Set of values	Hidden from the user
Structure	Hidden from the user
Set of operations	Explicit conversion Membership `in   not in` Qualification For `limited private`, only those operations defined in the corresponding package specification are true; for `private` types, assignment and tests for equality and inequality are also available.

Attributes	*Private types:*
	`Address`
	`Base`
	`Size`
	
	Private types with discriminants:
	Constrained

Predefined types	None

a user can `Set` the seed of the `Event` and then get `Uniform_Random` numbers by calling the appropriate subprogram. In addition, assignment of `Random.Number` objects to objects of the same type, along with tests for equality and inequality are permitted (by virtue of the `private` declaration). In no case, however, can a user apply `Float` operations such as multiplying or dividing two `Random.Number` objects. Such an attempt would not only violate our logical abstraction of such numbers but would also be prohibited by the language. Indeed, Ada detects such violations at compilation time.

Private types are thus the primary mechanism for creating abstract data types and hiding their implementation. Chapter 11 further describes the form of Ada's private types and their relationship to package declarations. For completeness, Table 6.7 provides a summary of the characteristics of private types.

Subtypes and Derived Types

Factorization of properties is one of the motivations for Ada's explicit typing. However, there may be cases where we need to factor our data even further than we can with the types introduced thus far. For example, we may have a `Month_Name` type and wish to speak only of the `Summer` months, or we may wish to distinguish between a `Fiscal_Year` and a `Calendar_Year`. Ada provides subtypes and derived data types for such occasions. These facilities aid in maintainability by further factoring type properties.

Subtypes   *A subtype* does not define a new type; rather, it provides a new name for another (potentially) constrained data type. Furthermore, except for a floating-point or fixed-point accuracy constraint, the constraints of a subtype need not be static but can be evaluated at run-time. For example, we can declare subtypes as:

```
type Month_Name is (January,    February, March,    April,
                    May,        June,     July,     August,
                    September, October,  November, December);
subtype Summer is Month_Name range June..August;
Current_Month : Month_Name;
Vacation_Time : Summer;
```

We have declared Summer as a subtype of Month_Name; Month_Name is known as the *base* type.

Since we have not created two distinct types, we can freely operate with objects of both the base type and the subtype. For example, the following are legal operations:

```
Current_Month := Vacation_Time;
Vacation_Time := Summer´Succ(Current_Month);
```

In the latter case, if Current_Month had a value other than May, June, or July, the exception Constraint_Error would be raised upon assignment to Vacation_Time, since the value would be out of bounds for the subtype. We can explicitly check whether the value of Current_Month is a value of Summer by using a membership test, as in:

```
if Current_Month in Summer then
   ...
end if;
```

The membership tests in and not in are defined for all types, not just scalar types. These tests allow us to explicitly check many of the constraints that, when violated, result in Constraint_Error being raised.

Subtypes are useful if our abstraction of the problem space defines subsets of a base type. Not only can range constraints be applied to base types, as above, but subtypes can also use accuracy constraints, index constraints, or discriminant constraints. For example, consider the following type declarations:

```
type Non_Negative is  range 0..Integer'Last;
type Weight is        delta 0.01 range 2000.0..3000.0;
type Vector is        array (Natural range <>) of Float;
type Sensor_Class is (Humidity, Pressure, Temperature);
type Sensor (Kind : Sensor_Class) is
  record
    Location : String(1..20);
    case Kind is
      when Humidity    => Humid     : Natural;
      when Pressure    => Press     : Float;
      when Temperature => Temporary : Integer;
    end case;
  end record;
```

We can declare subtypes as follows:

```
subtype Index is Non_Negative range 0..10;
    -- range constraint
subtype Coarse_Weight is Weight delta 10.0;
    -- accuracy constraint
subtype Vector_3d is Vector(1..3);
    -- index constraint
subtype Heat_Sensor is Sensor(Kind => Temperature);
    -- discriminant constraint
```

In each case above, we can declare objects of both the base type and the subtype and freely operate with any of them, as long as the subtype constraint is not violated. For example, we can add Index and Non_Negative objects, but if we ever try to assign a number greater than 10 to the Index object, the exception Constraint_Error will be raised. Although these examples do not indicate it, only the accuracy constraint must be a static expression.

Note also that every subtype declaration must satisfy the constraints of the base type. For example, we could not declare:

```
subtype Illegal_Index is Non_Negative range -1..1;
```

because the range constraint of the base type Non_Negative is violated. In general, the illegal declaration would produce a compile error. However, a subtype does not have to contain a constraint. In such cases, the subtype name is a synonym for the base type, such as:

```
subtype Not_Negative is Non_Negative;
```

We can also declare a subtype of a subtype (the same is true for derived types). For example:

```
subtype Big   is Non_Negative range 0..1_000_000;
subtype Small is Big range 0..10;
```

As a final note, if we ever need to refer to attributes of the base type, we use the attribute **Base** (which we can apply to any type). The **Base** attribute cannot stand by itself but must be used to refer to another attribute. For example:

```
Index'Base'Last
```

This evaluates to the largest value of the base type of **Index**. Note that this value need not be **Integer'Last** on all implementations. The base type of **Index** is selected by an implementation and thus is implementation dependent. The **Base** attribute can also be used to find the precision of the base type selected for real types:

```
type Mass is digits 15;
...
Mass'Base'Digits
Mass'Base'First
Mass'Base'Last
```

Derived Types   Unlike subtypes, *derived types* define distinct types. They are necessary when our abstraction of the problem space contains distinct objects that have a similar structure. For example, we can define objects of type **Mass** and **Weight**; they can both have the same underlying structure of a **Float** type but must be treated separately from each other. In Ada, these types can be declared as:

```
type Mass   is new Float;
type Weight is new Float;
```

Mass and **Weight** are derived from the existing type **Float**, which we call the parent type. Objects of type **Mass** and **Weight** can then be declared, but the language will not allow us to implicitly mix the objects. For example, we could not add values of a **Mass** object and a **Weight** object.

Formally, a derived type *inherits* the properties of its parent, including the parent's set of operations, attributes, and set of values, literals, and aggregates (if any). Thus, a derived type is of the same class as its parent. Additionally, a derived type can include constraints upon the parent type, much like the form of subtypes. For example:

```
type Budget is new Float range 0.0..12_000.0;
```

Budget has all the properties of **Float** objects, with the additional range constraint. Ada will enforce the abstraction that **Budget** objects have floating-point values, but they may not be implicitly combined with other `Float` objects. However, Ada defines an explicit type conversion between every derived type and its parent. Consider, for example, the following declarations:

```
Software_Budget : Budget;
Total_Budget    : Float;
```

We can explicitly convert the `Software_Budget` to the type of `Total_Budget`, as follows:

```
Total_Budget := Float(Software_Budget);
```

In general, any type can be derived. However, the definition of the parent type must be complete before derivation is permitted. This means that an incomplete type definition cannot be derived directly, nor can a private type (until after the private type is completed in the package private part).

As has been mentioned, a derived type inherits the operations applicable to the parent type. For a predefined type, the operations that are inherited are the corresponding predefined operations. For user-defined types, objects of a derived type also derive any visible subprograms that have a parameter or result of the parent type or one of its subtypes. Of course, a user can define subprograms unique to the derived type. For example:

```
type Date is ...
type My_Date is new Date;
function "+" (Left  : in Date; Right : in Date) return Date is ...
procedure Julian(A_Date : in Date; Number : out Integer) is ...
```

At the point of the derived type declaration for `My_Date`, the subprograms `"+"` and `Julian` are also derived (their names are thus overloaded). Objects of the type `My_Date` can use these derived operations. However, if we declared any other `Date` operations after the declaration of `My_Date`, these subprograms would not be derived.

The capabilities of derived types are best shown when deriving private types. An example would be deriving a stack data structure from a linked list data structure. Suppose linked lists are defined as follows:

```
package Linked_Lists is
  type List is private;
  ...
  function "&" (Left  : in Integer;
                Right : in List) return List;
  function "&" (Left  : in List;
                Right : in Integer) return List;
  ...
```

```
      function Head (Of_List : in List) return Integer;
      function Tail (Of_List : in List) return List;
   private
      type List is ...
   end Linked_Lists;
```

Since a stack can be viewed as a linked list where all operations are performed at one end of the list, we can derive the implementation of a stack from that of a linked list. For example:

```
with Linked_Lists;
package Stacks is
   type Stack is private;

   procedure Push (Item   : in Integer; Onto   : in out Stack);

   procedure Pop  (Item   : out Integer; Off_Of : in out Stack);
private
   type Stack is new Linked_Lists.List;
   -- At this point all the operations of the type
   -- List are defined for the type Stack.
end Stacks;

package body Stacks is
   procedure Push (Item : in Integer; Onto : in out Stack) is
   begin
      Onto := Item & Onto;
   end Push;
   procedure Pop (Item   : out Integer; Off_Of : in out Stack) is
   begin
      Item   := Head(Off_Of);
      Off_Of := Tail(Off_Of);
   end Pop;
end Stacks;
```

6.3   Object Declarations

In Ada, we can capture abstractions of the problem space with types. However, types form only templates. We must declare objects for our programs to manipulate. We have already used object declarations in earlier examples, but there are some details we have not yet discussed.

Objects are introduced in the declarative part of a program or in formal parameters of subprograms and generic program units. This is in contrast to types, which can appear only in declarative parts. Whenever we declare an object, we must explicitly give its type, such as:

```
Distance : Float;
Response : Character;
Number   : Integer;
Grades   : array (1..100) of Float;
```

Notice in the last example that the type of `Grades` does not have a name; we have created an anonymous data type. Such declarations are possible only for array objects—and only if the object stands alone. For example, record components cannot apply anonymous array declarations. As a style consideration, it is recommended that every type be given a name, although there may be some rare circumstances in which anonymous types are needed (e.g., a single object of a task type). A constraint can also be added to the type during object declaration. For example:

```
Name     : String(1..40);
Bottom   : Integer range -10..-1;
```

As a general style guideline, instead of providing a constraint at declaration time, it is recommended that the programmer create a subtype.

We mentioned previously that Ada is a strongly typed language, meaning that objects of different types cannot implicitly operate with one another. Ada uses *named type equivalence*. That is, two objects are of the same type if they are introduced as the same named type. For example:

```
type Distance is digits 4;
type Length   is digits 4;
Width  : Length;
Extent : Distance;
```

`Extent` and `Width` are objects of different types, although the types have the same underlying structure. In this way, the programmer can be assured that his or her named abstractions are enforced, even if there exist objects with structurally similar types.

We can also declare objects with default initial values, such as:

```
Extent : Distance := 0.0;
```

Ada does not define default initial values for objects (except for access objects, which are initialized to `null`); the programmer must initialize objects before they are used. One method of initializing an object is to assign it a value within the object's declaration, as shown by the declaration of `Extent`. Another method, applicable to record types, is to define default values for components of the object. For example, in the `Stack` record type from Chapter 4, the `Top` component of any objects of the type `Stack` will by default be given the value zero.

If we attempt to use an object before it receives a value, the program is said to be erroneous, meaning that the elect is implementation dependent. However, note that an implementation is free to raise the exception `Program_Error` if we try to access an object before it is given a value.

A programmer can also declare constant objects. These declarations have the same form as the previous declarations, with the addition of the reserved word `constant`. The type name can be omitted in the case of all numeric constants, which is the recommended practice. For example:

```
First_Month : constant Month_Name := January;
Pi          : constant           := 3.141_592_65;
Diameter    : constant           := 4;
```

In the case of constant numeric literals (which by definition are universal values), the values are converted implicitly to the appropriate user-defined type, depending upon the context of their use. In the previous example, we have introduced one object name per declaration, but Ada lets us create multiple objects using an identifier list. For example:

```
First, Index_J, K_Way : Integer;
```

introduces three objects. This declaration is actually equivalent to

```
First   : Integer;
Index_J : Integer;
K_Way   : Integer;
```

Identifier lists decrease maintainability; avoid using them.

Summary
- Data abstraction provides the fundamental mechanism for capturing design decisions regarding objects from the problem space.

- Ada identifiers consist of a letter followed by any number of letters, numbers, and nonconsecutive underscores.

- A type characterizes a set of values and a set of operations applicable to objects of the named type.

- Types are static; subtypes can denote dynamic constraints.

- Ada's classes of types include scalar, composite, access, and private types.

- Scalar types denote classes of objects with no components. Scalar types include integer, real, and enumeration types.

- Integer types denote a set of consecutive integers.

- Real types include definitions of relative accuracy (floating-point types) and absolute accuracy (fixed-point types).

- Enumeration types permit the developer to name values of the type explicitly.

- Composite types denote classes of objects with components. Composite types include arrays and records.

- Array types denote collections of homogeneous components; arrays can be constrained or unconstrained.

- Record types denote collections of potentially heterogeneous components; records can be simple or discriminated, or can contain a variant part.

- Access types denote values that designate other objects.

- Private types and limited private types permit the developer to hide the implementation of abstract data types.

- Subtypes and derived types permit factorization of the properties of other types. Derived types introduce new types; subtypes do not.

- Objects must be declared explicitly before they are used. Object declarations can contain default values, or they can be constant.

Exercises   *1. How does Ada's type mechanism support abstraction and information hiding?

2. What does a type characterize?

3. Write the declarations for the following scalar types:

(a) A Counter with only negative values.

(b) A Coefficient with 12 digits of significance.

(c) A Measurement with a coarseness of 1.0 centimeters.

(d) Same as (c), but with a range of 0.0 to 10.0 meters.

(e) The Colors_Of_Rainbow.

4. Is it possible to write a type definition for a number constrained to only the odd numbers? Defend answer.

5. Write the declarations for the following composite types:

(a) An array of 10 Coefficients.

(b) An unconstrained array of Measurements indexed by Colors_Of_Rainbow.

(c) Same as (b), but with an index constrained to the first three colors.

(d) A Personnel_Record showing Age, Weight, Height, and Name.

(e) Same as (d), but with a variant part. For a Child discriminant, include the values Mother_Name and Father_Name, and for the Adult discriminant, include the value Occupation.

6.   Declare an access type that can designate Personnel_Record objects.

7.   Take the declaration from 5(e) and change the type of Mother_Name and Father_Name to the access type from Exercise 6.

8.   Allocate three Personnel_Records and assign two of them as parents to the third, using the declaration from Exercise 7.

*9.   If we declared a package called Complex with a private type Number, which operations would be applicable to the type? Should we create a private type or a limited private type?

10.   Write the declarations for the following subtypes and derived types:

(a) A subtype of Coefficients with only 7 digits of accuracy.

(b) A further subtype from (a) with a range of positive numbers.

(c) Same as (a), but this time using a derived type.

(d) From 5(e), a subtype constrained as a Child.

(e) Same as (d), but this time using a derived type.

11.   Declare an object of each type given in Exercise 10 and provide an initial value for each.

CHAPTER 7

The Second Design Problem: Data Base System

Define the Problem
Identify the Objects
Identify the Operations
Establish the Visibility
Establish the Interface

The implementation of a data base system is not usually considered an embedded computer application; data base systems have traditionally been the domain of business data processing in COBOL and related languages. However, Ada is a general-purpose language and is suitable for such applications—and rightly so, for more and more massive real-time systems seem to require the manipulation of a data base as part of their solution.

In Chapters 7 through 10, we shall consider the construction of a simple data base system. In Chapter 7, we shall follow our object-oriented method up to the creation of the program unit interfaces. We shall then need other resources to finish the solution, so after studying Ada's subprograms and statements in Chapters 8 and 9, we shall complete the implementation of the problem solution in Chapter 10.

7.1   Define the Problem

Data bases appear as an element in a large number of applications. In this design problem we may wish to employ a data base to capture information about product orders or company personnel. In each of these cases, we may already have a data base management system that we can adapt to our needs. However, the data base system used by a given application need not be a general-purpose system. Rather, it may be more effective in the long run to develop an ad hoc data base that is intimately bound to the needs of the underlying problem. Indeed, this is the approach we shall take in this chapter, for it gives us an opportunity to explore how we might apply Ada to such a problem, and it exposes many new facilities of the language.

Imagine for a moment that we have a large collection of record albums. Over time, we may add new albums, get rid of ones we no longer want, and replace old albums with newer ones. As the number of albums increases, we may find it increasingly tedious to manually search through our collection to find particular songs, or songs of a certain style, or songs by a given artist. For this reason, we wish to build a simple data base system to help us keep track of our collection.

What are the requirements of our problem? Primarily, we need a data base that maintains Ada records of information about each album in our collection. For each album. we intend to keep track of the title, the artist, the style of music (for example, classical, jazz, or rock), the year of release, and the name and length of each song. We will need the usual data base management capabilities—the ability to create, open, and close the data base and the ability to add, delete, and modify individual albums. In addition we want to be able to generate reports about the albums in our data base. Specifically, we want to be able to search for albums according to any attribute. (For example, we may wish to find all the albums released in a particular year.) We also want to be able to sort the resulting records and then print a report. To have greater flexibility in our searching, we will permit the user to specify an arbitrary number of search criteria that must be met for each report. Thus, a user might search for the records by a particular artist, then search those found for all the albums released in a certain year. In this manner, the search proceeds over progressively smaller sets of records instead of the entire data base.

Clearly, we have not expressed all the requirements necessary for us to fully understand the problem. However, we do have enough information to proceed with an object-oriented method. Along the way, we shall expose the remaining requirements.

7.2   Identify the Objects

How might we proceed in creating a software solution to our problem? With a functional approach, we would start by identifying the major steps in the overall process. However, as we observed in Chapters 2 and 3, this approach often leads to solutions that neither parallel their problem domain nor are resilient to change. Instead, we shall start by identifying the objects and classes of objects that exist in the problem space, as we did for the concordance in Chapter 5.

Our description of the problem contained a number of nouns to describe the applicable entities. In particular, we mentioned the entities:

- Albums

- Database

- Reports

However, there are some important distinctions among these entities. In our data base, there may be many albums; hence, Albums really represents a class of objects. On the other hand, our description allowed for only one active data base; therefore, as we will discuss in Chapter 11, we characterize Albums as an abstract data type. Database represents an abstract-state machine.

There is no reason why we cannot build more than one report at a time, so we will treat Reports as the definition of an abstract data type.

As we mentioned in Chapter 4, Ada requires that every program have a subprogram that acts as the root of the system. The acting root is not really an object, but (as we shall see in a later section) the requirement causes us to introduce it as a separately compiled subprogram in our solution. Since invoking this subprogram is the action that initiates our application, we will name it with an active verb phrase, Process_Album_Database. As we did for the problem in Chapter 5, this main program will serve to process all user commands. Clearly, in a larger system, the user-machine interface can be encapsulated as an object-oriented design of its own.

7.3   Identify the Operations

We have identified the major objects of interest, but we are not yet ready to establish the architecture of our solution. First, we must consider the behavior embodied in each abstraction.

For example, let us examine the object Database. As our problem description stated, this object holds a collection of individual albums. We expect Database to be capable of undergoing the usual data base operations:

- Create   -- make a new data base
- Open   -- open an existing data base
- Close   -- close the current data base
- Add   -- insert a new record into the data base
- Delete   -- remove a record from the data base
- Modify   -- alter an existing record in the data base

These operations constitute the constructors that a data base can undergo. (Recall that constructors are operations that alter the state of an object.) Similarly, we need a set of selectors that let us retrieve the state of the data base. For example, we might include the selectors:

- `Size_Of`   -- return the number of records in the data base

- `Value_Of`   -- return the value of one particular record in the data base

Notice the parallelism: The constructor `Add` lets us insert a new record, and `Value_Of` lets us retrieve the value of a particular record.

How could we visit every record in the data base? We could include an iterator. An iterator is not a single operation; rather, it is defined by a set of operations that lets us visit all the items in a data base. Typically, an iterator includes the operations:

- `Initialize`   -- establish a starting point for the traversal

- `Get_Next`   -- advance the iterator to designate another item

- `Value_Of`   -- return the record currently being designated

- `Is_Done`   -- return True when all records have been visited

Note that iteration does not specify a particular order of traversal; iteration guarantees only that, when we are done, we have visited every record.

Whereas `Database` denotes an abstract-state machine, `Reports` represents an abstract data type. In order to start a report, we must include the operation:

- `Initialize`   -- start up the report so that it includes all the records
                      -- in the data base

Our problem permits a user to search for albums according to a particular category. Thus, we must include the constructor:

- `Find`   -- select the albums within a given report that satisfy
                  -- the given criteria

In particular, we will permit the user to select albums by title, artist, style, year of release, number of records, and name and length of song. Thus, we cannot export just one `Find` operation; we must offer a `Find` for each category.

As our problem description requires, `Find` progressively searches over smaller and smaller sets of albums. Thus, when we `Initialize` a report, we start with all the albums in the data base. As we call `Find` for a particular category, we retain only those albums in the report that satisfy the given value. For example, we may call `Find` for a particular album style and specify that only information about classical albums be retained in the report. Next we might call Find for a particular year and retain only information about classical albums that were released in that year. Clearly, we can establish a set of Find criteria that do not apply to any albums—calling Find for the year 1930 and also for the year 1950, for example. According to our problem statement, we need one other constructor:

- Sort   -- order the albums in the report according to the given criteria

The criteria should include the kind of ordering (ascending or descending) and the key to be used. In particular, we will allow reports to be sorted by title, artist, style, year, and the number of songs.

Just as we needed a selector for Database, we need a selector that tells us the size of a report object, plus an iterator:

- Length_Of -- returns the number of albums the report describes

We also need an iterator, so that we can visit every record in the report. Thus, we must include the operations:

- Initialize -- establish a starting point for the traversal

- Get_Next   -- advance the iterator to designate another item

- Value_Of   -- return the record currently being visited

- Is_Done   -- return True when all records have been visited

As we will see in a later section, the iterator allows us to print information about all the albums in a given report without altering the state of the report itself.

The last entity, Albums, defines a class of objects. However, we will use an approach to characterize its behavior that is different from our approach to Database and Reports. Specifically, we have defined Database and Reports as encapsulated abstractions; we will express Albums as an unencapsulated entity.

As we discussed in Chapter 6, Ada's *private* and *limited private* types hide the inside view (the implementation) of an abstraction. Therefore, such types are used to encapsulate design decisions and hide them from outside view. All of the other types provide unencapsulated abstractions; their structure is fully visible from the outside. As a rule of thumb, we tend to use encapsulation when it would be dangerous for a client to have access to the underlying representation of an entity. For example, if we allowed a client to manipulate the actual representation of the Database programmatically, it might be possible to put the object in an inconsistent state. On the other hand, the representation of an individual album is a pure structural abstraction. That is, our program object serves simply to collect other objects (in this case, a title, an artist, a year, etc.). Hence, there is little value in encapsulating the abstraction because there is little a client can do to corrupt its state.

Therefore, in this step, we shall not explicitly specify any operations for the class of objects defined by `Albums`. Rather, we shall only export some of Ada's primitive types and so implicitly export their corresponding predefined operations, as we described in Chapter 6.

We are not quite done with this step; there is another set of operations that we must consider. When building abstractions, we tend to capture their behavior by defining only primitive operations. Primitive operations are operations that we can implement only if we have access to the underlying representation of the type. Thus, `Add` is a primitive constructor for the `Database` because we can implement it only if we have an inside view of the abstraction. On the other hand, printing a particular record from the data base is not a primitive operation; we can implement it with only an outside view, since our abstraction of the album is unencapsulated.

This data base system is meant for human use, so it is necessary that we provide textual input and output facilities for all abstractions in our solution space. For example, we need some way to display album information to the user. Similarly, we need a mechanism that allows the user to name the find and sort criteria for a given report. Rather than including these operations as part of our specification of each abstraction, however, we choose to put them in a different place. In this way, we can keep each entity tightly coupled. For example, if we were to include the input/output operations for the report along with the entity `Reports`, we would actually be mixing two abstractions: the report itself and our I/O mechanism. Thus, if we changed the way we did I/O, we would have to alter every unit in our solution. On the other hand, it is possible for us to place such I/O operations in a different unit because the facilities we need are not primitive; they can be implemented with only an outside view of each entity.

For these reasons, we will introduce to our solution three additional units: `Album_IO`, `Report_IO`, and `Command_IO`. These units are not really objects; they are collections of subprograms, as we will discuss in Chapter 11. However, they are closely coupled to the objects we have already defined. Each of these new units serves as a nonprimitive utility built on top of more primitive abstractions. In particular, `Album_IO` and `Report_IO` parallel `Albums` and `Reports` directly. `Command_IO` parallels `Database`, but we have named it differently to reflect that this set of operations also includes the first line of user interaction (and thus must deal with user commands such as `Quit`).

7.4   Establish the Visibility

Now that we have characterized the behavior of each object and class of objects, we must consider how these objects relate to one another. In this problem, the connectivity of units is straightforward. To proceed with this step, we must ask: For each entity, what other objects or classes of objects must be visible?

It should be clear that `Albums` provides the central abstraction in this solution. `Albums` denotes the fundamental class of objects of the vocabulary of our problem space. Thus, `Albums` does not depend on any other unit, but it is the case that the following units must see `Albums`:

- Database
- Reports
- Album_IO

Similarly, the root of our solution, `Process_Album_Database`, must also see `Albums` to handle user-entered album data.

`Database` is the next highest entity in our layers of abstraction. Whereas `Database` depends on `Albums`, the following entities depend on `Database`:

- Reports
- Process_Album_Database

The main program must see both `Database` and `Reports`, because users can interact with these objects through commands that are processed in `Process_Album_Database`.

Two of the new units we introduced in the previous section, `Album_IO` and `Report_IO`, depend on the units `Albums` and `Reports`, respectively. In turn, the main program, `Process_Album_Database`, depends on these two units, and it also depends on `Command_IO` to process user requests.

Figure 7.1 uses the symbols we introduced in Chapter 4 to illustrate the structure of our system. Although in this solution the main program imports every other unit, this is not always the case. The present problem is fairly simple and demands this kind of interconnectivity, but the main programs of larger systems that are built in layers of abstraction can import only those units at one layer. (For example, see Chapter 13, in which we implement a lower layer of the problem we introduced in Chapter 5.)

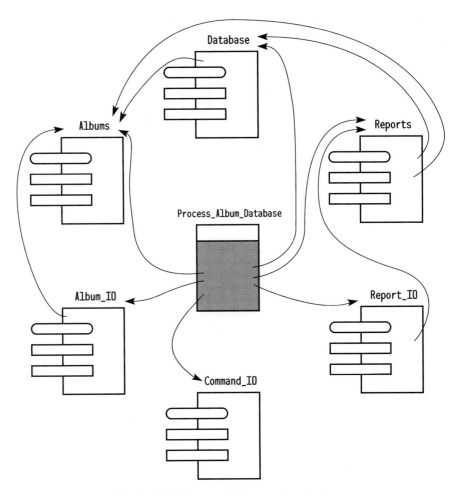

Figure 7.1 Design of `Process_Album_Database`

7.5   Establish the Interface

Now that we have created the high-level design of our solution, we can capture all the design decisions we have made to this point in the form of Ada package specifications.

Let us start with the interface to **Albums**. As we indicated, an **Album** includes information about title, artist, style, year of release, and the name and length of each song. This is a simple structural abstraction that we can represent with a record type. However, this abstraction is complicated by the fact that each record can contain a different number of songs. Happily, as Chapter 8 described, Ada permits us to declare discriminated records. In this manner, we might write the declaration:

```
type Album (Number_Of_Songs : Number := 10) is
  record
    The_Title  : Title;
    The_Artist : Artist;
    The_Style  : Style;
    The_Year   : Year;
    The_Songs  : Songs(1..Number_Of_Songs);
  end record;
```

Thus, a record describing a single album includes title, artist, style, and year components, as well as an array of songs, whose size is indicated by the discriminant Number_Of_Songs.

Notice that we have named each type explicitly; as we discussed in Chapter 6, it is safer to construct new types using the vocabulary of the problem space, rather than using predefined types.

To complete the interface to this unit, we need to know more about the nature of each piece of album information. For the purposes of this problem, we will assume that the title and artist are both strings of length 40. (However these strings are different types!) The name of a song is also a string of up to 40 characters. (This too is a different type.) We will assume that there is a fixed set of styles for each album, so we can represent them as an enumeration type. Finally, year of release, length of song, and number of songs are all numeric values. In fact, we can set the year 1877—the year of the invention of the phonograph by Thomas Edison—as the lower bound. The length of a song, on the other hand, is a real value. For our purposes, we shall use hundredths of a minute as the measure of song length.

Given these constraints on our abstraction of the problem space, we can capture our abstraction with the declarations:

```
package Albums is
  type Title is new String(1..40);
  type Artist is new String(1..40);
  type Style is (Classical, Jazz,      Rock,     Country,
                 Shows,     Religious, Ballroom, Patriotic,
                 Foreign,   Folk,      Blues,    Children);
  type Year is range 1877..Integer'Last;
  type Length is delta 0.01 range 0.0..60.0;
  type Name is new String(1..40);
```

```
      type Song is
        record
          The_Name   : Name;
          The_Length : Length;
        end record;
      subtype Number is Positive range 1..30;
      type Songs is array (Number range <>) of Song;
      type Album (Number_Of_Songs : Number := 10) is
        record
          The_Title  : Title;
          The_Artist : Artist;
          The_Style  : Style;
          The_Year   : Year;
          The_Songs  : Songs(1..Number_Of_Songs);
        end record;
  end Albums;
```

The style of package Albums demonstrates several points worth mentioning. Notice how the types Title, Artist, and Name all have the same structure; they are all strings of length 40. However, by declaring each as a unique type, we exploit Ada's rules of named typing. Thus, even though these types look the same, Ada rules will prevent us from mixing these abstractions during compilation. Notice also that the record type Album actually contains a nested record declaration—the component type of Songs is Song, which is itself a record. This structure leads to some possibly lengthy yet precise naming. For example, given an object The_Album of the type Album, we can refer to the name of the third song on the album with the expression:

```
The_Album.The_Songs(3).The_Name
```

Moving on, let us study the outside view of the entity Database. As we did in Chapter 5, we can take the operations we identified earlier and name them as subprograms that are exported from the package. The only complication in this solution is the way in which we expose the iterator. Recall that the iterator provides a mechanism that lets a client visit every album in the data base without altering its state. In effect, a client can view a data base as a list of albums, and the iterator acts as an index to this collection. As we advance the iterator, we simply advance the index in the collection. Along the way, we can save the value of this index through the iterator operation Value_Of. However, this only keeps our finger at a certain place in the data base. If we want to find information about the album at that place, we call a different `Value_Of` to retrieve the information. Because the four iterator operations are so intimately related, we shall place them in a package nested inside the specification of `Albums`. As we shall see in Chapter 11, this approach is primarily for the benefit of the human reader and does little to make Ada's rules work harder for us.

Thus, we can capture our design decisions in the package specification:

```
with Albums;
package Database is

   type Item is private;

   procedure Create (The_Name : in String);
   procedure Open   (The_Name : in String);
   procedure Close;

   procedure Add    (The_Album : in Albums.Album);
   procedure Delete (The_Album : in Albums.Album);
   procedure Modify (The_Album : in Albums.Album;
                     To_Be     : in Albums.Album);

   function Size return Natural;
   function Value_Of (The_Item : in Item) return Albums.Album;

   package Iterator is
     procedure Initialize;
     procedure Get_Next;
     function Value_Of return Item;
     function Is_Done  return Boolean;
   end Iterator;

private
   type Item is ...
end Database;
```

Since `Database` depends on `Albums`, we must explicitly import `Albums`, using a context clause.

Notice that we introduced the type `Item` as an encapsulated type. This type serves as our pointer in the list of albums. For example, while iterating through the data base, we may wish to "remember" a certain place. Since the iterator operation `Value_Of` returns an object of type `Item`—not `Albums.Album`—we can remember where we are by storing this value in an object of type `Item`, and then calling a different `Value_Of` to retrieve the related album information.

We shall defer the implementation of the private part of this package until Chapter 10, where we shall study the inside view of this application.

Databases denotes an abstract-state machine, so we do not export a type Database (there is only one data base). However, Reports denotes an abstract data type, so we must export a type Report as an encapsulated type. Thus, if we take the operations that we identified earlier, we can write the specification of this unit as:

```
with Albums;
package Reports is
  type Report is limited private;
  type Category is (Title,  Artist, Style, Year,
                         Number, Song,   Length);
  subtype Sort_Category is Category range Title..Number;
  type Order is (Ascending, Descending);
  procedure Initialize (The_Report   : in out Report);
  procedure Find (The_Title        : in      Albums.Title;
                  In_The_Report    : in out Report);
  procedure Find (The_Artist       : in      Albums.Artist;
                  In_The_Report    : in out Report);
  procedure Find (The_Style        : in      Albums.Style;
                  In_The_Report    : in out Report);
  procedure Find (The_Year         : in      Albums.Year;
                  In_The_Report    : in out Report);
  procedure Find (The_Number       : in      Albums.Number;
                  In_The_Report    : in out Report);
  procedure Find (The_Song         : in      Albums.Name;
                  In_The_Report    : in out Report);

  procedure Find (The_Length       : in      Albums.Length;
                  In_The_Report    : in out Report);
  procedure Sort (The_Report       : in out Report;
                  By_Category      : in      Sort_Category;
                  With_The_Order   : in      Order := Ascending);
  function Length_Of (The_Report   : in Report) return Natural;

  type Iterator is limited private;

  procedure Initialize (The_Iterator : in out Iterator;
                        With_The_Report   : in      Report);
  procedure Get_Next   (The_Iterator : in out Iterator);
```

```
    function Value_Of (The_Iterator : in Iterator)
      return Albums.Album;
    function Is_Done  (The_Iterator : in Iterator) return Boolean;
private
    type Report   is ...
    type Iterator is ...
end Reports;
```

Notice that we have introduced the enumeration types Category, Sort_Category, and Order primarily to support the interface to the constructor Sort. Also, we have intentionally overloaded the name Find so that it applies to each search category, since each requires a parameter of a different type.

The careful reader will realize that the Database iterator is subtly different from the Reports iterator. Since Database is an abstract-state machine, we have only one object; hence, we require only one iterator at a time. However, Reports provides the abstract data type Report, so we must be able to have many iterators. For this reason, we introduce the type Iterator, which is a parameter to the four iterator operations. We couple an iterator to a particular report object in the operation Initialize. The semantics of this operation make the iterator object denote all the items in the given data base.

The remaining three units—Album_IO, Reports_IO, and Command_IO—serve only as collections of subprograms. For example, according to our earlier description, Album_IO provides input and output facilities for each piece of album information:

```
with Albums;
package Album_IO is
    procedure Get (The_Title  : out Albums.Title);
    procedure Get (The_Artist : out Albums.Artist);
    procedure Get (The_Style  : out Albums.Style);
    procedure Get (The_Year   : out Albums.Year);
    procedure Get (The_Number : out Albums.Number);
    procedure Get (The_Song   : out Albums.Name);
    procedure Get (The_Length : out Albums.Length);
    procedure Get (The_Album  : out Albums.Album);
    procedure Put (The_Album  : in  Albums.Album);
end Album_IO;
```

The only complicated operation in this package is Get for an entire album; in this operation we can enter a different number of songs for each album. Report_IO takes on a similar form. We must provide I/O for various attributes of a report, including a find category, a sorting category, and a sorting order:

```
with Reports;
package Report_IO is
   procedure Get      (The_Category : out Reports.Category);
   procedure Get_Sort (The_Category : out Reports.Sort_Category);
   procedure Get      (The_Order    : out Reports.Order);
   procedure Put      (The_Length   : in  Natural);
end Report_IO;
```

Notice that we must introduce the name Get_Sort rather than use the overloaded name Sort, since Sort_Category is only a subtype of Category. As we will study further in the next chapter, Ada rules are such that an implementation could not distinguish calls of Sort for the type from calls of Sort for the subtype; hence, we must use distinct names to avoid ambiguity.

Command_IO is the last package of interest. Here we capture our design decisions about the ways in which a user can interact with the system. We can express this class of commands with a single enumeration type and one operation that gets a value from the user:

```
package Command_IO is

   type Command is (Create, Open,          Close, Add,  Delete,
                        Modify, Start_Report, Find,  Sort, Display_Report,
                        Quit);

   procedure Get (The_Command : out Command);
end Command_IO;
```

We have now specified the interface of each unit at this level of abstraction in our solution space. However, we have not yet studied the Ada facilities that permit us to fully express their implementation. Thus, we shall suspend the completion of our solution until Chapter 10. In Chapter 8, we shall discuss subprograms, and in Chapter 9, we shall consider statements as the vehicle for algorithmic control. Armed with these new resources, we shall then complete our solution for the data base system.

Exercises   1.   If we make a change in the interface of the package Database, what other units might be affected?

2.   Suppose that the requirements for our problem change, and we must also maintain information about the tempo of each song (fast, slow, danceable, etc.). Alter the units necessary to incorporate and take advantage of this change.

3. If we often sort on one category, such as artist, it may be useful to maintain indexed sequential access into the data base—in other words, a list of artists with pointers to their albums. Add this new abstraction to the solution.

4. How can we apply the use of indexed sequential access to any album component?

5. Have we really defined a safe abstraction for Database? Consider, for example, what happens if we call Open for a data base that is already open.

6. Identify all the other exceptional conditions for Database. Hint: Consider what might go wrong with each operation.

Algorithms and Control

Suit the action to the word, the word to the action...

Shakespeare
Hamlet [1]

Subprograms

The Form of Ada Subprograms
Subprogram Calls
Applications for Ada Subprograms

The primary activity of any computer program is to complete some amount of work, however that is measured. As we have seen, programs are both declarative and imperative in nature; that is, a user views a program as a collection of objects that interact with one another through a series of sequential or parallel actions. In their best form, these actions should directly reflect our abstraction of the algorithms in the real world. For example, a program to control a microwave oven should contain high-level operations such as Turn_On_Radiator, Read_Temperature_Probe, or Read_Power_Setting. By dealing with the program at this level, the readability and maintainability of the system is enhanced.

Of course, no general-purpose language could directly provide all the possible operations we would ever need. Instead, languages usually provide a mechanism built out of more-primitive instructions for defining algorithms at a high level. This mechanism is the *subprogram*. Just as we can create abstract data types from the facilities of primitive types, so can we specify high-level actions from simple statements, with the advantage of being able to defer the implementation of these actions to a lower level of abstraction. We have already used subprograms in our design examples, but in this chapter we shall take a closer look at their structure and applications.

8.1   The Form of Ada Subprograms

Subprograms form the basic executable units of Ada programs. They have two forms, namely:

- Procedures
- Functions

Simply stated, a *procedure* names a collection of statements that define a high-level action. *Functions* do the same, but their primary purpose is to return a calculated value. We also say that subprograms are *defined* in a declarative part and *invoked* (executed) by a subprogram call. Subprograms can be declared anywhere an object declaration is appropriate, such as in a package specification or in the declarative part of a block, subprogram body, task body, or package body.

In Chapter 4, we defined the symbols for an Ada subprogram, symbols that Figure 8.1 repeats. However, there is also another way to view subprograms, as shown in Figure 8.2. In this figure, we see that a subprogram is treated as a logical unit by the calling environment. In addition, the subprogram can have local objects that are hidden from the outside world, but there may be global objects visible to the subprogram. Communicating with entities that are outside the subprogram increases coupling among program units and is thus poor programming practice (see Chapter 2). Large, real-time systems may require the use of global variables for efficiency, however. Fortunately, the packaging mechanism of Ada can localize the effects of any global references. Indeed, we say that the scope of locally defined entities is limited to the inside of the subprogram.

It is better style to use parameters to pass objects to and from subprograms. The objects named in the parameter list of a subprogram call are called *actual* parameters; inside the subprogram, they are called *formal* parameters. Parameters can be passed in one of three modes:

- `in`   `-- Only the actual value is used; the subprogram cannot modify`
            `the value.`

- `out`   `-- The subprogram creates a value but does not use the value`
            `of the actual parameter.`

- `in out`   `-- The subprogram uses the value from the actual parameter and`
            `may assign a new value to it.`

Subprograms directly support the principles of modularity, abstraction, localization, and information hiding discussed in Chapter 2. They were originally used in first-generation languages to conserve memory space by

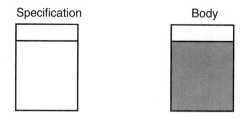

Figure 8.1 Symbols for an Ada subprogram

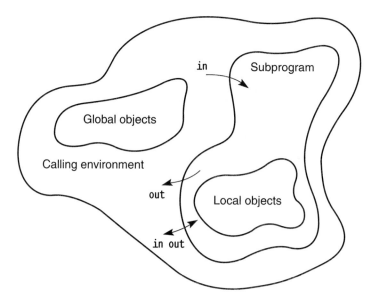

Figure 8.2 Model of an Ada subprogram

factoring out common statements, since we were often constrained by the address space of our machines. This is generally the wrong way to use them in Ada. Subprograms should reflect the operations in the high-level design of a problem solution. Rather than being constrained by the primitive facilities provided by a language, a programmer should name the high-level activities as needed, and then use subprogram definitions to implement the operations. This use of subprograms makes the language extensible; that is, it extends the language to express a solution in the problem's own terms.

Subprogram Specifications

Just like packages and tasks, subprograms can be divided into a specification part and a body. A subprogram specification defines the interface, or calling

convention, between a subprogram and the outside world. This interface
names the subprogram and lists zero or more parameters. Following the
strongly typed nature of the language, Ada subprograms also define the types
of each parameter directly in this interface. In the case of functions, the interface also specifies the type of the value returned by the subprogram. For
example, we can declare the following subprogram specifications:

```
procedure Count_Leaves_On_Binary_Tree;
procedure Push (Element : in     Integer; On      : in out Buffer);
procedure Rotate (Point : in out Coordinate; Angle : in      Radians);
function Cos (Angle : in Radians)       return Float;
function Random                         return Float;
function "*" (Left, Right : in Matrix) return Matrix;
```

The in mode is the default, and so can be omitted in the Cos function.
For readability, however, it is generally better practice to explicitly specify
the mode. Notice how we can mix the modes of our parameters. In the case
of functions, parameters can be passed only with the mode in, thus limiting
the possibility of side effects. For example, the Cos function should not normally modify the Angle—to do so would be an unexpected side effect—so
the in mode prevents us from taking this action. Normally, side effects
(caused by referencing a global object) are not desirable but are sometimes
necessary. For example, the Random function must modify a global seed
value, so we cannot pass the seed as simply an in parameter. As another
example, we might instruct our subprograms to increment a global variable
every time they are called. This is a common debugging technique, but it
requires us to reference a global object. If we must reference a global object,
we should do so only in a limited scope, and even then the design should
be explicitly documented.

It is good practice to keep the number of subprogram parameters to a
minimum, passing only the data that is necessary and sufficient for the
execution of that subprogram. Minimizing the number of parameters
enhances the readability of a subprogram declaration. Of course, with the
recommended use of meaningful and sometimes long names, subprogram
declarations may spill over onto successive lines. Readability can still be
maintained if we use a reasonable coding style, such as:

```
procedure Activate  (Process   : in out Process_Name;
                     Priority  : in     Natural;
                     Wait      : in     Duration);

procedure Print     (Banner    : in     String;
                     Centered  : in     Boolean := True;
                     Skip_Page : in     Boolean := True);
```

Notice in these examples that `Centered` and `Skip_Page` have been given default values. We shall see in a later section how default parameter values can affect a subprogram call.

As seen in the function examples given earlier, subprograms can also be named with symbols, known as *function designators*. This technique is called *overloading an operator*. We cannot use just any symbol but only the operator symbols described in Chapter 4 under Names and Expressions. (One exception is the inequality operator (`/=`) because it is implicitly declared when the equality operator (`=`) is overloaded.) Since Ada provides mathematical operations only for primitive data types such as `Integer` and `Float` (and derived numeric types), a programmer can use functions with designators to define the operations upon user-defined types, such as matrix multiplication or complex number arithmetic. Of course, Ada cannot guarantee the mathematical properties of user-defined operations, so it is important that the programmer adhere to the usual arithmetic conventions.

If we redefine the multiplication operator for, say, matrices, we have overloaded the operator symbol `*`. In other words, the same symbol has been used for different purposes. Actually, this is nothing new, since most languages overload their expression operators and their input/output procedures, such as `Read` and `Write`, for different types. For example, in Pascal the following subprogram calls can be used:

```
Writeln(Index);
Writeln("Enter your name: ");
```

Here, the same name is used to represent two different operations, namely, output of an object value and output of a string. In Ada, we can often overload subprogram names other than designators, such as:

```
type Levels is range 0..10_000;
procedure Set (Listing  : in Boolean);
procedure Set (Pixel    : in Color; Frame : in out Buffer);
procedure Set (Priority : in Levels);
procedure Set (Address  : in Natural);
```

A call to an overloaded subprogram is ambiguous if it is not possible for the compiler to identify exactly one subprogram specification. The compiler may take the types and order of the actual parameters, the name of formal parameters (if named parameter association is used), and the result type (for functions) to resolve an overloaded subprogram call. This process is called *disambiguation*. We may not use the presence or the values of defaults to distinguish between otherwise similar subprograms. For example, the following calls to the procedure `Set` are not ambiguous:

```
Set(Listing => True);
Set(Blue, My_Buffer);
```

However, the following is ambiguous, since 1372 could be an `Address` or a `Priority`:

```
Set(1372);
```

We can disambiguate the call by using named parameter association, such as:

```
Set(Address => 1372);
```

As we have said before, overloading should be used carefully. The unrestricted use of overloading will decrease the understandability of a program. Overloading should be used only when it is appropriate to name equivalent actions for different types.

Subprogram Bodies

For a subprogram declaration to be complete, both a specification, describing the subprogram interface, and a body, defining the algorithm itself, must be defined. A subprogram declaration is completed with a block containing a set of local declarations (possibly containing nested subprograms), followed by a sequence of statements delimited by `begin` and `end`. The subprogram body may include an exception handler, which will be discussed in Chapter 15. The overall subprogram structure directly supports information hiding by making the details of the subprogram inaccessible to the outside environment. Furthermore, these details are generally unimportant to a subprogram user. All that is important at a user's level of abstraction is that the named subprogram does what it is intended to do.

Although we have not covered all the details of Ada statements, the following examples provide several complete subprogram declarations using simple statements. Don't concern yourself with their details; they should be fairly obvious in form, and their exact meanings will be described in the following chapter.

Consider the following type declarations:

```
type List is array (Positive range <>) of Integer;
type Buffer(Total_Elements : Natural) is
  record
    Index : Natural := 0;
    Value : List(1..Total_Elements);
  end record;
```

For the `Push` subprogram described earlier, we can now complete the declaration as:

```
procedure Push (Element : in Integer; On : in out Buffer) is
begin
  On.Index           := On.Index + 1;
  On.Value(On.Index) := Element;
end Push;
```

Notice that we declared `Element` as a parameter with the mode `in`. Ada strictly enforces this abstraction and prevents the assignment of a value to such a parameter by noting an error at compilation time.

We can also declare subprograms with local objects, such as:

```
with Text_Io;
function Read_Flag return Boolean is
  User_Input : String(1..100) := (others => ASCII.Nul);
  Last_Char : Natural;
begin
  loop
    Text_Io.Get_Line(User_Input, Last_Char);
    if User_Input(1..3) = "yes" then
      return True;
    elsif User_Input(1..2) = "no" then
      return False;
    else
      Text_Io.Put_Line("Invalid response...try again");
    end if;
  end loop;
end Read_Flag;
```

In this example, we use the `return` statement to exit the subprogram and return a value, but, as you may have noticed, there are multiple exit points, which is normally not good practice. By introducing a switch, we can rewrite the function as:

```
with Text_Io;
function Read_Flag return Boolean is
  Result          : Boolean;
  User_Input      : String(1..100) := (others => ASCII.Nul);
  Last_Char       : Natural;
  Valid_Response  : Boolean := False;
```

```
    begin
      loop
        exit when Valid_Response;
        Text_Io.Get_Line(User_Input, Last_Char);
        if User_Input(1..3) = "yes" then
          Result := True;
          Valid_Response := True;
        elsif User_Input(1..2) = "no" then
          Result := False;
          Valid_Response := True;
        else
          Text_Io.Put_Line("Invalid response...try again");
        end if;
      end loop;
      return Result;
    end Read_Flag;
```

However, this version is not quite as readable as the first. Most of the time simpler is better, even if the structure seems to violate some rules of structured coding.

Although we used only simple object declarations (`Result`, `User_Input`, and `Valid_Response`) for local subprogram objects in this example, we can actually declare any item locally, such as types, subtypes, numbers, exceptions, renamed entities, packages, tasks, and even other subprograms. Chapter 20 takes a closer look at this approach.

If you look carefully, you will notice that the first line of each example (`Push` and `Read_Flag`) has a slightly different syntax from that first introduced for the subprogram specification. The subtle difference involves the word is instead of the semicolon, which acts as the prefix to the subprogram body. Actually, the subprogram body can stand alone, since it contains both an interface part (which must match an earlier specification for the subprogram, if one exists) and the implementation of the algorithm. In general, a subprogram body can appear anywhere a simple object declaration can appear (except that a body cannot appear in a package specification, although a subprogram specification can). A subprogram body can stand alone in a package body, or it can serve to complete a specification in the package's visible part.

A separate subprogram specification should be used as a sort of "forward" declaration when two subprograms must call each other. For example, consider the following declarations:

```
procedure First  (Some_Parameter    : in out My_Type) is
begin
  -- sequence of statements
end First;

procedure Second (Another_Parameter : in out Your_Type) is
begin
  -- sequence of statements
end Second;
```

If the First and Second procedures were in the same declarative part, the Second procedure could call the First, but not the other way around. This is a result of the scope rules of Ada, namely that an entity must be declared before it is used. To permit each subprogram to call the other, we can introduce the specifications and declare the subprograms as:

```
procedure First  (Some_Parameter    : in out My_Type);
procedure Second (Another_Parameter : in out Your_Type);
  -- other entities may be declared in between
procedure First  (Some_Parameter    : in out My_Type) is
  Yours : Your_Type;
begin
  ... Second(Yours); ...
end First;
procedure Second (Another_Parameter : in out Your_Type) is
  Mine : My_Type;
begin
  ... First(Mine);  ...
end Second;
```

Since the interface of the First and Second subprograms is known at the time their bodies are elaborated, each subprogram can now call the other. This feature is also useful if a programmer wishes to improve the readability of a program unit by grouping the subprogram specifications in one place and then textually separating the subprogram bodies, as in a package. Actually, in the example above, we do not need to include the specification for the First procedure, since the Second can already see the First. To keep a consistent style and thereby aid readability, the use of both specifications is recommended.

If a programmer does not wish to clutter the declarative part of a given unit, he or she can use subunits to complete the subprogram declaration. For example:

```
procedure Clip (Samples : in out Sample_Buffer) is separate;
```

Here, the specification is introduced and the body is placed in a separate compilation. As we shall see in Chapter 20, this facility directly supports top-down design methodologies.

8.2   Subprogram Calls

A call invokes the execution of a subprogram. Procedure calls can stand alone as primitive statements, but function calls can appear only in expressions, since they return a value. Using subprogram calls improves the readability of source code by invoking a named high-level action. It is therefore important that the programmer define meaningful names for subprograms.

Consider the following subprogram specifications:

```
procedure Search_File (Key   : in      Name;
                       Index : out     File_Index);
procedure Sleep        (Time  : in      Duration := 10.0);
procedure Sort         (Data  : in out Names;
                        Order : in      Direction := Ascending);
procedure Sort         (Data  : in out Numbers;
                        Order : in      Direction := Ascending);
procedure Turn_On      (Light : in      Location);
```

Notice that we have overloaded the name Sort for two subprograms, although there is no ambiguity, because of the different formal parameter types.

We can invoke these subprograms in any of three ways. First, we can call them using positional notation, which is the way most languages handle calls. In positional notation, the order of the actual parameters must match the order of the formal parameters, such as:

```
Search_File ("Smith, J", Record_Entry);
Sleep(120.0);
Sort(Personnel_Names, Descending);
Sort(Grades, Ascending);
Turn_On(Office_Lights);
```

If the static type of the actual parameter does not match the type of the formal parameter, a compilation error will be noted. At run-time, the exception Constraint_Error will be raised if an actual parameter value does not meet the constraint of the corresponding formal parameter.

The second way of invoking a subprogram, using named parameter association, can improve the readability of subprogram calls. For example:

```
Search_File (Key => "Smith, J", Index => Record_Entry);
Sleep(Time => 120.0);
Sort(Data => Personnel_Names, Order => Descending);
```

This facility makes subprogram calls almost self-documenting. Named and positional notation can be used in the same call, but once a named parameter is given, the rest of the parameters must be named. Named parameter association also permits the order of the actual parameters to differ from the order of the formal parameters, although it is not usually good practice to do so.

The third approach involves calling subprograms using default parameters. For example, we could call the subprogram Sort as:

```
Sort(Personnel_Names);
Sort(Grades);
```

Notice how we invoked the overloaded Sort subprogram. The Ada compiler can handle this seeming ambiguity by using the types of the actual parameters (which are different) to select the proper subprogram.

In both cases, the default order of Ascending would be applied. This is another language feature that must be used carefully. It is most useful when a subprogram has parameters whose actual values do not change over most calls. However, the use of default values may decrease program readability.

We can combine named parameter association and default parameters:

```
Sort(Data => Personnel_Names);
```

Function calls differ slightly from procedure calls. Consider the following specifications:

```
function Cos  (Angle       : in Radians)     return Float;
function Heat (Sensor      : in Sensor_Name) return Float;
function "+"  (Left, Right : in Matrix)      return Matrix;
```

We can call the subprograms as:

```
Distance := Length * Cos(1.5708);
Value    := Heat(Sensor => Wing_Tip);
Sum      := "+"(First_Matrix, Second_Matrix);
```

As we can see, both named and positional parameter associations are permitted for functions (as are as default parameters). In the last example, we used prefix notation to invoke the + function, but Ada permits us alternatively to write functions named with operator symbols using normal infix notation (assuming that the name of the operator is directly visible):

```
Sum := First_Matrix + Second_Matrix;
```

Here, we have invoked an overloaded function (+), but the compiler can determine by the types of the operands that we are referring to the operation defined for Matrix data.

Functions, like procedures, can be declared without any parameters. We often declare such functions when we need to express a predicate, for example:

```
function Is_Valid_Operation return Boolean;
function Access_Authorized return Boolean;
```

We call such functions without any actual parameter part:

```
if Access_Authorized then
  -- statements
end if;
```

Notice that a parameterless function call is indistinguishable from a simple object name.

8.3   Applications for Ada Subprograms

As we have seen, subprograms are executable program units that encapsulate algorithms. Subprograms do more than just textually collect statements. They have, in fact, three primary applications, namely:

- Main program units

- Definition of functional control

- Definition of operations for abstract data types

A discussion and examples of each of these applications is presented in the following sections

Subprograms as Main Programs

Ada does not have a separate construct for a main program. Rather, it requires that a subprogram be used as the part of an Ada system that can be called from the environment. How this main unit is called is not defined by the language but is left up to the environment. Of course, a particular implementation could require a pragma Main, but that feature would be contrary to the spirit of the language. Since the language does not prohibit it, a "main" subprogram could have parameters passed to and from the environment.

It is generally a good practice for large systems to have a "main" program devoid of any implementation details. As we discussed in Chapter 2, the principle of modularity suggests that high-level modules should describe the "what" of a solution, and lower-level modules should provide the "how." Thus, the subprogram at the highest level of a system would typically have only essential system types and objects, plus subprograms, packages, or tasks that provide the primary operations. For example, in a system that runs forever, periodically logging data, the highest level of the system might appear as:

```
with Recorder, Sensor;
procedure Record_Line_Conditions is
  Voltage : Sensor.Voltage_Type;
begin
  loop
    Sensor.Line(Measurement => Voltage);
    Recorder.Post (Voltage);
  end loop;
end Record_Line_Conditions;
```

Just as we saw in the first two design problems, the with clause imports library units (in this case, Recorder and Sensor). The resources of these units are available to the given procedure, but their implementation details are hidden from view. This encapsulation helps control the complexity of a large problem.

Definition of Functional Control

In traditional top-down functional design, an analyst will examine a problem starting at the highest levels, and then decompose a solution into its primary functions. This activity parallels the object-oriented design methodology for abstracting data.

Once these functions are determined, the next step is to create a subprogram that implements these actions. If a single value is to be returned, it is appropriate to consider a function subprogram; otherwise, procedure subprograms should be used. Since this functional allocation implies action, it is generally a good practice to name these subprograms accordingly. Subprograms should be named as active verb phrases, such as Initiate_Process, Retract_Probe, or Check_Limits. Functions are best named as nouns if they simply return an object value, such as Cos, Random, or Sensor_Value. If used as part of a test returning a boolean value, functions are best named as forms of the verb to be, such as Process_Is_Terminated, Probe_Is_Down, or Are_In_Limits.

At any given level in a program, only those subprograms that are critical to the solution should be visible. Of course, lower levels may require additional subprograms to implement higher operations, but these procedures and functions should be hidden. For example, in a simple data acquisition program, we might have:

```
with Sample;
procedure Analyze_Sensor_Values is
   Actual_Data : Sample.Values;
   Fitted_Data : Sample.Values;
   procedure Get_Samples (Data : out     Sample.Values) is separate;
   procedure Limit_Check (Data : in out Sample.Values) is separate;
   procedure Curve_Fit   (Data : in      Sample.Values;
                          Fit  : out     Sample.Values) is separate;
   procedure Report      (Data : in      Sample.Values) is separate;
begin
   Get_Samples(Actual_Data);
   Limit_Check(Actual_Data);
   Curve_Fit(Actual_Data, Fit => Fitted_Data);
   Report(Fitted_Data);
end Analyze_Sensor_Values;
```

Notice the use of the **separate** clause in each subprogram specification. The specification of each subprogram is directly visible, but their bodies are separately compiled and therefore textually and logically hidden. For example, the body of **Report** might appear as:

```
separate (Analyze_Sensor_Values)
procedure Report (Data : in Sample.Values) is
begin
   -- sequence of statements
end Report;
```

Using subprograms in this manner can improve the readability and therefore the maintainability of programs. Effective use of this technique requires a well-planned decomposition of the operations. However, in a real-time environment, having a great number of subprogram calls can impose too great a run-time overhead. To eliminate this overhead while at the same time maintaining the other benefits of subprogram modularization, we can use the **pragma** (compiler directive) called **Inline**. This directive has the effect of expanding a subprogram body in-line at each subprogram call. Thus, the code for the algorithm is placed at the calling point, without the overhead of parameter passing or other linkage. To the user, of course, the action still appears as a logical, encapsulated entity. The **Inline** pragma must appear in the same declarative part in which the named subprograms are declared and is coded as:

```
pragma Inline(Get_Samples, Limit_Check, Curve_Fit, Report);
```

The arguments of this pragma are subprogram names. By definition, the meaning of a subprogram is not affected by the pragma.

Definition of Operations for Abstract Data Types

As we noted in Chapter 6, a type is characterized by a set of values and a set of operations applicable to objects of that type. Primitive types (e.g., Integer) have implicit operations, but a programmer may wish to create a user-defined (abstract) type with unique applicable operations. Although we shall discuss the topic more fully in Chapter 11, we have already seen in the first two design problems how subprograms can be used to affect this definition. Packages are used to encapsulate and enforce a user's logical abstraction, such as:

```
package Linked_Lists is
   type List is limited private;
   procedure Add     (To      : in out List; Data : in     Integer);
   procedure Remove  (From    : in out List; Data : out    Integer);
   function  Is_Null (The_List : in      List) return Boolean;
   Null_List : exception;
private
   type List is ...
end Linked_Lists;
```

Typically, we use procedures as constructors (operations that alter an object) and functions as selectors (operations that return the value of an object). This package specification includes only the specification part of the subprograms. We would include the corresponding subprogram bodies in the package body. In the above example, we have created an abstract data type Linked_Lists. List that has only three available operations: Add, Remove, and Is_Null. The details of the subprogram implementations are hidden at this level.

In this chapter, we have examined subprograms as a means of encapsulating an algorithm. Of course, these high-level actions must be implemented by more-primitive operations. In the next chapter, we shall study Ada's statements as primitive operations in detail.

Summary
- Subprograms are the basic executable units of Ada programs.

- Subprograms are procedures or functions.

- A subprogram specification introduces an interface between a subprogram and the outside world.

- Subprogram parameters can be of an arbitrary type; each parameter has a mode that denotes the direction of data flow.

- A subprogram body repeats the specification and is followed by a block containing declarations, a sequence of statements, and (optionally) an exception handler.

- Subprograms are best applied as main programs, for functional decomposition, and as the definition of operations for abstract data types.

Exercises   1. Write the subprogram specification for an operation called `Normalize`, which takes an object of type `Float` and alters its value. (How it is altered is irrelevant.)

2. Write the subprogram specification for an operation called `Matrix_Multiply`, which multiplies two matrices. Rewrite this operation as a function using the designator `*`.

3. Write the specification for a subprogram called `Order_Dinner` with parameters denoting the various courses of the meal. Include default values for every parameter.

4. Write the declaration of a boolean function called `Is_Empty`, which is used to test for a stack underflow. The only parameter needed is an actual stack.

Expressions
and Statements

Names

Values

Expressions

Statements

I f we study programmer productivity in terms of lines of debugged code per day, we find that it is relatively constant and independent of the level of language used. For assembly language programming, the figure is roughly ten lines of code per day; the same number holds for high-order languages [1]. Since a single high-order instruction can do more than one assembly language statement, it is apparent that net productivity increases as we move to higher levels. In high-order languages, subprograms move us to the highest level by providing a facility for expressing user-defined algorithms that we can treat as primitive operations.

At some point we must implement these high-level algorithms, and we desire that such an implementation offer clarity. Just as abstract data types are constructed from more-primitive types, subprograms are constructed from simple statements that provide structures for the control of algorithms and facilities for calculating values. In this chapter, we examine Ada expressions and statements in detail.

9.1   Names

Before acting upon any object, we must be able to refer to that entity or its components by name. In Ada, a name formally denotes a declared entity, such as an object, number, type, subtype, subprogram, package, task, task entry, and exception. For example, in the following declarations each of the uppercase identifiers are legal Ada names:

```ada
type Process_Type is (Running, Ready, Blocked, Dead);
type Count       is array (Process_Type) of Natural;
type Count_Name  is access Count;
Process_State    : Process_Type;
Scheduler_Table : Count;
Local_Schedule  : Count_Name;
subtype Coefficient is Float digits 7 range -1.0..1.0;
subtype Size       is Integer range 1..4;
type Matrix        is array (Size, Size) of Coefficient;
Matrix_1, Matrix_2 : Matrix;
type Value is record
   Name        : String(1..10);
   Location    : String(1..10);
   Open        : Boolean;
   Flow_Rate   : Float;
end record;
subtype Total_Values is Integer range 1..100;
type Values        is array (Total_Values) of Value;
Value_Index  : Total_Values;
Value_Record : Values;
Pi           : constant := 3.141_592_65;
Is_Empty, Is_Active  : Boolean;
Voltage_1, Voltage_2 : Float;
Count_1, Count_2     : Total_Values;
type Radians is new Float;
function Cos (Angle : in Radians) return Float;
```

We shall use these declarations throughout the rest of this chapter in our expressions and statements.

To refer to a complete entity, we simply use its name (such as Matrix_1 and Value_Index). However, to reference only part of a composite entity, we must use a different notation. For array components and entries in a family of tasks (see Chapter 14), we use indexed component notation, which is simply a subscripted name. For example, given the previous declarations, we can refer to components such as:

```ada
Matrix_1(1, 4)
Scheduler_Table(Process_Type'Succ(Process_State))
Value_Record(37)
```

Notice in the `Scheduler_Table` example how we can also use expressions (with an attribute in this case) to index a component. If our index is outside the range of possible index values, the exception `Constraint_Error` is raised during execution.

Not only can we refer to single components, but we can also name a sequence of consecutive components in a one-dimensional array called a *slice*. The following examples illustrate the naming of slices:

```
Scheduler_Table(Ready..Dead)    -- 3 components
Value_Record(1..50)             -- 50 components
```

As before, if the value of the index falls outside the bounds of valid indices, the exception `Constraint_Error` is raised.

Slices are particularly useful if large blocks of data have to be moved from one array to another. For example, consider the following assignment statement:

```
Value_Record(1..20) := Value_Record(21..40);
```

This takes the 20 values starting at `Values(21)` and assigns them starting at `Values(1)`. Since Ada evaluates the sides of an assignment statement independently, we can have overlapping slices, such as:

```
Value_Record(1..10) := Value_Record(6..15);
```

The effect of this statement is as if we determined the values of `Value_Record(6..15)` first, and then assigned these values in order starting at `Value_Record(1)`.

Using array slices as subprogram parameters requires some care. For example, consider the declarations:

```
File_Name : String(1..32);
procedure Open (The_File : in String);
```

We might be tempted to write a statement in the body of `Open` such as:

```
if The_File(1) = ´:´ then ...
```

Most of the time, we would have no problem. However, if we invoked `Open` with a slice:

```
Open(File_Name(16..32));
```

the exception `Constraint_Error` would be raised, for 1 is not within the bounds of the slice. This is where attributes come to the rescue. It would be better to write:

```
if The_File (The_File´First) = ´:´ then  ...
```

Whenever we declare an entity, the language generally lets us refer to predefined characteristics called *attributes*. Attributes are defined for objects, types, subtypes, subprograms, and tasks. A complete list of predefined attributes and their meanings is provided in Appendix A. For example, given the previous declarations, we can refer to characteristics of these entities:

```
Process_Type'First        -- the value Running
Is_Empty'Address          -- the physical address of the object
Voltage_1'Size            -- number of bits in the object
Scheduler_Table'Range     -- shorthand for Scheduler_Table'First..
                          -- Scheduler_Table'Last
```

Like most other named entities, attributes can be used in further expressions.

For records and access values, we use selected component notation to refer to parts of an entity. This dot notation is also used with subprograms, packages, tasks, and blocks. For example:

```
Value_Record(7).Location
Value_Record(Value_Index).Flow_Rate
Local_Schedule(Running)
Local_Schedule.all
```

Notice how we combined indexed and selected component notation in the second example. In the third example, (Running) refers to just an indexed component of the designated object. In the last example, the all refers to the entire object designated by the access value.

As we have already seen, Ada permits us to overload certain names. This facility is particularly useful for subprograms and enumeration literals, although object names cannot be overloaded. Thus, within a given region of program text, we must take care so that names do not clash. For example, if the following declarations appear in the same declarative region:

```
procedure Clear (The_Values : in out Values);
procedure Clear (The_Matrix : in out Matrix);
```

we have legally overloaded the name Clear. However, the following is illegal because the enumeration literal A and the object name A clash:

```
type Simple is (A, B, C);
A : Integer;              -- illegal
```

These declarations are said to be homographs of each other. Two declarations are homographs if they both use the same identifier, and overloading is permitted for one of the two names at most.

9.2   Values

In order to generate new object values with expressions, we must first have some means of naming primitive values. Ada provides a means for naming both scalar values and composite values. For simple scalar values, we can use literals, such as:

```
1_024              -- an integer numeric literal
0.398_829_138      -- a real numeric literal
Blocked            -- an enumeration literal
"Warehouse"        -- a character string
null               -- null access value, referring to no object at all
´b´                -- a character literal
16#FFE#            -- a base 16 number
```

Numeric literals are of the types universal integer and universal real, and so are represented precisely in their literal form. Upon assignment to an object or when used in an expression to compute a new value, these literal values are converted to a model number of an appropriate type, depending upon the context. For example, if the object Matrix_1(1, 1), which is declared with seven digits of accuracy, is assigned the value 0.398_829_138, this real literal will be converted to a model number with at least seven digits of accuracy. This, then, is the benefit to the programmer: As far as he or she is concerned, numeric literals are of unbounded accuracy. For this reason, we recommend that numeric constants be declared as universal literals rather than being bound to a certain numeric type.

So far, we have handled atomic (single-component) values, but Ada also permits us to name composite values for arrays and records. These values, called *aggregates*, can be expressed using positional or named component notation. For example, for the one-dimensional array object Scheduler_Table, we can generate array values by listing the components, such as:

```
(7, 3, 1, 0)                -- positional notation
(Running => 7,              -- equivalent named notation
 Ready   => 3,
 Blocked => 1,
 Dead    => 0)
(Running..Dead    => 0) -- using a range
(Running | Dead    => 0, -- using a choice
 Ready   | Blocked => 1)
(Running | Ready..Blocked => 1, -- combination of range and choice
 Dead              => 3)
```

Notice the variety of options available. Generally, it is better to use named component notation since it is much more readable. Each index value can be named as in the second example, or we can use a range as in the third example. The last form is useful when several components have the same value. The `Running | Dead` construct means that both of these components get the value `0`. An `others` clause refers to every component that has not already been assigned a value. If an `others` clause appears in an aggregate, it must be the last choice mentioned (or it could be the only choice mentioned). When using the `others` clause, we must be certain that the context tells us what the bounds of the aggregate are.

It is important to note that if we are using named component notation, the aggregate expression is evaluated once for each index. Consider the aggregate:

```
(1..5 => new Count)
```

We would generate five objects of type `Count`, as opposed to all five components referring to the same `Count` object.

In the event that an aggregate (or for that matter, any expression) is ambiguous, a programmer can make the choice of values explicit with what is called a *qualified expression*. This expression has a form similar to an attribute, with the type mark followed by an apostrophe and the expression (which can be an aggregate). For example, we can have the following declarations:

```
type Dial_Setting is array (1..5) of Float digits 7;
type Polynomial   is array (1..7) of Float digits 15;
```

Let us name the value:

```
(1..3 => 10.1, others => 0.0)
```

The compiler will recognize that this is an ambiguous aggregate, since the aggregate could be of type `Polynomial` or `Dial_Setting`. We can remove this ambiguity with a qualified expression, such as:

```
Polynomial'(1..3 => 10.1, others => 0.0)
```

A qualified expression thus explicitly states the type of the prefixed expression and is particularly necessary when applying an `others` clause in array aggregates.

As is the case for subprogram actual parameters, if the elements of an aggregate do not match the constraints of their targets, the exception `Constraint_Error` will be raised upon assignment. Furthermore, any aggregate value must be complete; that is, values for every component must be provided.

For *n*-dimensional arrays, the aggregate must be broken into one-dimensional aggregate components. For example, for an object of the type

Matrix (a 4 x 4 matrix of type Coefficient), the following are appropriate aggregates for "zeroing" the matrix:

```
Matrix´((0.0, 0.0, 0.0, 0.0),
        (0.0, 0.0, 0.0, 0.0),
        (0.0, 0.0, 0.0, 0.0),
        (0.0, 0.0, 0.0, 0.0))
Matrix´(1..4 => (0.0, 0.0, 0.0, 0.0))
Matrix´(1..4 => (1..4 => 0.0))
Matrix´(others => (others => 0.0))
```

In the first case, we have written the aggregate as a collection of one-dimensional aggregates. In the second and third cases, we have named a range for the first index of the matrix, whose elements are then assigned the value of a one-dimensional aggregate. For multidimensional arrays, aggregates are written in order of their indices. In the last case, we use the others choice twice, to indicate that all components get the value zero.

Aggregates for records follow the same notation as for arrays, except that if we use an others clause, we must be referring to at least one element. In addition, all of the elements denoted by the others clause must be of a compatible type.

Given objects of the type Value introduced earlier, we can generate aggregates such as:

```
Value´("water ", "warehouse ", True, 37.65) -- positional notation

Value´(Name      => "water      ",          -- named notation
       Location  => "warehouse ",
       Open      => True,
       Flow_Rate => 37.65)
```

Of course, these aggregate forms can be combined. For example, to provide an initial value for the Value_Record object, we could name an aggregate such as:

```
Values´(1..100 => (Name      => "          ",
                   Location  => "          ",
                   Open      => False,
                   Flow_Rate => 0.0))
```

This aggregate names 100 instances of the initialized record aggregate. In this case, an others clause would be appropriate, such as:

```
Values´(1..100 => (Open      => False,
                   Flow_Rate => 0.0,
                   others    => "          "))
```

Since Ada does not define an initial value for any declared objects (with the exception of access types), you will often find aggregates used to provide default values in a composite object declaration.

9.3   Expressions

Now that we have a way to name objects and provide primitive values, we can turn to expressions as formulas that compute new values. Obviously, we cannot calculate values from any kind of named entity: Multiplying two subprogram names would be meaningless. Rather, the operands in expressions can be only what are called *primaries*. Primaries include:

```
"prompt"              -- string literal
10.125                -- numeric literal
(7, 3, 1, 0)          -- aggregate value
Matrix_1              -- a name
new Count'(0, 0, 0, 0) -- an allocator
Cos(37.5)             -- a function call
Integer(123.9)        -- a type conversion
Coefficient'(0.53)    -- a qualified expression
(3 * 4)               -- a parenthesized expression
null                  -- null value
```

Every primary has a value and a type. Following the strong typing rules of the language, operations are permitted only between primaries with the same types. Of course, as we saw in Chapter 6, an explicit type conversion is permitted for compatible types, namely derived types and all numeric types. In general, errors associated with static type conflict are detectable at compilation time. Furthermore, if, during the evaluation of an expression, the computed value is beyond the capability of the underlying machine to represent, the exception Numeric_Error will be raised:

```
Average := Total / Sum;    -- Numeric_Error raised if Sum = 0.0
```

If an expression produces a value that exceeds the constraints of a target object, the exception Constraint_Error will be raised upon assignment to that object:

```
type Limited_Range is range 0..10;
Small_Index : Limited_Range;

Small_Index := 100;    -- Constraint_Error raised at assignment
```

Of course, a good compiler may warn us about the exception condition at compilation time.

So far, we have described the valid operands in an Ada expression. The language also defines six classes of operators that can act upon these operands. In order of decreasing precedence, these operators are:

```
**          not  abs          -- highest precedence operator
*    /      mod  rem          -- multiplying operator
+    -                        -- unary adding operator
+    -      &                 -- binary adding operator
=    /=  <    <=  >  >=        -- relational operator
and  or  xor                  -- logical operator
```

It is important to note that these operators work with the accuracy of base types. For example, if we are multiplying two objects of type `Coefficient` (which is a subtype of `Float`), calculations will be done to the accuracy of `Coefficient'Base`, which is `Float`.

Any of these operator symbols (except for the operator `/=`) can be overloaded with a function declaration, as described in Chapter 8. For example:

```
function "/" (Left, Right : in Complex.Number) return Complex.Number;
```

Here we have overloaded the "/" operator, which we can invoke using prefix or infix notation. For example:

```
Result := "/"(First, Second);    -- prefix notation
Result := First / Second;        -- infix notation
```

Notice that if we use infix notation, the quotation marks are dropped. When we overload such operators, we do not change their precedence.

We can use infix notation only when the name is directly visible—that is, when it can be denoted by its simple name. As we will study in Chapter 11, visibility of operators is an issue we must deal with frequently when operators are exported across package boundaries.

In addition to the six classes of operators, Ada also has short-circuit logical operators. These have the same precedence as the basic logical operators. Membership tests (`in` and `not in`) are defined at the same level as the relational operators. We shall discuss these last two forms in detail later in this section. Finally, the predefined function `abs` is also provided for any numeric type; it returns the absolute value of an expression.

In general, operators with higher precedence are applied first. For a sequence of operators at the same level of precedence, the operators are applied from left to right or in any order that will give the same result. Of course, parentheses alter the order of precedence, since they are evaluated first. For example:

```
(1 >= 9) and (2 <= 10)  -- result is False
1.5 ** (-3)             -- result is -0.296_296_296...
2.5 / 0.5 + 2.0         -- result is 7.0
2.5 / (0.5 + 2.0)       -- result is 1.0
```

Since an optimizing compiler may alter the order of expression evaluation for operators with the same precedence, any program that depends upon a specific order of evaluation is considered erroneous. By *erroneous,* we mean that the Ada compiler may not detect the violation, and so the effect of running such a program is unpredictable. This may appear to be a constraining rule, but it is actually for the sake of portability and reliability. For purposes of readability, it is better practice anyway to explicitly parenthesize expressions, rather than expecting the reader to follow the implicit precedence rules. For example, compare the two expressions:

```
1.5 * X ** 2 + 6.5 * X + 4.7
(1.5 * (X ** 2)) + (6.5 * X) + 4.7
```

These expressions will produce the same result, but the use of parentheses and white space make the second expression much more readable.

Since Ada is a strongly typed language, the expression operators are predefined for only certain types, as indicated in Table 9.1 (see also package Standard in Appendix C). Since the use of most of these operators is consistent with that found in many high-order languages, we shall discuss only those rules unique to Ada. In all cases, these operators follow the usual mathematical meaning.

For the exponentiation operator (**), it is important to note that it is predefined only for integer powers. The language design team consciously omitted exponentiation to a real power, since they considered that function to be of limited use for the problem domain of embedded computer systems. Furthermore, an efficient exponentiation algorithm can be highly machine dependent. If a real power is desired, a programmer must write an appropriate overloaded function (or, better yet, use an exponential function from a mathematical package instantiated for the desired precision). The following are appropriate uses of the exponentiation operator:

```
3 ** 7       -- result is 2178
2.718 ** 3   -- result is 20.079_290_...
3.142 ** (-1) -- result is 0.318_268...
```

We may not raise an integer to a negative power, since the result would not be of an integer type. If, during execution, a program attempts to raise an integer to a negative power, the exception Constraint_Error is raised.

Table 9.1 Ada Predefined Operators

Operator	Operation	Operand Type		Result Type
**	exponentiation	L: integer	R: integer >= 0	integer
		L: floating	R: integer	floating
*	multiplication	integer		integer
		floating		floating
		L: fixed	R: integer	fixed
		L: integer	R: fixed	integer
		L: fixed	R: fixed	universal_fixed
/	division	integer		integer
		floating		floating
		L: fixed	R: integer	fixed
		L: fixed	R: fixed	universal_fixed
mod	modulus	integer		integer
rem	remainder	integer		integer
+	unary identity	numeric type		numeric type
−	unary negation	numeric type		numeric type
abs	absolute values	numeric type		numeric type
not	unary logical negation	Boolean		Boolean
		array of Boolean		same array type
+	addition	numeric type		numeric type
−	subtraction	numeric type		numeric type
&	catenation	one-dimensional array types		same array type
		array and component		same array type
		component and array		same array type
		component and component		any array type
=	equality	any type		Boolean
/=	inequality	any type		Boolean
<	less than	any scalar type		Boolean
		discrete array type		Boolean
<=	less than or equal	any scalar type		Boolean
		discrete array type		Boolean
>	greater than	any scalar type		Boolean
		discrete array type		Boolean
>=	greater than or equal	any scalar type		Boolean
		discrete array type		Boolean

▶

Table 9.1 Ada Predefined Operators *(continued)*

Operator	Operation	Operand Type		Result Type
in	membership	L: any scalar	R: range	Boolean
		L: any scalar	L: subtype indication	Boolean
not in	nonmember-ship	L: any scalar	R: range	Boolean
		L: any type	L: subtype indication	Boolean
and	conjunction	Boolean		Boolean
		array of Boolean		same array type
and then	conjunction (short circuit)	Boolean		Boolean
		array of Boolean		same array type
or	inclusive disjunction	Boolean		Boolean
		array of Boolean		same array type
or else	inclusive disjunction	Boolean		Boolean
		array of Boolean		same array type
	(short circuit)			
nor	exclusive disjunction	Boolean		Boolean
		array of Boolean		same array type

With the multiplication operators (`*`, `/`, `mod`, `rem`), integer operations provide exact results, while real operations are inexact. As we discussed in Chapter 6, Ada guarantees the minimal arithmetic properties for a given numeric type; so these inexact results will be converted to an appropriate model interval. Consider the following declarations:

```
type Fixed is delta 0.0001 range -1_000.0..+1_000.0;
Fixed_1    : Fixed := 0.1;
Fixed_2    : Fixed := 0.1;
Integer_1 : Integer := 2;
Integer_2 : Integer := 3;
Float_1    : Float := 1.0;
Float_2    : Float := 2.0;
```

The following are valid expressions with multiplying operators:

```
Fixed_1 * Fixed_2        -- result is model interval around 0.1
                         -- (of type universal_fixed)
Integer_1 / Integer_2  -- result is 0 (of type Integer)
Float_1 / Float_2        -- result is 0.5 (of type Float)
```

The `rem` operator returns the integer remainder, which takes the sign of the dividend (the left-hand side of the expression). The `mod` operator (modulus) returns a value with the sign of the divisor (the right-hand side of the expression). For example:

L	R	L rem R	L mod R
12	5	2	2
14	5	4	4
12	-5	2	-3
14	-5	4	-1
-12	5	-2	3
-14	5	-4	1
-12	-5	-2	-2
-14	-5	-4	-4

In general, the `mod` operator is the one most commonly used.

The unary operators (`+`, `-`, `not`, `abs`) are applied to a single operand and return a result of the same type. The identity (`+`) and negation (`-`) operators apply to any numeric type. It may seem strange that Ada defines `not` for an array of `Boolean` components, but this facility provides a means for performing bit operations. As we shall see in Chapter 16, `Boolean` arrays can be mapped in the underlying machine to a bit vector representation, and so operations on `Boolean` arrays are actually bit manipulations.

Unlike the unary operators, the binary operators (`+`, `-`, `&`) require two operands. These operators follow the normal arithmetic rules. In addition, the catenation operator is available for any type of one-dimensional array but is provided primarily in support of string operations. (*Catenation* is the action of combining the elements of two arrays to form one longer array.) Furthermore, this operator is overloaded to permit catenation with an array and one component. For example:

```
"Error message" & CR & LF  -- catenation of a string
                           -- and two literals
"A" & "BCDEFG"             -- catenation of two strings
Z + 0.1                    -- Z must be of a real type
```

The relational operators (`=`, `/=`, `<`, `>`, `<=`, `>=`) are provided to test for equality, inequality, ordering, and membership. The equality and inequality operators are provided for any data type that is not limited private. The operators that test for ordering are defined for any scalar type or any discrete array type. Finally, unlike the other operators, the membership operators (`in` and `not in`) do not have a primary for the right operand. Instead, the right operand can be a range (to test for in-bounds) or a type mark (to test for the satisfaction of any constraint). For example:

```
J not in 1..10   -- if J >= 1 and J <= 10, result is False
"AA" > "B"        -- result is False
X in Coefficient -- a subtype check
```

The logical operators (`and`, `or`, `xor`) provide the usual `Boolean` operations. Like the `not` operator, the logical operators are defined for both `Boolean` values and arrays of `Boolean` components, and so are useful for expressing bit manipulations within the high-level constructs of Ada. These simple logical operators are of the same precedence, and so it is necessary to parenthesize `Boolean` expressions with mixed operators.

If we need to impose an order on the evaluation of a compound `Boolean` expression, we can use the short-circuit form of these operators. In particular, the right-hand side of a short-circuit operation is evaluated only if the left-hand side is `True` (for the `and then`) or `False` (for the `or else`). For example:

```
Is_Running or Is_Ready      -- a simple Boolean operation
Y /= 0.0 and then X / Y > 5.0 -- a short-circuit operator (right-
                            -- hand side evaluated only if
                            -- left-hand side is True)
Is_Empty xor Is_Active      -- False if both sides have the
                            -- same value
```

In the second example, if we did not use the short-circuit form, an exception could be raised if Y had a value of 0.0. We could split this expression into two parts (with nested `if` statements), but in many cases, the short-circuit form offers greater clarity.

Before we complete our discussion of expressions, it is important to understand the concept of *static expressions*. A static expression is one that does not depend upon dynamically calculated entities, such as variables or dynamic attributes. An expression is static if its terms consist only of literals or literal expressions (including enumeration literals), constants initialized by static expressions, static attributes, or static qualified expressions. For example, the following are static expressions:

```
3                -- a numeric literal
Integer'First    -- a static attribute
abs(Pi ** 3)     -- a static expression
```

In the syntax charts in Appendix E, you will see several places where the language requires the use of a static expression.

Given this description of Ada's operators, the following are valid expressions:

```
Scheduler_Table(Ready) = 0
Value_Record(ValUe_Index).Flow_Rate not in 1.0..5.0
(Pi ** (Count_1 rem 4)) >= Matrix_1(1, 1)
Is_Active and then Scheduler_Table(Ready) = 0
(Matrix_1(1, 1) * Matrix_1(2, 2)) - (Matrix_1(3, 3) * Matrix_1(4, 4)) = 0.0
(Voltage_1 - Voltage_2) / 2.781 = 0.0
```

Now that we have a means of calculating new values, we can next examine statements as a means of expressing algorithmic control.

9.4   Statements

The execution of statements causes actions to be performed. Just as abstract data types are constructed from primitive types, statements provide the expression of primitive actions. We can create abstract actions with subprogram declarations and then treat these actions as if they were primitive. In addition, statements may alter the flow of control in a sequence of statements. C. Boehm and G. Jocopini [2] proved that only three basic control structures are needed to express any computable algorithm, namely:

- Sequential
- Conditional
- Iterative

In Ada each of these structures is characterized by one entry point and (usually) one exit. In the following sections, we shall examine most of Ada's statements as instances of these structures.

Sequential Control

In a sequential control structure, one statement is executed after another in a linear fashion. Actually, any sequence of statements can be considered sequentially, but some simple statements enforce a linear flow. In Ada, these statements include:

- Assignment
- Null
- Procedure call
- Return
- Block

In addition, we shall consider the infamous goto statement here, although it is not a purely sequential statement.

All of Ada's statements are terminated, not separated, by a semicolon. This rule makes it easier for compilers to recover from cascading syntax errors in the source program, and, in addition, the uniformity aids readability. Multiple statements can be placed on a single line, but it is better style to keep one statement per line. We offer other guidelines for the representation style of Ada's statements throughout this section, mainly in the area of statement layout and indentation (see also Appendix D, "Ada Style Guide").

To begin, an *assignment statement* replaces the current value of a variable with a new value specified by an expression. The basic structure of an assignment statement places an expression on the right-hand side and a variable object that will receive the new value on the left. The compound symbol := is used to separate them. In accordance with Ada's strong typing philosophy, the right- and left-hand sides of the assignment statement must be of the same type. Any static type violation is detectable at compilation time. Evaluation of the expression may raise the exception Numeric_Error if the computation is outside the representable bounds of the underlying machine. Upon assignment, if the expression value violates any constraint of the variable, then the exception Constraint_Error will be raised.

The following are valid assignment statements:

```
Voltage_1                   := Voltage_2 + 24.0;
Matrix_1                    := Matrix_2;
Local_Schedule.all          := Count'(0, 0, 0, 0);
Scheduler_Table(Ready)      := Scheduler_Table(Ready) + 1;
Value_Record(Count_1).Open  := True;
Value_Record(1..10)         := Values'(1..10 =>
                                  (Name     => "spare     ",
                                   Location => "warehouse ",
                                   Open     => False,
                                   Flow_Rate => 0.0));
```

In the last example, note the use of a slice assignment that takes a composite value (the aggregate) and assigns it to a slice of Value_Record. Of course, each slice must be of the same size.

Following the Ada philosophy that no action occur implicitly, the language provides a sequential statement that explicitly states inaction—the null statement. In a sense, the null statement is similar to a document with a page marked "This page intentionally left blank." Obviously, the page is not blank, but the statement is there to assure us that nothing has been left out. The effect of the null statement is such that control simply passes to the next statement. There need be no run-time overhead associated with this action. For all practical purposes, the statement is provided for the sake of readability. The form of this statement is:

```
null;
```

As will be demonstrated later, this statement is often used in the case statement for unimportant choices, a record declaration indicating an empty variant part, or in the body of a subprogram stub.

The next purely sequential statement is the *procedure call*. We have already discussed its form in Chapter 8, so we shall not repeat the syntax here. However, we will reiterate the importance of the procedure as an expression of an abstract action. Although the algorithm for a given procedure will be implemented inside the body of the procedure, a user will view that algorithm through its name as a primitive action.

The next statement of interest is the return statement. This is associated primarily with subprograms. Basically, a return statement terminates the execution of a procedure or function. A function must include at least one return statement and can contain multiple return statements. In the case of a procedure, the form of this statement is:

```
return;
```

Upon execution of this statement, execution of the procedure ceases and control returns to the calling environment. At that time, values of any out or in out formal parameters are copied out to the calling environment. If the subprogram terminates abnormally, the values are not copied out. The same basic action is performed for functions, but in addition, a value is returned through the name of the function itself. For example, note the use of the return statement in the following function:

```
function Is_Odd(Value : in Integer) return Boolean is
begin
  if (Value rem 2) = 0 then
    return False;
  else
    return True;
  end if;
end Is_Odd;
```

The basic form of a return statement in a function is the keyword return, followed by an expression. The expression must return a value of the type described for the return in the function declaration. Otherwise a syntax error may be flagged or Constraint_Error may be raised at execution time. If a function reaches the end of its body without encountering a return, the predefined exception Program_Error is raised.

In the above example, if `Value` was 2, then `(Value rem 2) = 0` would evaluate to `True` and `Is_Odd` would return the expression value `False`. In this case, the `else` part of this conditional control structure would never be executed.

Generally, it is good practice to have only one `return` per subprogram, but sometimes it is clearer to include multiple returns. We can easily rewrite a subprogram with multiple returns by adding another variable (see Chapter 8), but sometimes the clarity suffers. In the previous example, we can take advantage of the fact that the returned value is `Boolean` and rewrite it as:

```
function Is_Odd(Value : in Integer) return Boolean is
begin
   return (Value rem 2) /= 0;
end Is_Odd;
```

The last purely sequential control structure is the *block.* A block statement permits us to textually encapsulate a sequence of statements, along with local declarations and an exception handler, if desired. Since such data is local to a given block, resources for that data are allocated only when the block is entered (elaborated). Furthermore, any data local to a block is hidden from the outside.

Although a block and subprogram seem to be similar, the basic difference is that a procedure is callable by any number of other program units, while a block is limited in scope to its immediate lexical level and cannot be called. By *scope,* we mean that region of program text over which an entity is in existence. For example, if we declare an object local to a subprogram, that object is in scope from the point where we first named it until the end of the subprogram body. The same is true for objects declared inside a block; their scope extends from the point where we first name them until the end of the block in which they were declared. As a result of these rules, we cannot call a block; it is just executed sequentially.

A common use of the block is to encapsulate a section of code in order to provide a local exception handler or to declare some local objects or types that cannot then be used by other program units. The following is an example of a block structure:

```
Swap:
 declare
   Temporary : Float;
 begin
   Temporary := Voltage_1;
   Voltage_1 := Voltage_2;
   Voltage_2 := Temporary;
 end Swap;
```

The basic structure of a block is delimited simply by a `begin ... end` pair, although a block name (`Swap`, for example) can be included for readability. It is generally good style to explicitly name blocks if they are nested and include local objects, for, as we shall see, the block name gives us a handle to reference otherwise hidden entities (see Chapter 20). For example, consider the following structure:

```
Outer:
  declare
    Temporary : Float;                      ⎤
  begin                                     │  Scope of Outer.Temporary
    ...                                     │
    Inner:                                  │  A
      declare                              ⎤ │
        Temporary : Float;                 │ │
      begin                                │ │  Scope of Inner.Temporary,
        ...                                │ │  which hides Outer.Temporary   B
      end Inner;                           ⎦ │
    ...                                      │  C
  end Outer;                                ⎦
```

At points A and C, only the declaration of `Outer.Temporary` is in scope and visible. By *visible*, we mean that the object has a unique name with which we can reference it. At point B, both `Outer.Temporary` and `Inner.Temporary` would be in scope and visible. The scope rules of Ada state that if an inner declaration hides an outer declaration (by using the same name, such as `Temporary`), and if the choice of the objects cannot be determined by context, the compiler assumes the local declaration. For example, if at point B we just used the name `Temporary`, the compiler would assume that we were referring to the closest declaration namely, `Inner.Temporary`. Using selected component notation, however, permits a programmer to explicitly refer to either object. At point B, then, `Outer.Temporary` would refer to the outer declaration, and `Inner.Temporary`, or simply `Temporary`, would refer to the inner object. These scope rules apply to all structures in Ada; we will discuss these rules in more detail in Chapter 20.

Actually, the above example is rather artificial. It is generally poor practice to have such a nested block structure. However, since Ada is designed for the domain of large, complex problems, a programmer cannot always control the names of objects external to his or her area of concern. Scope rules such as the above provide precise control over the visibility of objects.

The final sequential statement we shall discuss, the `goto`, is not purely sequential, but its nature places it better here than in any other category. We could fill rooms with rhetoric about the pros and cons of the use of the `goto`. For our purposes, we shall simply say that `goto`s are probably not essential in an Ada system and that we could use other structured constructs to implement our algorithms. However, if we must use the goto, we should limit its scope and always document the construct.

Ada restricts the scope of a goto such that its execution cannot transfer control into a compound statement (namely, an if, loop, accept, case, block, or accept statement) or an exception handler; nor from parts of one if, case, or select statement to another; nor from one corresponding exception handler to another; nor back into block, subprogram, task, or package bodies. As a general rule, gotos can transfer control only within the same lexical level. The general form of a goto is:

```
goto Shut_Down;
```

The goto statement consists of the literal goto, followed by a label. Every statement can have a label delimited by << and >> such as:

```
<<Shut_Down>> Start_Power_Down_Sequence;
```

Conditional Control

The next class of control structures provides conditional control, which is the selection of one of a number of alternative sequences of statements. This selection is based upon some condition or expression. In Ada, there are two statements designed for conditional control, namely:

- if
- case

The if statement selects for execution one or none of a number of sequences of statements, depending upon the truth value of one or more corresponding conditions. These conditions are Boolean expressions, that is, expressions that return the value True or False. There are three basic forms to the if statement:

```
if Count_1 < 5 then          -- a simple if-then
   Count_1 := 9;
end if;
```

```
if Value_Record(1).Open then    -- an if-then-else construct
   Value_Record(2).Open := True;
   Value_Record(3).Open := False;
else
   Value_Record(2).Open := False;
   Value_Record(3).Open := True;
end if;
```

```
if Voltage_1 > Voltage_2 then      -- a parallel if structure
  Voltage_1 := Voltage_2;
elsif Voltage_1 < Voltage_2 then
  Voltage_2:= Voltage_1;
end if;
```

In all three examples, note that each if statement is bracketed with an end if and that the sequence of statements for each part is bracketed by the reserved words. Also, only one or none of a corresponding sequence of statements will be selected for execution. In the first example, if Count_1 is less than 5, then the next statement (Count_1 := 9;) will be selected; control will then pass to the end of the if statement. If the expression evaluates to False, control passes immediately to the end of the if statement. In the second example, the same control flow is followed, except that the sequence of statements following the else part is selected if the condition evaluates to False. In the final example, only one of the sequence of statements is selected, depending upon the value of the corresponding conditions, which are mutually exclusive. This form of the if statement can include any number of elsif branches as well as an optional ending else part.

The case structure, like the if structure, provides for the selection of alternative paths of control. Unlike the if statement, however, the case statement selects one from many alternative sequences of statements, based upon the value of a discrete expression. (A *discrete expression* is one that returns the value of an integer or an enumeration type.) For example:

```
case Process_State is
  when Running => Scheduler_Table (Running) := 1;
                  Is_Active := True;
  when Ready   => Scheduler_Table(Ready) := Scheduler_Table(Ready) + 1;
                  Is_Active := False;
  when Blocked => Scheduler_Table(Blocked) := Scheduler_Table(Blocked) + 1;
                  Is_Active := False;
  when Dead    => Scheduler_Table(Dead) := Scheduler_Table(Dead) + 1;
                  Is_Active := False;
end case;
case Count_1 is
  when 1      => Value_Record(Count_1).Open := True;
  when 2 | 3  => Value_Record(Count_1).Open := False;
  when 5..10  => Value_Record(Count_1).Open := False;
  when others => Value_Record(Count_1).Open := True;
                  Value_Record(Count_1).Flow_Rate := 1.0;
end case;
```

In both examples, only one alternative will be selected, depending upon the value of the expression after the word **case**. We refer to this expression as the *case selector*. Within the **case** statement, there must be one and only one alternative for every value of the expression's type (or just the subtype, if that subtype is static). The alternatives must be exhaustive and mutually exclusive. Thus, if the type of the case selector is **Size** (which we defined earlier with a range of 1 to 4), we must have alternatives to cover all four values. As in the last example, several choices can be declared for the same sequence of statements (e.g., 2|3), or we can indicate a range of values (e.g., 5..10). Finally, the choice **others** can be included to cover all values not given in previous choices, and so it must be the last choice (if given). This feature is useful, particularly if the type of the expression has a large number of possible values (such as a case selector of type **Integer**).

The reason that **case** statement choices must be static is so that the compiler can check, during compilation, that the choices are exhaustive. This makes the **case** statement, in some sense, a "strongly typed" statement: Its semantics depend on the type of the expression being evaluated. We can use this checking performed by the compiler to our advantage. Suppose that we added another value to the type **Process_Type**. Then the first **case** statement above would no longer be valid Ada, indicating that we have not accounted for the new value everywhere in our program. Indeed, the **case** statement is one of the many ways we can use Ada's strong typing to simplify program modification.

As a general style guideline, use the **case** statement when there are conditions based upon scalar values. The **if** statement must be used for other situations, including ones involving complex logical expressions.

Iterative Control

The final class of control structures permits a sequence of statements to be executed zero or more times. Ada provides three explicit iterative control structures that implement the one-entry, (usually) one-exit form, including:

- Basic loop
- **for** loop
- **while** loop

Associated with the loop is the **exit** statement, which we also discuss in this section.

The basic loop is the simplest form of iteration; it is structured to loop forever. For example:

```
loop
   -- sequence of statements
end loop;
```

The above forms an infinite loop with one entry but no exit. This form is most often found in the outer loop of a task, such as in a data-sampling system that must continue forever once initiated.

To leave a loop, we use the `exit` statement. When the `exit` statement is executed, the execution of the enclosing loop terminates. Control then resumes just after the end of the loop. This statement has several forms, including:

```
exit;                          -- exit enclosing loop
exit Outer;                    -- exit named loop
exit when Temp > Max_Temp;     -- exit enclosing loop if
                               -- condition is True
exit Outer when Is_Active;     -- exit the named loop
                               -- when the condition is True
```

As we can see, the `exit` statement can include a loop name and/or a condition. If the name is omitted, the immediately enclosing loop is assumed. If a condition is omitted, an unconditional exit is assumed.

If we have several levels of loops, we can name them to explicitly exit a given level. For example:

```
Outer_Loop:
   loop                                    ⎤
      ...                          ⎤    A  |
      Inner_Loop:                  |       |
         loop              ⎤       |       |
            ...            | B     |       |
         end loop Inner_Loop; ⎦    |       |
      ...                          ⎦    C  |
   end loop Outer_Loop;                    ⎦
```

The rules for exiting a loop are similar to the scope rules listed earlier. At points A or C, if we say simply `exit` or `exit Outer_Loop`, then control will pass to the end of the `Outer_Loop`. At point B, if we say `exit` or `exit Inner_Loop`, then control passes to the end of the `Inner_Loop`, but we are still inside the control of `Outer_Loop`. However, if at point B we say `exit Outer_Loop`, then control passes immediately to the end of the `Outer_Loop`. As is true with the `return` statement, we can have multiple `exit` statements in a given loop.

The second type of iterative control structure is the `for` loop. A `for` loop is also known as a *counting* loop, since the loop repeats a countable number of times. This loop structure is formed by taking the basic loop and preceding it with a `for` iteration clause. Such a clause contains an implicitly declared control variable that steps through the range of the count in unit increments. The value of the control variable can be used inside the loop (for an array index, for example), but it cannot be modified (for example, by assignment). Furthermore, the control variable is local only to the loop; it is undefined outside the loop. For example:

```
for Index in Running..Dead
  loop
    Sum := Sum + Scheduler_Table(Index);
  end loop;

for Index in reverse Total_Values
  loop
    Value_Record(Index).Open := False;
  end loop;
```

In the first example, `Index` will step through the values `Running`, `Ready`, `Blocked`, and `Dead`, in that order, since that is the order in which we declared the enumeration literals. The loop will repeat four times. In the second example, `Index` will step through 100 down to 1; the loop will repeat 100 times.

Although we have not shown it, the expression for the control variable need not be static; it could be of the form:

```
for Index in 1..Count_1
  loop
    -- sequence of statements
  end loop;
```

Here the value of `Count_1` is established outside the loop. It is important to note that the range of the control variable is determined only once, at the point the loop is entered. Thus, in the above example, if `Count_1` had an initial value of 10, we would iterate 10 times, even if `Count_1` was modified inside the loop.

If we need to iterate over the entire range of a type, we can express the range in one of several forms, such as:

```
for Index in Values'range
  loop
    ...
  end loop;

for Index in Values'First..Values'Last
  loop
    ...
  end loop;
```

The effect of both forms is the same. Note again that we do not have to declare the loop parameter I, but rather it is implicitly declared; the compiler will determine the correct type of the loop parameter.

The final type of iteration structure is the while loop. In this form, a sequence of statements is repeated as long as some condition is True. This form of iteration is essential when we do not know the number of iterations in advance or if the iteration depends upon some logical condition. The iteration is formed by preceding the basic loop with a while construct:

```
while (Value_Record(1).Flow_Rate > 10.0) and (not Is_Empty)
  loop
    ...
  end loop;
```

In this example, we enter the loop only if the selected flow rate is greater than 10.0 and if Is_Empty is False. If the entire condition initially evaluates to False, the entire loop is bypassed. Otherwise, we enter the loop, and the sequence of statements bracketed by the basic loop is repeated as long as the while condition is True. One final note about this structure: The condition is tested at the top of the loop. If you need to test a condition at a different point, you must use the exit statement. For example, the statements in the following loop will be executed one or more times:

```
loop
  ...
  exit when (Value_Record(1).Flow_Rate > 10.0)
        and (not Is_Empty);
end loop;
```

In this chapter, we have presented some of Ada's facilities for calculating new values and describing the flow of control in an algorithm. With these new tools, we shall be ready in the next chapter to complete the data base system started in Chapter 7.

Summary

- Names denote declared entities.

- Certain names can be overloaded, including subprograms, enumerative literals, and operator symbols.

- Simple literals can be used to name scalar values, and aggregates can be used to name composite values.

- Expressions are used to create new values. Expressions combining primaries with various operators can be predefined or user defined.

- Ada's statements include facilities for expressing sequential, conditional, and iterative control.

- Sequential statements express a linear flow of control. Sequential statements include assignment, `null`, procedure call, `return`, and block statements.

- Conditional statements express alternative paths of execution. Conditional statements include forms of the `if` and `case` statements.

- Iterative statements express a repetitious flow of control. Iterative statements include various forms built around a basic `loop` statement.

Exercises   1. Declare a three-dimensional array object called `Cube` whose components are of type `Float` and which has a range of 10 elements to a side. Next, write the names for the eight corners of the `Cube`.

2. Declare a record object called `Condition_Code` with the `Boolean` elements `Carry`, `Zero`, and `Negative`. It also has a component called `Priority` with an `Integer` range of 0 to 31. Next, write the name for the `Priority` component.

3. Declare an access object that points to `Condition_Code`. Next, write the names referring to the access object, the entire designated object, and the `Zero` component of the designated object.

4. Write an aggregate for the `Cube` object so that one face of the object has a value of 1.0 and all other components have a value of -1.0.

5. Write an aggregate for the `Condition_Code` object setting `Carry` and `Zero` to `False`, `Negative` to `True`, and `Priority` to the value 7.

6. Write an Ada expression for the following equations:

   (a) The area of a circle.

   (b) The volume of a sphere.

   (c) The product of a matrix row times a matrix column.

*7. Write the sequence of statements for the following:

   (a) Calculating the sum of two matrices.

   (b) A function whose parameter is a `Natural` value and whose result is the same value but with the digits transposed (for example, 12345 as the parameter yields a result of 54321).

   (c) Searching the `Cube` object and calculating the sum of all the elements.

   (d) Searching the `Cube` object and setting a `Boolean` called `Found` to the value `True` if a `Cube` component with a negative value is found.

   (e) Same as (d), but this time count the number of negative components.

   (f) Same as (d), but this time stop the iteration as soon as a component with a value of `0.0` is found.

CHAPTER 10

The Second Design Problem: Continued

The Problem Revisited
Evaluate the Objects
Implement Each Object

N ow that we have studied Ada's subprograms and statements as vehicles for expressing action and control, we can complete a solution to the problem we started in Chapter 7.

10.1   The Problem Revisited

Let us review the problem statement for the data base system we introduced earlier. Specifically, our task is to build a data base system that maintains records about each album in our collection. For each album, we maintain information about the title, the artist, the style of music, the year of release, and the name and length of each song on the album. We need to be able to create, open, and close data bases as well as add, delete, and modify individual album entries. Finally, we want to be able to make reports about the albums described by a particular data base. For these reports, we need to be able to select records based on certain criteria. For example, we may want to find all the albums we have that were released in a particular year. We also need to be able to sort the records.

Figure 10.1 illustrates the architecture of our solution. The package Albums is the central abstraction; this unit provides several unencapsulated types that characterize the information we maintain for each album. Database is an abstract-state machine that acts as the repository for all album

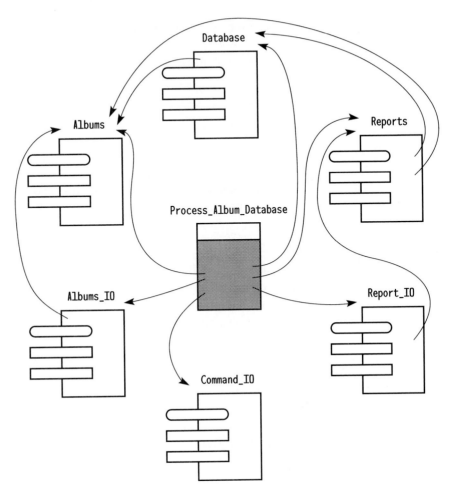

Figure 10.1 Design of Process_Album_Database

records. This unit exports operations such as Open, Close, Add, and Delete as well as an iterator, which gives us a way to visit every record in the data base without destroying its state.

Reports is the remaining major unit at this level of abstraction. It builds on top of Albums and Database, and provides an abstract data type named Report. This package exports several overloaded Find procedures, a Sort procedure, and an iterator.

10.2   Evaluate the Objects

In this section we introduce three simple heuristics for evaluating objects. It is often very difficult to identify and define objects. This extra step of evaluating objects helps us to gain confidence that, first, we have identified the objects of our problem and, second, we have defined them properly. The heuristics are summarized as follows:

- *Minimize coupling.* If an object is dependent on more than 5 to 7 other objects, there are probably more objects to be identified.

- *Maximize cohesion.* Each object should present only one level of abstraction.

- *Separate constructors and selectors.* To increase understandability, it should be clear which operations modify object values and which operations simply view object values.

Minimize Coupling

When establishing the visibility between objects, we produce diagrams such as that in Figure 10.1. Here we see that no object (other than the main subprogram) is dependent on more than two other objects. That is, there are no more than two outgoing arrows from any package. This decoupling, or separation of objects, is critical to maintainability.

In larger systems, where it is not uncommon for many dozens of objects to be identified, we can get into a situation where an object is dependent on too many other objects. This generally indicates that the object is too large and needs to be further decomposed into smaller objects.

Maximize Cohesion

When establishing object interfaces, we begin to make concrete our abstractions by declaring types. If the interface of an object requires the declaration of many types, the object again may be too large. This is true especially if the interface declares multiple private or limited private types. Objects that declare multiple private types are often trying to work at two levels of abstraction at once.

Consider the **Albums** object. Its interface is defined as a package specification. The specification defines nine types and one subtype. We certainly could have defined each of these types in its own object. For example, the object **Years** could be defined as:

```
package Years is
   type Year is range 1877..Integer'Last;
end Years;
```

Notice, however, that most of the types defined in **Albums** are rather primitive; that is, they have simple declarations. Declaring many small objects, like Years above, would most likely complicate our design with no apparent advantage. In other words, increasing the number of objects complicates the design, regardless of the simplicity of the individual objects.

When evaluating tradeoffs such as whether Years should be an object in our design, we should refer back to the fundamental goals of software engineering covered in Chapter 2. Would our design be more modifiable if Years was declared? How likely is it that Year will later change? Additionally, how likely is it that Year can be reused elsewhere? In this example, we have decided that Year is neither likely to change nor likely to be reused, so we will increase maintainability by minimizing the number of objects in our design.

Separate Constructors and Selectors

A constructor is an operation that modifies an object. For example, Database.Add modifies Database; Add changes the abstract value of the data base. A selector does not change the value, but rather views an aspect of the value. Size and Value_Of are selectors of the Database object. Operations that are both constructors and selectors are generally complicated to understand and use. We should try to define operations that are either constructors or selectors, but not both. A very common example of an operation that is both is the stack operation Pop, when defined as follows:

```
procedure Pop (Top_Item :    out Item;
               Off_Of   : in out Stack);
```

Pop both modifies the stack by removing its top item and views the old stack by returning its top item.

Two additional methods of evaluating objects will be discussed in Chapter 13.

10.3   Implement Each Object

All that remains is to implement the main program and the bodies of each package mentioned in Figure 10.1.

Let us start with the root of this system, Process_Album_Database. This parameterless procedure serves as a main program. As we decided in Chapter 7, the activity of this subprogram is to coordinate all user interaction. Hence, we will write its body as a basic loop. Within the loop, we can call Command_IO.Get to obtain a user command. Next, we can apply a case statement to select a particular course of action based on this command. For example, if the user asks to start a new report, our action is to call the procedure Reports.Initialize for a specific report object. Some actions require a bit more user response. For example, if the user wants to open a data base, we must use a `Text_IO` procedure to read a line of input from the user. Similarly, if the user wants to select items from a report, we must first call `Reports.Get` to obtain the search criteria from the user.

All of this user interaction requires that we declare a number of objects locally. For example, if the user starts a search based on an artist name, we must have a local object that maintains the value of this artist name. Indeed, we must have one object for every possible class of user input.

Finally, our design as expressed in Figure 10.1 indicates that this main program imports a number of units. For this reason, we must have a fairly lengthy context clause to make all of these units visible.

We can write the body of this main procedure as:

```
with Text_IO, Albums, Database, Reports, Album_IO, Report_IO, Command_IO;
procedure Process_Album_Database is
   The_Command     : Command_IO.Command;
   The_Parameter   : String(1..80);
   Last_Character  : Natural;
   The_Album       : Albums.Album;
   The_New_Album   : Albums.Album;
   The_Title       : Albums.Title;
   The_Artist      : Albums.Artist;
   The_Style       : Albums.Style;
   The_Year        : Albums.Year;
   The_Number      : Albums.Number;
   The_Song        : Albums.Name;
   The_Length      : Albums.Length;
   The_Category    : Reports.Category;
   The_Order       : Reports.Order;
   The_Report      : Reports.Report;
   The_Iterator    : Reports.Iterator;
begin
  loop
    Command_IO.Get(The_Command);
    case The_Command is
      when Command_IO.Quit =>
        Text_IO.Put_Line("Leaving the database manager.");
        exit;
      when Command_IO.Create =>
        Text_IO.Put("Enter the database name: ");
        Text_IO.Get_Line(The_Parameter, Last_Character);
        Database.Create(The_Parameter(1..Last_Character));
        Text_IO.Put_Line(The_Parameter(1..Last_Character)
                  & " has been created");
```

```
when Command_IO.Open =>
  Text_IO.Put("Enter the database name: ");
  Text_IO.Get_Line(The_Parameter, Last_Character);
  Database.Open(The_Parameter(1..Last_Character));
  Text_IO.Put_Line(The_Parameter(1..Last_Character) & "is open");
when Command_IO. Close =>
  Database.Close;
  Text_IO.Put_Line("Database has been closed");
when Command_IO.Add =>
  Text_IO.Put_Line("Enter an album description:");
  Album_IO.Get(The_Album);
  Database.Add(The_Album);
  Text_IO.Put_Line("Item added to the database");
when Command_IO.Delete =>
  Text_IO.Put_Line("Enter an album description:");
  Album_IO.Get(The_Album);
  Database.Delete(The_Album);
  Text_IO.Put_Line("Item removed from the database");
when Command_IO.Modify =>
  Text_IO.Put_Line("Enter an album description:");
  Album_IO.Get(The_Album);
  Text_IO.Put_Line("Enter the new value:");
  Album_IO.Get(The_New_Album);
  Database.Modify(The_Album, To_Be => The_New_Album);
  Text_IO.Put_Line("Item has been modified");
when Command_IO.Start_Report =>
  Reports.Initialize(The_Report);
  Text_IO.Put_Line("Report has been started");
when Command_IO.Find =>
  Report_IO.Get(The_Category);
  case The_Category is
    when Reports.Title =>
      Album_IO.Get(The_Title);
      Reports.Find(The_Title, The_Report);
    when Reports.Artist =>
      Album_IO.Get(The_Artist);
      Reports.Find(The_Artist, The_Report);
    when Reports.Style =>
      Album_IO.Get(The_Style);
      Reports.Find(The_Style, The_Report);
```

```
            when Reports.Year =>
                Album_IO.Get(The_Year);
                Reports.Find(The_Year, The_Report);
            when Reports.Number =>
                Album_IO.Get(The_Number);
                Reports.Find(The_Number, The_Report);
            when Reports.Song =>
                Album_IO.Get(The_Song);
                Reports.Find(The_Song, The_Report);
            when Reports.Length =>
                Album_IO.Get(The_Length);
                Reports.Find(The_Length, The_Report);
            end case;
            Report_IO.Put(Reports.Length_Of(The_Report));
        when Command_IO.Sort =>
            Report_IO.Get_Sort(The_Category);
            Report_IO.Get(The_Order);
            Reports.Sort(The_Report, The_Category, The_Order);
            Text_IO.Put_Line("Sorting completed");
            Report_IO.Put(Reports.Length_Of(The_Report));
        when Command_IO.Display_Report =>
            Text_IO.Put_Line("Database report follows:");
            Reports.Initialize(The_Iterator, The_Report);
            loop
                exit when Reports.Is_Done(The_Iterator);
                Album_IO.Put(Reports.Value_Of(The_Iterator));
                Reports.Get_Next(The_Iterator);
            end loop;
            Report_IO.Put(Reports.Length_Of(The_Report));
        end case;
    end loop;
end Process_Album_Database;
```

There are two more points we need to consider about this implementation. First, the careful reader will realize that we have provided a somewhat user-hostile implementation. Specifically, consider what happens if the user enters an invalid Find criterion (perhaps by misspelling *artist*). Additionally, we may have trouble if the user calls Modify for a record that does not exist in the data base. As we studied in Chapter 4, under such conditions, an exception might be raised. Since we shall not study Ada's exception-handling facilities in detail until Chapter 15, we have not used defensive programming to deal with such problems. As a result, our solution expects perfect user input—a dangerous thing to expect. On one hand, this allows us to simplify our solution, but on the other hand, this does not make for a usable program. For the purposes of this chapter, we shall continue to ignore the processing of exceptional conditions. A complete solution to this problem would add exception processing as a means of defensive programming.

The other point we need to consider concerns our use of the iterator. Focus for a moment on the sequence of statements associated with processing the user command `Display_Report`. Recall that the purpose of an iterator is to let us visit every item of a structure. In this case, we iterate across the object `The_Report` in order to print every album record in the report we have built. It is important that iteration be nondestructive—that it not alter the state of `The_Report`. Why? We may want to process this report further, yet still provide interim printouts.

Our solution demonstrates the classical use of an iterator. First, we must call `Reports.Initialize`, which, as we introduced in Chapter 7, attaches the iterator (the object `The_Iterator`) to denote the items in the given report object (`The_Report`). Next, we apply a loop, which we maintain until we have exhausted the iteration (denoted when `Reports.Is_Done` evaluates to `True`). Within this loop, we can apply `Reports.Value_Of` to retrieve information about the record to which the iterator is currently pointing. Additionally, we must call `Reports.Get_Next` to advance the iterator to the next record.

Let us move on to the implementation of another unit. `Albums` needs no further work, since here we have only a collection of unencapsulated declarations; no explicit operations remain to be implemented. However, the abstract-state machine of `Database` does require that we implement each operation introduced in its specification. To review, we repeat this specification from Chapter 7:

```
with Albums;
package Database is
   type Item is private;
   procedure Create (The_Name : in String);
   procedure Open   (The_Name : in String);
   procedure Close;
   procedure Add    (The_Album : in Albums.Album);
   procedure Delete (The_Album : in Albums.Album);
   procedure Modify (The_Album : in Albums.Album;
                     To_Be     : in Albums.Album);
   function Size  return Natural;
   function Value_Of (The_Item : in Item) return Albums.Album;
```

```
      package Iterator is
        procedure Initialize;
        procedure Get_Next;
        function Value_Of return Item;
        function Is_Done  return Boolean;
      end Iterator;
  private
    type Node;
    type Item is access Node;
  end Database;
```

This gives us the outside view of our abstraction. However, in this step, we must now turn to its inside view. There are actually two entities we must deal with: the external representation of the data base and its internal representation. By *external* we refer to data base records stored in a permanent way. Happily, Ada's I/O facilities provide us with the right abstraction. Because we have no requirement that this stored form of the data base be readable by humans, we shall use Sequential_IO (instead of Text_IO) in the manner described in Chapter 4.

Thus, in the body of Database, we must instantiate Sequential_IO to provide facilities for Albums.Album storage, and we must also declare a File_Type object. We can write the framework of this package body as:

```
with Sequential_IO;
package body Database is
  type Node is
    record
      The_Album : Albums.Album;
      Next      : Item;
    end record;
  package Album_IO is new Sequential_IO(Albums.Album);
  The_Items        : Item;
  The_File         : Album_IO.File_Type;
  Has_Been_Modified : Boolean := False;
  procedure Create (The_Name : in String) is separate;
  procedure Open   (The_Name : in String) is separate;
  procedure Close is separate;
  procedure Add    (The_Album : in Albums.Album) is separate;
  procedure Delete (The_Album : in Albums.Album) is separate;
  procedure Modify (The_Album : in Albums.Album;
                    To_Be     : in Albums.Album) is separate;
```

```
    function Size return Natural is separate;
    function Value_Of (The_Item : in Item) return Albums.Album is separate;
    package body Iterator  is separate;
end Database;
```

We shall discuss the details of I/O processing in Chapter 18. For our present purposes, we need only simple Open, Close, Get, and Put file operations, whose semantics are obvious.

Notice that we have also introduced the local object Has_Been_Modified. We shall use Has_Been_Modified to help decide when to save changes to The_File. Thus, as we call Add or Modify, we will set this object to True. Therefore, when we Close the data base, we will write changes to external storage only if Has_Been_Modified is True.

We should realize that it is the existence of The_File and Has_Been_Modified in the body of Database that makes this unit an abstract-state machine. These two objects form the state of the package because they are declared directly inside the package—not inside a subprogram. We shall discuss the implications of this approach in the next chapter.

The_File gives us an abstraction of the external representation of the database, but we also need an internal representation. One obvious solution is to use a linked list of albums. Initially, this list is empty, but as we call Add to introduce new items, we insert a new node in the list. Remove requires that we traverse this list and delete the node that matches our criterion. Modify also requires that we traverse this list, but when we find a match, we simply replace that node.

The type Item introduced in the specification of Database forms one part of this abstraction. Notice that the outside view of Item is an encapsulated type. We must complete this declaration in the private part, according to Ada's rules. As we did in Chapter 6, we used an incomplete type declaration to defer our declaration of the type Node to which Item objects point. Thus, the private part of Database includes the declarations:

```
type Node;
type Item is access Node;
```

In the body of Database, we completed the declaration of Node as:

```
type Node is
  record
    The_Album : Albums.Album;
    Next      : Item;
  end record;
```

Here we have a recursive definition, since Node objects themselves may point to other Node objects. Paralleling the state The_File, we will also locally declare an object—The_Items of type Item—to denote the internal representation of the data base.

Now that we have completed our design of the data structures used in Database, we can continue with the algorithms that manipulate those structures. The operations Create, Open, and Close mainly affect the object The_File and so are built on top of operations available from the instantiation of Sequential_IO named Album_IO. (Do not confuse this instantiation with the separately compiled unit of the same name. In this case we have a locally declared unit that is visible only in the body of Database.) Specifically, Create in turn calls Album_IO.Create. Similarly, Open calls the Album_IO operation of the same name, but this procedure must also build an initial linked list. Close reverses this action, and if the data base has been modified, it traverses the linked list and writes the album information back to the file. Thus, we can write:

```
separate ( Database )
procedure Create (The_Name : in String) is
begin
  Album_IO.Create(The_File, Album_IO.In_File, The_Name);
end Create;

separate ( Database )
procedure Open (The_Name : in String) is
  The_Album : Albums.Album;
begin
  Album_IO.Open(The_File, Album_IO.In_File, The_Name);
  loop
    exit when Album_IO.End_Of_File(The_File);
    Album_IO.Read(The_File, The_Album);
    The_Items := new Node´(The_Album => The_Album, Next => The_Items);
  end loop;
end Open;

separate ( Database )
procedure Close is
begin
  if Has_Been_Modified then
    Album_IO.Reset(The_File, Album_IO.Out_File);
    loop
      exit when The_Items = null;
      Album_IO.Write(The_File, The_Items.The_Album);
      The_Items := The_Items.Next;
    end loop;
```

```
        Has_Been_Modified := False;
    end if;
    Album_IO.Close(The_File);
end Close;
```

Add, **Delete**, and **Modify** primarily affect the internal representation of the data base. Specifically, **Add** simply requires that we allocate a new node to the linked list The_Items:

```
separate ( Database )
procedure Add (The_Album : in Albums.Album) is
begin
    The_Items := new Node'(The_Album => The_Album, Next => The_Items);
    Has_Been_Modified := True;
end Add;
```

Here again we have not used the best defensive programming practices; consider what happens if we enter album information that duplicates a record that we already have in the data base. In a final implementation, we would provide a slightly more complicated algorithm that uses exceptions to defend against this possibility.

Delete and **Modify** require that we traverse this linked list to find a matching album. (As with **Add**, we have not defended ourselves against not finding a match.) Recall from the outside view that we apply an iterator to nondestructively traverse every item in the data base. We can do exactly the same from the inside. Thus, the first loop in **Delete** and **Modify** is one in which we walk down the list The_Items until we find a match. **Delete** simply throws away this node (being careful if it finds that the match is the first node in the list). **Modify** simply replaces the album information. Thus, we can write:

```
separate ( Database )
procedure Delete (The_Album : in Albums.Album) is
    Previous_Item : Item;
    The_Iterator  : Item := The_Items;
    function "=" (Left, Right : in Albums.Album) return Boolean
        renames Albums."=";
begin
    loop
        exit when The_Iterator = null
            or else The_Iterator.The_Album = The_Album;
        Previous_Item := The_Iterator;
        The_Iterator  := The_Iterator.Next;
    end loop;
```

```
    if Previous_Item = null then
      The_Items := The_Items.Next;
    else
      Previous_Item.Next := The_Iterator.Next;
    end if;
    Has_Been_Modified := True;
  end Delete;

  separate ( Database )
  procedure Modify (The_Album : in Albums.Album;
                    To_Be     : in Albums.Album) is
    The_Item     : Item;
    The_Iterator : Item := The_Items;
    function "=" (Left, Right : in Albums.Album) return Boolean
      renames Albums."=";
  begin
    loop
      if The_Iterator = null then
        exit;
      elsif The_Iterator.The_Album = The_Album then
        The_Item := The_Iterator;
        exit;
      else
        The_Iterator := The_Iterator.Next;
      end if;
    end loop;
    The_Item.The_Album := The_Album;
    Has_Been_Modified  := True;
  end Modify;
```

There are two points of style we must discuss. First, notice that we initialized the object. The_Iterator when we declared it. We did this without fear of an exception being raised, and freedom from exceptions resulted in simpler procedure bodies. Next, notice that we included a renaming declaration to make the equality operator directly visible. As we will discuss further in the next chapter, entities exported from a package are not directly visible; they must be either qualified by the package name or made visible with a use clause or a renaming declaration. We prefer the latter approach. Unlike the use clause, a renaming declaration makes only one name directly visible.

Size_Of and Value_Of are the only two selectors for the data base. Their implementation is straightforward: Size_Of traverses the linked list represented by The_Items and counts the number of codes along the way, and Value_Of returns the album information associated with an object of type Item:

```
separate ( Database )
function Size return Natural is
  The_Count    : Natural := 0;
  The_Iterator : Item     := The_Items;
begin
  loop
    if The_Iterator = null then
      return The_Count;
    else
      The_Count    := The_Count + 1;
      The_Iterator := The_Iterator.Next;
    end if;
  end loop;
end Size;

separate ( Database )
function Value_Of (The_Item : in Item) return Albums.Album is
begin
  return The_Item.The_Album;
end Value_Of;
```

Implementation of the data base iterator is the only remaining task. The body of this nested package should come as no surprise, for it parallels our use of the iterator in Modify and Delete. Thus, we can write:

```
separate ( Database )
package body Iterator is
  The_Iterator : Item;
  procedure Initialize is
  begin
    The_Iterator := The_Items;
  end Initialize;
  procedure Get_Next is
  begin
    The_Iterator := The_Iterator.Next;
  end Get_Next;
  function Value_Of return Item is
  begin
    return The_Iterator;
  end Value_Of;
```

```
function Is_Done return Boolean is
begin
  return The_Iterator = null;
end Is_Done;
end Iterator;
```

This completes our implementation of Database; now let us turn to
Reports, which builds on top of this abstraction.

Reports provides an abstract data type named Report. From the inside
view, Report can be seen as a collection of data base items. In its simplest
representation, we might use an array whose components are of the type
Database.Item. However, it is impossible for us to know how many items a
data base may have; thus, we must in some manner be able to declare
report objects containing varying numbers of items. The solution to this
problem is similar to a solution we examined in Chapter 6: We can use an
unconstrained array whose components are of type Database.Item. However,
this is only part of the solution. Since a report object, over its lifetime, may
be attached to data bases of different sizes, we must add one level of indirection. Thus, we will wrap a discriminated record around this array. We
can express these design decisions with the declarations:

```
type Items is array (Positive range <>) of Database.Item;
type Node (The_Size : Natural) is
  record
    The_Items  : Items (1..The_Size);
    The_Length : Natural := 0;
  end record;
```

But we can even do better. From the outside view, it would be best if
a user were not concerned with the size of a data base before declaring an
object of type Node (since we must constrain it). Hence, we will add one
more level of indirection: Instead of representing the type Report as just a
Node, we will make Report a pointer to a Node. As we initialize a new report,
we first allocate a new Node, which is constrained to the size of the currently active data base. Thus, in the private part of Reports, we can complete the
declaration of Report as follows:

```
type Node (The_Size : Natural);
type Report is access Node;
```

We can hide the representation of the type Node by placing its full declaration in the body of Reports along with the declaration of the type Items.
Since the type Iterator is also declared in the specification of Reports, we
must also complete its declaration in the private part. Here, we choose to
represent this type as a record with two components: One component is a

record object, and the other is an index that indicates to where in the list of items our iterator is currently pointing. Thus, we can write:

```
type Iterator is
  record
    The_Report : Report;
    The_Index  : Natural;
  end record;
```

Let us turn to the body of Reports. For example, the constructor Initialize requires that we build a new report containing all the items in the current data base. Here, we must use the data base iterator to traverse the data base. Rather than saving the album information itself, we maintain objects of type Database.Item as pointers to individual album records. Thus, in the body of Initialize, first we allocate a new object of type Node, which is constrained to the current size of the data base. Then we use the iterator to visit every item:

```
separate ( Reports )
procedure Initialize (The_Report : in out Report) is
  function "=" (Left, Right : in Database.Item) return Boolean
    renames Database."=";
begin
  The_Report := new Node(The_Size => Database.Size);
  Database.Iterator.Initialize;
  loop
    exit when Database.Iterator.Is_Done;
    The_Report.The_Length := The_Report.The_Length + 1;
    The_Report.The_Items(The_Report.The_Length) :=
      Database.Iterator.Value_Of;
    Database.Iterator.Get_Next;
  end loop;
end Initialize;
```

Following Initialize are a number of overloaded Find procedures, which simply select items from the current report. Our strategy will be to introduce a local object, The_Index, to visit every item in the current report. Starting at one end of The_Items array, we check that the value of that item matches the given criteria. For example, if we call Find for an album title, we see whether there is a match with this value and the title component of the designated item. If there is a match, then we do nothing and retain the item in the report. If we do not have a match, we must throw away this item. To do so, we can use array slice assignment to overwrite the offending item, then reduce the length of the report by 1. We can express this algorithm as:

```
separate ( Reports )
procedure Find (The_Title     : in      Albums.Title;
                In_The_Report : in out Report) is
  The_Index : Natural := In_The_Report.The_Length;
  function "=" (Left, Right : in Albums.Title) return Boolean
    renames Albums."=";
begin
  while The_Index > 0
  loop
    if Database.Value_Of(In_The_Report.The_Items(The_Index)).The_Title
      = The_Title then
      The_Index := The_Index - 1;
    else
      if The_Index < In_The_Report.The_Size then
        In_The_Report.The_Items
        (The_Index..(In_The_Report.The_Length - 1)) :=
          In_The_Report.The_Items((The_Index+ 1)..In_The_Report.The_Length);
      end if;
      The_Index := The_Index - 1;
      In_The_Report.The_Length := In_The_Report.The_Length - 1;
    end if;
  end loop;
end Find;
```

We shall not include the implementation of the remaining Find operations, since their bodies are almost identical to the one above.

The next procedure, Sort, takes advantage of our decision to maintain a report as a collection of items that designate albums rather than saving the information as individual records. The major benefit is that we have to define only one occurrence of each record.

We choose to use the quick-sort algorithm. Thus, we can write:

```
separate ( Reports )
procedure Sort (The_Report     : in out Report;
                By_Category    : in     Sort_Category;
                With_The_Order : in     Order := Ascending) is
  function Incorrect_Order (Left  : in Albums.Album;
                            Right : in Albums.Album) return Boolean
    is separate;
```

```
procedure Quicksort (Sort_Array : in out Items) is
  Front : Natural := Sort_Array'First;
  Back  : Natural := Sort_Array'Last;
  procedure Exchange (First, Second : in out Database.Item) is
    Temporary : constant Database.Item := First;
  begin
    First  := Second;
    Second := Temporary;
  end Exchange;
  pragma Inline (Exchange);
  procedure Partition is
    Mid_Point : constant Natural := (Front + Back) / 2;
    Mid_Value : constant Database.Item := Sort_Array (Mid_Point);
  begin
    Outer:
    loop
      loop
        exit when Incorrect_Order(Database.Value_Of(Sort_Array (Front)),
                                  Database.Value_Of(Mid_Value))
              or Front = Sort_Array'Last;
        Front := Front + 1;
      end loop;
      loop
        exit when Incorrect_Order(Database.Value_Of(Mid_Value),
                                  Database.Value_Of(Sort_Array(Back)))
              or Back = Sort_Array'First;
        Back := Back - 1;
      end loop;
      if Front <= Back then
        if Front < Back then
          Exchange (Sort_Array(Front),Sort_Array(Back));
        end if;
        if Front /= Sort_Array'Last then
          Front := Front + 1;
        end if;
        if Back /= Sort_Array'First then
          Back := Back - 1;
        end if;
      end if;
```

```
                    exit Outer when (Front > Back)
                                or (Front = Sort_Array'Last
                                    and Back  = Sort_Array'First);
                end loop Outer;
            end Partition;
        begin -- Quicksort
            if Sort_Array'Length > 1 then
                Partition;
                if Sort_Array'First < Back then
                    Quicksort (Sort_Array (Sort_Array'First..Back));
                end if;
                if Front < Sort_Array'Last then
                    Quicksort (Sort_Array (Front..Sort_Array'Last));
                end if;
            end if;
        end Quicksort;
    begin -- Sort
        Quicksort(The_Report.The_Items(1..The_Report.The_Length));
    end Sort;
```

Quicksort sorts arrays of type Items. Thus our Sort subprogram does nothing more than select the actual items of the report and pass them to Quicksort.

Quicksort begins by deciding whether the array is long enough to require sorting (SortArray'Length > 1). The basic idea of Quicksort is to exchange components that are far apart. The array is partitioned in the middle, and components on opposite sides are exchanged. This process is repeated on slices of the array, using recursion.

Notice how we make use of object attributes in the body of Quicksort. Quicksort is called with arrays of many different sizes. It is the use of attributes that allows the subprogram to work correctly on any size array.

The function Incorrect_Order is used to determine whether components need to be exchanged. Incorrect_Order must be passed two Albums.Album objects, which we can obtain (given an object of type Database.Items) by using the data base selector Value_Of. Additionally, Incorrect_Order depends on the sorting category (By_Category) and order (With_The_Order), which are global to this function. Thus, we can write:

```
separate ( Reports.Sort )
function Incorrect_Order (Left  : in Albums.Album;
                          Right : in Albums.Album)
    return Boolean is
    use Albums;
```

```
begin --Incorrect_Order
  if With_The_Order = Descending then
    case By_Category is
      when Title  => return Left.The_Title   < Right.The_Title;
      when Artist => return Left.The_Artist  < Right.The_Artist;
      when Style  => return Left.The_Style   < Right.The_Style;
      when Year   => return Left.The_Year    < Right.The_Year;
      when Number => return Left.Number_Of_Songs < Right.Number_Of_Songs;
    end case;
  else
    case By_Category is
      when Title  => return Left.The_Title   > Right.The_Title;
      when Artist => return Left.The_Artist  > Right.The_Artist;
      when Style  => return Left.The_Style   > Right.The_Style;
      when Year   => return Left.The_Year    > Right.The_Year;
      when Number => return Left.Number_Of_Songs > Right.Number_Of_Song;
    end case;
  end if;
end Incorrect_Order;
```

The main action of `Incorrect_Order` involves two large case statements that determine the correct relational test to apply.

`Length_Of` is the only selector exported by `Reports`. Its body is simple, since the state it references is directly accessible:

```
separate ( Reports )
function Length_Of (The_Report : in Report) return Natural is
begin
  return The_Report.The_Length;
end Length_Of;
```

The iterator exported by `Reports` is similar to that exported by `Database`, except that in `Reports` we have an abstract data type, not an abstract-state machine. Actually, the implementation of each iterator operation parallels that from `Database`, except that the iterator object used is passed in as a parameter. Thus, we can write:

```
separate ( Reports )
procedure Initialize (The_Iterator    : in out Iterator;
                      With_The_Report : in      Report) is
begin
  The_Iterator := (The_Report => With_The_Report, The_Index => 1);
end Initialize;
```

```
separate ( Reports )
procedure Get_Next (The_Iterator : in out Iterator) is
begin
   The_Iterator.The_Index := The_Iterator.The_Index + 1;
end Get_Next;

separate ( Reports )
function Value_Of (The_Iterator : in Iterator)
  return Albums.Album is
begin
   return Database.Value_Of
     (The_Iterator.The_Report.The_Items(The_Iterator.The_Index));
end Value_Of;

separate ( Reports )
function Is_Done (The_Iterator : in Iterator) return Boolean is
begin
   return The_Iterator.The_Index > The_Iterator.The_Report.The_Length;
end Is_Done;
```

This completes our implementation of the body Reports. The remaining packages—Album_IO, Report_IO, and Command_IO—all have simple implementations. As we discussed in Chapter 7, these packages collect all the textual operations for their associated abstractions. For example, for the body of Command_IO, we build on top of the package Text_IO. Thus, the body of the procedure Get involves the use of only Put and Get procedures. We can write the body of Command_IO as:

```
with Text_IO;
package body Command_IO is
  package IO is new Text_IO.Enumeration_IO(Command);
  procedure Space (Count : Positive) is
  begin
    Text_IO.Put (String'(1..Count => ' '));
  end Space;
  procedure Get (The_Command : out Command) is
    Prompt : constant String := "Possible commands are: ";
  begin
    Text_IO.New_Line;
    Text_IO.Put (Prompt) ;
```

```
        for A_Command in Command
          loop
            IO.Put(A_Command, Set => Text_IO.Lower_Case);
            if (Command'Pos(A_Command) mod 4) = 3 then
              Text_IO.New_Line;
              Space(Count => Prompt'Length);
            else
              Space(Count => Command'Width + 1 - Command'Image(A_Command)'Length);
            end if;
          end loop;
        Text_IO.New_Line;
        Text_IO.Put("Waiting for command: ");
        IO.Get(The_Command);
        Text_IO.Skip_Line;
      end Get;
    end Command_IO;
```

The Get procedure prints the Command names, and then reads a Command from the user's input. Commands are printed four per line. Notice how we use the Pos attribute and mod to determine when we have printed four Command names. Also notice the use of the Width, Image, and Length attributes to correctly space the Command names.

We will not finish implementing Report_IO and Album_IO, since they depend only on Ada's predefined I/O facilities. (We shall not complete our study of these resources until Chapter 18.)

Exercises   1. Modify this system so that the user can search for albums that match a range of values. For example, find all the albums released between 1970 and 1979.

2. Reports permits the existence of more than one active report at a time, but currently our system does not take advantage of this facility. Modify the system so that the user can merge the contents of two reports.

3. Currently, Sort applies to only one key at a time. Modify this constructor so that a secondary sort key can be used. For example, the user may wish to sort albums by year, then sort alphabetically by title within each year.

4. Identify what might go wrong with each operation in the body of Reports.

*5. Clearly, we could have designed this system in more of a FORTRAN style, instead of carefully separating each abstraction. What are the advantages and costs of the FORTRAN-style approach?

6. The `Delete` operation of the data base will indicate that the data base has been modified even if the item to be deleted is not in the data base. Which goals of software engineering—modifiability, efficiency, reliability, and understandability—are in jeopardy here?

7. What prevents the data base from being updated while a report is being prepared?

PACKAGE

4

Packaging Concepts

It was clear that a most powerful addition to any programming language would be the ability to define new higher level entities in terms of previously known ones, and then to call them by name. This would build the chunking right into the language. Instead of there being a determinate repertoire of instructions out of which all programs had to be explicitly assembled, the programmer could construct his own modules, each with its own name each usable anywhere inside the program, just as if it had been a built-in feature of the language.

D.R. Hofstadter
Gödel, Escher, Bach:
An Eternal Golden Braid[1]

CHAPTER

11

Packages

The Form of Ada Packages
Packages and Private Types
Applications for Ada Packages

Y our house has a plumbing problem and you need to do some repair work. You could use the resources you have at home—at three o'clock in the morning almost anything can be made to stop a drip. However, it will be better in the long run to go to a hardware store in the morning and get the package of materials needed to do the job correctly and efficiently. Finally, at home, you can collect the tools you need and put them to use. It isn't important how the tools work, just that they do work.

Ada isn't going to stop your leaky faucets, but there is a parallel here. In Ada, a programmer can collect logically related resources in a package. The first two design examples have both used packages in their solutions, so by now you should have an intuitive feel for the use of this language feature. This chapter takes a closer look at packages and examines their structure and applications.

11.1   The Form of Ada Packages

A package forms a collection of logically related entities or computational resources. Formally, we say that a package *encapsulates* (puts a wall around) these resources. In Chapter 4, we introduced the symbols for an Ada package, repeated here in Figure 11.1. From this figure we see that a

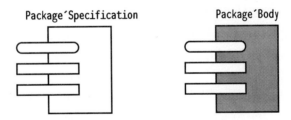

Figure 11.1 Symbols for an Ada package

package consists of two parts, the specification and the body. The specification identifies the visible parts of the package; formally, we say that the package exports these entities. We have used two different symbols in the package specification to distinguish between exporting objects and types (the rounded rectangle) and exporting operations (the regular rectangle).

In a sense, this package specification is the contract between the implementor of the package and the user. This interface specifies which parts of the package can be used and, furthermore, how they can be used. It is not important for a user to understand how these operations are actually implemented. In addition, a package user can refer only to these visible entities. For example, the human interface to a car includes the steering wheel, brakes, and accelerator; these are the resources that are visible. The driver does not need to know how these resources work—that is an implementation detail. In Ada, similar details can be hidden in the package body.

This structure directly supports the principles of modularity, abstraction, localization, and information hiding. Of course, good programmers can apply these principles in other languages, including FORTRAN or even assembly languages. The difference between Ada and most other programming languages is that Ada packages enforce and encourage these principles. The language rules do not permit a package user to do anything more than what the package specification allows. If the user tries, he or she will be stopped at compilation time with semantic errors.

Since the specification and body can be compiled separately, it is a simple matter to create the specification early in the software design and then add the body later. Indeed, this is the essence of using Ada as a design language, as we discussed in Chapter 3. Furthermore, it is good practice to separate the two parts physically—and to hide supporting information consistently. Perhaps most importantly, though, Ada packages help the programmer control the complexity of software solutions by giving him or her a mechanism with which to physically group related entities into a logical chunk.

Package Specifications

A package specification takes the form:

```
package Some_Name is
   ...
end Some_Name;
```

A package specification can itself be further divided into two parts, the *visible* part and the *private* part. The visible part declares the resources that can be used outside the package; the package is said to *export* these entities. A package can export any of a number of items, including objects, types, subtypes, subprograms, tasks, numbers, exceptions, constants, renamed entities, and even other packages. It is good practice to keep package specifications small and to export only a single logical chunk. Later in this chapter, we shall discuss how this grouping can best be chosen.

The private part appears only at the end of the package specification and is introduced by the reserved word **private**. The private part is textually available to a package user and, like the visible part, consists of declarative items. However, the private part cannot be referenced outside the package. It exists in the specification part to support the separate compilation unit mechanism. Its use will be explained later in a section on private types.

A program unit can use the resources of any package that is visible. For example, consider the package **Complex** introduced in Chapter 4:

```
package Complex is
   type Number is private;
   procedure Set (A_Number       : out Number;
                  Real_Part      : in  Float;
                  Imaginary_Part : in  Float);
   function "+" (Left, Right : in Number) return Number;
   function "-" (Left, Right : in Number) return Number;
   function Real_Part (A_Number : in Number) return Float;
   function Imaginary_Part (A_Number : in Number) return Float;
private
   type Number is
     record
       Real_Part,
       Imaginary_Part : Float;
     end record;
end Complex;
```

Package **Complex** is visible to another program unit, P, if it is declared in an inner or outer scope of P and is not hidden by another declaration. There are more detailed scope rules; these are discussed in Chapter 20. For an example of the general case, we have:

```
procedure Main_Program is
   procedure First is begin ... end First;
           -- start of the declarative part
   package Complex is ... end Complex;
           -- specification of the package
   package body Complex is ... end Complex;
           -- body of the package
   procedure Second is ...                    -- another declarative item
      procedure Third is begin ... end Third;  -- a nested procedure
   begin ... end Second;
begin     -- Main_Program
   -- sequence of statements
end Main_Program;
```

Complex is visible inside Main_Program from the point at which it is first named. As a result of the scope and visibility rules of Ada, the First procedure cannot see the Complex package; however, the procedures Second and Third, along with the Main_Program body, can use the resources of the Complex package.

Another, and usually preferred, method of establishing visibility is through the with clause. Thus, the package Complex can be compiled separately and can be used by other program units, as we saw in Chapter 4 and as illustrated in the following example:

```
with Complex;
procedure Main_Program is ...
```

Main_Program is said to *import* the unit Complex. Complex is then visible throughout Main_Program, and the type Number and various subprograms are available. The benefit of this approach is that it supports the principles of modularity and localization and so helps limit the scope of any changes that may be made during software maintenance. Another, more subtle, benefit is that it encourages the transportability of software units. Eventually, you will be able to go to your local software package store, specify the interface you need, and then receive these packages for use with your program units. The structure of Ada packages clearly facilitates the development of an industry of transportable software modules.

Once a package is visible, parts of its specification can be identified with selected component notation (the visible parts only). For example:

```
with Complex;
procedure Some_Program is
  Number_1, Number_2 : Complex.Number;
begin
  -- sequence of statements
end Some_Program;
```

Notice how our choice of names made the declaration of Number_1 and Number_2 quite readable. This notation can be used with other names, such as:

```
Complex.Set(Number_1, 37.861, -40.25);
Number_1 := Complex."+"(Number_1, Number_2);
```

The last example looks a bit awkward, since the addition operator is not directly visible and must be selected. Normally, we would like to write our equations using infix rather than prefix notation. Alternatively, we can gain direct visibility through the use clause. Application of this clause permits components to be referenced without requiring the package name as a prefix (as long as the component name is not ambiguous). For example:

```
with Complex;
procedure Another_Program is
  Number_3, Number_4 : Complex.Number;
  use Complex;
begin
  Number_3 := Number_3 + Number_4;
end Another_Program;
```

In this example, the addition operator refers to the operation exported from the package Complex, not the predefined addition operator for numeric types. The addition operator is directly visible, and so we can use infix notation and drop the quotation marks. We say that the addition operator is *overloaded,* and, as long as the compiler can determine the operator to which we are referring (by examining the actual parameters of the call, for example), we can freely use any such overloaded entity. Note another style issue: Ada permits the declaration of several objects at the same time (Number_3, Number_4) in what is called an *identifier* list. In most cases, however, it is recommended that a programmer use only one object name per declaration in order to improve readability.

The use clause is sometimes convenient to apply since it permits shorter names, but it can cause a loss of clarity and could introduce a name clash (the condition in which there are two or more entities at the same level with the same name). The use clause does not prohibit prefixing the package name, however, so Number_3 and Number_4 could still be declared as Complex.Number to improve readability. Generally, it is still good practice to avoid the **use** clause in order to minimize the number of names directly visible at one time.

As we discussed in Chapter 4 and shall study in greater detail later in this chapter, private types implicitly export the operations of assignment and test for equality and inequality. However, Ada treats the visibility of these operations differently; herein lies a common problem. As our previous two examples have indicated, assignment of a private type is directly visible with or without the **use** clause. On the other hand, equality and inequality follow the same rules of visibility as all the other operator symbols we have studied. Thus, in the presence of a **use** clause, equality (and inequality) operators are made directly visible, so we can write:

```
if Number_1 = Number_2 then ...
```

However, if the equality operator is not directly visible, we must use prefix notation such as:

```
if Complex."="(Number_1, Number_2) then ...
```

Applying the **use** clause just to gain direct visibility to the equality and inequality operations has the undesirable side elect of making everything exported from the package directly visible; this effectively pollutes the name space. Fortunately, a *renaming declaration* provides an approach we can use to selectively gain visibility to exported entities. Using a renaming declaration, we might write:

```
with Complex;
procedure Main is
  function "=" (Left, Right : Complex.Number) return Boolean
    renames Complex."=";
  Number_5, Number_6 : Complex.Number;
begin
  if Number_5 = Number_6 then ...
end Main;
```

The renaming declaration thus provides a simple alias for the fully qualified name `Complex.Number`. We can then use infix notation to compare two numbers, but the remaining operations (such as `Set`) must be fully qualified. We will study all the options for renaming declarations in Chapter 20.

Package Bodies

A package body takes the form:

```
package body Some_Name is
   ...
end Some_Name;
```

Note that the package body name must correspond exactly to its specification name. Every package specification must have a corresponding body unless the specification contains only types and objects, and then the body is optional. The elements in a package body are not accessible (visible) outside the package, thus supporting the principle of information hiding.

A body has a form somewhat similar to a subprogram. It consists of a declarative part, followed by an optional block with a sequence of statements and an optional exception handler. If we introduce any subprogram, task, or package specifications in this package's specification, their bodies must be completed in the declarative part (unless we define them as subunits, as Chapter 20 describes). Like subprogram bodies, any local declarations and local program units can be introduced in a package body.

When a package body is elaborated, its declarative part is elaborated first, and then its sequence of statements, if any, are executed. This last feature is useful if any package initialization must be accomplished.

We can complete the body of the package Complex as:

```
package body Complex is
   procedure Set (A_Number        : out Number;
                  Real_Part       : in  Float;
                  Imaginary_Part : in  Float) is
   begin
     A_Number := (Real_Part, Imaginary_Part);
   end Set;
   function "+" (Left, Right : in Number) return Number is
   begin
     return (Left.Real_Part      + Right.Real_Part,
             Left.Imaginary_Part + Right.Imaginary_Part);
   end "+";
   function "-" (Left, Right : in Number) return Number is
   begin
     return (Left.Real_Part      - Right.Real_Part,
             Left.Imaginary_Part - Right.Imaginary_Part);
   end "-";
   function Real_Part (A_Number : in Number) return Float is
   begin
     return A_Number.Real_Part;
   end Real_Part;
```

```
      function Imaginary_Part (A_Number : in Number) return Float is
      begin
        return A_Number.Imaginary_Part;
      end Imaginary_Part;
    end Complex;
```

In this example, we required no package initialization. If we have a package that creates a log file, however, we could use initialization to create the file. This can be expressed in the package body as follows:

```
    package Log is
      procedure Write (Item : in String);
    end Log;
    with Text_IO;
    package body Log is
      use Text_IO;
      The_File : File_Type;
      procedure Write (Item : in String) is
      begin
        Put_Line(The_File, Item);
      end Write;
    begin
      Create(The_File, Out_File, "my_log");
    end Log;
```

In this case, when we elaborate the Log package, we will initialize The_File, which is a local object. Notice the meaningful names we applied to this package; we call the procedure as Log.Write.

If more than one unit depends upon the same package (denoted by a with clause), it is important to note that it is elaborated only one time. Thus, if four library units reference the package Log by naming Log in a context specification, Log will be elaborated once before any of the four units are elaborated. In this manner, packages are shared as library units by every using occurrence within a program.

Before we can call any subprograms declared in the visible part of a package specification, both the specification and the body must be elaborated. For packages that are nested inside other units, we can textually separate the specification and body, provided that the specification appears first. This is quite a normal style, as the following indicates:

```
    procedure Yet_Another_Program is
      package First is               -- specification of First
        ...
      end First;
```

```
procedure Second;              -- specification of Second
procedure Third;               -- specification of Third
package body First is ...      -- body of First
procedure Second is ...        -- body of Second
procedure Third is ...         -- body of Third
begin
  -- sequence of statements
end Yet_Another_Program;
```

In this manner, we specify the interfaces of each program unit first and then group their bodies at the end of the declarative part. However, one problem with placing each complete unit body at the end is that it tends to make the main unit quite lengthy and difficult to read. To reduce the length of the program text and to consistently hide the implementation of each local unit, a preferred method is to introduce a subunit, as in the following example:

```
procedure Still_Yet_Another_Program is
  package First is

    ...

  end First;
  package body First  is separate;
  procedure    Second is separate;
  procedure    Third  is separate;
begin
  -- sequence of statements
end Still_Yet_Another_Program;
```

In this example, the body of each unit is compiled independently, although the specification is directly visible. Further use of this method is discussed in Chapter 20.

11.2   Packages and Private Types

Earlier, we mentioned that packages can enforce the principle of abstraction. Often, a programmer wishes to create an object whose logical properties must be maintained outside a package but whose structural details are irrelevant. This is accomplished primarily with private types. A private type definition can appear only in the visible part of a package.

There exist two classes of private types:

- Simple private types

- Limited private types

For simple private types, the only information available outside the package is that given in the visible part of the package in which it was declared. Thus, the type name is available, but the set of values or the structure applicable to the type is hidden. The only operations available to objects of the private type are those applicable subprograms declared in the visible part, plus the assignment operator and tests for equality and inequality. For limited private types, the same rules apply, except that even assignment and tests for equality and inequality are not available outside the package. Of course, within the private part and body of the same package, the structure of the private type is visible, which means that its structure can be referenced.

If a package contains a private type definition, then the specification must also contain a private part that completes the type definition. A private part can contain more than the definition of the private type (although this is generally not good style). Furthermore, a package without a private type can include a private part.

Within a package specification, not only can we define private types but we can also declare constants of a private type (although we cannot define objects of the private type until the elaboration of the private part). For example, we may wish to create a package that issues passwords and also checks their validity. As we create Password objects, we want to initialize them to some Null_Password value, which we can declare as a private constant:

```
package Manager is
   type Password is private;
   Null_Password : constant Password;
   function Get return Password;
   function Is_Valid (A_Password : in Password) return Boolean;
private
   type Password is range 0..7_000;
   Null_Password : constant Password := 0;
end Manager;
```

We have chosen to declare Password as a **private** type, as opposed to **limited private**, to permit users to assign passwords to one another. However, we cannot directly name values of the type, since the complete type declaration is hidden from us.

Even though we have hidden the implementation of the constant, we can freely use Null_Password outside the package. For example, when declaring Password objects, we can indicate a default value:

```
use Manager;
My_Password : Password := Null_Password;
```

Private and limited private types therefore permit a programmer to exercise complete control over the operations available on an exported type. This feature is particularly useful when creating abstract data types, which we discuss in the next section.

There is a subtle interaction between some of the rules for access types and those for private types. Ada rules require that a private type introduced in a package specification be completed with a full type declaration in the private part; in other words, by the time we finish the package specification, we must have provided a complete implementation for any private types. However, Ada permits us to split the definition of incomplete types across package specification and body boundaries. For example, if in the private part of the package `Manager`, we chose to represent the type `Password` as an access type, we might have written:

```
type Node;
type Password is access Node;
```

Then, in the body of the package `Manager`, we might have completed the declaration of the incomplete type `Node` as:

```
type Node is range 0..7_000;
```

In this manner, we can defer the implementation of our abstractions even further.

11.3   Applications for Ada Packages

Ada is a general-purpose language with considerable power, but it still does not prevent a programmer from abusing certain features of the language—it is definitely possible to write unreadable, unstructured Ada code. To avoid this trap, each language construct must be applied in a purposeful manner. This is clearly true for Ada packages, since they form an essential element of any software system. Ada packages should be logically small, that is, they should export only a single, small chunk. We recommend four different applications for Ada packages, namely:

- Named collections of declarations
- Groups of related program units
- Abstract data types
- Abstract-state machines

These applications are further characterized by the kinds of entities they usually export:

- *Named collections of declarations*
  Export objects and types
  Do not export other program units

- *Groups of related program units*
  Do not export objects and types
  Export other program units

- *Abstract data types*
  Export objects and types
  Export other program units
  Do not maintain state information in the body

- *Abstract-state machines*
  Do not export objects and types
  Export other program units
  Maintain state information in the body

Note that these represent the purest forms of application; in practice, we may find hybrid versions. The following sections provide a discussion and examples of each of these general applications.

Named Collections of Declarations

One of the simplest uses of packages is for the logical grouping of objects and types. This application benefits maintainability by factoring out common data, objects, and types and placing their definition in one location. This definition can then be used by any other program unit. As changes are made, only the one package must be altered, thus ensuring consistency.

For example, in a system that requires an earth model, such as a guidance program or a mapping application, it is important to maintain a set of constants that every other program unit can reference. We can package this set as follows:

```
package Metric_Earth_Constants is
   Equatorial_Radius    : constant := 6_378.145;      -- km
   Gravitation_Constant : constant := 3.986_012E5;    -- km**3/sec**2
   Speed_Unit           : constant := 7.905_368_28;   -- km/sec
   Time_Unit            : constant := 806.811_874_4;  -- sec
end Metric_Earth_Constants;
```

In this example, there are no other program units defined in the specification, so we can omit the package body. As an even better (safer) implementation, we could export types defining kilometers and seconds, and then declare the numbers as constants of that specific type. In this manner, we would prevent a user from applying a constant with the wrong units. To ensure portability, predefined types such as `Float` should not be used. In fact, in our example above, we used numeric constants (of type universal real) instead of naming constants of type `Float`.

As another application, it is often useful to collect a set of logically related types. In a system that manipulates dates, it would be useful to package day, month, and year types. For example:

```
package Date_Information is
  type Day_Name   is
    (Monday, Tuesday, Wednesday, Thursday, Friday, Saturday, Sunday);
  type Day_Value  is range 1..31;
  type Month_Name is
    (January,   February, March,      April,   May,       June,
     July,      August,   September, October, November, December);
  type Year_Value is range 0..Integer'Last;
end Date_Information;
```

Again, a package body is not required to complete the package declaration.

A few comments on style are in order here. In the example above, note that we chose to apply meaningful names, even though they take longer to write. We do this to enhance understandability. Note also that the packages in both examples are relatively small. If package specifications are made too large, they become unreadable and difficult to understand. In such a case, the programmer probably missed factoring the data one more level. It would then be appropriate to create *subpackages* (packages nested within another package). Also, if packages are used as collections of declarations, they should not be used as if they were `FORTRAN COMMONs` or `JOVIAL COMPOOLs`. Such an application turns them into nothing more than named pools of global data, which then makes Ada programs reflect the topology of first- or second-generation languages. This clearly is not in the spirit of Ada, and furthermore, it defeats much of the power of the language.

Groups of Related Program Units

In the previous examples, we were able to group logically related data. It is also possible to group program units, namely subprograms, tasks, or even other packages. For example, since Ada does not have predefined trigonometric functions, we might need to specify such a package. (Actually, a programmer would not normally have to write such a package; he or she would most likely just reference it as a predefined library unit.) We could specify the package as follows:

```
package Transcendental_Functions is
  function Cos (Angle : in Float) return Float;
  function Sin (Angle : in Float) return Float;
  function Tan (Angle : in Float) return Float;
end Transcendental_Functions;
```

Actually, in a production environment, we could increase the utility of the package by adding a generic part so that the package could operate at accuracies defined by the user. We shall do so in the next chapter.

Since this specification includes entities other than objects, constants, and types, a package body is required. Of course, a user of the package need not see the body—how the functions execute is an implementation detail. It would be good practice for the package implementor to compile the package separately. This has the added benefit that if the transcendental algorithms were ever modified (for reasons of efficiency), the change would not affect any program units that use the package. We provide one implementation of a package body in the following example, in which a trigonometric series is used to calculate values. The implementation is not rigorously designed to account for all accuracy considerations (we leave that up to the numerical analysts), but it is sufficient to illustrate Ada's control features:

```
package body Transcendental_Functions is
  Series_Length : constant := 5;
  function Odd (Index : in Integer) return Boolean is
    -- return True if Index has an odd value
  begin
    return (Index mod 2) /= 0;
  end Odd;
  function Factorial (Value : in Positive) return Positive is
    -- determine Value! using a recursive function
  begin
    if Value = 1 then
      return 1;
    else
      return Value * Factorial(Value - 1);
    end if;
  end Factorial;
  function Term (Angle  : in Float;
                Power  : in Integer;
                Number : in Integer) return Float is
    -- calculate a term of the trigonometric series
```

```
      begin --Term;
        if Odd(Number) then
          return -(Angle ** Power) / Float (Factorial(Power));
        else
          return +(Angle ** Power) / Float (Factorial(Power));
        end if;
      end Term;
      function Cos (Angle : in Float) return Float is
        -- calculate the cosine of Angle
        Answer : Float;
        Power  : Integer;
      begin
        Answer := 1.0;
        for Index in reverse 1..Series_Length
          loop
            Power := Index * 2;
            Answer := Answer + Term(Angle, Power, Index);
          end loop;
        return Answer;
      end Cos;
      function Sin (Angle : in Float) return Float is
      -- calculate the sine of Angle
        Answer : Float;
        Power  : Integer;
      begin
        Answer := Angle;
        for Index in reverse 1..Series_Length
          loop
            Power := (Index * 2) +1;
            Answer := Answer + Term(Angle, Power, Index);
          end loop;
        return Answer;
      end Sin;
      function Tan (Angle : in Float) return Float is
        -- calculate the tangent of Angle
      begin
        return Sin(Angle) / Cos(Angle);
      end Tan;
    end Transcendental_Functions;
```

In this implementation, note particularly the use of the Series_Length constant that determines the length of the trigonometric series. Declaring this value as a constant makes it easier for a programmer to modify the package later. Furthermore, the body does not have the optional sequence of statements for initialization, but three local subprograms are declared to complete the implementation. These functions, Odd, Factorial, and Term, are hidden in the body and therefore cannot be accessed outside the package. Within Cos and Sin, we step through the series from the smallest term to the largest (to minimize roundoff errors). For the Tan subprogram, the facilities provided by Cos and Sin are used.

Graphics packages demonstrate another application of Ada packages as collections of subprograms. Since transformations (Rotate, Scale, and Translate) are common graphics algorithms, a user might be provided with the following package specification:

```
package Two_D_Transform is

  type Coordinate is
    record
      X, Y : Float;
    end record;
  procedure Rotate    (Point : in out Coordinate; Angle : in Float);
  procedure Scale     (Point : in out Coordinate; X, Y  : in Float);
  procedure Translate (Point : in out Coordinate; X, Y  : in Float);
end Two_D_Transform;
```

We say that Coordinate is an unencapsulated type since it is neither private nor limited private. We have somewhat violated our philosophy of never using predefined types such as Float, but we have done so here to simplify our solution and also to show some more applications of type transformations.

Our package will need the resources of the Transcendental_Functions, but we can hide the reference in the Two_D_Transform body. We apply the use clause to permit shorter names in the implementation; since the package specification is small, there is little chance of ambiguity. One possible body is as follows:

```
with Transcendental_Functions;
use Transcendental_Functions;
package body Two_D_Transform is
  procedure Rotate (Point : in out Coordinate;
                    Angle : in    Float) is
    -- rotate the Point by Angle radians about the origin
    Temporary :  Coordinate := Point;
```

```
      begin --Rotate
        Point := (X => (Temporary.X * Cos(Angle)) +
                       (Temporary.Y * Sin(Angle)),
                  Y => -(Temporary.X * Sin(Angle)) +
                       (Temporary.Y * Cos(Angle)));
      end Rotate;
      procedure Scale (Point : in out Coordinate;
                        X, Y  : in      Float) is
        -- scale the Point by a factor of X and Y
      begin
        Point := (X => Point.X * X, Y => Point.Y * Y);
      end Scale;
      procedure Translate (Point : in out Coordinate;
                            X, Y  : in      Float) is
        -- translate the Point by a distance of X and Y
      begin
        Point := (X => Point.X + X, Y => Point.Y + Y);
      end Translate;
    end Two_D_Transform;
```

As before, package initialization is not required.

So far, we have shown applications of packages as collections of subprograms, but it is also reasonable to use packages to collect other packages or tasks. In fact, that is precisely the application we used in the second design problem.

Abstract Data Types

As we indicated in Chapter 6, Ada has a wealth of primitive data types. Of course, this set of types is not all-encompassing. Thus, the language provides a mechanism whereby a user can create an abstract data type and then encapsulate it in such a manner that the language enforces the abstraction. As we have discussed, this mechanism involves the use of packages and private types. When creating abstract data types, it is a good practice to export only one type (or a small set of highly related types) per package. Thus, a package specification would contain only one private or limited private type, the subprograms that define the operations applicable to the type, and the specification private part.

The package Complex described earlier is one example of an abstract data type. However, this abstraction is not enforceable, since the type is not private and its structure is therefore visible. A user could violate this abstraction by adding the imaginary and real parts of a number, for example. The language would not be able to detect the infraction.

To enforce a logical abstraction, we must use private types. For the graphics package we could declare the type `Coordinate` as private and move the implementation of the type to a private part. Since we could no longer refer to its structure directly, we would have to add other operations, such as `Put_Y_Part` and `Return_Y_Part`. The complete specification of `Two_D_Transform` is left as an exercise.

Within the language, Ada does not define any queue data structures, such as first-in-first-out (FIFO) buffers. What is needed is a `Queue` data type that can be treated as a primitive type. Additionally, we would like to be able to declare queues of differing lengths. To simplify the problem, we define queues that use only `Integer` elements, although it would be a simple task to create a generic `Queue` for any type of element (as will be seen in the next chapter). We define this abstract data type in the following package specification:

```
package Queues is
   type Queue (Size : Positive) is limited private;
   procedure Clear (The_Queue      : in out Queue);
   procedure Add   (The_Item       : in Integer;
                    To_The_Queue   : in out Queue);
   procedure Remove(The_Item       : out Integer;
                    From_The_Queue : in out Queue);
   function Length_Of (The_Queue : in Queue) return Natural;
   Overflow, Underflow : exception;
private
   type List is array (Positive range <>) of Integer;
   type Queue (Size : Positive) is
      record
         The_Items : List(1..Size);
         The_Back  : Natural := 0;
      end record;
end Queues;
```

Notice how we have used a record discriminant in the private type declaration to express dependencies among components of the `Queue` record. In addition, we gave `The_Back` a default value so that whenever we declared objects of type `Queues.Queue`, a stable initial state would be guaranteed, namely, an empty queue. The operations defined for this abstract type include the constructs `Clear`, `Add`, `Remove`, and the selector `Length_Of`. We consciously declared `Queue` as a limited private type to prohibit a user from assigning `Queue` objects to each other or comparing two Queue objects. We also export two exceptions, `Overflow` and `Underflow`, to detect any attempted `Add` on a full buffer or `Remove` from an empty buffer. It would also be useful to export the boolean functions Is_Empty and Is_Full, but we omit them here, since Length_Of can be used for these purposes, and for simplicity. In the next chapter, we shall see how to make this a general-purpose abstract FIFO queue by adding a generic part to parameterize some Item type. As before, a user does not need to see how the operations are implemented.

Several implementations exist for FIFO buffers, including the use of dynamic linked lists or simple arrays. In the following package body, we implement the Queue as an array. Without knowing the details of our representation, the user can thus declare objects such as:

```
My_Buffer   : Queues.Queue(70);         -- a queue of size 70
Your_Buffer : Queues.Queue(Size => 32); -- a queue of size 32
```

The use of the private discriminant has been exploited to enable the user to declare queues of different sizes. Notice the distinction between size and length. We can evaluate both measures:

```
My_Buffer.Size
Queues.Length_Of(My_Buffer)
```

Both expressions return an integer value. The first indicates how many items the buffer *can* hold while the second indicates how many items the buffer *does* hold.

The implementation of the package body is as follows:

```
package body Queues is
  procedure Clear (The_Queue : in out Queue) is
  begin
    The_Queue.The_Back := 0;
  end Clear;
  procedure Add (The_Item     : in      Integer;
                 To_The_Queue : in out Queue   ) is
  begin
    To_The_Queue.The_Items(To_The_Queue.The_Back + 1) := The_Item;
    To_The_Queue.The_Back := To_The_Queue.The_Back + 1;
  exception
    when Constraint_Error => raise Overflow;
  end Add;
  procedure Remove (The_Item     :     out Integer;
                    From_The_Queue : in out Queue   ) is
    Back : Natural renames From_The_Queue.The_Back;
  begin
    if Back = 0 then
      raise Underflow;
```

```
      else
        The_Item := From_The_Queue.The_Items(1);
        Back := Back - 1;
        From_The_Queue.The_Items(1..Back) :=
            From_The_Queue.The_Items(2..Back + 1);
      end if;
    end Remove;
    function Length_Of (The_Queue : in Queue) return Natural is
    begin
      return The_Queue.The_Back;
    end Length_Of;
  end Queues;
```

A user of this package can explicitly Clear any declared Queue. This operation sets the back pointer to its initial state. In a Remove operation, we first check for Underflow, and then we extract the front of the queue. Then we slide each item to the previous location. An Add operation will raise Constraint_Error if The_Back + 1 is outside the range 1...Size. If Constraint_Error is detected, the exception Overflow is raised. Notice that the queue's integrity is not destroyed upon Overflow; this permits the user to gracefully recover from the error.

Let us examine another application of Ada packages as abstract data types. When modeling a process control system, a programmer may need to abstract entities such as storage tanks. Ada obviously does not have them as a primitive type, but private types can be used to provide the abstraction. A package user might see storage tank types as:

```
package Storage is
  type Tank    is limited private;
  type Percent is delta 0.01 range 0.0..100.0;
  procedure Add    (Amount : in Percent; To   : in out Tank);
  procedure Remove (Amount : in Percent; From : in out Tank);
  function  Level  (Place  : in Tank) return Percent;
  Is_Empty,
  Is_Full : exception;
private
  type Tank is new Percent;
end Storage;
```

Again, we have used subprograms to provide the operations on our abstract data type. The subprograms were arranged as constructors (the procedures) and selectors (the functions).

Notice that Tank has a simple representation. Encapsulating it, however, prevents a user from violating the abstraction by, for example, directly adding two Tank objects together. Also, the limited private declaration makes it impossible to assign one Tank object to another. Instead, we must Remove from one Tank object while adding to another. Additional safety is built in with the use of exceptions. Exceptions need to be raised *before* anything illegal is attempted (such as filling a Tank too full). We shall see how this works after examining the following implementation:

```
package body Storage is
  procedure Add (Amount : in Percent; To : in out Tank) is
    -- add the Amount to the Tank object To
  begin
    To := To + Tank(Amount);
  exception
    when Constraint_Error => raise Is_Full;
  end Add;
  function Level (Place : in Tank) return Percent is
    -- return the Level of the Tank object Place
  begin
    return Percent(Place);
  end Level;
  procedure Remove(Amount : in Percent; From : in out Tank) is
    -- delete the Amount from the Tank object From
  begin
    From := From - Tank(Amount);
  exception
    when Constraint_Error => raise Is_Empty;
  end Remove;
end Storage;
```

Even though the algorithms in the implementation are trivial, they are shielded from the user. We have had to apply several type transformations, but this too is shielded from the user. Note how the predefined exception (Constraint_Error) is captured and then passed on as the user-defined exceptions Is_Empty and Is_Full. It is important to note that we capture the error before the damage is done. Thus, if we try to Add to an almost full Tank object, the Add subprogram will attempt the assignment, but an exception will then be raised. Since we did not complete the assignment (and thus no values would have been copied to the in out parameters), the Tank object will retain the value it had before the exception was raised, thus simplifying error recovery.

Abstract-State Machines

A *state machine*, or *automaton*, is an entity that has well-defined states and operations for changing from state to state. Additionally, there is a means of detecting the current state of the machine. We can think of abstract-state machines as simple "black box" objects. A user can act upon the box (with procedures) or examine the attributes of the box (via functions). The latter are considered to be the state. Of course, any actions on the box may change its state.

In terms of form, packages as abstract-state machines do not export types or (usually) objects. In a sense, they look like abstract data types or simple collections of program units. However, the essential difference is that packages used as abstract-state machines have retained state information in the package body. For example, the Transcendental_Functions package declared earlier consisted of several subprograms, but calling one subprogram did not affect any state. In fact, each subprogram was quite independent, and its outcome could never affect the other. For state machines, however, the operations applied do affect the state. For example, we may abstract a Furnace to the user as:

```
package Furnace is
   procedure Set(Temperature : in Float);
   procedure Shut_Down;
   function Is_Running return Boolean;
   function Temperature_Is return Float;
   Overtemp : exception;
end Furnace;
```

As we can with abstract data types, we can categorize our operations as constructors or selectors. The package user can apply only the four given subprograms to either change the state of Furnace or determine the current Temperature. Clearly, the order in which these subprograms are called makes a difference, due to the retained data. Since no types or objects are exported, this package defines only one object. Furthermore, since the package specification defines several subprograms, a complete package body must eventually be supplied.

Another typical example of a state machine is a *lexical analyzer,* which is a machine that can recognize and classify a stream of characters. Such machines are necessary tools for compilers and communication systems. For example, as part of a compiler, we may wish to create a state machine that can recognize identifiers or numbers. A state transition diagram for such a machine is shown in Figure 11.2.

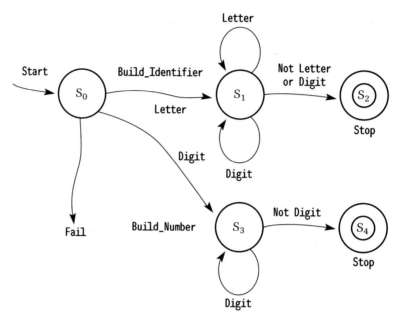

Figure 11.2 State machine for `Lexical_Analyzer`

As seen in the diagram, the machine is initially in a `Start` state. When the first symbol is received, it moves to a `Build_Identifier` state if it is a `Letter` and to a `Build_Number` state otherwise. The machine stays in either state as long as a stream of letters or digits (for `Build_Identifier`) or just digits (for `Build_Number`) is received. Once a different symbol is received, the machine moves to a `Stop` state; at that point, the token has been recognized.

We can define the interface to this abstract state machine as:

```
package Lexical_Analyzer is
   type Token is (None, Invalid, Identifier, Number);
   procedure Set_Start_State;
   procedure Receive_Symbol(A_Character : in Character);
   function Value return Token;
end Lexical_Analyzer;
```

Notice that we have identified the accepting conditions as enumeration literals. A user of this package can continue to send symbols to the state machine without the overhead of explicitly checking to see whether the token has been accepted. If desired, we could easily pass the accepting information as a parameter through `Receive_Symbol`. We have included an `Invalid` literal, which is used if the first symbol is neither a `Letter` nor a `Digit`. We have also included the operation `Set_Start_State` so that the user can reinitialize the state machine.

We can implement our state machine as follows:

```
package body Lexical_Analyzer is
  type State is (Start, Build_Identifier, Build_Number, Stop);
  Present_State : State := Start;
  The_Result : Token := None;
  subtype Alpha is Character range 'A'..'Z';
  subtype Digit is Character range '0'..'9';
  procedure Set_Start_State is
    -- initialize state machine
  begin
    Present_State := Start;
    The_Result    := None;
  end Set_Start_State;
  procedure Receive_Symbol(A_Character : in Character) is
    -- accept a symbol from the transmitter
  begin
    case Present_State is
      when Start =>
        case A_Character is
          when Alpha => Present_State := Build_Identifier;
          when Digit => Present_State := Build_Number;
          when others => The_Result := Invalid;
        end case;
      when Build_Identifier =>
        case A_Character is
          when Alpha | Digit => null;
          when others => Present_State := Stop;
                         The_Result := Identifier;
        end case;
      when Build_Number =>
        case A_Character is
          when Digit => null;
          when others => Present_State := Stop;
                         The_Result := Number;
        end case;
      when Stop => null;
    end case;
  end Receive_Symbol;
  function Value return Token is
  begin
    return The_Result;
  end Value;
end Lexical_Analyzer;
```

This completes our implementation of a simple lexical analyzer. Since we defined State as an enumeration type, it would be quite simple to modify the machine to accept other tokens.

Ada packages derive their power from their ability to encapsulate a local entity and then enforce that abstraction. In the next chapter, we shall study additional packaging concepts involving generic program units.

Summary

- Packages form collections of logically related entities.

- Packages can have two parts—the specification and the body—which can be compiled separately.

- Package specifications can have two parts. The visible part denotes all entities that are exported from the package, and the private part is hidden from outside view.

- Packages can exist as library units or nest inside other units.

- The specification and body of a package must be elaborated before any visible operations are invoked. Library packages are elaborated only once, even though they can be referenced by many other units.

- Entities exported from a package can be made directly visible with a use clause or a renaming declaration.

- Packages that export private or limited private types are said to provide encapsulated types, whose behavior is expressed in the visible part of the package and whose implementation is hidden from the outside view.

- Packages are typically used as named collections of declarations, groups of related program units, abstract data types, or abstract-state machines.

Exercises

1. Create a package specification called Complex which exports a private type called Number. Complete the package by describing a body that includes the operations of addition, subtraction, multiplication, division, setting and retrieving values, and determining angle and length.

2. Create a package, called Metric_English_Conversion, that exports the types Liter and Gallon, Inch and Centimeter, along with constants with the appropriate universal real values needed for conversion.

3. Write the package specification for a unit that brings in the current date in month-day-year form and returns an equivalent Julian date. (A Julian date includes the year number and the day of the year. For example, 128 83 is the 128th day of 1983.)

4. Rewrite the factorial routine in `Transcendental_Functions` without using recursion.

5. Write the package specification for three-dimensional transformations (scale, rotate, translate).

*6. Rewrite the body of `Queues`, this time using access types as the underlying implementation for the `Queue`.

*7. Modify `Lexical_Analyzer` so that an exception occurs whenever an invalid character is received.

*8. Modify `Lexical_Analyzer` so that we can recognize delimiters such as =, +, and -.

9. Explain how abstract-state machines can generally be rewritten as abstract data types. Do such a rewrite for the abstract-state machines presented in this chapter.

CHAPTER 12

Generic
Program Units

The Form of Ada Generic Program Units
Generic Parameters
Applications for Ada Generic Program Units

A s we break down any software system into modules, we usually find subprograms or packages that are similar in purpose. For example, in a situation similar to our data base problem from Chapters 7 and 10, we may need a subprogram to sort values of a specific type prior to producing an output report. This operation can easily be provided with an Ada subprogram, even if the size of the array varies. The following subprogram specification could be used:

```
type Integer_Array is array (Positive range <>) of Integer;
procedure Sort(My_Array : in out Integer_Array);
```

To sort an array having some other type of component, we must create a separate subprogram. This is because Ada's strong typing rules require us to specify the type of every object at compilation time. Thus, we might be forced to write the additional declarations:

```
type Real_Array is array (Positive range <>) of Float;
procedure Sort(My_Array : in out Real_Array);
```

This is an undesirable situation, since we must explicitly create separate forms of packages and subprograms in order to process objects of different types, even if the algorithms are identical. This increases the complexity of these system and thereby degrades the clarity, modifiability, and reliability of the solution. What is needed is the ability to create templates of program units that can be written just once and then tailored to particular needs at translation time. As we shall see, Ada provides a general and very powerful tool to do just this through the use of generic program units.

12.1 The Form of Ada Generic Program Units

Ada permits the creation of generic packages and subprograms. As we shall see later, to achieve the effect of a generic task, we must embed the task inside a package. Generic program units define a unit template, along with generic parameters that provide the facility for tailoring that template to particular needs at translation time.

Since generic units are just templates, they are not executable, and so they cannot be used directly. We must first create instances of the generic unit, and then we can use the corresponding subprogram or package as if it were an ordinary program unit. In a sense, generic units are to subprograms and packages as types are to objects. Figure 12.1 illustrates how our graphic representation of Ada subprograms and packages can be modified to denote a generic unit.

Generic Definition

To create a generic program unit, we can simply take a package or subprogram specification and then add a prefix, called the *generic part*, that defines all of the generic parameters (if any). For example, we can create the following regular subprogram that exchanges two elements of an Integer type:

```
procedure Integer_Exchange(First, Second : in out Integer) is
  Temporary : constant Integer := First;
begin
  First := Second;
  Second := Temporary;
end Integer_Exchange;
```

If this application is needed to exchange other types of elements, it is not necessary to create a new subprogram for every situation. Since in each case the algorithm is identical, we can factor out this similar operation by adding the following generic part to the procedure specification:

```
generic
  type Element is private;
  procedure Exchange(First, Second : in out Element);
```

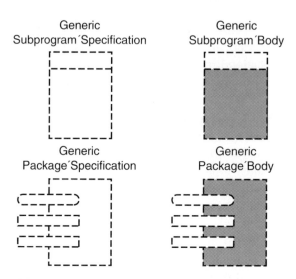

Figure 12.1 Symbols for Ada generic program units

We now write the body as:

```
procedure Exchange(First, Second : in out Element) is
  Temporary :  constant Element := First;
begin
  First := Second;
  Second := Temporary;
end Exchange;
```

Note that the algorithm expressed in the body of this subprogram is identical to that of Integer_Exchange, except for the data types. In the generic part, we declared Element. This forms the parameter for the subprogram template. At every point that the type name Integer was previously used, we (conceptually) substitute the parameter Element. As we shall see later, Ada provides a general generic facility. This permits the declaration of several classes of generic parameters other than types, including values, objects, and other subprograms.

Since a generic program unit can also be a compilation unit, we can submit the Exchange subprogram for compilation. Ada rules require that the names of such units be unique; within a given declarative region, generic unit names may not be overloaded. However, only partial compilation will be achieved until we match the generic formal parameters with the actual parameters from some parent program unit. Since Exchange defines just the template of a regular program unit, we cannot use its facilities directly; we must first create an instance of the generic unit.

Unlike its treatment of nongeneric packages, Ada permits an implementation to require that both a generic unit specification and a body be compiled before we use the generic unit. Creating a generic program unit from an already completed nongeneric unit is actually quite simple. For example, in Chapter 11, we defined a `Queues.Queue` for `Integer` elements. To make this a generic unit, we prefix the original package specification with a generic part that introduces the name of a formal parameter. Then, in the rest of the package specification and body, this name is used to denote the element type. For example, the generic package specification for `Queues` can be written as:

```
generic
   type Item is private;
package Queues is
   type Queue (Size : Positive) is limited private;
   procedure Clear  (The_Queue      : in out Queue);
   procedure Add    (The_Item       : in     Item;
                     To_The_Queue   : in out Queue);
   procedure Remove (The_Item       : out    Item;
                     From_The_Queue : in out Queue);
   function Length_Of (The_Queue : in Queue) return Natural;
   Overflow, Underflow : exception;
private
   type List is array (Positive range <>) of Item;
   type Queue (Size : Positive) is
     record
       The_Items : List(1..Size);
       The_Back : Natural := 0;
     end record;
end Queues;
```

Similar action is taken for the package body, replacing every occurrence of the `Integer` element with the formal name `Item`:

```
package body Queues is
   procedure Clear (The_Queue : in out Queue) is
   begin
     The_Queue.The_Back := 0;
   end Clear;
   procedure Add (The_Item    : in     Item;
                  To_The_Queue : in out Queue) is
```

```
begin --Add
  To_The_Queue.The_Items(To_The_Queue.The_Back + 1) := The_Item;
  To_The_Queue.The_Back := To_The_Queue.The_Back + 1;
exception
  when Constraint_Error => raise Overflow;
end Add;
procedure Remove (The_Item       : out    Item;
                  From_The_Queue : in out Queue) is
  Back : Natural renames From_The_Queue.The_Back;
begin
  if Back = 0 then
    raise Underflow;
  else
    The_Item := From_The_Queue.The_Items(1);
    Back := Back - 1;
    From_The_Queue.The_Items(1..Back) :=
                From_The_Queue.The_Items(2..Back + 1);
  end if;
end Remove;
function Length_Of (The_Queue : in Queue) is
begin
  return The_Queue.The_Back;
end Length_Of;
end Queues;
```

In the next section, we shall see how this formal program unit can be used for many different types of actual elements.

Generic Instantiation

Instantiation is defined here as the process of creating an instance of a generic subprogram or package. As part of the instantiation process, we provide an identifier that will name the regular program unit. We must also match the generic parameters with actual parameters (as we match actual and formal parameters in subprograms). We fill in the generic template by making a one-to-one substitution of every occurrence of a generic formal parameter with the corresponding actual parameter. From that point, elaboration of the completed template continues as if a regular subprogram or package had been defined.

Using the example from the previous section, we can declare several instances of the generic units Exchange and Queues:

```
procedure Integer_Exchange   is new Exchange(Integer);
procedure Float_Exchange     is new Exchange(Element => Float);
procedure Character_Exchange is new Exchange(Element => Character);
```

Note that the form in which the generic actual parameters are defined is syntactically similar to a subprogram invocation:

```
package Integer_Queues   is new Queues(Item => Integer);
package Character_Queues is new Queues(Item => Character);
```

As before, we have used named parameter association in the last two examples to improve the readability of the declaration. Note also that a generic instantiation can be invoked at any point that a subprogram or a package can be declared. Of course, the name of the generic unit must be visible at the point of instantiation.

Now that we have created instances of the generic unit Exchange, we can use the regular program units directly, as the following illustrates:

```
My_Character, Your_Character : Character;
```

```
Character_Exchange(My_Character, Your_Character);
```

As we will discuss further in Chapter 18, the predefined package Text_IO exports a number of nested generic units. Like packages and subprograms, generic units need not be library units, but they can be nested inside other units. For example, Text_IO.Integer_IO is a nested generic package that provides I/O facilities for integer types. Before we use these resources, we must instantiate this nested generic with an appropriate type, such as:

```
type Index is range 0..1_000_000;
package Index_IO  is new Text_IO.Integer_IO(Index);
package Positive_IO is new Text_IO.Integer_IO(Positive);
```

12.2   Generic Parameters

In this section, we examine the various classes of generic parameters. The different kinds of parameters can be categorized as:

- Generic type parameters
- Generic value and object parameters
- Generic subprogram parameters

It is important to note that *generic parameters are never static*; hence, they cannot be used in static expressions.

Generic Type Parameters

As was observed in the discussions on subprograms and packages in Chapters 8 and 11, respectively, Ada permits us to pass only object values to such program units. However, as we saw in the previous section, it is sometimes necessary or convenient to pass types as parameters. Although the strong typing rules do not permit us to pass types to regular program units at execution time we can achieve the same effect through the use of generic type parameters. Just as there are actual and formal subprogram parameters, there are also actual and formal generic parameters.

Since Ada provides a rich variety of type constructs, we can use a number of different generic type parameters. In any event, the formal parameter must always be matched with a compatible actual parameter. Ada enforces this rule so that we can be assured of the safety data typing offers us, even across separately compiled units. If the two types are incompatible, a compiler will mark a semantic error (if the error can be detected at compilation time), or the system will raise the exception Constraint_Error (if the error is detected at elaboration time).

The following list summarizes the form of all generic type parameters and defines a compatible actual parameter. The names starting with an uppercase letter are not reserved, nor do they have special significance in Ada; they represent only their structural function.

```
type General_Purpose is limited private;
    -- matches any data type
type Element is private:
    -- matches any type that permits assignment and
    -- tests for (in)equality
type Link is access Some_Object;
    -- matches any access type designating the same type
    -- of object
type Enumeration is (<>);
    -- matches any discrete (integer and enumeration) type
type Integer_Element is range <>;
    -- matches any integer type
type Fixed_Element is delta <>;
    -- matches any fixed-point type
type Float_Element is digits <>;
    -- matches any floating-point type
type Constrained_Array is array (Some_Index) of Some_Element;
    -- matches any constrained array of the same
    -- dimensions, index types, and type of components
```

```
type Unconstrained_Array is array (Some_Type range <>)
   of Some_Element;
   -- matches any unconstrained array of the same
   -- dimensions, index types, and type of components
```

In the body of a generic unit, the operations and attributes that are available for an actual type are also available for a corresponding generic type. Thus, for example, if we use Float_Element as declared above, the body of the generic unit can apply any of the predefined floating-point operators. Correspondingly, for a private generic type, only assignment and test for (in)equality are available. For limited private generic types, no operators are available except those defined as generic subprogram parameters.

Unlike its rules for subprogram parameters, Ada permits the definition of dependencies among generic type parameters. For example, we can define the following general-purpose sort routine:

```
generic
   type Element is (<>);
   type List is array (Positive range <>) of Element;
procedure Sort(Table : in out List);
```

In this generic subprogram declaration, the component of the array type List is also a generic formal parameter. We can provide a subprogram instantiation as follows:

```
type Color is (Black, Green, Red, Blue, White);
type Color_Table is array (Positive range <>) of Color;
procedure Sort_Color is new Sort (Element => Color,
                                  List    => Color_Table);
```

In the following chapter, we shall examine a moderately complex example using generic type parameters. In addition, in Chapter 18, we shall see that Ada relies heavily upon this generic facility to accommodate input/output processing.

Generic Value and Object Parameters

Ada also permits the definition of values and objects as generic formal parameters. The declaration of such a parameter takes the form of a variable declaration, with the addition of the key words in (for a value parameter) or in out (for an object parameter). The mode out is not available for generic object parameters. If desired, a previously declared generic type parameter can be used as the type of a generic value or object parameter.

When using a generic value parameter, we must match the formal parameter with a constant or a variable of the same type. Ada then treats the value as a constant for the remainder of the program unit. The benefit of this class of generic parameter is that we can instantiate a program unit and provide constant limits to our algorithms or object abstractions. In a sense, this facility permits the creation of high-level language macros. (A *macro* is a template that can be called as if it were a primitive feature of the target language.) For example, we can define the following package, which defines a generic terminal as an abstract data type:

```
generic
   Rows    : in Integer := 24;
   Columns : in Integer := 80;
package Terminal is...
```

We may then create several instances of this generic package:

```
package Micro_Terminal is new Terminal(24, 40);
package Word_Processor is new Terminal(Rows => 66, Columns => 132);
package Programmer_Terminal is new Terminal;
```

Notice how we have used several forms of the generic instantiation. In the first example, we used positional parameter association; in the second example, we used named parameter association to improve the clarity of the declaration. Since we provided default values to the generic parameters, it was not necessary to insert any actual parameters in the third example.

To declare a generic object parameter, we use the key words **in out**. We must match the formal parameter with a variable of the same type. The effect of an instantiation is to rename the formal parameter to the actual parameter. As a result, this facility permits us to access an object global to the subprogram or package, which is not normally recommended programming practice. A generic object parameter may not be given a default expression value. Generic value parameters and discriminated types can be used to achieve similar purposes. For example, earlier in this chapter, in the generic Queues package, we parameterized the type with the discriminant Size. In the same manner, we could give each object of the type Queue a unique maximum length. What advantage would we gain if we wrote the following code?

```
generic
   type Item is private;
   The_Size : in Positive;
package Queues is ...
```

The generic value parameter The_Size could be used to establish the maximum size of all objects declared of the type Queue. Thus, we have a tradeoff: By using a discriminant, each object can be parameterized with different values, but by using generic value parameters, all objects from the same instantiation share the same characteristics.

Generic Subprogram Parameters

Ada also permits us to pass subprograms as parameters to generic units. For example, the Terminal package defined previously may need to Send and Receive data using different protocols, depending upon the kind of physical terminal it is associated with. We would still like to use a generic package, since our logical abstraction of every terminal is virtually the same in regard to the way we format a screen. We can then treat Send and Receive as generic subprogram parameters:

```
generic
   Rows    : in Integer := 24;
   Columns : in Integer := 80;
   with procedure Send   (Value : in Character);
   with procedure Receive(Value : out Character);
package Terminal is ...
```

When we instantiate Terminal, we must provide the names of two sub-programs whose declarations are compatible with Send and Receive. (*Compatible* means here that the actual subprogram has parameters of the same type, mode, order, and constraints as the formal subprogram, plus a matching return value if we are dealing with functions.) For example:

```
procedure Micro_Send   (Value : in Character) is ...
procedure Micro_Receive(Value : out Character) is ...
package Micro_Terminal is new
   Terminal (Rows     => 24,
             Columns => 40,
             Send    => Micro_Send,
             Receive => Micro_Receive);
```

Ada also permits the declaration of defaults for generic subprogram parameters, using one of two forms. In the first case, we use the key word is, followed by the name of the default subprogram. For example:

```
with Text_IO;
generic
   Rows    : in Integer := 24;
   Columns : in Integer := 80;
   with procedure Send (Value : in Character) is Text_IO.Put;
   with procedure Receive(Value : out Character) is Text_IO.Get;
package Terminal is ...
```

In the other form, we use the key word is, followed by the compound symbol <>. In this case, we can omit the corresponding actual parameter if a subprogram with the same name as and having a specification compatible with specification the generic subprogram parameter is visible at the point of instantiation. For example, consider the following declarations:

```
generic
   Rows    : in Integer := 24;
   Columns : in Integer := 80;
   with procedure Send   (Value : in Character) is <>;
   with procedure Receive(Value : out Character) is <>;
package Terminal is ...
```

We can instantiate the package if we have compatible Send and Receive subprograms visible at that point. (Again, compatible means that the subprogram declarations are identical, without considering the names of formal parameters or the presence or values of defaults.) For example:

```
procedure Send   (Value : in Character);
procedure Receive(Value : out Character);
package Dumb_Terminal is new Terminal;
```

Since the local Send and Receive are visible at the point of instantiation, we do not have to provide any actual parameters to match the generic formal subprograms.

These last two forms of subprogram parameter defaults are primarily a convenience for the programmer. Since they reduce the clarity of the generic instantiation somewhat—they make it more difficult to determine what is actually being imported by the instantiation—it is generally better practice to explicitly name the actual subprogram parameter.

12.3   Applications for Ada Generic Program Units

There are three classical models for applying generic units:

- Using generic units as reusable software components
- Using generic units as state machine templates
- Using generic units to control visibility

The following sections examine each of these models.

Generic Units as Reusable Software Components

As we have seen with the generic Queues package, generic units permit us to parameterize nongeneric units so that they can be applied to a wide range of uses. The units are reusable components that permit developers to construct large, complex systems out of existing generic units. The primary benefit of this approach is that developers do not have to write as much new code. In addition, developers can have a higher level of confidence in the quality of solutions by building them from components whose behavior is well defined.

For example, we have already examined how to write the specification for a general-purpose sorting procedure, but we can do even better. The example presented earlier applied only to elements of a discrete type. Consider the following example:

```
generic
   type Item is private:
   type Index is (<>);
   type Items is array (Index) of Item;
   with function "<" (Left, Right : in Item) return Boolean is <>;
procedure Sort(The_Items : in out Items);.
```

Here we sort arrays of any constrained index type and of any nonlimited component type. By virtue of importing the type Item as a private type, we implicitly make operations of assignment and tests for equality and inequality available. In addition, since importing a private type does not implicitly import any relational operations, we must explicitly import the operator "<" so that the body of Sort compares individual items of the array The_Items. As in Chapter 10, the quick-sort algorithm is used:

```
procedure Sort (The_Items : in out Items) is
   Front : Index := The_Items'First;
   Back  : Index := The_Items'Last;
   procedure Swap is new Exchange (Item);
   pragma Inline(Swap);
   procedure Partition is
      Mid_Point : constant Index := Index'Val
         ((Index'Pos (Front) + Index'Pos (Back)) / 2);
      Mid-Value : Item renames The_Items (Mid_Point);
   begin
      Outer:
      loop
         while (The_Items (Front) < Mid-Value)
            and (Front /= The_Items'Last)
         loop
            Front := Index'Succ (Front);
         end loop;
```

```
          while (Mid_Value < The-Items (Back))
            and (Back /= The_Items'First)
          loop
            Back := Index'Pred (Back);
          end loop;
          if Front <= Back then
            if Front < Back then
              Swap (The_Items (Front), The_Items (Back));
            end if;
            if Front /= The_Items'Last then
              Front := Index'Succ (Front);
            end if;
            if Back /= The_Items'First then
              Back := Index'Pred (Back);
            end if;
          end if;
          exit Outer when (Front > Back)
            or ((Front = The_Items'Last)
           and (Back = The_Items'First));
        end loop Outer;
      end Partition;
    begin
      if Items'Length < 2 then
        return;
      end if;
      Partition;
      if The_Items'First < Back then
        Sort (The_Items (The_Items'First..Back));
      end if;
      if Front < The_Items'Last then
        Sort (The_Items (Front..The_Items'Last));
      end if;
    end Sort;
```

Notice the use of type and object attributes. The attributes Pred and Succ
are used where addition and subtraction were used in Chapter 10. Also consider the calculation of the midpoint of the array. Since Index is declared
using a discrete type template, it can be instantiated with an enumeration
type. Because addition and division are not defined for enumeration types,
we use the Pos attribute to convert Index values to integer values, and the Val
attribute to convert integer values to Index values. Lastly, notice that Mid_Value
simply renames the middle Item, rather than declaring a new Item object.

The generic formal subprogram parameter ("<") is used in the `while` loops of procedure `Partition`. Since this operation has been imported into `Sort`, it is directly visible in the body.

With this unit, we can now provide an instantiation that sorts characters in ascending order.

```
procedure String_Sort is new Sort(Item  => Character,
                                  Index => Positive,
                                  Items => String,
                                  "<"   => "<");
```

To sort in descending order, we simply change the actual parameter for "<":

```
procedure Descending_Sort is new Sort (Item  => Character,
                                       Index => Positive,
                                       Items => String,
                                       "<"   => ">");
```

In the previous chapter, we introduced the package `Transcendental_Functions`, which exported `Cos`, `Sin`, and `Tan` functions. We make this unit generic simply by extracting all type-dependent information, just as we did in `Sort`:

```
generic
   type Real is digits <>;
package Transcendental_Functions is
   function Cos(Angle : in Real) return Real;
   function Sin(Angle : in Real) return Real;
   function Tan(Angle : in Real) return Real;
end Transcendental_Functions;
```

In this manner, we instantiate the package to provide `Sin`, `Cos`, and `Tan` functions to any desired accuracy. Again, type and object attributes are the key to writing the body of this unit so that it adapts to any actual instantiation.

Using Generic Units as State Machine Templates

Consider the `Furnace` abstract-state machine from the previous chapter. This package does not define a `Furnace` data type; rather, the state of the entire package represents the furnace. Using a package such as this, a program could include at most one `Furnace`, since packages cannot be replicated like data type values can.

By making the package into a generic unit, we can produce multiple furnaces. Notice that making `Furnace` generic involves only a one-line change to its specification, and no change to its body:

```
generic
package Furnace is

   ...

end Furnace;
```

Notice that we have an empty generic part: No generic parameters are declared. The only purpose in making the unit generic is so that we can replicate the state in its body. The following are example instantiations of this generic unit:

```
package Car_Heater    is new Furnace;
package Garage_Heater is new Furnace;
package Home_Furnace  is new Furnace;
```

Using Generic Units to Control Visibility

Generic units are usually created as reusable software components, but they can also be used to decouple parts of a large program. For example, in Chapter 5, we studied the design of a program that built a document concordance. As Figure 12.2 illustrates, the program uses the packages `Words` and `Lines` in every other unit. However, it may be desirable to decouple the design of the abstractions for `Words` and `Lines` from such packages as `Concordance`. Decoupling allows each component to be independent.

For example, the package `Concordance` can be defined independently of any abstraction (`Words` or `Lines`) as long as we use generic parameters to import the resources that `Concordance` needs. In this sense, we use the generic parameters to explicitly indicate the resources that we must make visible to the package. Thus, instead of writing the package `Concordance` as a regular package, we can express it as the generic:

```
generic
   type Word is private;
   type Line is private;
   with function Value_Of (The Word : in Word) return String;
   with function Image_Of (The_Line : in Line) return String;
package Concordance is
   procedure Start;
   procedure Add (The_Word : in Word;
                  The_Line : in Line);
   procedure Make_Report;
   Overflow : exception;
end Concordance;
```

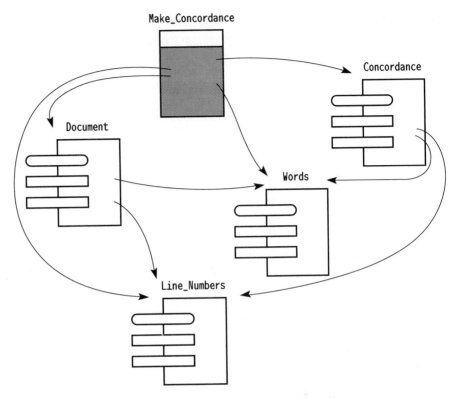

Figure 12.2 Architecture of Make_Concordance

To achieve flexibility we imported Word and Line as private types. In addition, we must import two functions, Value_Of and Image_Of, which enable the package Concordance to produce the report.

We cannot use this unit directly; we must instantiate it. For example, in the main program Make_Concordance, we might include the following nested instantiation:

```
package Local_Concordance is new Concordance
   (Word     => Words.Word,
    Line     => Lines.Line,
    Value_Of => Words.Value_Of,
    Image_Of => Lines.Line'Image);
```

Notice that we can apply an attribute to the actual generic parameter that matches Image_Of, because Ada rules treat attributes as if they were special functions. (Because we have decoupled the design of the packages Lines and Words from the unit Concordance, we can freely alter the units Lines and Words without affecting Concordance, although we may have to recompile the instantiation.

Summary
- Generic units include generic packages and generic subprograms. They serve as templates of nongeneric units.

- An instantiation creates an instance of a generic unit.

- Generic parameters serve as imports to a generic unit.

- Generic parameters include generic type parameters, generic value and object parameters, and generic subprogram parameters.

- Generic units are usually used to form libraries of reusable software components from which larger, more complex systems may be composed. In addition, generic units can be used to decouple the visibility among units of a large system.

Exercises

1. Write an instantiation for the generic Transcendental_Functions program unit, with Real having 10 digits of significance. First use positional notation and then named parameter association.

*2. What changes must be made to the body of Transcendental_Functions in order to incorporate the requirements of Exercise 1?

3. Modify the generic part of Transcendental_Functions to import Series_Length. What changes must be made to the body?

4. Write the specification for a matrix package in which we can add, subtract, and multiply matrices. Next, add a generic part to parameterize the type of the matrix components. Will your generic unit work for complex and imaginary numbers?

5. Rewrite the specification for Lexical_Analyzer from the last chapter, adding a generic part that permits the user to specify the accepting characters in the set of Alpha and in the set of Digits. Provide an instantiation to demonstrate its use.

*6. Complete the implementation of the generic form of Transcendental_ Functions.

7. Write a generic stack package.

*8. Modify the generic Sort procedure so that it applies to structures other than arrays.

*9. Can a generic apply to either fixed-point or floating-point actual parameters?

*10. Write the specification (including generic part) for a matrix operations package that will work with integer, floating-point, fixed-point, or coplex number components.

*11. Exchange specifications written for Exercise 10 with another student. Write the body for the other student's specification. Did he or she leave out any needed generic formal parameters?

CHAPTER

13

The Third Design Problem: Generic Tree Package

Define the Problem
Identify the Objects
Identify the Operations
Establish the Visibility
Establish the Interface
Evaluate the Objects
Implement Each Object

P ackages and generic program units are powerful facilities that assist the programmer in managing the complexity of a software solution. As we observed in Chapter 12, generic units facilitate the reuse of software components. Such components extend the power of the Ada language by packaging new abstractions in a form that can be easily applied across problem domains.

In this chapter, we shall apply our object-oriented method to build one such reusable component, the binary tree. A tree is not a primitive type in Ada, so we must build our own abstract data type. Furthermore, we want this abstraction to apply to trees of many types; indeed, we want to reuse our abstraction for trees of integers, trees of records, and perhaps even trees whose values are objects of another abstract data type. When we are done constructing this component, we will see how we can apply our generic tree unit by completing the body of the package Concordance from Chapter 5.

13.1   Define the Problem

Programmers use trees in a number of diverse applications, including data base retrieval, the intermediate representation of computer programs, game planning, and natural language translation. In the real world, we find many objects that exhibit treelike behavior: An organization chart, the outline of

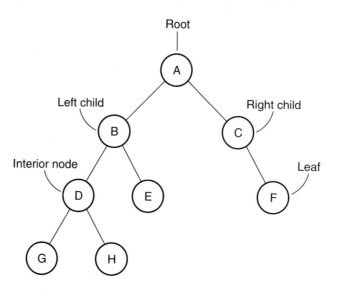

Figure 13.1 A binary tree

a speech, and a genealogy are but a few examples. Trees derive much of their value from the fact that they can represent a hierarchy among items. This capacity distinguishes them from abstractions such as queues, which are one-dimensional.

As we see in Figure 13.1, a tree can be represented as a collection of nodes arranged in a hierarchical fashion. Each node can have a value; in this figure we see eight nodes labeled from A to H. Node A is designated as the root of the tree. (Abstract trees are drawn with their root at the top, unlike their organic counterparts.) A simple path connects each node with its adjoining node on the next level. Thus, we say that B and C are the children of node A; A is the parent of nodes B and C, and B and C are siblings. In a binary tree, each node can have two children at most, and they are designated as the left or right child. If a node has no children (such as E), it resides on the frontier of the tree and is called a leaf or a terminal node. Otherwise, the node is an interior node.

Our job is to develop a generic unit that captures this abstraction of the binary tree. Furthermore, we will add the requirement that the unit we design must apply to trees whose node values are of any type.

13.2   Identify the Objects

We have defined the problem sufficiently; the problem contains one object of primary interest. We shall name this class of objects the type **Tree**. Certainly, we could define a simple type declaration for Tree, such as the one we defined in Chapter 6, but simply exporting an unencapsulated type does not capture our abstraction. Rather, we need to hide the representation of the type Tree in a package and then export only those operations that support our abstraction of a tree.

Notice that the problem also contains an object of secondary interest. We mentioned earlier that each node of a tree can have a value; therefore, we must concern ourselves with the class of objects from which these values are drawn. For the moment, assume that node values can be of any non-limited type. As we shall soon see, this decision will play an important part in defining the outside view of our component. Indeed, it is this decision that makes it possible for us to generalize our tree abstraction and provide it as a generic unit.

We have also eliminated the possibility of using our tree component for node values that are of a limited private type. Our rationale is quite sound. Limited private types disallow the operations of assignment and the test for equality. These operations would make it clumsy for us to assign and retrieve the values of a tree node. However, nonlimited types (which include all other classes of types) are not restricted in this way; we can apply our tree to the widest classes of types while placing only minimal restrictions on the node value type, which we will call Item.

13.3   Identify the Operations

This step is critical in the construction of our abstraction. Indeed, identifying the operations establishes the behavior of our abstraction as viewed from the outside. As is the case with all the other abstractions we have examined, we can classify these operations as selectors or constructors.

Tree constructors include all those operations that alter the state of an object. In particular, we need an operation that copies one tree to another and a second operation that makes an empty tree:

- Copy   Copy one tree object to another.
- Clear   Make the tree empty.

We also need an operation that adds a new node to a given tree. The challenge here is to specify this operation so that we cannot lose track of any existing nodes. Our approach will be to create a new node and make it the root of the tree. We will attach the old root as one of the children of the new node:

- Construct   Create a new node with the given value and make it the new root; take the old root and attach it as a child of the new root.

To give the greatest degree of flexibility, we will let the client of this operation choose to which child we attach the old root. Construct gives us one way to alter the shape of a tree by adding new nodes, but we also need an operation that lets us reorganize the relationships among nodes. Thus, we will include an operation that swaps one of the children of the root node with another tree:

- Swap_Child   Swap the named child of the root node with another tree.

Like Construct, the semantics of this operation are defined so that we cannot easily lose track of any nodes. Thus, when we replace the child of the root node with the tree, instead of just throwing that child subtree away, we save it by attaching it as the root of the second tree.

We need one other constructor. Given that a node has a value, we need some way to alter that value. Thus, we will include the operation:

- Set_Item   Set the value of a node to the given value.

Turning to the selectors for this abstraction, our approach will be to provide a full complement of operations that roughly parallel the collection of constructors. Thus, since we include a constructor that copies one tree to another, we also include a selector that tests whether two trees have equal values. Similarly, Clear makes a tree empty. As a result, we shall include a selector that tests whether a tree is indeed empty:

- Is_Equal   Return True if the two given trees have an equal value.
- Is_Null   Return True if the given tree is empty.

Paralleling the constructor Swap_Child, we must include an operation that returns a child of the root node of a given tree. Since a child of a node is itself a tree, this operation actually returns an object of type Tree:

- Child_Of   Return a child of the root node of the given tree. The name of the child (left or right) is specified by the client.

Finally, we need an operation that parallels the constructor Set_Item:

- Item_Of   Return the value of the root of the given tree.

As we have done in all our previous design examples, we must now consider the exceptional conditions. Specifically, we must consider the possibility of running out of storage with operations such as Copy and Construct. In addition, there are some operations that require the use of a nonempty tree. In particular, Set_Item, Swap_Child, Item_Of, and Child_Of all require that a nonnull tree be used. For example, Set_Item clearly could not proceed if there were no root node.

We can divide these exceptional conditions into two classes:

- Overflow   There is not enough storage left to complete the desired operation.
- Tree_Is_Null   The desired operation cannot proceed because the given tree is empty.

This completes our characterization of the type Tree, but we must also consider the type Item. To do so, we must reverse our perspective of the type Tree. Rather than worrying about what operations we must export, we must consider what operations Item must import to our generic tree package. As we discussed, we want to make this component as general as possible, and so we have defined the type Item as any nonlimited type. Thus, at a minimum, we must permit assignment and test for equality for objects of this type. This is not as hard as it sounds, for as we shall see in a later section, Ada generic parameters give us the precise mechanism for expressing these imports.

13.4   Establish the Visibility

In this problem, establishing the visibility of our objects of interest is straightforward: We will export only the type Tree and its operations from this generic package, but the package itself cannot see anything except the type Item. In this manner, we are building a component that is very loosely coupled.

This situation is fairly common among generic units. As we studied in the previous chapter, generic units are not only useful in building reusable software components, but they also serve to control the visibility among compilation units. As we see here, by defining our tree abstraction as independent of any other abstraction (except the type Item), we effectively decouple it from every other unit in our solution space.

13.5   Establish the Interface

At this point, we can capture our design decisions regarding the tree abstraction in a generic unit:

```
generic
  type Item is private;
package Trees is
  type Tree is private;
  type Child is (Left, Right);
  Null_Tree : constant Tree;
  procedure Copy     (From_The_Tree : in     Tree;
                      To_The_Tree   : in out Tree);
  procedure Clear    (The_Tree      : in out Tree);
  procedure Construct(The_Item      : in     Item;
                      And_The_Tree  : in out Tree;
                      On_The_Child  : in     Child);
  procedure Set_Item (Of_The_Tree   : in out Tree;
                      To_The_Item   : in     Item);
  procedure Swap_Child (The_Child    : in     Child;
                        Of_The_Tree  : in out Tree;
                        And_The_Tree : in out Tree);
  function Is_Equal (Left  : in Tree;
                     Right : in Tree) return Boolean;
  function Is_Null (The_Tree : in Tree) return Boolean;
  function Item_Of (The_Tree : in Tree) return Item;
  function Child_Of (The_Tree  : in Tree;
                     The_Child : in Child) return Tree;
  Overflow,
  Tree_Is_Null : exception:
private
  ...
end Trees;
```

As we have done with many other abstract data types, we have written our constructors as procedures, selectors are exported as functions, and exceptional conditions are explicitly declared. Also, notice how we have imported the type Item: By using a private type, we have asserted that we can instantiate this component with any nonlimited type. As we studied in the previous chapter, this declaration also implicitly provides the operations of assignment and the test for equality, as our problem demands.

13.6   Evaluate the Objects

In Chapter 10 we discussed three methods of evaluating objects. These methods involved coupling, cohesion, and classification of operations. In this chapter we present two more methods involving the classification of operations:

1. *Identify exceptional conditions.* Most operations will have special cases in which they cannot be used. These cases should be considered, and exceptions defined for them.

2. *Exceptional conditions should have a corresponding selector.* Special cases that are treated as exceptions should have an associated operation that can be used to observe the case.

Identify Exceptional Conditions

One of the fundamental goals of software engineering is reliability. As we discussed in Chapter 2, reliable software prevents failure. The first step in prevention is to identify the conditions that can cause failure. Further, again from Chapter 2, reliability must be built from the start—from the design. It is not possible to build a reliable implementation for an unreliable interface. Conditions that can cause failure should be identified at the interface level.

Many failure, or exceptional, conditions can be identified simply by restricting the values on which an operation will work. This can be done using types. Consider a square root function:

```
function Square_Root (Radicand : Float) return Float;
```

This function will fail to return a meaningful value when applied to negative numbers. We can explicitly state this condition using a subtype:

```
subtype Non_Negative is Float range 0.0..Float'Last;
function Square_Root (Radicand : Non_Negative) return Non_Negative;
```

While better defining the values on which Square_Root will operate, we have also better defined the values it will return.

Other exceptional conditions cannot be so easily defined. In these cases an interface can declare an exception that identifies the condition. There is no way for the Trees unit to ensure that Item_Of will never be called with a null tree. Yet the function Item_Of must act reliably and predictably in such a call. Exceptions are Ada's mechanism for allowing Item_Of to be reliable without returning a value.

Exceptional Conditions Should Have a Corresponding Selector

If we were to explain to a user when the exception Tree_Is_Null is raised, we would inevitably mention the condition of a tree being null. We have made this condition explicit in our abstraction by defining the boolean function

Is_Null. By defining both the exception and its corresponding condition, we make the abstraction more complete and self-documenting. Also, we provide users with the flexibility of checking the condition themselves, rather than waiting for the exception to be raised. Suppose we had a Tree object named T and we wanted to examine every item on its leftmost branch. This algorithm could be written using either the exception or the condition:

```
begin                                 while not Is_Null(T) loop
   loop                                  ... Item_Of(T)...
      ... Item_Of(T)...                  T := Child_Of(T, Left);
      T := Child_Of(T, Left);         end loop;
   end loop;
exception
   when Tree_Is_Null => null;
end;
```

The left-hand example is considered bad coding style because it essentially uses the exception as an implicit goto. Reaching the end of the tree is neither "exceptional" nor an error; we fully expect it to happen every time we execute the code. The right-hand example is explicit and understandable.

Actually, notice that we have exported the "is null" condition twice: once as a function and once as T = Null_Tree. Generally, exporting any operation more than once is bad practice, since it reduces the maintainability of the interlace.

13.7   Implement Each Object

Let us turn to the inside view of this component and consider its complete implementation. First, we must decide on an implementation of the type Tree, which will then drive the form of the rest of our solution. The most obvious approach is to implement the type Tree in a manner that literally reflects its abstraction in the problem space. Thus, we can represent Tree as a pointer to a node, where the type Node is a record containing an item and two subtrees. This implementation involves recursive types, and so we must apply an incomplete type, as Ada rules demand. However, we can take advantage of this requirement and hide the full definition of the incomplete type. Thus, in the private part of this package, we can write:

```
type Node;
type Tree is access Node;
Null Tree : constant Tree := null;
```

In the component body, we can complete the definition of the type Node as:

```
type Node is
  record
    The_Item      : Item;
    Left_Subtree,
    Right_Subtree : Tree;
  end record;
```

Let us now examine the implementation of each operation in the order in which it appears in the package body. As we shall see, we need only apply some simple algorithms. Some of these algorithms are also quite elegant as a result of the recursive nature of the tree. However, do not be fooled by this simplicity. Indeed, the critical reader might wonder why we are bothering to build the tree as a private type. There is a good reason for encapsulating our design decisions. By specifying the outside view of our abstraction, we insulate any clients from the bothersome details of our implementation decisions. This approach gives us, the implementors, the freedom to choose whatever representation we wish, as long as it satisfies the semantics of the outside view. We can alter these implementation details without disturbing any clients (although we may force them to be recompiled).

Copy is the first operation we shall study. Because a tree is recursive (that is, a binary tree is defined as a root node with maximum of two subtrees as children), we can implement Copy recursively. Our algorithm proceeds by first seeing if the source tree is empty. If it is, we simply make the destination tree empty. Otherwise, we allocate the new node as the root of the destination tree and call Copy again to copy first the left and then the right subtrees:

```
procedure Copy (From_The_Tree : in     Tree;
                To_The_Tree   : in out Tree) is
begin
  if From_The_Tree = null then
    To_The_Tree := null;
  else
    To_The_Tree :=
      new Node'(The_Item      => From_The_Tree.The_Item,
                Left_Subtree  => null,
                Right_Subtree => null);
    Copy(From_The_Tree.Left_Subtree, To_The_Tree.Left_Subtree);
    Copy(From_The_Tree.Right_Subtree, To_The_Tree.Right_Subtree);
  end if;
```

```
exception
   when Storage_Error => raise Overflow;
end Copy;
```

Notice how we can use an aggregate to establish the value of a newly created node in just one statement. Since this allocator might raise the exception Storage_Error, we must include an exception handler that captures this exception and then raises an exception with a meaningful name (Overflow).

The body of Clear is simple: It applies our convention that an empty tree is one whose value is null:

```
procedure Clear (The_Tree : in out Tree) is
begin
   The_Tree := null;
end Clear;
```

Construct proceeds much like the beginning of Copy, by allocating a new node. However, since the given tree may already contain nodes, the semantics of this operation require that we save the existing nodes by attaching them as a subtree of the new node. Thus, the procedure includes a parameter that specifies which child to use:

```
procedure Construct (The_Item    : in     Items
                     And_The_Tree : in out Tree;
                     On_The_Child : in     Child) is
begin
   if On The Child = Left then
      And_The_Tree := new Node'(The_Item       => The_Item,
                                Left_Subtree   => And_The_Tree,
                                Right_Subtree => null);
   else
      And_The_Tree := new Node'(The_Item       => The_Item,
                                Left_Subtree   => null,
                                Right_Subtree => And_The_Tree);
   end if;
exception
   when Storage_Error => raise Overflow;
end Construct;
```

Notice how, as we did with Copy, we must include an exception handler to deal with a possible Overflow condition.

Set_Item requires only one statement. We must simply set The_Item value of the root node. In the event Of_The_Tree is empty, this statement raises Constraint_Error, which we handle by raising the exception Tree_Is_Null:

```
procedure Set_Item (Of_The_Tree : in out Tree;
                    To_The_Item : in      Item) is
begin
  Of_The_Tree.The_Item := To_The_Item;
exception
  when Constraint_Error => raise Tree_Is_Null;
end Set_Item;
```

Swap_Child is the last constructor we must implement. Like Construct, this operation includes a parameter that designates which child of the source tree to replace with the destination tree. Notice that we must introduce a temporary object; we use it to save the child subtree while we replace the child with the destination tree. Rather than just throwing this tree away, we save it as the destination tree:

```
procedure Swap_Child (The_Child   : in       Child;
                       Of_The_Tree : in out Tree;
                       And_The_Tree : in out Tree) is
  Temporary_Node : Tree;
begin
  if The Child = Left then
    Temporary-Node            := Of_The_Tree.Left_Subtree;
    Of_The_Tree.Left_Subtree := And_The_Tree;
  else
    Temporary_Node            := Of_The_Tree.Right_Subtree;
    Of_The_Tree.Right_Subtree := And_The_Tree;
  end if;
  And_The_Tree := Temporary_Node;
exception
  when Constraint_Error => raise Tree_Is_Null;
end Swap_Child;
```

Turning now to the tree selectors, we find that Is_Equal has a simple recursive algorithm that follows the pattern we found in the constructor Copy. Our algorithm checks that the root of each given tree matches. If so, we recursively call Is_Equal to test for equality of the two subtrees:

```
function Is_Equal (Left  : in Tree;
                   Right : in Tree) return Boolean is
begin
  if Left.The_Item /= Right.The_Item then
    return False;
```

```
      else
         return Is_Equal(Left.Left_Subtree, Right.Left_Subtree)
                    and then
                 Is_Equal(Left.Right_Subtree, Right.Right_Subtree);
      end if;
   exception
      when Constraint_Error => return False;
   end Is_Equal;
```

The remaining selectors all have simple bodies. Is_Null checks for
equality with null, and Item_Of and Child_Of both hide direct access to components of the Node record. For these last two selectors, we must defend
ourselves against a possible Constraint_Error, which would be raised if the
given tree was empty. We include an exception handler that raises
Tree_Is_Null in its place:

```
   function Is_Null (The Tree : in Tree) return Boolean is
   begin
      return The_Tree = null;
   end Is_Null;

   function Item_Of (The_Tree : in Tree) return Item is
   begin
      return The_Tree.The_Item;
   exception
      when Constraint_Error => raise Tree_Is_Null;
   end Item_Of;

   function Child_Of (The_Tree : in Tree;
                      The_Child : in Child) return Tree is
   begin
      if The_Child = Left then
         return The Tree.Left_Subtree;
      else
         return The_Tree.Right_Subtree;
      end if;
   exception
      when Constraint_Error => raise Tree_Is_Null;
   end Child_Of;
```

This completes our implementation of the tree package. Before we
leave this chapter, however, let us consider a significant application.

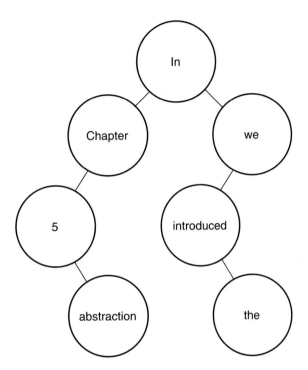

Figure 13.2 Representation of The_Concordance

In Chapter 5, we introduced the abstraction of a concordance as an object. Our program feeds one word and line number at a time to this abstract-state machine, and the concordance must save them in some manner. As we see in Figure 13.2, one strategy is to use a tree. Thus, as we accumulate words, we add them to the tree in alphabetical order. At first glance, this figure may not appear to have words in alphabetical order, but notice that for each node, the value of its left subtree is always less than the value of its right subtree. The figure shows the state of the concordance after we have recorded the first few words of this paragraph. Consider then how we add the next word, *of.* Starting at the root of the tree, we ask if the current word *(of)* is less than, equal to, or greater than the value of the node. In this case, its value is greater, so we move to the right child. Asking the same question, we then move to the left child (since the string *of* is less than the string *we).* At the next node (labeled by *introduced,* we choose to move again to the right, since *of* is larger. Looking at the node labeled *the,* we note that *of* is smaller. However, this time, there are no children. Since we are at the frontier of the tree and have found no match, we construct a new node and attach it as the left child of the node labeled *the.*

We reverse the process to recreate an alphabetical ordering of words. Starting at the root node, we move to the left. If there is a left child, we recursively call this algorithm. If not, we print the value of the node, then recursively call this algorithm for the right child.

This traversal is a very common form of tree searching and is called an in-order traversal. The advantage of this approach is that we expend little effort in inserting each new word. When we are done building the concordance, we do not have to sort all the words; we only need to walk the tree to re-create the alphabetical ordering.

Let us turn to the body of the package Concordance. Actually, the value of each node in the tree must be slightly more complicated than what we have described. Since a given word may appear more than once in a document, we must somehow save all word references. Happily, we already have a component that will do the job. In the previous chapter we built a generic version of the package Queues. Applying the same concept, we can treat word references as a queue of line numbers. Thus, as we encounter a word, we add the line number to a queue associated with this word. When we are ready to display the concordance, we simply extract the line numbers from the front of the queue, which returns them to us in the order in which we entered them in the queue.

A node in the concordance tree is thus a record consisting of a word and a queue of line numbers. We can express our design decisions about the framework for the package body Concordance as:

```
with Text_IO, Queues, Trees;
package body Concordance is
  package Line_Number_Queue is new Queues(Line_Numbers.Number);
  type Reference is access Line_Number_Queue.Queue(100);
  type Node is
    record
      The_Word        : Words.Word;
      The_References : Reference;
    end record;
  package Word_Tree is new Trees(Node);
  The_Concordance : Word_Tree.Tree;
  procedure Start is ...
  procedure Add (The Word   : in Words.Word;
                 The_Number : in Line_Numbers.Number) is ...
  procedure Make_Report is ...
end Concordance;
```

Notice how we must constrain the declaration of objects of type Queue, since the type requires a discriminant. The decision to make 100 references the maximum for any word is arbitrary.

Turning to the implementation of each of the procedures, we begin to see how we can use the resources provided by our reusable software components. For example, Start sets the state of this package as a stable initial value. In this case, the only state associated with this package body is the object The_Concordance. Thus, Start can build on top of the tree constructor Clear:

```
procedure Start is
begin
  Word_Tree.Clear(The_Concordance);
end Start;
```

Add is passed a word and a line number. In its body, we simply call another procedure, which we will declare locally to the package body:

```
procedure Add(The_Word   : in Words.Word;
              The_Number : in Line_Numbers.Number) is
begin
  Insert(The_Word, The_Number, In_The_Tree => The_Concordance);
exception
  when Word_Tree.Overflow => raise Overflow;
end Add;
```

The reason we added this level of indirection will become clear in a moment. Before we study the body of the local procedure Insert, however, let us add one more local function that we will need later. Recall that the relational operations for String compare two string objects on an item-by-item basis. However, we may encounter words of a different case as we build the concordance. (Ada's rules for relational operations define the words *Ada* and *ada* as unequal, for example.) Thus, we must add an operation that normalizes a string by converting all the characters to lowercase:

```
function Lower_Case (The_String : in String) return String is
  Result : String(1.. The_String'Length) := The_String;
  Offset :constant := Character'Pos ('a') - Character'Pos ('A');
begin
  for Index in Result'Range
    loop
      if Result(Index) in 'A'..'Z' then
        Result(Index) := Character'Val(
                                     Character'Pos(Result(Index)) + Offset);
      end if;
    end loop;
  return Result;
end Lower_Case;
```

Insert can now follow the recursive algorithm we described earlier. First, let us examine Insert in more detail. Given a tree, we see if it is empty. If so, we call Construct to build a new node. Otherwise, we check to see whether the given word is less than, equal to, or greater than the word of the current root. If it is equal, we simply add the given line number to the queue of line numbers by calling the queue constructor Add. If the word is less than the current roots, we move to the left child; otherwise, we move to the right child. In either case, we save a pointer to the current node, and then call Insert recursively. When we return from Insert, we know that the given tree (Temporary_Tree) has been updated, so we reattach it to the child we last visited:

```
    procedure Insert (The_Word    : in      Words.Word;
                      The_Line    : in      Line_Numbers.Number;
                      In_The_Tree : in out Word_Tree.Tree) is
  Temporary_Node : Node;
  Temporary_Tree : Word_Tree.Tree;
begin
  if Word_Tree.Is_Null(In_The_Tree) then
    Temporary_Node :=
      Node'(The Word        => The Word,
            The_References => new Line_Number_Queue.Queue(100));
    Line_Number_Queue.Add(The_Line, Temporary_Node.The_References.all);
    Word_Tree.Construct(Temporary_Node,
                        And_The_Tree => In_The_Tree,
                        On_The_Child => Word_Tree.Left);
  else
    Temporary_Tree := In_The_Tree;
    Temporary_Node := Word_Tree.Item_Of(Temporary_Tree);
    if Lower.Case (Words.Value.Of(The.Word)) =
       Lower-Case(Words.Value.Of(Temporary_Node.The_Word)) then
         Line_Number_Queue.Add(The_Line, Temporary_Node.The_References.all);
    elsif Lower_Case(Words.Value_Of(The_Word)) <
          Lower_Case(Words.Value_Of(Temporary_Node.The_Word)) then
      Temporary_Tree := Word_Tree.Child_Of(In_The_Tree, Word_Tree.Left);
      Insert(The_Word, The_Line, Temporary_Tree);
      Word_Tree.Swap_Child(Word_Tree.Left,
                           Of_The_Tree  => In_The_Tree,
                           And_The_Tree => Temporary_Tree);
    else
      Temporary_Tree := Word_Tree.Child_Of(In_The_Tree, Word_Tree.Right);
      Insert(The_Word, The_Line, Temporary_Tree);
```

```
      Word_Tree.Swap_Child(Word_Tree.Right,
                           Of_The_Tree  => In_The_Tree,
                           And_The_Tree => Temporary_Tree);
    end if;
  end if;
end Insert;
```

Notice how we leverage the resources of our tree component. In the absence of this component, our implementation would be much more complex since the developer would have to duplicate much of our earlier work.

Turning to the implementation of Make_Report, we apply a recursive algorithm:

```
procedure Make_Report is
  procedure Display (The Tree : in Word_Tree.Tree) is ...
  procedure Traverse (The Tree : in Word_Tree.Tree) is ...
begin
  Text_IO.New_Line;
  Traverse(The_Concordance);
end Make_Report;
```

Display is a locally declared procedure that, given a node, displays the value of the word and all the line numbers associated with it. Here, we can apply some facilities from Text_IO to provide the formatting we want; we will discuss these facilities further in Chapter 18. We have complicated our algorithm slightly by introducing the object Previous_Line. Rather than repeating references that appear on the same line, we output a new line number only if its value is not equal to the last one we printed:

```
procedure Display (The_Tree : in Word_Tree.Tree) is
  Temporary_Node : Node;
  The_Line       : Line_Numbers.Number;
  Previous_Line  : Line_Numbers.Number := Line_Numbers.Number'Last;
  function "=" (X, Y : Line_Numbers.Number) return Boolean
    renames Line-Numbers."=";
begin
  Temporary_Node := Word_Tree.Item_Of(The_Tree);
  Text_IO.Put(Words.Value_Of( Temporary_Node.The_Word));
  Text_IO.Set_Col(20);
  while Line_Number_Queue.Length_Of
    (Temporary_Node.The_References.all) > 0
  loop
    Line_Number_Queue.Remove (The_Line, Temporary_Node.The_References.all);
```

```
      if The_Line /= Previous_Line then
        Text_IO.Put(Line_Numbers.Number'Image (The_Line));
        Previous_Line := The_Line;
      end if;
    end loop;
    Text_IO.New_Line;
  end Display;
```

Finally we turn to the body of Traverse. This procedure implements the in-order traversal that we described earlier:

```
procedure Traverse (The_Tree : in Word_Tree.Tree) is
begin
  if not Word_Tree.Is_Null(The_Tree) then
    Traverse(Word_Tree.Child_Of(The_Tree, Word_Tree.Left));
    Display(The_Tree);
    Traverse(Word_Tree.Child_Of(The_Tree, Word_Tree.Right));
  end if;
end Traverse;
```

Exercises * **1.** Rewrite the in-order traversal algorithm used in the body of Concordance so that it is generic.

2. How might we modify the body of Concordance so that we also display the number of times a word appears?

*3. How might we modify our generic tree so that it applies to arbitrary trees (that is, trees with an arbitrary number of children)?

4. Add an operation to the tree package that, given a tree, returns the tree that is its parent. How must we alter the representation of the type Node to make this operation efficient?

5. Whenever we Clear a tree, we create the potential to generate garbage by throwing away nodes. How could we alter the body of Trees to maintain a free list of unused nodes?

6. Is it possible to lose track of part of a tree? In particular, what happens if we assign a value to a tree object that already has a value?

7. Modify the body of Concordance so that words are displayed in order of increasing number of references.

*8. In the Trees package we introduce the identifiers Left and Left_Subtree. Generally, introducing a term (Left) more than once indicates a missing type or subtype. Argue that the type Node would be better defined as:

```
type Children is array (Child) of Tree;
type Node is
  record
    The_Item    : Item;
    The_Children : Children;
  end record;
```

Problems   In this section we define a number of larger exercises, called problems.

1. Geothermal prospecting

   A file will be supplied that contains values of one or more 25 x 25 matrices. The components of the matrices are integers that represent heat intensities in the range 0–99.

   Allow the user to define (at least) four subranges of heat and a character to be associated with each range, for example:

Range	Character
0 .. 10	.
11 .. 30	_
31 .. 55	o
56 .. 99	*

   Ensure that the subranges entered are nonoverlapping. Then read the matrices from the file and display them using the appropriate subrange characters. Also, allow the user to specify an intensity level, t. Find all 5 x 5 squares in which all intensity values are greater than or equal to t.

   Modify your program so that it can process matrices of any size, not just 25 x 25.

2. Air traffic control

   Simulate an airport's landing and takeoff patterns. The airport has a number of runways and a number of holding patterns for each runway. When a plane reaches the airport, it is assigned an ID and placed in one of the holding patterns. The plane informs the airport of the number of time units that the plane can remain in a holding pattern (before it runs out of fuel).

   If a plane wants to take off, it is assigned a runway and placed in a wait queue for that runway. Planes in the takeoff queues are also assigned an ID.

   Design the program so that the user can decide the number of runways, the number of holding patterns per runway, and the number of planes that want to land and take off per time unit. Try to minimize the number of planes in queues. Also try to minimize the number of planes that run out of fuel and crash.

For each time unit during the execution of the simulation, display the number of planes in each takeoff queue, the number of planes in each landing queue, and the number of time units remaining for each plane in a holding pattern.

Exchange program source code with another student. Evaluate the program's reliability, understandability, and modifiability. Test the implementation to determine the maximum number of incoming planes that can be handled per time unit at an airport that has two runways, two holding patterns per runway, and up to three planes per holding pattern.

PACKAGE

5

Concurrent Real-Time Processing

If it were done, when 'tis done,
then 'twere well
It were done quickly.

Shakespeare
Macbeth [1]

CHAPTER 14

Tasks

The Form of Ada Tasks
Task Statements
Applications for Ada Tasks

I n the problem space of the real world, there are usually a number of logical activities that occur at the same time. For example, an aircraft autopilot may be continuously monitoring air speed and angle-of-attack sensors, waiting for user requests, and controlling several independent devices, such as control surfaces and throttles. In addition, some devices, such as navigation aids, may use asynchronous hardware interrupts to request service.

If we were to develop a software solution for such a problem, we would find that most existing high-order languages provide little or no support for expressing such concurrent activities. Instead, we would have to resort to the facilities of the host operating system, or we would have to write some unique multitasking assembly language routines.

Either case is usually an unacceptable alternative. When we step outside of the high-order languages, the resulting software is not portable and is often difficult to maintain because of the many disjoint pieces. Furthermore, writing multitasking software is a complex activity. When programming in an assembly language, it is difficult if not impossible to explicitly express timing relationships or to reliably control the interactions among different tasks (see Chapter 2).

In Ada, a *task* is simply an entity that operates in parallel with other program units. Logically, we can conceptualize a solution consisting of many independent tasks. Physically, tasks may execute on multicomputer systems, multiprocessor systems, or with interleaved execution on a single processor. No matter what the physical representation, the abstraction of a solution with many tasks is quite natural, and is drawn directly from our abstraction of the problem space. What we desire is the ability to represent these real-world parallel activities within all levels of our solution. Today we are quite comfortable with manipulating real numbers instead of fooling around at the bit level; we should become as comfortable with creating tasks instead of creating purely sequential solutions.

Unless the tasks are totally independent, there must be some means of expressing communication among them. Ideally, we would like this communication to be explicit and reliable. For example, consider a system that has two tasks, one of which samples a keyboard and collects entire lines of text (the Producer); the other task then takes the buffered characters and transmits them across a modem (the Consumer). Obviously, the timing interactions between the two tasks cannot be predicted. We may be waiting for keyboard input for several minutes, or we may suddenly get a burst of input data at 80 words per minute. Additionally, we must accomplish the proper handshaking with the modem and perhaps take care of retransmission in case of errors.

Basically, there are two methods that express communication between these two tasks. The first method is similar to sending a letter through the mail. The Producer builds a collection of keyboard inputs and then, when an entire line is assembled, deposits that collection in a common buffer area known to both tasks (the *mailbox*). It then raises some sort of flag to indicate that the mailbox contains a message. The Consumer picks up complete messages from the mailbox as they become available.

According to the rules of this type of communication, only one task can enter the mailbox at a time (*mutual exclusion*), and if both try to enter at the same time, one has to wait so as not to interfere with the other. Additionally, as long as no input exists, the Consumer waits at the mailbox. On the other hand, if the Consumer is busy processing a message, the Producer simply continues to drop messages in the mailbox and returns to its activities.

In terms of programming languages, we would implement such a communications scheme by using what are called *monitors* or *semaphores*. As shown in Figure 14.1, the mailbox can be considered as a resource, protected by a critical section of code, that only one task can enter at a time. In this case, the flag is a semaphore, raised by an operation marked V and lowered by the operation P. For simple task communication, this method is quite acceptable. However, it does not handle complex cases very well.

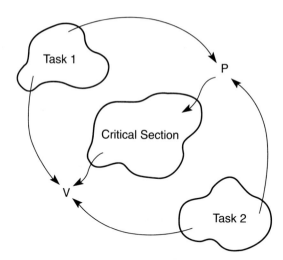

Figure 14.1 Task communication with semaphores

When several producers and consumers are needed, rather than just two, some priority system for the allocation of the resource is necessary. Furthermore, this kind of task communication is unsynchronized. It is therefore difficult to express a solution that meets specific timing requirements, such as "The keyboard data shall be transmitted across the modem within 500 milliseconds after receipt of a complete line." Since one task cannot readily recognize the existence of the other (each task sees only the semaphore, not the other tasks), it is difficult if not impossible for one task to detect a failure in the other. Conceivably, the Consumer task could fail, and the Producer would just keep creating lines of input data that would be lost.

A more natural method of handling task interaction is to treat each task as a communicating sequential process [1], as illustrated in Figure 14.2. Instead of being unsynchronized, such tasks are synchronized in time and space when they communicate, much like the process of two people talking to each other. Using our example, after the Producer has created a line of input, it calls an entry of the Consumer, thus signaling that it is ready to communicate. As soon as the Consumer accepts the entry, a message is passed (in one or both directions), and then the two tasks resume their independent actions until the Producer is ready to deliver another message.

Such explicit synchronization is known as a *rendezvous*. In this model, if one task is ready to enter or accept before the other is at the rendezvous point, that task has three options: It can wait indefinitely, it can wait for a specified period, or it can enter/accept another task that is ready to communicate. One advantage of this method is that communication can be more reliable. If one task were to fail or become delayed, it is possible for another task to detect the inaction and take appropriate measures. Further-

Figure 14.2 Tasks as communicating sequential processes

more, if the task communication is synchronized, we can more easily express the timing relationships of the two tasks.

Ada contains constructs that let us directly express the structure of multitasking solutions through the use of communicating sequential processes. Unlike most other high-order languages, it is not necessary to step outside the host language to implement tasking. In this chapter, we shall examine the form and application of Ada's tasks.

14.1   The Form of Ada Tasks

A task is one of Ada's three primary program units (the other two are subprograms and packages). We consider a main program unit to be a task implicitly, but a programmer can declare other tasks explicitly within the other units. A programmer can introduce tasks in the declarative part of any unit, such as a block, subprogram body, task body, or library package. An independent task cannot be compiled separately, but it can be encapsulated inside a library package to achieve the same effect. A task cannot stand alone; it depends upon its parent, which is essentially the unit in which the task is declared.

In Ada, we do not have to explicitly initiate a task. Instead, a task is activated after its body has been elaborated, at the end of the declarative part of the parent. If several tasks are declared in the same declarative part, they will all be activated at the end of the declarative part, although the order of activation is nondeterministic.

On the other hand, a task parent will not terminate until all of its task children have terminated. A task normally terminates when its execution reaches the end of the task body and all of its dependent tasks, if any, have terminated. We shall discuss this and other issues of termination in detail in a later section.

A task has a two-part form similar to a package declaration, as Figure 14.3 indicates. A task includes a specification, which defines the interface between this task and other units, and the task body, which consists of that task's executable part. Just like packages and subprograms, each part of a task can be textually separated.

Specification   Body

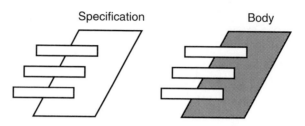

Figure 14.3 Symbols for an Ada task

Task Specifications

A task specification introduces the name of the task object (or task type, as we discuss later), along with the entries visible to users of the task. In a sense, the specification part defines the communication paths (entries) available to other tasks. For example, for the Consumer task defined earlier, the specification might look like the following:

```
task Consumer is
  entry Receive_Message(A_Message : in String);
end Consumer;
```

An entry declaration has a form similar to a subprogram specification, namely the entry name is followed by formal parameters that describe the type of the parameters (messages) that are passed during rendezvous. These formal parameters may have the modes in, out, or in out, just like subprograms, and this mode defines the direction in which a particular message is passed, relative to the task owning the entry declaration.

A task entry can be called from any point at which a subprogram call is permitted, such as in a subprogram, task, package body (including the main program), or block, although it makes no sense for a task to invoke its own entry. If a task tries to communicate with itself, a deadlock condition may be created, since a rendezvous is impossible. A deadlock occurs when tasks are waiting for a resource that can never become free.

Consider the following more complex task specification:

```
task Protected_Stack is
    entry Pop (Element : out Integer);
    entry Push(Element : in Integer);
end Protected_Stack;
```

Several characteristics of this declaration are worth noting. First, a task specification can contain only entry calls (and representation specifications), unlike a package that can export many different kinds of entities. Like that of a package, a user of a task must refer to specific entries, using selected component notation. The use clause is not applicable to task entries, so it is always necessary to prefix entry calls with the task name. For example:

```
Protected_Stack.Pop(My_Value);
Protected_Stack.Push(36);
```

A call to an entry is indistinguishable from the form of a subprogram invocation. In fact, entries can be renamed as procedures. For example:

```
procedure Protected_Pop (Element : out Integer) renames
    Protected_Stack.Pop;
```

We can then simply invoke Protected_Pop. Since we may not apply a use clause to a task, the renames construct is useful, especially when the task and entry names are long and we wish to provide a shorter yet meaningful name for the entry action.

Although an entry call looks like a subprogram call, the semantics of the invocation are quite different. If several tasks can call the same subprogram, then several tasks may actually be executing the same subprogram at one time; we speak of the subprogram code as being *reentrant*. However, associated with every entry declaration is an implicit queue. If several tasks call the same entry, only one task (starting with the one that called the entry first) would be permitted to rendezvous at a time. All other tasks would wait in the implicit queue in the order in which they arrived (first-in-first-out), not according to their priority. In the event that two tasks called the entry at identical times, the selection would be arbitrary. As we shall see later, it is possible for a task to leave the implicit queue before it completes the rendezvous. This may occur in the event of a timeout condition (where some maximum waiting time has expired) or if a different rendezvous is immediately possible.

Once activated, a task can be in one of five states:

- Running: the task is currently assigned to a processor.

- Ready: the task is unblocked and waiting for processing.

- Blocked: the task is delayed or waiting for a rendezvous.

- Completed: the task has finished executing its sequence of statements.

- Terminated: the task never was, or is no longer, active.

Figure 14.4 illustrates the interaction of these states. Here, we see that, like any other declaration, a task is elaborated first; it becomes activated only at

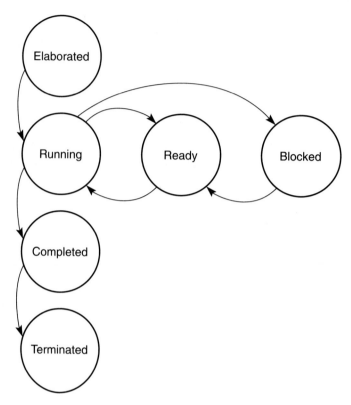

Figure 14.4 Task states

the end of the elaboration of the enclosing declarative region. During its active lifetime, the state of a task can be running, ready, and blocked. *Running* implies that the task has processing resources; *ready* implies that the task is waiting for processing resources but is otherwise ready to run. *Blocked* means that the task is waiting for some event, such as a rendezvous. As we shall discuss in more detail later, Ada semantics do not require that task scheduling apply a time-slicing algorithm. Thus, once a task is running, it can continue running until some higher priority task becomes ready. Once a task has finished executing its sequence of statements, it is *completed* and waits for any of its dependent tasks to complete. After completion, a task can no longer participate in any rendezvous. When there are no active task children, the task is *terminated*. Associated with every task, including the main program, is a static priority that indicates a degree of urgency. A user can explicitly specify this priority using the pragma priority. The pragma takes an integer value of type Priority (from package System) that has an implementation-defined range. A higher value indicates a greater urgency. If a Priority is not specified explicitly for a given task, the compiler will assign a value. `Priority` does not affect the order in which a queued task will be served, since Ada's queues are first-in-first-out.

The effect of a priority is to assist in the allocation of processing resources, such as processors or memory space, to parallel tasks when there are more tasks ready for execution than can be supported with the available resources. Thus, if two or more tasks with different priorities are in the ready state, the task with the highest priority will be selected for running. If only tasks with equal or undefined priorities are ready, the scheduling order is not defined within Ada, and the decision is left to the implementation. Although this scheduling algorithm is outside the domain of the language, the definition of Ada tasking requires that this scheduling be "fair"—that is, it will not permit a task to starve. Note that `Priority` should be used only to indicate the relative degree of urgency among tasks. It is poor practice to use this pragma to achieve task synchronization, since the exact meaning of different task priorities is highly machine dependent.

A task does not have to have any defined entries. For example, consider the following:

```
task Producer;
```

This defines a task that has no visible communication paths; the definition is similar to the condition of the main program unit. We can classify such tasks as *actor tasks,* since they do not provide any services to other units but are instead fully active. Of course, an actor task can still call the entries of another task, as long as the other task entries are visible.

This classification points out that Ada task communication is asymmetrical. At one extreme, we have actor tasks that have no entries; at the other extreme, we have passive *server tasks* that have entries but do not invoke the entries of any other task. Of course, Ada permits the creation of intermediate cases. Thus, we may have a task that both calls entries of other tasks and also provides a service to other units (a sort of transducer).

This asymmetry is also evident in the visibility of actor/server tasks. A calling task must know the name of the entered task. On the other hand, a called task does not know the name of the calling tasks. Recalling the Ada rule that objects must be declared before they are used, we may think that it is impossible to permit two tasks to mutually call entries of the other. Actually, this is not the case. For example, consider the following declarations:

```
task First_Task is
    entry Service;
end First_Task;
```

```
task Second_Task is
    entry Service;
end Second_Task;

task body First_Task is
begin
    ...
  Accept Service ...
    ...
end First_Task;

task body Second_Task is
begin
    ...
  Accept Service ...
    ...
end Second_Task;
```

Since a task specification and body can be textually separated, both task specifications can be declared first, so that their entries are visible to the bodies of both. Thus, the First_Task body can call the entry named Second_Task.Service and vice versa.

We conclude our discussion of entries with the topic of *families* of entries. Essentially, a family defines a set of peer entries, indexed by a discrete value much like an array index. For example:

```
type Importance is (Low, Medium, High);
task Message is
  entry Get(Importance)(A_Message : out Message_Type);
  entry Put(Importance)(A_Message : in  Message_Type);
end Message;
```

We can then refer to specific entries, such as:

```
Your_Message, My_Message : Message_Type;

Message.Get(High)(Your_Message);
Message.Put(Low)(My_Message);
```

In a later section, we shall discuss how families of entries are commonly used as tasks that act as schedulers.

So far, we have only mentioned the declaration of task objects. Consider the following:

```
task Terminal_Driver is
  entry Get(A_Character : out Character);
  entry Put(A_Character : in Character);
end Terminal_Driver;
```

This declaration is actually equivalent to:

```
task type Anonymous_Type is
  entry Get(A_Character : out Character);
  entry Put(A_Character : in  Character);
end Anonymous_Type;
Terminal_Driver : Anonymous_Type;
```

Here, the name Anonymous_Type denotes a type that is not visible to any user. Like a data type, a *task type* defines a template that can be used to create several instances of task objects. A task type is a limited private data type and so cannot be assigned or tested for equality or inequality, although it can be used as an in-parameter to a subprogram or task entry.

The only operations applicable to objects of a task type are the entries defined in the task type specification. Given a task type, we can then declare task objects. For example:

```
task type Resource is
    entry Release;
    entry Seize;
end Resource;
Buffer  : Resource;
Segment : array (1..100) of Resource;
```

We can then refer to entries of specific objects, such as:

```
Buffer.Release;
Segment(7).Seize;
```

This last example, illustrating a family of tasks, is different from one using a family of entries. For families of entries, we define only one task with a set of different entries (communication paths). In the case of the object Segment, we have actually defined a collection of several tasks (100 different tasks), each with entries called Release and Seize.

We can also use task types in other declarations, such as:

```
task type Resource is
    entry Release;
    entry Seize;
end Resource;
type Locked_Data is
  record
    Element : Integer;
    Key     : Resource;
  end record;
```

```
My_Data : Locked_Data;
type Heap is access Resource;
```

With the declaration objects of a task type such as My_Data, activation proceeds according to the rules we have already stated: The declaration is elaborated first, and the task object becomes activated only at the end of the enclosing declarative region. We can name its entries:

```
My_Data.Key.Release;
My_Data.Key.Seize;
```

As the Heap example indicates, defining an access type to a task type is useful if we do not know how many tasks we shall eventually need, or if we need to exchange task identities. Here, the rules for task activation are different: A task is activated when the allocator is executed. The following code shows how this kind of execution works:

```
Pool : Heap;
Pool := new Resource; -- task is activated
```

We can call an entry of the task as follows:

```
Pool.Release;
Pool.Seize;
```

To conclude our discussion of task specifications, note that several attributes exist for task objects and task types, namely:

```
T'Address      -- Start address for the task.
T'Callable     -- True when T is not completed or terminated.
T'Size         -- Storage space needed for T.
T'Storage_Size -- Storage space reserved for an activation of T.
T'Terminated   -- True when T is no longer active.
```

Appendix A describes each of these attributes in detail.

Task Bodies

Associated with every task specification is a task body that defines the action of the task. The form of a task body is similar to that of a subprogram body, consisting of a declarative part followed by a sequence of statements with an optional exception handler. When a task is activated, the items in the declarative part of the task body are elaborated, then the action associated with the sequence of statements is initiated. Since we often want the task to continue processing indefinitely, these statements may take the form of an infinite loop. For example, we may define a simple watchdog task as:

```
task Water_Monitor;
task body Water_Monitor is
begin
  loop
    if Water_Level > Maximum_Level then
      Sound_Alarm;
    end if;
    delay 1.0;
  end loop;
end Water_Monitor;
```

This task will continue forever and trigger an alarm whenever the sampled water level is too high. The delay statement makes the task wait (a condition program developers describe as *going to sleep*) for at least one second, and so the loop repeats no faster than once per second. Actually, we may have violated good programming practice by permitting this task to access the global objects Water_Level and Maximum_Level, especially if other tasks set and use these objects. We shall discuss the problem of shared variables in a later section.

If we have defined entries for a task, its task body should contain at least one accept statement corresponding to each entry (although the language does not enforce this). For example, consider the task specification:

```
task Consumer is
  entry Transmit_Message(A_Message : in String);
end Consumer;
```

The following would be an appropriate task body:

```
task body Consumer is
begin
  loop
    accept Transmit_Message(A_Message : in String) do
      Text_IO.Put(Modem, A_Message);
    end Transmit_Message;
  end loop;
end Consumer;
```

With a nonactor task, two conditions are required for a simple rendezvous, namely an entry call from outside the task and a corresponding accept in the task body. According to the rules of Ada rendezvous, if Task_1 is ready to rendezvous before Task_2, then Task_1 will wait until Task_2 is ready. Generally, a task will put itself to sleep rather than execute a busy wait. A *busy wait* is a task using processing resources, without doing any useful work, while waiting for some event. A *sleeping wait* means that the task is still waiting for an event, but the process has been suspended until that event occurs. Once the rendezvous is initiated, the sequence of statements associated with the accept statement (if any) are executed. When the server task completes execution of these statements, the rendezvous is complete, and the two tasks are released to continue in parallel.

For every entry, a task body can contain one or more accept statements. An accept statement must appear directly in a task body; according to an Ada rule, it cannot be embedded inside another subprogram, for example. This rule is necessary to prevent one task from executing the accept statement of another task. An accept statement takes the form of the reserved word accept, followed by the entry name with optional subscripts (for a family of entries) and its formal part, if any. The actions associated with the rendezvous are defined next, delimited by the accept...do...end clause. If there are no actions, the do...end clause can be omitted. For example:

```
task Sequencer is
  entry Phase_1;
  entry Phase_2;
  entry Phase_3;
end Sequencer;
task body Sequencer is
begin
  accept Phase_1;
  accept Phase_2;
  accept Phase_3 do
    Initiate_Launch;
  end Phase_3;
end Sequencer;
```

Here, we have forced an order to our task communication. We must rendezvous at Phase_1, then Phase_2, then Phase_3, until we can finally execute the statement Initiate_Launch. During the intermediate rendezvous, no action is performed other than the synchronization tasks.

14.2   Task Statements

Since Ada was designed primarily for real-time applications, it is understandable that it contains constructs for expressing events in time. In particular, the language definition includes a package Calendar that exports a Time type and a predefined function Clock that returns the time of day. In addition, package Standard includes a predefined Duration type, used for expressing units of seconds (see Appendix C for the specification of these units). We can use a simple expression that yields a value of type Duration in a delay statement, such as:

```
delay 10.0; -- delay 10 seconds
delay Next_Time - Calendar.Clock; -- delay for some delta time
```

In our example, Calendar.Clock is the function call that returns the time of day. The effect of a delay statement is to suspend (put to sleep) further execution of the unit that executes it for at least the given time interval. Continuing, we can define our own Seconds, Minutes, and Hours constants to improve the readability of the delay statement, such as:

```
Seconds : constant Duration := 1.0;
Minutes : constant Duration := 60.0;
Hours   : constant Duration := 3600.0;
delay 2*Hours + 7*Minutes + 36*Seconds;
```

The following statement is illegal, however, because of a type mismatch:

```
delay 4.5*Minutes;      -- illegal!
```

The expression 4.5*Minutes involves the multiplication of a universal real value and a fixed-point value, which (as Chapter 6 discussed) yields a universal fixed value, which is not of the type Duration. The solution is to either use a type conversion or declare Minutes as an integer type.

Notice that we did not say that a delay statement suspends processing for an exact amount of time, but rather that it expresses a minimum delay. If we have a solution that contains several tasks running on a single processor, a task that is ready to run may have to wait further for processing resources. The actual delay thus becomes the minimum delay plus the time overhead necessary to wake up the previously delayed task. However, in an embedded application, we may need to have a process that takes an exact amount of time, such as when sampling sensors.

The following is an example of an improper use of the delay statement to achieve a regular loop:

```
-- an invalid algorithm
loop
   -- some timed action
   delay 30*Seconds;
end loop;
```

In this case, the loop will take at least 30 seconds to complete, plus the execution time of the action. However, we cannot be assured that the loop will start execution every 30 seconds, because of the nondeterminism associated with task scheduling and the fact that several other jobs may be competing for the same resources.

A better solution is to calculate the time that the next loop should start, and then delay only the amount required to meet this time. With this strategy we shall be assured that a loop, on the average, will take an exact amount of time to process:

```
declare
  Seconds       : constant Duration := 1.0;
  Time_Interval : constant Duration := 30*Seconds;
  Next_Time     : Calendar.Time := Calendar.Clock;
begin
  loop
    delay Next_Time - Calendar.Clock;
    -- some actions taking less than Time_Interval to process
    Next_Time := Next_Time + Time_Interval;
  end loop;
end;
```

As we shall see in Chapter 15, an even better way to achieve a regular loop is with a timed interrupt.

So far, we have examined the basic elements of task activation and termination and the semantics of task rendezvous. We achieve "simple" task communication with the paired entry/accept constructs. We call such communication simple because a task that reaches the rendezvous point first must wait for the other to arrive at the same point. However, our problem space is often not quite so simple. Rather, we may be concerned with the actual time of events and, instead of permitting a task to wait forever for a rendezvous, we may wish a task to quit the attempted rendezvous after a specified delay period. Furthermore, one task may have to choose from several different entry calls from users requesting service. To handle such cases, Ada provides some statements that are similar in form to the sequential statements presented in Chapter 9. These statements, however, are designed for tasks only.

The classes of Ada task communication can be summarized as follows:

- Simple communication
- Selective rendezvous by the server
- Selective rendezvous by the caller

We shall introduce the Ada statements for each form of task communication, using the simulation of a bank teller and customers. The philosophy of Ada's tasking maps closely to a model of human communication, and so we have chosen this informal example first. In the last section of this chapter, we shall formalize these concepts and present several embedded systems applications.

Clearly, a bank teller and a customer form independent tasks that are synchronized at some points in time. During the day, a customer will be engaged in such activities as waking, eating breakfast, going to work, and, perhaps, going to a bank to make a deposit. The teller will also wake in the morning and eat breakfast, but certainly not at the same time or place as the customer. Later, the teller will go to work and wait for customers. These two entities, the teller and the customer, only interact when the customer comes into the bank to make a transaction. Initially, let us assume that we have a very dedicated teller—once he or she is at the bank, the teller will forever wait upon customers. We can abstract this problem as:

```
-- Teller task
accept Make_Deposit (Id : in Integer; Amount : in Float) do
  Balance(Id) := Balance(Id) + Amount;
end Make_Deposit;

-- Customer task
  Teller.Make_Deposit (Id => 1273, Amount => 1.0);
```

This is an example of simple Ada task communication. Notice how we named the task entry, Make_Deposit, to indicate an abstract action. If the Customer reaches the entry call first, he or she will wait (a blocked task) until the Teller accepts the message. Conversely, if the Teller reaches the accept statement before a Customer is ready to rendezvous, the Teller will wait until a Customer arrives to make a deposit. Once the two tasks have rendezvoused, then the sequence of statements associated with the server's (the Teller's) accept statement—bracketed by the do...end clause—is executed and the messages are exchanged.

In this example, the Teller simply updates the appropriate Balance. In the event that several Customer tasks call Make_Deposit, they will enter the implicit queue defined for that particular entry in the order in which they called the Teller. If the President_Customer (with a high priority) arrives after the Average_Customer (a lower priority), the Average_Customer will still be served first by the Teller, since the Average_Customer arrived first.

This abstraction does not describe the most efficient Teller: If there are only a few Customers during the day, the Teller task will most often simply be waiting for some Customer to Make_Deposit. Simple task communication does not permit us to keep the Teller active, so we must provide the Teller (a server) with more things to do, such as serving drive-up window customers.

We can treat this as another task entry and write the code for the `Teller` processing as:

```
task Teller is
  entry Make_Deposit (Id : in Integer; Amount : in Float);
  entry Make_Drive_Up_Deposit (Id : in Integer; Amount : in Float);
end Teller;
task body Teller is
begin
  loop
    select
      accept Make_Deposit (Id : in Integer; Amount : in Float) do
        ...
      end Make_Deposit;
    or
      accept Make_Drive_Up_Deposit (Id : in Integer; Amount : in Float) do
        ...
      end Make_Drive_Up_Deposit;
    end select;
  end loop;
end Teller;
```

In Ada, we call this construct a *selective wait.* In this case, the `Teller` can select from two possible entries or wait until one of the entries is ready for service. At the top of the `select` statement, the `Teller` examines the queues for each entry (via the tasking mechanism). If there are no `Customers` waiting to rendezvous, the `Teller` waits at the top of the `select` statement. Once the `Teller` determines that it is possible to immediately rendezvous with a `Customer` who is calling `Make_Deposit` or `Make_Drive_Up_Deposit`, the `Teller` selects that entry. In the event that customers call both entries at the same time, the `Teller` makes an arbitrary choice. We cannot depend upon servicing an entry based on the order of the selection, because of the nondeterminism of task scheduling. Furthermore, the order in which the `accept` statements are placed does not affect the task selection. However, keep in mind that an implementation is free to choose among any `accept` statements. Thus, it is legal for an implementation to try the `accept` statements in the order in which they appear. A better legal approach employs round-robin scheduling.

This is still not quite good enough for our `Teller`. In the event that there are absolutely no transactions occurring, we wish to keep the `Teller` busy, doing some filing perhaps. We can add an `else` clause to the above solution to achieve this effect:

```
task body Teller is
begin
  loop
    select
      accept Make_Deposit (Id : in Integer; Amount : in Float) do

        ...

      end Make_Deposit;
    or
      accept Make_Drive_Up_Deposit (Id : in Integer; Amount : in Float) do

        ...

      end Make_Drive_Up_Deposit;
    else
      Do_Filing;
    end select;

    ...

  end loop;
end Teller;
```

This construct is known as a *selective wait with an else part*. In this case, if the Teller cannot rendezvous immediately, then the Teller will perform the sequence of statements indicated after the **else** part. Otherwise, the semantics of this **select** statement are identical to that given earlier. Note that the **else** part statements cannot be interrupted. Even if other tasks request services, the Teller_Task first completes this sequence of statements and then loops to the start of the unit.

We can still do better. For example, a Teller should not permit a Customer to Make_Deposit during nonbanking hours. For this example, we shall assume that the hours for the drive-up deposit are different. To indicate that these services may be temporarily unavailable, the code for the Teller can be expressed as follows, using what are called *guards:*

```
task body Teller is
begin
  loop
    select
      when Banking_Hours =>
        accept Make_Deposit (Id : in Integer; Amount : in Float) do

          ...

        end Make_Deposit;
    or
      when Drive_Up_Hours =>
        accept Make_Drive_Up_Deposit (Id : in Integer;
                                      Amount : in Float) do

          ...

        end Make_Drive_Up_Deposit;
```

```
      else
         Do_Filing;
      end select;
      ...
   end loop;
end Teller;
```

This construct is called a *select with guards*. If an alternative does not have a guard, or if the boolean expression on a particular guard (indicated by the when clause) evaluates as True, we consider that accept alternative to be open. If the expression evaluates as False, the alternative is closed, and we do not even consider it for selection; it is as if the alternative did not exist. Of course, the state of the guard can change over time, as it does in our example. Note that these guards are not evaluated continually; evaluation occurs only when we are at the top of the select statement, calculating our next action. Guards can be used only for accept statements, not for the else part. Furthermore, if it is possible for all alternatives to be closed, Ada requires the existence of an else part; otherwise, the exception Program_Error will be raised—an efficient Teller just can't cope with having no work to do.

Let us go one step further. Obviously, a Teller is only human and can wait for a Customer for only so long. In the event that the Teller has not had a Customer enter for two hours, we would like the Teller to be able to Take_A_Break. We can express this scenario as follows:

```
task body Teller is
begin
  loop
    select
      when Banking_Hours =>
        accept Make_Deposit (Id : in Integer; Amount : in Float) do
           ...
        end Make_Deposit;
    or
      when Drive_Up_Hours =>
        accept Make_Drive_Up_Deposit (Id : in Integer;
                                      Amount : in Float) do
           ...
        end Make_Drive_Up_Deposit;
    or
      delay 2*Hours;
      Take_A_Break;
    end select;
    ...
```

```
      end loop;
    end Teller;
```

We call this form of the selective rendezvous a *select with a delay alternative*. In our example, if the Teller does not rendezvous with any task within at least 2*Hours, the sequence of statements following the delay will be executed. As is the case with the else part, these statements may not be interrupted.

The language rules state that several alternatives in a select statement can have a delay part. Clearly, the alternative with the shortest delay will always be chosen over the others. A select with a delay statement cannot contain an else part, since the delay alternative would never be selected. Aside from this restriction, we can combine each of these possible forms of communication to meet our needs, including:

- Select with an else
- Select with delay
- Select with guards
- Simple selection

If we wanted the Teller to service Make_Deposit only and sit idly for a maximum of 30 minutes, we might form the Ada solution as:

```
task body Teller is
begin
  loop
    select
      accept Make_Deposit (Id : in Integer; Amount : in Float) do

        ...

      end Make_Deposit;
    or
      delay 30*Minutes;
      Take_A_Break;
    end select;

    ...

  end loop;
end Teller;
```

We must have some way of terminating our Teller. There are three ways to deal with task termination. First, the language rules state that a task can terminate normally only when the task parent has reached the end of its sequence of statements and all dependent tasks are either terminated or ready to terminate. In other words, all the tasks within a given declaration must be either already terminated or waiting to terminate together. For example, given the declaration:

```
task Outer;
task body Outer is
  task Inner;
  task body Inner is
  begin
    -- sequence of statements
  end Inner;
begin -- Outer
  -- sequence of statements
end Outer;
```

The task Outer completes when it finishes execution of its sequence of statements. However, Outer does not terminate until its child task (Inner) also terminates or becomes ready to terminate. These rules have some important implications when dealing with subprograms. Suppose we declared A_Task inside A_Subprogram instead of in a library unit:

```
procedure A_Subprogram is
  task A_Task;
  task body A_Task is
  begin
    -- sequence of statements
  end A_Task;
begin -- Program
  -- sequence of statements
end Program;
```

Even though A_Subprogram completed its sequence of statements, Ada rules require that we not return from A_Subprogram until A_Task is terminated.

In the case of tasks that involve multiple entries, it is typical to have task bodies in the form of a loop with a nested select statement, the form of the body of Teller. Here, the degree of task communication is much more complex, making it awkward to write a task body so that it naturally ends execution of a sequence of statements. For this reason, and to provide graceful termination in the presence of equally complex child tasks, Ada permits the use of a terminate alternative within a select statement. Only one terminate alternative per select statement is permitted, however, and it cannot be combined with a delay statement or an else alternative. An example of a terminate alternative is:

```
task body Teller is
begin
  loop
    select
      accept Make_Deposit (Id : in Integer; Amount : in Float) do
        ...
      end Make_Deposit;
    or
      terminate;
    end select;
    ...
  end loop;
end Teller;
```

In this case, the Teller's terminate alternative can be implicitly selected. The task can terminate only when the parent task is ready to terminate and when any tasks dependent on the Teller are ready to terminate also. The parent task is ready to terminate if it is waiting at a terminate or is waiting at its final end clause. This method is perhaps the most graceful way to deal with task termination, especially if there are a number of tasks in the solution. As a general rule, applying a terminate statement to every server task achieves this graceful termination. If all the tasks in a given set are finished with their actions and are ready to accept their terminate, all of the tasks terminate at once.

Ada rules allow a select statement to include either a terminate statement, delay statements, or an else clause (or none of these). The three are mutually exclusive. Thus, we cannot have a terminate alternative as well as an else part within the same select statement.

A second way to deal with task termination is to provide an entry that is called when we want to explicitly terminate a task. For example, we could add the entry called Shut_Down to our Teller task and, when the message is accepted, just exit the loop. If things become truly desperate and we have a rogue Teller (the third alternative), we can abnormally terminate a given task by executing an abort statement, such as:

```
abort Teller;
```

A task can be aborted as long as it is visible at a given location. This has the effect of prematurely killing a given task and all of its dependent tasks. Aborting a task is a rather ungraceful means of task termination and should be done only when all other means fail.

A more graceful way to kill a task is to try to rendezvous with a Shut_Down entry previously defined for that server task, delay for a period of time, and then abort the task (just to make certain of finishing it off). For example:

```
Teller.Shut_Down;
delay 30*Seconds;
abort Teller;
```

Since we announce to the Teller that we are going to terminate it (through the Shut_Down entry call) and we then wait awhile, this technique is known as *giving the task its last wishes.*

So far, we have examined selective rendezvous for the server; there are similar options for the Customer task. For example, a Customer will wait only so long to be serviced by a Teller; we want the actor task to quit the attempted rendezvous after some maximum delay. For example:

```
-- Customer task
select
  Teller.Make_Deposit(Id => 1273, Amount => 1_000.0);
or
  delay 10*Minutes;
  Take_A_Hike;
end select;
```

This construct is known as a *timed entry call.* In this case, when we start execution of this **select** statement, we wait for a rendezvous with the Teller. If the Customer is not served within at least 10 minutes, we remove our request from the Make_Deposit entry queue (thus affecting the Count attribute in the Teller). We then execute the sequence of statements associated with the **delay** part, and the Customer will then Take_A_Hike. If the Customer is served within 10 minutes, then, after the rendezvous, execution resumes after the end of the **select** statement.

In the event we have a very impatient customer who will wait for no one, the situation can be expressed as:

```
-- Customer task
select
  Teller.Make_Deposit(Id => 1273, Amount => 1_000.0);
else
  Run_Away;
end select;
```

We call this construct a *conditional entry call.* This structure is semantically equivalent to a timed entry call with a zero delay, but Ada includes a distinct form to explicitly indicate the lack of a delay. Note that there are only subtle differences in the syntax of these two statements (an **else** in place of an **or**).

This completes the collection of task-specific statements. At this point, we have presented a grab bag of tools; in the next section, we shall examine tasking applications.

14.3   Applications for Ada Tasks

In our examination of subprograms in Chapter 8 and packages in Chapter 11, we discussed not only the form of each construct but also the proper application of each. Since tasking is a feature that is not present in most high-order languages, it is particularly appropriate that we present the use of Ada tasks in the form of several application models. In general, subprograms represent abstract actions, and packages permit us to collect logically related entities. When used properly, both of these constructs should reflect the structure of the problem space. The same is true of tasks. They should reflect the nature of the various processes in the problem space.

The application of Ada's tasks can be divided into four areas:

- Concurrent actions

- Rooting messages

- Managing shared resources

- Interrupt handling

Each of these applications will be presented, along with examples, in the following sections.

Concurrent Actions

One of the basic uses of Ada tasks is the expression of concurrent processes. As was mentioned in the introduction to this chapter, few languages permit the expression of concurrency. Ada does so with great clarity. As we go through our object-oriented design method, we may find actions that logically occur in parallel with other actions. At the highest level of our solution, such actions can be encapsulated inside a task.

For example, consider an automobile computer system that monitors engine parameters such as oil pressure and water temperature. These are clearly independent actions. The problem may require the sounding of an alarm whenever either value goes over predefined limits. The two tasks can be introduced in the declarative part of a main program:

```
task Oil_Monitor;
task Water_Monitor;

task body Oil_Monitor is
  Pressure : Float;
begin
  loop
    Get (Pressure);
    if Pressure > Maximum_Pressure then
      Activate_Alarm;
    end if;
  end loop;
end Oil_Monitor;

task body Water_Monitor is
  Temperature :  Float;
begin
  loop
    Get (Temperature);
    if Temperature > Maximum_Temperature then
      Activate_Alarm;
    end if;
  end loop;
end Water_Monitor;
```

Although not indicated in this example, the names Max_Pressure and Max_Temperature would probably denote constant values declared in the main program. In addition, Activate_Alarm might be the entry to another task or simply a subprogram that turns on a visual or audible warning. In either case, neither monitor defines any entries, and so both are purely actor tasks as defined earlier. If the underlying machine contained only one processor, these two tasks could trade use of the processor (perhaps with a time-slice strategy). On the other hand, if we had as many processors as tasks, all the tasks could truly run concurrently. However, keep in mind that an implementation is free to do its own brand of task scheduling for tasks that have equal priority. Thus, it is legal for an implementation to give processing resources to Oil_Monitor and never let Water_Monitor run, since Oil_Monitor never blocks. Clearly, this is not a useful implementation. A better (and also legal) implementation uses time slicing so that Oil_Monitor and Water_Monitor each run for a certain amount of time. Thus, Oil_Monitor runs for several milliseconds and then—even though it did not block—it is marked as ready. Processing resources are then given to the Water-Monitor task. For the sake of portability, it is common to introduce delay statements of short duration into such tasks to force a task that seldom blocks to block for a short amount of time; this coerces the implementation's task scheduler into making other ready tasks active.

The use of tasks does not have to be restricted to the higher levels of solutions. Rather, we may find simple algorithms containing components that can operate in parallel. For example, matrix algebra is often used in the solutions to scientific and engineering problems. Many phases of such calculations are independent and so can logically be completed in parallel with one another. One common calculation in aerodynamics is the multiplication of a matrix and a vector. We may wish to form the following product:

$$\begin{vmatrix} X(1,1) & X(1,2) & ... & X(1,C) \\ ... & ... & ... & ... \\ ... & ... & ... & ... \\ ... & ... & ... & ... \\ X(R,1) & X(R,2) & & X(R,C) \end{vmatrix} * \begin{vmatrix} U(1) \\ \cdot \\ \cdot \\ \cdot \\ U(C) \end{vmatrix}$$

This operation yields a value of the form:

$$\begin{vmatrix} X(1,1)*U(1) & + & X(1,2)*U(2) & +...+ & X(1,C)*U(C) \\ & & ... & & \\ & & ... & & \\ & & ... & & \\ X(R,1)*U(1) & + & X(R,2)*U(2) & +...+ & X(R,C)*U(C) \end{vmatrix}$$

The matrix of size R by C multiplies a vector of size C by 1, producing a vector of size R by 1. On studying the algorithm used to form the product, we notice that each row can be calculated independently. The task that calculates the value of a single row is quite simple.

The first part of a strategy for a `Partial_Product` task will be to `Send_Values` needed for the calculation. Next, we will produce the product, and then we will `Receive_Value` back to the parent task. This can be expressed as follows:

```
type Matrix_Row is array (Integer range <>) of Float;
type Pointer    is access Matrix_Row;
task type Partial_Product is
   entry Receive_Value(Result : out Float);
   entry Send_Values  (First, Second : in Matrix_Row);
end Partial_Product;
Size : constant := 10;
type Matrix is array (1..Size) of Matrix_Row(1..Size);
A_Matrix      : Matrix;
```

```
Source_Vector  : Matrix_Row(1..Size);
Product_Vector : Matrix_Row(1..Size);
task body Partial_Product is
  Product  : Float;
  Vector_1 : Pointer;
  Vector_2 : Pointer;
begin
  accept Send_Values(First, Second : in Matrix_Row) do
    Vector_1 := new Matrix_Row'(First);
    Vector_2 := new Matrix_Row'(Second);
  end Send_Values;
  Product := 0.0;
  for Index in Vector_1.all'Range
    loop
      Product := Product + Vector_1(Index) * Vector_2(Index);
    end loop;
  accept Receive_Value(Result : out Float) do
    Result := Product;
  end Receive_Value;
end Partial_Product;
```

We have defined two entries for this task. One entry, Send_Values, is used to transmit the two vectors to the task for processing, and the other entry, Receive_Value, is used to get a partial product. Notice how this task is applicable to any size array: We defined the formal parameters of the entries to be unconstrained array types (of type Matrix_Row). When matched with the actual parameters, they become constrained, and we can refer to their size through the attribute Range. Within the task body, we must first accept the Send_Values entry, and then we save the values of First and Second in designated access objects. We had to use access types because we could not be certain of the size of the array until execution time. Next, we loop for the length of each vector, calculating the partial product along the way. After this product is completed, we accept the entry Receive_Value.

Assuming that this task type is visible, the general form of the matrix-vector multiplication algorithm can be written as follows. We shall assume that the A_Matrix is a square array of type Matrix, with each row of the type Matrix_Row and constrained to a certain length. Additionally, we shall assume the vector Source_Vector to be visible and also declared of the type Matrix_Row with the same length as for the rows of the Matrix. We shall declare the vector Product_Vector to hold the result. These arrays were formally named above in their proper place before the task body.

```
declare
  Parallel_Product : array (Source_Vector'range) of Partial_Product;
begin
  for Index in Source_Vector'range
    loop
      Parallel_Product(Index).Send_Values(A_Matrix(Index), Source_Vector);
    end loop;
  for Index in Source_Vector'range
    loop
      Parallel_Product(Index).Receive_Value(Product_Vector(Index));
    end loop;
end;
```

In this example, the family of task objects (`Parallel_Product`) is in existence only within the scope of this local block. We first `Send_Values` to each task by sending a component of `A_Matrix` and the entire `Source_Vector`. We then loop until we `Receive_Value` from each task. Then we place the partial product in the appropriate component of `Product_Vector`. Note that this method is practical only when the underlying system contains more than one processor. On a single processor there would be too much overhead in switching from task to task. This same technique is applicable to collections of independent equations.

Routing Messages

Another typical application area for Ada's tasks is that of message routing; we may wish to route messages to other tasks or to physical devices. In the simplest form of message routing, a task can be defined for each peripheral; the tasks are then used to buffer data transfers. For example, we can spool output for a printer. As another task puts characters on the printer, the spooling task accepts the entry and takes the characters so that the first task can be released to continue its processing. The spooling task will then send the characters to the printer as long as there are no further requests. If the spooling buffer is not full, the task accepts characters for printing. However, if the buffer is full, that task closes the entry alternative and forces putting tasks to wait until the buffer is open again.

In our problem solution, we have chosen to implement an internal buffer using the generic `Queues` package created in Chapter 12 using `Character` elements. In addition, we shall assume that the output to the printer is available through a file named `"printer"`. The code can be written as follows:

```
task Spool is
  entry Put(A_Character : in Character);
end Spool;
task body Spool is
  package Character_Queue is new Queues(Item => Character);
  use Character_Queue;
  Buffer      : Character_Queue.Queue(Size => 100);
  A_Character : Character;
  Printer     : Text_IO.File_Type;
begin
  Clear(Buffer);
  Text_IO.Open(File => Printer,
               Mode => Text_IO.Out_File,
               Name => "printer");
  loop
    select
      when Length_Of (Buffer) < 100 =>
        accept Put(A_Character : in Character) do
          Add(A_Character, Buffer);
        end Put;
      else
        if Length_Of(Buffer) > 0 then
          Remove(A_Character, Buffer);
          Text_IO.Put(Printer, A_Character);
        end if;
    end select;
  end loop;
end Spool;
```

Since the language rules do not permit the declaration of tasks as library units, we often encapsulate a task inside a package. We then make such a package visible through a **with** clause in a context specification. For example, we can write a package specification for the Spool task as:

```
package Spooled_Print is
  procedure Put(A_Character : in Character);
end Spooled_Print;
```

The corresponding package body can be written as:

```
with Text_IO, Queues;
use Text_IO;
```

```
package body Spooled_Print is
  task Spool is
    entry Put(A_Character : in Character);
  end Spool;
  task body Spool is
    package Character_Queue is new Queues(Item => Character);
    use Character_Queue;
    Buffer        : Character_Queue.Queue(Size => 100);
    The_Character : Character;
    Printer       : Text_IO.File_Type;
  begin
    Clear (Buffer);
    Text_IO.Open(File => Printer,
                 Mode => Text_IO.Out_File,
                 Name => "printer");
    loop
      select
        when Length_Of (Buffer) < 100 =>
          accept Put(A_Character : in Character) do
            Add(A_Character, Buffer);
          end Put;
      else
        if not Is_Empty(Buffer) then
          Remove(The_Character, Buffer);
          Text_IO.Put(Printer, The_Character);
        end if;
      end select;
    end loop;
  end Spool;
  procedure Put(A_Character : in Character) is
  begin
    Spool.Put(A_Character);
  end Put;
end Spooled_Print;
```

Notice that we have called the entry Spool.Put within the procedure Put. In this way, the implementation (task versus subprogram) is hidden from the user.

In a more complicated example of message passing, we may have a task that routes messages to other tasks, as in a distributed processing system. Such a task would be an actor/server in the sense that it would have defined entries and would also call the entries of other tasks. In this example, we shall assume that the information passed by this task is of the type

Message. Furthermore, a calling task can route a message to one of three destinations. Additionally, the task can indicate a priority for the message, with higher-priority messages being serviced first. We thus need the following entities visible to our task:

```
procedure Main is
   type Message is ...
   my_message, your_message : Message;
   type Priority is (Low, Medium, High);
   type Place    is range 1..3;
   task Destination_1 is
      entry Send(A_Message : in Message);
   end Destination_1;
   task Destination_2 is
      entry Send(A_Message : in Message);
   end Destination_2;
   task Destination_3 is
      entry Send(A_Message : in Message);
   end Destination_3;
```

Here, we assume that each destination processes the message in a different manner. If, instead, the processes are identical, we can use a family of tasks.

For the routing task, the processing for each level of priority is identical, so we use a family of entries. The task specification can be defined as:

```
task Transmit is
   entry Routed_Priority(Priority)(The_Message : in Message; To : in Place);
end Transmit;
procedure Route(The_Message : in Message; To : in Place) is separate;
task body Destination_1 is separate;
task body Destination_2 is separate;
task body Destination_3 is separate;
task body Transmit is separate;
```

Because of the naming conventions used, notice how readable a call to this task is:

```
begin
   ...
   Transmit.Routed_Priority(Medium)(My_Message, To => 1);
   Transmit.Routed_Priority(Low)(Your_Message, To => 3);
   ...
end Main;
```

An even better style would be to declare an enumeration type for `Place` instead of using an integer value.

For the task body, our algorithm will use a **select** statement to choose among the possible entries. In addition, as long as there are higher-priority messages, the alternatives must be closed to the lower priorities. This can be accomplished by using a **select** with guards. Since the algorithm for selecting the destination is the same for each priority, we can first write the subprogram:

```
separate (Main)
procedure Route(The_Message : in Message; To : in Place) is
begin
  case To is
    when 1 => Destination_1.Send(The_Message);
    when 2 => Destination_2.Send(The_Message);
    when 3 => Destination_3.Send(The_Message);
  end case;
end Route;
```

It is not a problem that multiple tasks call this procedure, since Ada requires that subprograms be reentrant.

If `Route` is visible to `Transmit`, we can next complete the body of `Transmit`:

```
separate (Main)
task body Transmit is
begin
  loop
    select
      accept Routed_Priority(High)(The_Message : in Message;
                                    To          : in Place) do
        Route(The_Message, To);
      end Routed_Priority;
    or
      when Routed_Priority(High)'Count = 0 =>
        accept Routed_Priority(Medium)(The_Message : in Message;
                                        To          : in Place) do
          Route(The_Message, To);
        end Routed_Priority;
    or
      when Routed_Priority(High)'Count = 0 and
           Routed_Priority(Medium)'Count = 0 =>
```

```
        accept Routed_Priority(Low)(The_Message : in Message;
                                    To           : in Place) do
            Route(The_Message, To);
        end Routed_Priority;
    end select;
  end loop;
end Transmit;
```

Notice how we used the `Count` attribute to ensure that there were no higher-priority tasks waiting to be serviced. The semantics of `Count` are such that `Count` is zero if there are no tasks that have called a particular entry.

Controlling Resources

When we decompose a problem into its functional parts and then implement each action using subprograms, it is generally poor programming practice to let such entities use global data. As we discussed in Chapter 2, the use of global data increases the coupling among program modules, thereby making the entire system less maintainable and less reliable. Instead, it is better practice to pass only the data that a particular module sets or uses. In the case of tasks, however, we may have a situation where two or more tasks need to access the same data concurrently. Since several tasks may try to read the value while others may be writing it at the same time, we must have some way of excluding all but one task from accessing the value.

If two or more tasks must access a global entity (not recommended), the following can be applied:

```
pragma Shared (variable_name);
```

We can apply this `pragma` to any scalar object, such as:

```
pragma Shared (Index);
```

To allow multiple tasks to set or use the value of `Index`, this `pragma` must be applied. The `Shared` pragma does provide task synchronization and is necessary to ensure that shared data is properly referenced by two or more tasks, since an optimizing compiler may affect the run-time location of certain entities.

Instead of using global variables, a task can be used to seize or release a given resource. For example, when updating an element of a data base, we would permit only one task to access a given record at a time, such as:

```
Seize_Resource;
-- update the data here
Release_Resource;
```

The `Seize_Resource` and `Release_Resource` entries act as semaphores. If one task has already taken the resource, other tasks will wait at the `Seize_Resource` entry in the order of the request until the task inside the critical section enters `Release_Resource`. We can implement the semaphores as:

```
task Semaphore is
  entry Seize_Resource;
  entry Release_Resource;
end Semaphore;
task body Semaphore is
  In_Use : Boolean := False;
begin
  loop
    select
      when not In_Use =>
        accept Seize_Resource;
        In_Use := True;
    or
      when In_Use =>
        accept Release_Resource;
        In_Use := False;
    end select;
  end loop;
end Semaphore;
```

If it is necessary to protect the access of several data objects, a better approach to shared data is to create a task type for controlling resources, such as:

```
procedure Main is
  task type Resource is
    entry Seize;
    entry Release;
  end Resource;
```

The body of this task type would be equivalent to the body of the task `Semaphore`. For those elements to be shared among tasks, we can create a record such as:

```
type Protected_Data is
  record
    Data_Item    : Data;
    The_Resource : Resource;
  end record;
```

Since a task type is limited private, we could not copy or assign a value to objects of type Protected_Data. Instead, we would apply the following algorithm:

```
Shared_Data : Protected_Data;
task body Resource is separate;
begin
  ..
Shared_Data.The_Resource.Seize;
-- update Shared_Data.Data_Item here
Shared_Data.The_Resource.Release;
  ...
end Main;
```

We may still be forced at some point to communicate using global data, perhaps for efficiency reasons. Such an approach has the same side effects as the unsynchronized type of communication mentioned earlier in the chapter. This approach is primitive and unstructured, and so it is easy to produce an erroneous algorithm. The best approach is to encapsulate the shared data in a task, such as:

```
task Protected_Item is
  entry Set(An_Item :  in Item);
  entry Get(An_Item : out Item);
end Protected_Item;
task body Protected_Item is
  Local_Item : Item;
begin
  loop
    select
      accept Set(An_Item : in Item) do
        Local_Item := An_Item;
      end Set;
    or
      accept Get(An_Item : out Item) do
        An_Item := Local_Item;
      end Get;
    end select;
  end loop;
end Protected_Item;
```

In this case, several tasks may be trying to Set or Get the object at the same time, but this task prevents simultaneous access. Although we do not indicate the solution here, this task can be modified to permit multiple readers and writers.

Interrupts

In embedded systems, we must often respond to asynchronous events indicated by a hardware or software interrupt. In most other languages, we would have to resort to an assembly language routine to handle the interrupt. In Ada, however, we can treat interrupts as calls to entries of a task. Assuming that the underlying machine permits vectored interrupts, an Ada task can be attached to the interrupt. For example:

```
with System;
procedure main is
  task Power_Failure is
    entry Fail;
    for Fail use at 16#1FE#;
  end Power_Failure;
  task body Power_Failure is
  begin
    loop
      accept Fail;
      -- do some actions
    end loop;
  end Power_Failure;
begin -- Main
  ...
end Main;
```

In this example, we have attached the `Power_Failure` interrupt to the hardware location 1FE hexadecimal, even though the task body may be elsewhere in memory. When we receive a hardware interrupt and the machine execution jumps to this location, the action is equivalent to calling the entry `Fail`. The task can then accept the entry and act as an interrupt service routine. The `for` clause is an example of a representation specification that allows us to use machine-dependent facilities. We shall study these features in greater depth in the next chapter.

Summary ■ Tasks are entities that operate in parallel with other program units.

■ Intertask communication is provided by the rendezvous. One task must call the entry of another, which in turn must accept the entry.

- Tasks include a specification and a body. Both can be compiled independently. A task cannot be compiled alone, however. Rather, it must be compiled in the context of another unit such as a library package or a subprogram.

- Task specifications include entries, which define the communication paths available to other tasks.

- When a task calls the entry of another task, it is serviced immediately if the called task is waiting at an **accept**. Otherwise, the calling task is placed in an implicit entry queue to be serviced in the order in which it was called.

- A task is activated at the end of the elaboration of the enclosing declarative region. A task completes when it finishes executing its sequence of statements, then terminates after any dependent tasks have completed.

- Task bodies define the action of a task.

- A number of statements provide various kinds of task communication. The simplest form is a single **accept** statement. Advanced forms include the selective wait, the selective wait with an **else** part, the selective wait with guards, the **select** with a **terminate** alternative, the timed entry call, and the conditional entry call.

- Tasks are usually used to express concurrent actions, for routing messages, for managing shared resources, and for interrupt handling.

Exercises

1. Subprograms can be used to express abstract action, while packages can be used to express abstract objects or data types. How would you best classify a package that contains a task?

2. Sending a parcel across the country takes at least three independent actors: the sender, the carrier, and the receiver. Write the task specifications for all three of these entities. We can represent the sender as an actor task (no entry calls), the carrier as a transducer (one entry call named Receive_Parcel, plus the need to call the entry of another task), and the receiver as a server task (one entry call named Accept_Parcel).

3. Write the bodies of the above three tasks, using simple task communication. Assume that the parcel is of type Parcel_Kind.

4. Rewrite the task bodies from Exercise 3, this time adding a return receipt path. In other words, once the receiver gets the parcel, the carrier returns a message to the sender indicating successful delivery. You will need to add entry calls to the sender and the carrier.

5. Modify the task bodies from Exercise 4 so that the sender will wait only five seconds for the return receipt. Raise an exception (called `Complain_About_Service`) if the receipt does not arrive in time.

*6. Modify the task bodies from Exercise 5 so that if the carrier cannot deliver the message to the receiver within one second, the carrier will then deliver the parcel to another receiver. Send a receipt back to the sender telling it who finally received the parcel.

*7. Add `terminate` alternatives to each of the above tasks so that they die gracefully once the parcel is delivered and the return receipt is accepted.

*8. The task named `Spool` presented earlier in this chapter has a flaw: If the `Buffer` is empty and the `Producer` is not sending any characters, the `Spool` task is in a busy wait. Rewrite the `Spool` task body to eliminate the busy wait.

*9. In the discussion of the `Read_Flag` function in Chapter 8, we argued that readability is usually increased by simplicity. In light of this, argue that the following is a better implementation of the `Semaphore` task:

```
task body Semaphore is
begin
  loop
    select
      accept Seize_Resource;
      accept Release_Resource;
    or
      terminate;
    end select;
  end loop;
end Semaphore;
```

15

Exception Handling

Declaring and Raising Exceptions
Handling Exceptions
Applying Exceptions

I n embedded computer systems, run-time reliability is an important factor: If we have a software system in a satellite or a nuclear power plant,
we cannot afford any errors. However, there are sometimes exceptional
situations beyond our control, such as hardware failures in peripheral
devices or unexpected bursts of input data. We cannot predict when such
situations might occur, but, in a reliable system, they must be planned for.
In a sense we must always program defensively.

In Ada terminology, an *exception* names an event that causes suspension of normal program execution. This event might be an error, such as
the predefined `Numeric_Error`, or it might be an exceptional condition that
requires special attention, such as a buffer overflow. In the best case, we
would like the program to be able to respond to the exception. In the worst
case, in which total recovery is beyond our control, such as the failure of a
peripheral device, we would like to gracefully degrade. That is, we wish to
continue processing with reduced capability. *Raising* an exception brings
the condition to our attention; we call the response *handling the exception*.

When we step through our object-oriented development method, we
can recognize exceptional conditions associated with the logical properties
of our high-level objects, such as an `Overflow` exception during a `Put` on a
queue. For lower-level data structures, such as arrays or even integer
objects, many conditions related to logical violations are available as the

predefined exceptions. In either case, it is generally good practice to explicitly recognize such conditions as exceptions and plan for them in solutions.

15.1 Declaring and Raising Exceptions

As we have seen, Ada permits us to declare user-defined exceptions, but it also includes several predefined exception conditions. Five predefined exceptions are declared as part of package `Standard`: `Constraint_Error`, `Numeric_Error`, `Program_Error`, `Storage_Error`, and `Tasking_Error`. Later in this section, we shall discuss the conditions under which these exceptions are raised. In Chapter 18, we shall examine a number of predefined exceptions associated with Ada's I/O facilities.

Technically an exception is not an object, but user-defined conditions can be declared anywhere an object declaration is appropriate (except as a subprogram or generic unit parameter). A user-defined exception declaration takes a form similar to an object declaration. It consists of an identifier list, a colon, and the reserved word `exception`, as the following examples indicate:

```
Above_Limits, Below_Limits : exception;
Parity_Error               : exception;
Fatal_Disk_Error           : exception;
```

The name of a user-defined exception has the same scope as an object declaration (see Chapter 20), although the effect of an exception may extend beyond its scope.

A program signals a user-defined exception by executing an explicit `raise` statement, as the following illustrates:

```
raise Fatal_Disk_Error;
raise Above_Limits;
raise;
```

The last of the examples above can be used only in an exception handler and it re-raises the exception that caused the exception handler statement to be executed. We will discuss exception handlers in more detail in the next section.

A predefined exception is raised implicitly by the run-time system, as the following illustrates;

- `Constraint_Error` Raised when a range, index, or discriminant constraint is violated.

- `Numeric_Error` Raised when a numeric operation cannot yield a value (i.e., `Any_Value / 0`) or yields a value outside the bounds of the implemented range.

- **Program_Error** Raised when all alternatives of a **select** statement having no **else** part are closed. Also raised if an attempt is made to access a subprogram, package, or task before it is elaborated, or if an attempt is made to exit a function without returning a value. An implementation can also raise this exception if an erroneous condition is detected.

- **Storage_Error** Raised when the available dynamic storage is exhausted.

- **Tasking_Error** Raised when exceptions arise during intertask communication.

A `Constraint_Error` is raised in a number of situations, such as when the range of an object is exceeded:

```
procedure Out_Of_Range is
  Count : Natural := 0;
  Value : Natural := 1;
begin
  Count := Value - 4;  -- the result, - 3, is not a value of Natural.
end Out_Of_Range;
```

Referencing a component that does not exist in the current context will also raise `Constraint_Error`:

```
with Text_IO; Use Text_IO;
procedure Does_Not_Exist is
  type Text is access String;
  type Value (Valid : Boolean := False) is
    record
      case Valid is
        when False => null;
        when True  => N : Integer;
      end case;
    end record;
  package Value_IO is new Integer_IO(Integer);
  use Value_IO;
  Name   : Text;  -- Name has value null.
  Result : Value; -- Result.Valid is False.
begin
  Put(Name.all);  -- Name.all does not exist, raises Constraint_Error
  Put(Result.N);  -- Result.N does not exist, raises Constraint_Error
end Does_Not_Exist;
```

There are situations where it is not clear whether `Constraint_Error` or `Numeric_Error` will be raised. For example:

```
Too_Big : Integer := Integer'Last + 1;
```

In such situations the defensive programmer must be ready to handle either exception.

Because `Constraint_Error` can be raised in so many ways, it is considered good practice to be explicit about the errors you plan to handle. For example, consider a stack that is implemented as an array with an index to the top of the stack:

```
with Text_IO; use Text_IO;
procedure Explicit is
   subtype Item is Natural range 0..10;
   type List is array (Positive range <>) of Item;
   Max_Size : constant := 20;
   type Stack is
     record
       Items : List (1 .. Max_Size);
       Top   : Natural := 0;
     end record;
   Overflow : exception;
   A_Stack  : Stack;
   procedure Push (The_Item : in Item; Onto : in out Stack) is separate;
begin
   for Count in 1..25
     loop
       Push ( 5, A_Stack );
     end loop;
end Explicit;
```

An attempt to push an item onto a stack will fail if there are already `Max_Size` items on the stack. The `Push` procedure could be implemented by implicitly detecting when the stack is full:

```
separate(Explicit)
procedure Push (The_Item : in Item; Onto : in out Stack) is
begin
   Onto.Top := Onto.Top + 1;
   Onto.Items(Onto.Top) := The_Item;
exception
   when Constraint_Error => raise Overflow;
end Push;
```

The second assignment statement will raise `Constraint_Error`, when indexing the array, if `Onto.Top` is greater than `Max_Size`. The author of the procedure should have made this condition explicit in order to increase understandability and modifiability. Further, since we have partially updated the stack (i.e., we have incremented `Top`) before checking this condition, we will return a corrupt stack if `Overflow` is raised, because `Top` is now greater than `Max_Size`. It is better simply to check for the condition under which `Overflow` is raised at the beginning of the procedure:

```
separate(Explicit)
procedure Push (The_Item : in Item; Onto : in out Stack) is
begin
  if Onto.Top = Max_Size then
    raise Overflow;
  else
    Onto.Top := Onto.Top + 1;
    Onto.Items(Onto.Top) := The_Item;
  end if;
end Push;
```

As was mentioned previously, one of the conditions under which the exception `Program_Error` is raised includes detection of an erroneous condition. An *erroneous condition* is one in which the effect is unpredictable, such as attempting to use a function that has not been given a value upon return.

It is important to note that when an exception is raised, the only information available is the fact that an exception did occur. In a sense, an exception is only a symptom of a problem; it is the responsibility of the programmer to develop an appropriate algorithm to respond to the cause.

Detecting exceptional conditions imposes a run-time overhead, the extent of which is somewhat dependent on the particular implementation. Nevertheless, it is a good practice to use exceptions to promote increased understandability, reliability, and maintainability. Greater gains in execution are generally achieved by the use of a better macrostructure, as opposed to the microefficiency of suppressing run-time exception detection.

However, if there is some compelling reason to do so, such as very critical space or time considerations, Ada permits the suppression of various run-time checks. We can use the `pragma Suppress` in the declarative part of a program unit or block. This pragma's first argument is an identifier that represents the check to be suppressed, followed by an optional second argument giving the name of a type, an object, or a unit for which no run-time checks are desired. If the second argument is not given, the run-time check is suppressed over the remaining declarative region. The following check names can be used:

- *Suppression of* Constraint_Error *checks*

  Access_Check
  Discriminant_Check
  Index_Check
  Length_Check
  Range_Check

- *Suppression of* Numeric_Error *checks*

  Division_Check
  Overflow_Check

- *Suppression of* Program_Error *checks*

  Elaboration_Check

- *Suppression of* Storage_Error *checks*

  Storage_Check

For example, if we want to suppress the run-time check for range constraints on a type called Index, we can write the following:

```
pragma Suppress (Range_Check, On => Index);
```

Notice how the second argument is included using named association notation. Again, we do not recommend the use of this pragma.

15.2   Handling Exceptions

When an exception such as a divide-by-zero condition occurs in most languages, normal processing is suspended and control returns to the operating system. In any reliable system, we cannot permit a program to come to an abnormal finish; we must have some way to intercept the exception. To satisfy this need, Ada permits us to write exception handlers to capture both predefined and user-defined exceptions. When an exception is raised in a given unit, processing of that unit is abandoned and control passes to its exception handler. Exception handlers appear after the reserved word exception, which is an optional end of any frame. (A frame is any begin sequence_of_statements end;.) For example, a frame occurs in a block statement and in the body of a subprogram, package, or task.

The optional exception part of a frame has a form similar to a case statement. Each when clause represents an exception handler and designates the action in response to a particular exception. For example:

```
with Text_IO; use Text_IO;
procedure Block_Example is
  procedure Open_Valve is
  begin
    Put_Line ("open valve");
  end Open_Valve;
  procedure Sound_Alarm is
  begin
    Put_Line ("sound alarm");
  end Sound_Alarm;
  procedure Close_Valve is
  begin
    Put_Line("close valve");
  end Close_Valve;
  procedure Log_Unknown_Error is
  begin
    Put_Line("log unknown error");
  end Log_Unknown_Error;
begin
  -- any sequence of statements
  declare                   -- the start of a block statement
    Low_Fluid_Level : exception;
  begin
    null;    -- any sequence of statements
  exception                 -- marks the beginning of exception part
    when Low_Fluid_Level => -- one exception handler
      Open_Valve;
      Sound_Alarm;
    when Numeric_Error =>    -- a second exception handler
      Close_Valve;
      raise;
    when others =>          -- the last exception handler
      Log_Unknown_Error;
  end;
  -- any sequence of statements
end Block_Example;
```

In the above example, to support the exceptions occurring in the sequence of statements for the given block statement, the handler can name any visible exceptions (such as Low_Fluid_Level and any predefined exceptions) and then list a sequence of statements to be executed in response to each particular exception. An `others` clause handles all exceptions previously unnamed in this handler or any exceptions whose names are not known in this scope of declaration. If the exception `Low_Fluid_Level` is raised in the block, the exception handler would respond by executing the statements `Open_Valve` and then `Sound_Alarm`. `Numeric_Error` is handled by calling `Close_Valve` and then re-raising the same exception. All other exceptions are handled by calling `Log_Unknown_Error`.

It is important to note that once the exception has been recognized by an exception handler the exceptional condition no longer exists and the exception is said to be lowered. When an exception handler has completed its processing, control does not return to the point where the exception was raised, but simply continues past the bottom of the frame in which the exception was handled. In the next section, we will examine how to try an operation again. If no exception is raised, processing continues normally and we eventually fall through the bottom of the frame without executing any of the exception handler statements.

In the above discussion, we assumed that every frame would contain an exception handler to capture all local exceptions. However, in terms of program design this is usually not the best approach. Instead, it is better programming practice to apply the principle of levels of abstraction, just as we did for data types. Thus, a preferable approach is to design exception handlers to capture exceptions at the lowest possible level at which the program can properly respond to the error. Often, at lower levels, the response to predefined exceptions is simply to raise a user-defined exception, thus promoting the exception to the appropriate level of abstraction.

For example, in a matrix-processing package, we may encounter a divide-by-zero condition when inverting a matrix; the exception `Numeric_Error` might be raised locally in response to the error. The package cannot properly respond to the condition, since it cannot know the purpose of the inversion. Instead, we could export an exception `Is_Singular` to the calling routine in response to the local exception.

On the other hand, it may be preferable to capture the exception at a lower level, such as in an I/O driver routine. A program that is trying to write to a serial I/O port should not have to be concerned with the details of the communication, such as responding to parity or framing errors; these exceptions should be handled locally within the driver.

If we do not respond to an exception in the frame where it is raised, the exception is propagated until it reaches a level where the exception can be handled. For example, we may have the following main program:

```
with Text_IO; use Text_IO;
procedure Main is                                        ⎤ Subprogram
  procedure Do_Something is
  begin
    Put_Line("do something");
  end Do_Something;
  procedure Do_Something_Else is
  begin
    Put_Line("do something else");
  end Do_Something_Else;
  procedure Do_Something_More is
  begin
    Put_Line("do something more");
  end Do_Something_More;
begin
  -- any sequence of statements
  declare                          ⎤
    Local_Error : exception;       | Local block
  begin                            |
    -- any sequence of statements  |
  exception                        |
    when Local_Error =>            |
      Do_Something;                |
  end;                             ⎦
  -- any sequence of statements
exception
  when Constraint_Error =>
    Do_Something_Else;
  when Numeric_Error =>
    Do_Something_More;
end Main;
```

Since the predefined exceptions in the above example are declared in package Standard, they are visible both to the subprogram body and within the block statement. We also defined an exception named Local_Error, which is local to the block statement. If Local_Error is raised inside the block, the local exception handler will capture the error and Do_Something. Then, control will pass to the end of the block because of the control flow defined for exceptions.

On the other hand, if Constraint_Error is raised inside the block statement, the exception is propagated to the containing body. In the subprogram, we capture the locally raised Constraint_Error and then Do_Something_Else. Also, if Numeric_Error is raised inside the local block statement, there is no local exception handler; thus, the exception is propagated up to the unit that contains a handler for Numeric_Error.

In the final case, if the exception Program_Error is raised in the local block statement (or in the subprogram), perhaps during the elaboration of the declarative part of the block statement, we would find no exception handler at all. Control would then pass to the calling environment (the operating system). Generally, we can nest block statements, each with or without its own exception handler. An exception that is raised at a given block statement and not handled locally will propagate to the level of the containing block statement until it is handled.

A similar rule for exception propagation occurs for subprograms that are not the main program. Consider the following:

```
with Text_IO; use Text_IO;                              Outer
procedure Main is                                       subprogram
   ...
   type Small is digits 5 range 0.0.. 10.0;
      ...
   function Inverse(I : Float)
           return Small is              Local
   begin                                subprogram
     return Small(1.0/I);
   exception
     when Numeric_Error =>
       return 10.0;
   end Inverse;
      ...
   procedure Calling is                 Local
     X : Float := 0.0;                  subprogram
     Y : Small;
     procedure Do_Something is
     begin
       Put_Line("do something");
     end Do_Something;
   begin
      ...
     Y := Inverse ( X );
      ...
   exception
     when Constraint_Error =>
       Do_Something;
   end Calling;
begin
   ...
   Calling;
   ...
end Main;
```

In this example, if we called `Inverse` with an actual parameter of 0.0, the exception `Numeric_Error` will be raised in the subprogram. Since there exists a local exception handler to capture the error, the handler would execute and return the value 10.0. On the other hand, if we tried to obtain the `Inverse` of 0.0001, the exception `Constraint_Error` will be raised inside the subprogram `Inverse`. According to the rules of the language, since the local exception handler does not capture this exception, this same exception will be raised at the point of the call inside the procedure `Calling`. `Calling` has an exception handler for `Constraint_Error`; the exception is lowered and the statement `Do_Something` is executed.

Note also that if an exception occurs during the elaboration of the declarative part of a subprogram, the exception is raised at the point of the call. If this subprogram is the main program, execution of the unit is abandoned. Actually, this is a reasonable strategy since, if the entities in the declarative part of a main program are elaborated with errors, we cannot be assured of the program's initial state, and further processing would be unreliable.

We now consider the rules of exception handling for package and task units. If a given package is not a library unit and if an unhandled exception occurs in the sequence of statements of a package body or during the elaboration of that package's declarative part, the exception is propagated to a point immediately following the package body in the unit containing the package declaration. On the other hand, if the package is a library unit and an exception occurs, execution of the main program is abandoned for the same reason cited in the previous paragraph.

If an exception is raised when the declarative part of a task is elaborated, the exception `Tasking_Error` will be raised at the point of task activation, and the task will be marked completed. If an unresolved exception is raised during the execution of the body of the task, that task is completed and the exception is propagated no further, as we discussed in Chapter 14.

We must also handle the special case of an exception occurring during task rendezvous. In conjunction with the asymmetry of Ada's tasking mechanisms, the language rules state that the exception `Tasking_Error` is raised in the calling task at the point of the entry call if the called task is not active when the entry is called or if it completes before accepting the entry call.

If the called task terminates abnormally during a rendezvous, then the exception `Tasking_Error` is also raised in the calling task. If the calling task is aborted during a rendezvous, no exception is propagated to the called task. Finally, if an exception is raised in an `accept` statement but not handled within that `accept` statement, execution of the accept statement is abandoned, and the same exception is raised in the task containing the abandoned **accept** statement. The exception is also raised in the calling task at the point of the entry call.

Before leaving this section, we need to elaborate on the idea of propagating an exception beyond its scope. In other words, an exception, whose name is known locally, can be propagated beyond the unit in which it was declared to a point where the exception has no name to which we can refer. Consider the following situation:

```
with Text_IO; use Text_IO;
procedure Local is
  procedure Do_Something is
  begin
    Put_Line("do something");
  end Do_Something;
  procedure Do_Something_Else is
  begin
    Put_Line("do something else");
  end Do_Something_Else;
begin
  ...
  declare                                          Outer
  ...                                              block
  begin
    ...
    declare                           Local
      Local_Exception : exception;    block
    begin
      ...
      raise Local_Exception;
      ...
    end;
    ...
  exception
    when Numeric_Error =>
      Do_Something;
    when others =>
      Do_Something_Else;
  end;
  ...
end Local;
```

The Local_Exception is known only inside the local block. If we raise Local_Exception, it will be propagated outside the block, since we have not provided a local exception handler. In the outer block, we cannot know the name of this exception, since we are outside the scope of the block statement in which Local_Exception was declared. We can capture it only by using the others clause.

15.3   Applying Exceptions

As is the case with every Ada construct discussed so far, there are proper and improper ways to apply exceptions. For example, we should not use exceptions to provide some sort of implicit goto facility. Rather, when modeling solutions, we should try to recognize the possible error states of our objects and algorithms and explicitly use exceptions only to plan for their resolution.

When an exception is raised, there are several alternative courses of action, namely:

- Abandon the execution of the unit.

- Try the operation again.

- Use an alternative approach.

- Repair the cause of the error.

The use of the first alternative (abandonment, just ignoring an exception) is not normally considered good programming practice; if an error occurs, we should take some sort of action. Abandonment is appropriate, however, if it is impossible to continue processing the current unit or block statement. For example, if we have a fatal error in a peripheral device that prevents us from doing any further I/O, our action would be to cease processing and report the condition.

As the following example indicates, we can export exceptions as part of a package specification:

```
package IO_Interface is
  procedure Put (A_Character : in Character);
  Timeout : exception;
end IO_Interface;
package body IO_Interface is
  Milliseconds : constant Duration := 0.01;
  task IO_Driver is
    entry Send (C : in Character);
  end IO_Driver;
```

```
task body IO_Driver is
begin
  loop
    ...
    accept Send ( C : in Character ) do
      -- peripheral dependent code
    end Send;
    ...
  end loop;
end IO_Driver;
procedure Put (C : in Character) is
begin
  select
    IO_Driver.Send(C);
  or
    delay 5*Milliseconds;
    raise Timeout;
  end select;
end Put;
end IO_Interface;
```

In this case we defined an IO_Interface that queues requests to Put
character values; inside the package body is a task that implements the
spooled communication. When we Put a value, we are indirectly calling the
task through the subprogram. If the peripheral device fails to respond within the stated delay, we will assume a physical device failure. In our algorithm, we choose to raise the exception Timeout, which will be exported to
the point where the subprogram Put was called. Since we named the exception Timeout in the package specification, users of this package can write an
exception handler that names this exception.

Rather than abandon an operation, we can choose the second alternative, to repeat an operation after an exception is raised. The technique we
use to repeat the operation is to declare a local block statement that encapsulates the algorithm we want to defend, and then place the block inside a
loop that repeats the operation. For example, the following code implements recovery from human input of an enumeration value:

```
with Text_IO; use Text_IO;
procedure Second_Alternative_1 is
  type Response is (Up, Down, Left, Right);
  package Response_IO is new Enumeration_IO ( Response );
  use Response_IO;
  User_Request : Response;
```

```
begin
  loop  -- repeat the operation
    begin   -- start of the defended code
      Put(">");
      Get (User_Request) ;
      Skip_Line;
      exit;              -- exit if there is no exception
    exception
      when Data_Error =>
        Skip_Line; -- skip the bad input
        Put_Line("Invalid response; enter only Up, Down, Left, or Right.");
    end;
  end loop;
end Second_Alternative_1;
```

When we enter the block, we issue a prompt and then wait for a User_Request input. If the input is valid, we proceed to the next statement and exit the loop. If the user enters something other than Up, Down, Left, or Right, the exception Data_Error will be raised by the I/O package (see Chapter 18 for further details). After we display the error message, execution of the block is abandoned. However, since the block is inside a loop, we return to the top of the loop and reenter the block, repeating the process until the user enters a valid response, which lets us exit the loop.

Looping until a user input is valid is probably a reasonable design decision. However, there are some cases in which we wish to retry an operation only a certain number of times—such as when we are trying to communicate with a peripheral device. As an example, we modify our original protected input routine to retry an operation five times only:

```
with Text_IO; use Text_IO;
procedure Second_Alternative_2 is
  type Response is (Up, Down, Left, Right);
  package Response_IO is new Enumeration_IO ( Response );
  use Response_IO;
  User_Request : Response;
begin
  for Repeat_Count in 1..5 -- repeat the operation
  loop
    begin                 -- start of the defended code
      Put(">");
      Get(User_Request);
```

```
        Skip_Line;
        exit;                   --exit if there is no exception
    exception
      when Data_Error =>
        Skip_Line;
        if Repeat_Count < 5 then
          Put_Line("Invalid response; " &
                      "enter only Up, Down, Left, or Right.");
        else
          Put_Line("You tried too many times... Up is assumed.");
          User_Request := Up;
        end if;
      end;
    end loop;
  end Second_Alternative_2;
```

In this case, if the exception Data_Error is raised, the exception handler determines how many times we have already retried the operation and prints an appropriate message. Rather than repairing the user's error we could also have raised an exception to pass on the condition to the next higher program unit.

We next consider the third course of action in response to an exception using an alternative approach. For an example we use a critical message–routing system in which a high degree of reliability may be required; here we design a number of redundant communication tasks. Thus, if we try to enter a given task and receive a Tasking_Error exception that indicates a failure in the communications path, we try an alternative route. Consider this example:

```
begin
  Send_Message_To_Path_1 (Critical_Message);
exception
  when Tasking_Error => Send_Message_To_Path_2 (Critical_Message);
end;
```

As before, notice how we used a block statement with a local exception handler to defend a section of code.

If we apply a family of tasks instead of using individual communicating tasks, we can combine this alternative approach with the previous method of retrying an operation:

```
with Text_IO; use Text_IO;
procedure Task_Error is
  task type Message_Task is
    entry Put( Message : String );
  end Message_Task;
  Send_Message : array ( 1..10 ) of Message_Task;
  task body Message_Task is
  begin
    loop
      accept Put ( Message : String ) do
        Text_IO.Put_Line ( Message );
      end Put;
    end loop;
  end Message_Task;
  procedure Send_Alert_To_Operator is
  begin
    Put_Line ("Can not send message");
  end Send_Alert_To_Operator;
begin  -- Task_Error
  for Index in Send_Message´range
    loop
      begin
        Send_Message( Index ).Put( "Critical_Message" );
        exit;
      exception
        when Tasking_Error =>
          if Index = Send_Message´Last then
            Send_Alert_To_Operator;
            raise; -- propagate Tasking_Error
          end if;
      end;
    end loop;
end Task_Error;:
```

In this example, we try to send a message to one of ten possible message tasks. If we fail to pass the message ten times (for example, if the called tasks are all terminated), then we Send_Alert_To_Operator. In addition, we raise the same exception (Tasking_Error) to propagate it to the next handler.

The fourth alternative approach for Ada exceptions is to repair the cause of the error. For an exception handler within a subprogram, all of the local subprogram objects, including the formal parameters, are visible to us. We can use these objects to repair the cause of the error. For example, in a control system, we can call a subprogram to command the movement of a control surface. There will certainly be a feedback mechanism to relay the effect of this command: If we send too large a command, we may exceed the limitations of the control surface movement. An exception then needs to be raised before we destroy the control surface. This can be achieved via the following code:

```
with Text_IO; use Text_IO;
procedure Main is
  procedure Move_Rudder(Amount : in Integer) is
    Rudder_Stressed : exception;
  begin
    -- send command to rudder servomechanism,
    -- the local exception may be raised here
    if Amount > 0 then
      raise Rudder_Stressed;
    else
      return;
    end if;
  exception
    when Rudder_Stressed =>
      Put_Line("reduce amount");
      Move_Rudder ( Amount / 2 ); -- retry
  end Move_Rudder;
  begin  -- Main
    Move_Rudder(10);
  end Main;
```

Summary

- Reliable systems often need be programmed defensively by anticipating and handling exceptional conditions.

- Exceptions can be handled by one of several techniques: abandonment, by trying again, by using an alternative approach, or by repairing the cause of the exception.

Exercises

1. Assume that we have a subprogram called Sample_Line that samples line voltage. It detects out-of-limit conditions by raising Under_Voltage or Over_Voltage. Write a package containing a subprogram that continuously calls Sample_Line. If Sample_Line counts ten exceptions, abandon processing

of the subprogram and raise an exception called Noisy_Line, which is exported from the package.

2. Modify the package from Exercise 1 so that the exception Noisy_Line is raised only if ten exceptions are detected within a one-minute period.

Machine Representations

Representation Specifications
System-Dependent Features
Unchecked Conversion

Whereas assembly languages force us to work at the most primitive machine levels, high-order languages usually constrain us to work only at more abstract levels. Since programming in a high-order language is much more productive than programming in an assembly language, this is generally not a problem. However, we must sometimes refer to system-dependent features, such as the location of an input/output port or the representation of some data structure in memory. In the past, because high-order languages did not provide appropriate expressive power, we were forced to use a combination of high-order and assembly language programs in solutions, an approach that complicated the solutions and hindered readability and maintainability.

Ideally, we prefer a language that provides a means of expressing low-level machine features in a high-level fashion. Ada supports software development at both of these levels. In this chapter, we will study language constructs for system-dependent programming.

16.1   Representation Specifications

Representation specifications describe how the entities in solutions are mapped to the underlying machine. Such specifications can appear in the declarative part of a unit or in the specification part of Ada tasks and packages. It is important to note that each data type can have one and only one representation. Furthermore, we can establish representation specifications only after we have declared the type and before we even declare any objects of the type or use the entity (as an expression).

Representation specifications should be applied only:

- For purposes of efficiency

- To permit us to refer to a low-level feature with usual Ada names

- When required for interfacing with other extant or external systems

When we do need to apply these low-level features, Ada lets us create abstractions about them in high-level terms. Bear in mind, however, that representation specifications are implementation dependent: Different compilers may implement the same representation specification differently. Thus, programs that use such low-level features are inherently nonportable. If a compiler cannot provide the semantics of a representation specification, the specification is illegal on that compiler.

We can explicitly list global criteria for the representation of data structures and for the optimization of code, using two predefined pragmas:

```
pragma Pack(Some_Type);
pragma Optimize(Time);
pragma Optimize(Space);
```

In the first case, the pragma indicates that objects of the type Some_Type (for example, an array of boolean elements) will be packed to remove any gaps in their storage. The last two directives provide the compiler with guidance concerning the primary optimization criteria for a given compilation. These and the remaining predefined pragmas are described in detail in Appendix B.

Ada provides four clauses for specifying representations, namely:

- Length

- Enumeration

- Record

- Address

A length clause controls the amount of storage associated with a particular entity and takes the form:

```
for attribute use simple_expression;
```

Here, the attribute indicates the kind of length specification, and the expression yields some numeric value whose meaning is dependent upon the attribute. The attributes appropriate to this representation specification include Size, Storage_Size, and Small. Each of these attributes is described in detail in Appendix A. In particular, using the Size attribute, we can specify an upper bound to the number of bits allocated to objects of a given type, as the following illustrates:

```
Bits : constant := 1;
type My_Integer is range -100..100;
for My_Integer'Size use 8*Bits;
```

Notice the declaration of the constant named Bits, which is introduced to improve readability. As a result of this declaration, every object of type My_Integer will occupy no more than 8 bits of storage. Most compilers interpret this to mean exactly 8 bits. The user of such a specification should realize that specifying a small size for a type will have differing effects on the referencing code, which may affect execution speed. Illegal length clauses are possible, such as specifying the size of My_Integer to be 4 bits: these 201 values simply cannot be represented with only 4 bits.

We can also specify the amount of storage permitted for a collection of allocated objects or for the activation of a task object. For example:

```
procedure Main is
  Bits : constant := 1;
  type My_Integer is range -100..100;
  for My_Integer'Size use 8*Bits;
  Bytes      : constant := 8*Bits;
  Kilo_Bytes : constant := 1024*Bytes;
  type Buffer;
  type Record_Pointer is access Buffer;
  for Record_Pointer'Storage_Size use 100*Bytes;
  task type Watchdog_Task is
    ...
  end Watchdog_Task;
  for Watchdog_Task'Storage_Size use 3*Kilo_Bytes;
  type Buffer is
    record
      B : String(1..100);
    end record;
```

```
task body Watchdog_Task is
begin
   ...
end Watchdog_Task;
begin
   ...
end Main;
```

In the case of the Record_Pointer, the representation specification reserves 100 bytes of storage for all objects designated by Record_Pointer access values. For the task, Storage_Size refers to the amount of storage set aside for the activation (including the data, not the code) of the given task.

Note that the Storage_Size attribute is specified in terms of the number of storage units allocated, where *storage unit* generally denotes the machine's most manipulable data size. The predefined package System defines a constant named Storage_Unit that denotes the number of bits per storage unit. (The specifications for package System are given in Appendix C.) Note that System.Storage_Unit may differ from machine to machine. In the case of the Storage_Size attribute, the exception Storage_Error is raised in the event that the space reserved is exceeded.

A final use of the length clause is to specify the actual delta of a fixed-point numeric type, as the following indicates:

```
type Radians is delta 0.001 range 0.0..1.0;
for Radians'Small use 0.001;
```

In this case, the value for Small given in the length clause must be less than or equal to the delta given in the type declaration. That is, a length clause can increase, but not decrease, the precision of a fixed-point type.

The second case of representation specifications is for enumeration types. This specification indicates the internal codes for values of that type. The form resembles a length specification but uses an aggregate to specify the mapping from enumeration type values to internal codes. For example:

```
type Response is (Up, Down, Left, Right);
for Response use (Up    => 1,
                  Down  => 2,
                  Left  => 4,
                  Right => 8);
```

For an enumeration type representation, all literals of the type must be given unique internal codes. Further, internal codes can be noncontiguous (as in the above example). Whatever the internal representation, the relationship of

```
Up < Down < Left < Right
```

must still hold true.

Note that internal codes for an enumeration type are not visible from within Ada; an enumeration representation clause does not affect the Pos, Val, Pred, or Succ attributes of the type. For example, the Pos of Up, Down, Left, and Right will still be 0, 1, 2, and 3 respectively. Internal codes are intended to be used only when enumeration values are passed "outside" of Ada, to hardware or to code written in another language. Indeed, package Standard specifies the internal codes of the predefined type Character to conform with the ASCII standard (see Appendix C).

A third case involves the representation of record data types. In particular, we can describe the alignment of the entire record in terms of numbers of storage units, plus the location of each record component within those storage units. A typical use of this construct is to describe at a high level the addressable hardware structures on our machine. For example, our abstraction of a memory port along with a status word can be described as follows:

```
type IO_Port is
  record
    Data                : Integer range 0..255;
    Ready,
    Interrupts_Enabled : Boolean;
  end record;
```

Assuming that each storage unit in our machine is 1 byte wide and that IO_Port objects are 2 contiguous bytes of memory, the record representation can be written as follows:

```
for IO_Port use
  record at mod 2;
    Data              at 0 range 0..7;
    Ready             at 1 range 3..3;
    Interrupts_Enabled at 1 range 7..7;
  end record;
```

In this kind of representation specification, we use the at mod construct to specify the alignment of the record in terms of whole storage units needed. Here, IO_Port objects will have starting addresses that are multiples of 2. The at clause specifies the relative location of a component, expressed in storage units. The above example indicates that the Ready component of IO_Port objects is located in the second byte of the object. (Numbering of bytes—storage units—begins at zero.) Finally, the range construct specifies the actual bits within the byte used by the component. (Note that the first bit is also numbered zero.) In our example, the Interrupts_Enabled component is located in bit 7 of the second byte, and occupies only 1 bit. Such a layout can be depicted as follows, where unused bits are shaded:

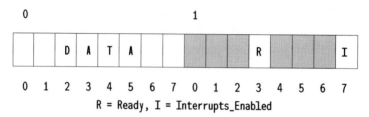

R = Ready, I = Interrupts_Enabled

The last kind of representation that Ada provides for is the specification of addresses. This construct takes a form similar to the other specifications. For example, the location of a variable or constant can be specified as follows:

```
D_To_A_Converter : IO_Port;
for D_To_A_Converter use at 16#177F6#;
```

In this case, we have declared an object of type IO_Port and specified that it is located at the absolute address 16#177F6#. The value given after use at must be a value of the type System.Address, a system-dependent type. For simplicity, the address clause examples in this chapter assume that System.Address is an integer type. In actuality, System.Address need not be an integer type; it can be any type that the system designer chooses to represent the addressing scheme for a particular piece of hardware. For some systems it may be a record that contains an address segment number and an offset.

```
type Address is
  record
    Segment : Word;
    Offset  : Offset_Type;
  end record;
```

For specific information about any implementation, check Appendix F of the *Ada Reference Manual* provided by the vendor.

Address clauses can also be used to indicate the starting address of a program unit such as a subprogram, package, or task. The specified address points to the start of the machine code associated with the body of the program unit. For example, the operating system of our underlying machine may have a machine routine located at the absolute address 8#76# that executes a graceful system power-down. In order to refer to this routine in the usual Ada terms, we declare the following:

```
procedure Power_Down;
for Power_Down use at 8#76#;
```

Thus, when we call Power_Down from Ada programs, we are actually invoking a machine language routine.

A final application of the address clause associates an interrupt with a task entry, as described in Chapter 14. For example:

```
task Air_Conditioner_Failure is
  entry Temperature_Interrupt;
  for   Temperature_Interrupt use at 16#3E#;
end Air_Conditioner_Failure;
task body Air_Conditioner_Failure is
begin
  loop
    accept Temperature_Interrupt do
      Power_Down;
    end Temperature_Interrupt;
  end loop;
end Air_Conditioner_Failure;
```

In this example, if we have a hardware interrupt at location 3E (hexadecimal), the task `Air_Conditioner_Failure` will capture the signal and call `Power_Down`. Note that we may not associate more than one task entry with a given interrupt; if we do, the program is considered erroneous.

So far, we have emphasized that Ada permits only one representation for each type. However, there may be situations in which two representations are more efficient or perhaps map our view of the world better. For example, we may want to manipulate a large collection of telemetry records. When we save a record on disk, we may want to pack the data to save space. Performing calculations on packed data is inefficient, since we are continually unpacking and repacking the data. Our solution would be to have one computational representation and one storage representation. This would allow the programmer to explicitly control the data packing.

For example we can declare a `Telemetry` record without a representation specification, allowing the compiler to select its optimal representation. Then we would declare a packed representation of the same record:

```
type Telemetry is
  record
    ...
  end record;
type Compressed_Telemetry is new Telemetry;
pragma Pack (Compressed_Telemetry);
```

We now have two related types with different representations. (We could write a test program to evaluate the size attributes of these types, to determine just how much space we have saved by packing.) As noted in Chapter 6, we could apply a type conversion between a derived type and its parent:

```
    subtype Unpack is Telemetry;
    subtype Pack   is Compressed_Telemetry;
    Computational_Data : Telemetry;
    Storage_Data       : Compressed_Telemetry;
begin
    Computational_Data := Unpack(Storage_Data);
    Storage_Data       := Pack(Computational_Data);
end Main;
```

Note that the use of subtypes renders the type conversions very readable.

16.2   System-Dependent Features

Being able to control the representation of program entities is an important feature of Ada, without which we would have to step outside the language to perform any low-level processing. Ada goes even further, however, permitting us to refer to machine-dependent features at a high level. For example, Ada includes a package named System, which provides a collection of system-dependent constants.

In addition, we can specify configurations of our system through the use of pragmas (such as System_Name and Storage_Size), or we can reference system-dependent characteristics by using attributes (such as Machine_Radix and Position). A given implementation has the right to provide its own set of system pragmas aud attributes but must implement at least the minimum set as defined in Appendices A and B.

In some applications, perhaps in a highly time-critical subprogram, we may need to write our code in assembly language. We should avoid starting at this level. Rather, we should design our system using high-level constructs first, and then recode only those parts of the system that are the resource bottlenecks.

Ada optionally provides a means of writing low-level statements. We place these machine code statements in a subprogram that contains no other declarations or statements. The predefined package Machine_Code (if provided) exports a record or records abstracting the machine's instruction set. This package is, of course, highly system dependent. For example:

```
package Machine_Code is
    Bits : constant := 1;
    Word : constant := 8;
    type Opcode is (Mov, Sub, Add);
    for Opcode´Size use 2*Bits;
```

```
            for Opcode use (Mov => 2#00#,
                            Sub => 2#01#,
                            Add => 2#10#);
            type Register is range 0..7;
            for Register'Size use 3*Bits;
            type Instruction is
              record
                Command     : Opcode;
                Source      : Register;
                Destination : Register;
              end record;
            for Instruction use
              record at mod 1;
                Command     at 0*Word range 0..1;
                Source      at 0*Word range 2..4;
                Destination at 0*Word range 5..7;
              end record;
          end Machine_Code;

          with Machine_Code;
          use Machine_Code;
          procedure Copy_3 is
          begin
            Instruction'( Command => Mov, Source => 0, Destination => 1 );
            Instruction'( Mov, Source => 0, Destination => 2 );
            Instruction'( Mov, 0, 3 );
          end Copy_3;
```

We may then call the machine code procedure as:

```
          Copy_3;
```

The code statements used in such a routine take the form of qualified expressions. The package `Machine_Code` contains only declarations; `Copy_3` executes the defined low-level statements.

16.3   Unchecked Conversion

The final low-level construct available in Ada permits us to relax the typing rules of the language. Use of this facility is machine dependent, and it is therefore up to the programmer to ensure that these features are used safely. Ada defines two generic subprograms to achieve this "unchecked" programming:

```
generic
  type Object is limited private;
  type Name   is access Object;
procedure Unchecked_Deallocation (X : in out Name);

generic
  type Source is limited private;
  type Target is limited private;
procedure Unchecked_Conversion (S : Source) return Target;
```

These generic units are library units and thus must be named in a context clause to be used. These units provide the benefit of explicitly indicating the use of nonportable programming methods. For example:

```
with Unchecked_Deallocation;
with Unchecked_Conversion;
```

Unchecked_Deallocation explicitly instructs the system to free and reuse the space of a dynamically allocated object. After a call to an instance of Unchecked_Deallocation, the actual parameter will have the value null. The language, however, cannot guarantee that the space formerly used is actually freed and reused by the system.

The danger of this construct is that the deallocation process does not ensure the preservation of the identity of other access objects that may be pointing to the object. For example:

```
with Unchecked_Deallocation;
procedure Dangerous is
  type Buffer is array (1.. 100) of Character;
  type Pointer is access Buffer;
  procedure Free_Buffer is new Unchecked_Deallocation(Buffer, Pointer);
  Head : Pointer := new Buffer;
  Tail : Pointer;
begin
  ...
  Tail := Head;
  ...
  Free_Buffer(Head);
  ...
end Dangerous;
```

The last statement deallocates the object pointed to by Head and sets Head to null. However, Tail is not affected, and so it points to a nonexistent object; thus, the value of Tail.all is undefined.

The Unchecked_Conversion unit permits us to convert data freely from one type to another. It should be noted that some implementations may restrict its use, depending on the relative sizes of the source and target object's type. This feature is necessary if we want to map one type into an incompatible type. Unchecked_Conversion is often used, for example, when interfacing Ada code to code written in another language. The effect of this function is to return the uninterpreted bit string of the parameter as a value of the target type. This procedure usually generates no code and thus no run-time overhead, but is necessary to satisfy Ada's strong typing rules. For example:

```
with Unchecked_Conversion;
procedure Main is
  type Integer_16 is range -32_768..32_767;
  for Integer_16'Size use 16;
  type Word is array (1..16) of Boolean;
  pragma Pack(Word);
  for Word'Size use 16;
  function Image (Int : Integer_16) return String is
    function To_Bits is new Unchecked_Conversion(Integer_16, Word);
    Bits   : constant Word := To_Bits(Int);
    Map    : constant array (Boolean) of Character := ('0', '1');
    Result : String(Bits'range);
  begin
    for Index in Result'range loop
      Result(Index) := Map(Bits(Index));
    end loop;
    return Result;
  end Image;
begin
  ...
end Main;
```

In this case we convert an integer to an array of boolean values in order to easily generate a textual image of its bit pattern. Unchecked_Conversion is intended to be used with source and target types of the same size. The result of using this generic procedure with types of different sizes is undefined. In all cases, it is the programmer's responsibility to ensure that such conversions maintain the properties of the target type. For example, the following conversion does not do so:

```
with Unchecked_Conversion;
procedure Main is
  type Byte is range 0..255;
  for Byte'Size use 8;
  function Byte_To_Character is new Unchecked_Conversion (Byte, Character);
```

```
C : Character := Byte_To_Character(255);
-- C probably does not contain a Character value.
begin
   ...
end Main;
```

Summary

■ Representation specifications can be used to map high-level constructs to the underlying machine. The effect of such clauses is machine dependent.

■ Length specifications can be used to establish the size of entities. Enumeration and record type representations establish the underlying structure of such objects. Address specifications force an object to reside at a certain location in memory.

■ Unchecked_Conversion relaxes Ada's typing rules.

■ Unchecked_Deallocation provides a machine-specific means of freeing memory.

Exercises

1. Create a record type declaration for a 16-bit program status word containing a priority field in bits 0 to 3, the zero flag at bit 9, a negative flag at bit 10, a carry flag at bit 11, and an overflow flag at bit 12. Declare an appropriate object and write an address specification to place it at memory location 8#777_776#.

*2. Write a type declaration for an array of 32 elements (indexed by an integer value) with components of type Binary. Assume that Binary is an enumeration type with values Zero and One. Write the representation specifications (not the pragma) needed to pack objects of the array type into two 16-bit words.

*3. Is it possible to write a procedure that, in the presence of an arbitrary exception, outputs the exception name?

4. Compare and contrast the use of exceptions with the use of explicit testing of possible error conditions.

5. Given the declaration for the type Binary in Exercise 2, write subprograms that convert an object of the type Binary to the type Integer and vice versa.

The Fourth Design Problem: Environment Monitoring

Define the Problem
Identify the Objects
Identify the Operations
Establish the Visibility
Establish the Interface
Evaluate the Objects
Implement Each Object

M‍ost embedded computer systems have four unique processing capabilities:

- Concurrency

- Real-time control

- Exception handling

- Unique input and output

As we have discussed, many high-order languages such as FOR-TRAN, Pascal, and C do not have constructs that correspond directly to these capabilities. Instead, the developer must access underlying facilities of the target system via assembly language or special operating system calls. The result is a program that is not portable. In general, such a program is poorly suited to large problems. Ada is well designed for this class of applications and, since we have completed our study of the facilities Ada provides for tasking and low-level programming, we are ready to examine a real-time application. In this chapter, we shall examine the problem of an environment monitoring system.

17.1   Define the Problem

Business processing systems are usually input/output bound, and most scientific applications are compute bound. With embedded systems, however, the primary concern is often the control or monitoring of real-time processes. Thus, embedded systems must often meet stringent timing requirements and be able to respond gracefully to exceptional conditions—conditions that may be caused by hardware failures. As we have with the other problems we have examined, we shall use our object-oriented method to evolve a complete Ada solution.

Figure 17.1 illustrates the problem space. Although this particular system involves monitoring temperature sensors, it should be clear that this solution is extensible to other systems involving different sensors, such as those that monitor pressure, voltage, or fluid levels.

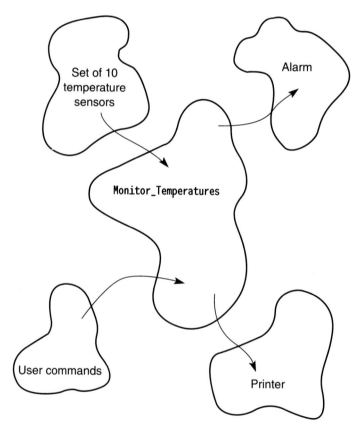

Figure 17.1 The environmental monitor problem

Our problem involves several temperature sensors in various rooms of a building. These sensors continuously sample the ambient temperature. If a particular sensor detects a temperature above some limit, our system triggers an alarm. A sensor also shows the temperature and whether or not it is within limits. A user can interact with the system by setting the alarm limits for a particular sensor and by reading the status of all sensors. When an alarm sounds, a user can quickly find where the abnormal temperature condition exists. Periodically, our system must print the current reading of each sensor to a permanent log. Since printers have the nasty habit of running out of paper at the worst possible time, we have judged the printer to be the least reliable device in our system. Our system must also be able to detect a device error and trigger an alarm.

For the moment, assume that our application runs on a target computer that uses memory-mapped I/O. Thus, sensors can be sampled by reading from a specific memory location, and the alarm can be sounded by writing to a specific location. We have not yet defined any performance requirements. We shall examine these as we go deeper into our design.

17.2   Identify the Objects

By considering the nouns that we used in our description of the problem space, we quickly extract the objects and classes of objects that are of interest in our design. In particular, we have mentioned:

- A set of sensors

- A printer

- An alarm for out-of-limits conditions and printer errors

- Memory-mapped I/O ports

- A user

The set of sensors really defines a class of objects, whereas our system includes only one printer and one alarm. As a result, we can abstract the sensors as abstract data types and consider the printer and the alarm as abstract-state machines. However, we can generalize even further. Various kinds of sensors have one thing in common: They all measure physical attributes of the real world. Thus, as we shall see, it is possible to abstract a sensor independently of the kinds of physical measurements it makes. Our abstraction of a sensor applies equally to temperature sensors, pressure sensors, and fluid-level sensors. Therefore, not only can we classify this set of sensors as an abstract data type, but we can also treat our solution as a generic abstraction and instantiate it to our particular application. We can then reuse this abstraction in other applications as the need arises. Indeed, as the requirements of the present problem change, generalization makes it much easier to modify our solution.

Notice also that we have collected as a single object the abstraction of the memory-mapped I/O ports. Not only is this a logical grouping, but as we shall see, this approach isolates most of the implementation-dependent characteristics of our solution. Isolation is desirable, for if we were to port our application to a different target machine (with different I/O port addresses), we would need to modify the application.

Finally, we should distinguish the user as an object slightly different from any other in the problem space. A user exists outside our application, and the user can interact with the system via commands. Thus, our solution will not contain a software object that directly parallels this organic abstraction. Rather, as is typical with user-driven systems, we shall delegate the user interface to the main thread of control. All other objects will exist as distinct entities in the architecture of our solution.

17.3   Identify the Operations

In this step, we must consider the behavior of each object as viewed from the outside. Here, not only will we specify the operations that each object must undergo, but we must also identify the concurrency of each. In particular, we must decide whether a given object is an actor, a transducer, or a server. As we shall see, this is an important decision because it affects the connectivity of objects.

We shall abstract a sensor as a concurrent entity. Its primary role is to continuously monitor the temperature in a given room. Since we have multiple sensors, continuous measurement by each sensor object gives rise to the need for constructing sensors as tasks. One alternative is to treat each sensor as a passive entity and have a single process poll each sensor. Indeed, this is the traditional approach that older languages such as FORTRAN or Pascal use. However, by using Ada tasks explicitly, we capture the reality of concurrency in the problem space and embody it in our solution in a natural manner. Also, as we shall see, Ada gives us much more flexibility in tuning the timing behavior of our system.

Let us now consider what operations a sensor can undergo. At first, it may appear that a sensor undergoes no operations; rather, a sensor serves as an actor task. In fact, this could be one reasonable design. Instead, we will allow clients a bit more control over a sensor by characterizing a sensor as a transducer task. On the one hand, a sensor invokes operations of other objects—for example, a sensor can trigger an alarm. On the other hand, given that we permit user interaction, we must be able to set the alarm limits of a specific sensor and monitor the status of a sensor; that is, we must be able to obtain the current temperature value and determine whether it is or is not within allowable limits. Thus, we can include these activities as operations on a sensor object. Therefore, we permit the following operations:

- Start   Initiate sensor activity.

- Set_Limit   Establish a value for triggering the alarm.

- Get_Status   Return the current sensor value.

- Shut_Down   Terminate the sensor.

The existence of Set_Limit and Get_Status should be no surprise. But why should we include operations to explicitly start and stop a sensor? As we discussed in Chapter 14, Ada embodies specific rules regarding the activation and termination of tasks. In our application, however, we would like to have explicit control over the lifetime of each object. For this reason, we include operations for Start and Shut_Down.

The need for Shut_Down should be clear; it represents the classical approach for specifying the graceful termination of a task. Start does not really activate a task, since activation is implicitly started when any task's master begins execution. We use Start to prevent the object from doing anything until we are ready for it to begin. In addition, as we shall see, this operation solves the problem of telling a task its own name. Given that we have chosen to characterize the sensors as objects drawn from a class of sensors, our solution must be able to distinguish among different task objects. Each sensor must measure the temperature in a different location.

We have also chosen to characterize this class of sensors as generic, so it is relevant for us to consider what operations a sensor requires. As we mentioned earlier, this approach helps us to identify the things that our generic unit must import. As we did in Chapter 13, our strategy is to consider what common requirements we can identify among all sensor objects, and then extract them as generic parameters. In particular, we will import:

- Name   Type used to identify a specific sensor.

- Value   Type that identifies the class of measurement values.

- Sense_Rate   How often the sensor samples the environment.

In addition, we must also import an operation that permits a specific sensor to read a memory-mapped I/O port, as well as an operation that sounds an alarm:

- **Value_Of**   Read a specific I/O port.

- **Sound_Alarm**   Sound the temperature out-of-limits alarm.

By importing these operations, we have effectively decoupled our abstraction of the sensor from all other objects in the problem space.

Now consider the behavior of the printer. A printer is a single object characterized as an abstract-state machine. We shall treat the printer as a concurrent entity since it must interact with other tasks. Indeed, the need to establish concurrent entities is a common consequence of concurrent systems in Ada; it is hard to write just one task. Once a developer has decided to introduce concurrency, the behavior of all objects in the presence of multiple tasks must be considered. For example, it is not safe to encapsulate a device such as a printer as a sequential entity, because of problems of mutual exclusion.

The printer is wholly a server object; it can invoke no operations. From the outside, we shall allow a printer to undergo the following operations:

- **Put_Line**   Print one line.

- **Shut_Down**   Terminate the printer.

Just as we did with the sensors, we have included an operation that lets us explicitly control the termination of this task. However, we need not include a **Start** operation; there is only one object, so we do not need to tell this task its name.

The alarm has characteristics similar to those of the printer. The alarm can be abstracted as a server object with the operations:

- **Report_Out_Of_Limits**   Sound an over-temperature alarm.

- **Report_Printer_Error**   Sound a printer alarm.

- **Shut_Down**   Terminate the alarm.

Again, since there is only one alarm object, we need a **Shut_Down** operation but not a **Start** operation.

Notice that we have not included an operation to turn off the alarm. We shall assume for a moment that this is outside our software solution. Assume that our application need only write a value to a particular memory location to trigger the alarm and that the user turns it off.

Let us consider the last major object in our problem space: the I/O ports. Clearly this object is at a lower level of abstraction than any other we have examined. Nevertheless, we discuss I/O ports because they are important elements of the problem space. This object encapsulates several objects, namely the individual I/O ports for each sensor and the alarm. Actually, this kind of encapsulation is quite common when dealing with embedded systems. From the perspective of an assembly language, it is useful to define macros that mask the use of physical addresses. Our abstraction is the high-level-language analogue to assembly language. Thus, this object exports no operations explicitly; we need it only to assign and retrieve values from simple variables.

17.4   Establish the Visibility

Now that we have characterized the behavior of each major object in our problem space, we must consider the relationships among them. In particular, we can state that our abstraction of the sensor is completely isolated from any other object. However, the instantiation of this component is coupled to other abstractions. If we call the instantiation Temperature_Sensors:

- Temperature_Sensors must see Printer and Alarm.

The inverse, of course, is not true: neither Alarm nor Printer can see the instantiation. Similarly, Alarm and Printer are decoupled from one another.

As required by Ada, our application must contain a main subprogram that serves as the root of the system. We shall call this subprogram Monitor_Temperatures, and it will contain the instantiation of the sensors. Additionally, this unit will be responsible for user interaction. As a result:

- Monitor_Temperatures must see Printer and Alarm.

Figure 17.2 illustrates these relationships. We have used a special symbol in the body of Monitor_Temperatures to indicate that this unit is further divided into subunits. Monitor_Temperatures not only contains the instantiation of the sensors, but if we zoom in, as in Figure 17.3, we see three subunits: one subprogram to support the instantiation (Value_Of), one subprogram to handle user interaction (Process_Commands), and one task to force the periodic logging of sensor readings (Monitor).

The careful reader will wonder what happened to the I/O ports. As we discussed, this abstraction falls at a lower level in our system. As we see in Figure 17.4 on page 357, these ports (which we place in a package called Definitions) are visible only to the bodies of two units.

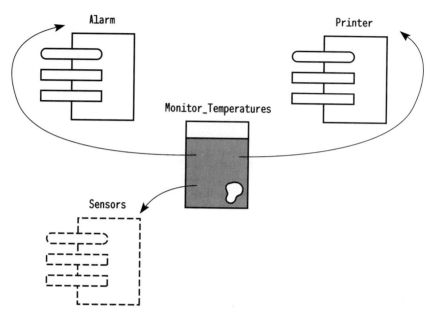

Figure 17.2 Design of `Monitor_Temperatures`

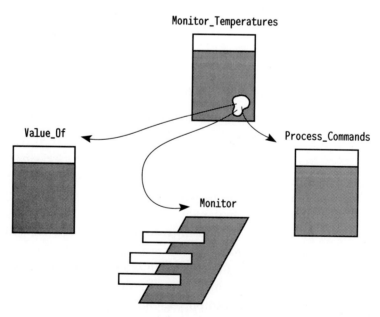

Figure 17.3 Body of `Monitor_Temperatures`

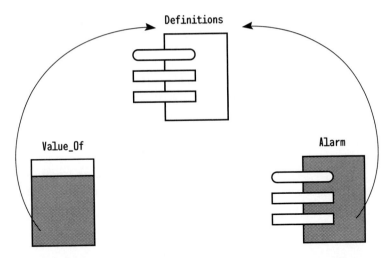

Figure 17.4 `Monitor_Temperatures` at a lower level of abstraction

17.5   Establish the Interface

We are now ready to capture our design decisions, using Ada as a design language. Let us start with a simple object and later take on more complex ones. We can express the outside view of the printer with the package specification:

```
package Printer is
   task The_Printer is
      entry Put_Line (The_Item : in String);
      entry Shut_Down;
   end The_Printer;
end Printer;
```

Notice how we have directly declared a task object. As we mentioned in Chapter 14, Ada rules require that tasks be declared in the context of an enclosing unit, such as the library package we have here. It is not necessary for us to export anything else; the entries of this task provide the operations our abstraction demands.

An alternative to this approach is to hide the task in the package body and export only subprograms, which in turn call the appropriate entries. Indeed, this is exactly the approach we took in our example of the package `Spooled_Print` in Chapter 14. We do not use this approach here so that clients of this package can use timed entry calls to determine when the printer has failed.

The outside view of the alarm is similar to the view of the printer:

```
package Alarm is
   task The_Alarm is
      entry Report_Out_Of_Limits;
      entry Report_Printer_Error;
      entry Shut_Down;
   end The_Alarm;
end Alarm;
```

The interface to the sensors is similar, except that we must make this unit generic and import the items we specified earlier:

```
generic
   type Name is (<>);
   type Value is range <>;
   Sense_Rate : in Duration;
   with function Value_Of (The_Name : in Name) return Value;
   with procedure Sound_Alarm;
package Sensors is
   task type Sensor is
      entry Start      (The_Name  : in  Name);
      entry Set_Limit  (The_Value : in  Value);
      entry Get_Status (The_Value : out Value; Out_Of_Limits : out Boolean);
      entry Shut_Down;
   end Sensor;
end Sensors;
```

The declaration of the task type Sensor looks just like what we declared for Printer and Alarm. Of course, here we have a task type and not a task object; therefore, we must declare objects of that type. We shall declare the objects in the main program. The unit does not export task objects, which lets us defer the decision as to how many sensors actually exist. If the requirements of our application changed so that there were a different number of sensors, we would not have to alter this generic unit.

Since the generic part of this package is reasonably complex, we will consider it in detail. As in the tree generic in Chapter 13, we have imported types (Name and Value). Here, however, we have constrained these types to be discrete and integer, respectively. Recall from Chapter 12 that this means we implicitly import a set of discrete and integer operations (such as assignment and test for equality) as well as the relational operators (and others). The generic parameter Sense_Rate is a generic value parameter. We must match it with a value of type Duration, thus indicating how often our sensors sample the environment. Finally, Value_Of and Sound_Alarm are generic subprogram parameters. By using these parameters, we effectively decouple this unit from a specific alarm or sensing mechanism. Thus, we will be able to reuse this abstraction for other applications.

Even though it is at a lower level of abstraction, consider the outside view of the memory I/O ports. As we indicated, this abstraction is really a high-level view of physical memory locations. Clearly, the location of these ports depends on our target machine. By specifying these values in this package alone, we effectively isolate any target dependencies from the rest of our system. Happily, Ada's representation specifications are sufficiently powerful to specify the exact size and address of each of these ports. For the purpose of this problem, we assume that the location of these ports has been given to us by the hardware designers. Thus, we can express the outside view of this abstraction as:

```
package Definitions is
   type Byte is range 0..255;
   for Byte'Size use 8;
   package Sensor_Ports is
      Lobby,   Main_Office,   Warehouse, Stock_Room,   Terminal_Room,
      Library, Computer_Room, Lounge,    Loading_Dock, Clean_Room      : Byte;
      for Lobby         use at 16#30#;
      for Main_Office   use at 16#32#;
      for Warehouse     use at 16#34#;
      for Stock_Room    use at 16#36#;
      for Terminal_Room use at 16#38#;
      for Library       use at 16#3A#;
      for Computer_Room use at I6#3B#;
      for Lounge        use at 16#3C#;
      for Loading_Dock  use at 16#3D#;
      for Clean_Room    use at 16#3E#;
   end Sensor_Ports;
   package Alarm_Ports is
      On : constant Byte := Byte'Last;
      Out_Of_Limits, Printer_Error : Byte;
      for Out_Of_Limits use at 16#80#;
      for Printer_Error use at 16#100#;
   end Alarm_Ports;
end Definitions;
```

Notice how we have used nested package declarations to logically group the two major classes of ports. With the representation clauses we have included, a client can assign a value to the object Printer_Error to effectively write 8 bits to the physical location 16#100#. Notice also the use of based numbers to express a memory location in a form more convenient from the hardware view of the abstraction. Similarly, by referencing an object such as Lobby, our application effectively reads 8 bits from the location 16#30#.

17.6   Evaluate the Objects

In Chapters 10 and 13 we introduced five simple heuristics for evaluating designs. We will apply them to our design:

- *Minimize coupling.* Our major concurrent objects—sensors, printer, and alarm—have been separated into library packages. Furthermore, the generic nature of the sensor package greatly decouples these objects from the hardware I/O ports. A coupling that might be reduced is that between Monitor and the main program.

  If we were to move Monitor to its own package, how much of the main program would have to be moved with it? Certainly Monitor would need visibility to the instantiation of Sensors and to the array of sensor tasks—a large part of the main program. Thus, we will leave Monitor nested within the main program.

- *Maximize cohesion.* Whenever we see packages nested in another package's specification, we should consider whether or not the packages belong together. Thus, we might question the cohesiveness of the Definitions package. Since the main purpose of the Definitions package is to isolate all I/O port addresses in our solution, we accept that Sensor_Ports and Alarm_Ports should both be included as part of the Definitions package.

- *Separate constructors and selectors.* In this problem, we are mainly dealing with concurrent objects, rather than abstract data types. Therefore we do not have many selectors. Servers and actors tend to have constructors but few selectors. For example, the printer has two constructors (Put_Line and Shut_Down) and no selectors.

  Sensors have constructors and a selector. The selector Get_Status has been separated from the constructors.

- *Identify exceptional conditions.* The main exceptional conditions in this design are the printer being out of paper (or not responsive for any reason) and a temperature above a set limit. Although these conditions were not explicit in the design as Ada exceptions, the use of alarms makes them obvious. In our design we have chosen to make the printer a simple server, a server unaware of whether it is operating normally. We have decided that users of the printer must detect printer problems and have allowed users to do so using timed entry calls.

The second exceptional condition, out-of-limit temperatures, is handled by both an alarm and a printed report. We have made sensors "smarter" than the printer in that the sensor itself detects this condition.

- *Exceptional conditions should have a corresponding selector.* The exceptional condition of the printer is implicit, or detected by users. The exceptional condition of a sensor is exported by the selector Get_Status. Note that both the sensors themselves and Monitor will detect out-of-limit temperatures. In our design we have decided that both will report the condition, but in different ways. The sensor will sound an alarm and Monitor will print a report.

17.7   Implement Each Object

We have finished capturing the outside view of each relevant abstraction, and we now turn to the inside view. Since we have just finished studying the package Definitions, let us study the body of a unit that builds on top of this abstraction. In particular, the body of Alarm requires that we write to the two Alarm_Ports defined earlier. However, this body is a bit more complicated because we must deal with the existence of a task.

As is true for many real-time applications, it is common to have processes that run indefinitely. Thus, we can write the body of the task The_Alarm as a basic loop with a nested **select** statement. In this case, the client can select from three entries, given earlier in the task specifications and shown below nested in a **select** statement:

```
with Definitions;
package body Alarm is    task body The_Alarm is
    On : Definitions.Byte renames Definitions.Alarm_Ports.On;
  begin
    loop
      select
        accept Report_Out_Of_Limits;
        Definitions.Alarm_Ports.Out_Of_Limits := On;
```

```
      or
        accept Report_Printer_Error;
        Definitions.Alarm_Ports.Printer_Error := On;
      or
        accept Shut_Down;
        exit;
      end select;
    end loop;
  end The_Alarm;
end Alarm;
```

Since the package **Alarm** uses the resources of **Definitions**, we must mention this package in a context clause.

Notice how we handle task synchronization. Writing to an I/O port is done outside the **accept** statement, so that the calling task is freed immediately after acceptance of the rendezvous. This is a common approach when dealing with parameterless entries. Notice also that to sound an alarm, we need only assign a value (**On**) to a specific variable, thus effectively writing to that memory location.

The package **Alarm** handles termination using the entry **Shut_Down**. When this entry is accepted, **The_Alarm** exits the loop, an action that causes the task to complete and then terminate.

The body of the package **Printer** looks much the same as that of **Alarm**, except that we create a text file that actually sends a string to the physical device. The actual name of the printer is system dependent. Since the entry **Put_Line** involves a parameter, the corresponding **accept** statement includes a sequence of statements to process its value:

```
with Text_IO;
package body Printer is
  task body The_Printer is
    type String_Access is access String;
    Local     : String_Access;
    Print_File : Text_IO.File_Type;
  begin
    Text_IO.Create( File => Print_File, Name => "PRN": );
                                        -- system dependent
    loop
      select
        accept Put_Line ( The_Item : in String ) do
          Local := new String'( The_Item );
        end Put_Line;
        Text_IO.Put_Line( Print_File, Local.all );
```

```
      or
        accept Shut_Down;
        exit;
      end select;
    end loop;
    Text_IO.Close(Print_File);
  end The_Printer;
end Printer;
```

We have taken care in writing the code for The_Printer. When the printer is out of paper, or not responsive for any reason, the execution of the string-to-printer statement will suspend indefinitely. If the code that sends the string to the printer were included in the accept statement, the caller would also be suspended. We cannot allow the suspension of the calling task; the importance of this will become apparent later, when we implement The_Printer's client.

Now that we have seen these task bodies, the body of the package Sensors seems less complex. The basic function of a sensor task is to continuously sample the environment, taking samples every Sense_Rate seconds. Thus, the core of this body involves a loop with a nested select statement, a structure similar to those in Alarm and Printer. The difference is that we want something to happen periodically, not just when an entry is called.

The solution we shall use involves the creation of a timed loop similar to the one in Chapter 14. Recall that there is the possibility of concurrent entry calls to Set_Limit, Get_Status, or Shut_Down. We do not want to delay any clients. To avoid delay, we apply a select statement with a delay alternative, in which the delay is calculated every time around the loop. Thus, at the top of the loop, we calculate the next time we should measure the environment. Our algorithm waits at the top of the select statement. If an entry is called, it will be accepted eventually. But if nothing happens by the calculated time, the delay alternative is selected and the sensor is measured. Additionally, it is at this time that we determine whether a sensor is out-of-limits and sound an alarm if necessary.

Clearly, each sensor must maintain some state (Current_Value, The_Limit, or Next_Time) that tells when a measurement should be taken. Additionally, a sensor task must know its name. The naming of a task is a typical Ada design problem. We want to write one task body but have each task instance do something slightly different. In our application, the difference is that each task samples a different physical port. In the specification of the Sensors package, we imported the operation Value_Of, but a caller of this operation must be able to identify itself. Thus, as we Start a task we must give it a name. Then, when we call Value_Of, we pass this name to the function so that it can look up the proper port. Therefore, each task must maintain Sensor_Name, another piece of state information. Given these requirements for the behavior of the task body, we can write:

```
with Calendar;
package body Sensors is
  task body Sensor is
    Sensor_Name    : Name;
    Current_Value  : Value := Value'First;
    The_Limit      : Value := Value'Last;
    Next_Time      : Calendar.Time := Calendar.Clock;
    use Calendar;
  begin
    select
      accept Start (The_Name : in Name) do
        Sensor_Name := The_Name;
      end Start;
    or
      terminate;
    end select;
    loop
      select
        accept Set_Limit (The_Value : in Value) do
          The_Limit := The_Value;
        end Set_Limit;
      or
        accept Get_Status (The_Value    : out Value;
                           Out_Of_Limits : out Boolean) do
          The_Value := Current_Value;
          Out_Of_Limits := Current_Value > The_Limit;
        end Get_Status;
      or
        accept Shut_Down;
        exit;
      or
        delay Next_Time - Calendar.Clock;
        Current_Value := Value_Of(Sensor_Name);
        if Current_Value > The_Limit then
          Sound_Alarm;
        end if;
```

```
        Next_Time := Next_Time + Sense_Rate;
      end select;
    end loop;
  end Sensor;
end Sensors;
```

The main loop at the end of the task Sensor looks much like the loop in The_Printer and The_Alarm, but Sensor has a delay alternative. The Start entry is called only once and we need not concern ourselves with it during the rest of the object's lifetime. However, notice that the accept for Start is written in a different select statement. Why? Because we wish to defend ourselves against catastrophic failure. Note that we have included a terminate alternative; if a task instance does not receive a Start entry call, the task can still terminate gracefully.

We are now ready to build the body of the main program (Monitor_Temperatures). Recall that this unit provides the instantiation of the Sensors package, as well as user interaction.

```
with Sensors, Printer, Alarm;
procedure Monitor_Temperatures is
  type Sensor_Names is (Lobby,         Main_Office,   Warehouse,
                        Stock_Room,    Terminal_Room, Library,
                        Computer_Room, Lounge,        Loading_Dock,
                        Clean_Room);
  subtype Value is Natural;
  Once_Per_Second : constant Duration := 1.0;
  function Value_Of (The_Name : in Sensor_Names) return Value is separate;
  package Temperature_Sensors is new Sensors
    (Name        => Sensor_Names,
     Value       => Value,
     Sense_Rate  => Once_Per_Second,
     Value_Of    => Value_Of,
     Sound_Alarm => Alarm.The_Alarm.Report_Out_Of_Limits);
  The_Sensors : array (Sensor_Names) of Temperature_Sensors.Sensor;
  function Format ( Name         : Sensor_Names;
                    Reading      : Value;
                    Out_Of_Limits : Boolean) return String is separate;
  task Monitor is
    entry Shut_Down;
  end Monitor;
  task body Monitor is separate;
```

```
    procedure Process_Commands is separate;
begin -- Monitor_Temperatures
  for Index in Sensor_Names
    loop
      The_Sensors(Index).Start(The_Name => Index);
    end loop;
  Process_Commands;
  Monitor.Shut_Down;
  for Index in Sensor_Names
    loop
      The_Sensors(Index).Shut_Down;
    end loop;
  Printer.The Printer.Shut_Down;
  Alarm.The_Alarm.Shut_Down;
end Monitor_Temperatures;
```

The bulk of this main program involves its declarative part. First, we provide several declarations (Sensor_Names, Value, Once_Per_Second, and Value_Of) that support the instantiation of the Sensors package. Next, we declare an array of sensors (The_Sensors). Final declarations include a function for formatting sensor readings, a Monitor task that periodically logs the value of each sensor, and a procedure that handles user interaction.

The statements associated with this program allow for orderly task activation and termination. We know that the tasks imported in the **with** clause (The_Printer and The_Alarm) will be activated before the declarative part of the main program is elaborated. This earlier activation is safe, for these tasks are just server tasks; they make no entry calls of their own. Tasks of The_Sensors are all activated by the end of the elaboration of the declaration region of the main program. The same is true for the task Monitor. Even though tasks of The_Sensors are active at this point, they are all suspended at the accept for Start. Thus, in the body of Monitor_Temperatures, we first name each task by calling the Start entry and then call Process_Commands. When we return from this procedure (when the user stops the system), we shut down the Monitor task to prevent any more samples from being printed. Next we shut down each sensor, then we shut down the Printer and Alarm tasks. If we shut down the Printer and Alarm tasks earlier, we could create problems. Specifically, if Monitor were still trying to print measurements as the Printer task completed, Monitor would receive a Tasking_Error and terminate ungracefully.

The function `Format` is used by the `Monitor` task and by the `Process_` `Commands` subprogram. `Format` converts sensor readings into strings which are sent either to the printer or to the user. A tabular format for readings can be generated as follows:

```
with Calendar;
separate (Monitor_Temperatures)
function Format (Name         : Sensor_Names;
                Reading       : Value;
                Out_Of_Limits : Boolean) return String is
   Message : array ( Boolean ) of String (1..15) :=
               (False => (others => Ascii.Nul),
                True  => ":   OUT OF LIMITS");
   function Pad_Left (Item    : String; Length : Positive) return String is
   begin
      return String'(1..Length - Item'Length => ' ') & Item;
   end Pad_Left;
   function Pad_Right (Item   : String; Length : Positive) return String is
   begin
      return Item & String'(1..Length - Item'Length => ' ');
   end Pad_Right;
   function Format(The_Time : Calendar.Time) return String is separate;
begin
   return Format(Calendar.Clock) & ' '                              &
      Pad_Right(Sensor_Names'Image(Name), Sensor_Names'Width) &
      " sensor value is"                                       &
      Pad_Left(Value'Image(Reading), Value'Width)             &
      " degrees" & Message(Out_Of_Limits);
end Format;
```

The nested `Format` function, for `Time`, is left as an exercise for the reader.

We used subunits in the main program to simplify implementation and to further restrict dependencies on the `Definitions` package. Now let us consider these subunits. `Value_Of` takes a sensor name and returns its current value by reading the corresponding I/O port. A `case` statement looks up the appropriate I/O port based on the name:

```
with Definitions;
separate (Monitor_Temperatures)
function Value_Of (The_Name : in Sensor_Names) return Value is
```

```
begin
  case The_Name is
    when Lobby        =>
      return Value(Definitions.Sensor_Ports.Lobby);
    when Main_Office  =>
      return Value(Definitions.Sensor_Ports.Main_Office);
    when Warehouse    =>
      return Value(Definitions.Sensor_Ports.Warehouse);
    when Stock_Room   =>
      return Value(Definitions.Sensor_Ports.Stock_Room);
    when Terminal_Room =>
      return Value(Definitions.Sensor_Ports.Terminal_Room);
    when Library      =>
      return Value(Definitions.Sensor_Ports.Library);
    when Computer_Room =>.
      return Value(Definitions.Sensor_Ports.Computer_Room);
    when Lounge       =>
      return Value(Definitions.Sensor_Ports.Lounge);
    when Loading_Dock =>
      return Value(Definitions.Sensor_Ports.Loading_Dock) ;
    when Clean_Room   =>
      return Value(Definitions.Sensor_Ports.Clean_Room);
  end case;
end Value_Of;
```

Notice that we must use a type conversion in each **return** statement since each sensor port is of the type **Byte** rather than the type **Value**.

The body of the **Monitor** task employs a timed loop so that each sensor is periodically sampled and its state is printed. We must defend ourselves against printer problems. Earlier, we saw how the **Printer** task could be suspended indefinitely, but we took care that **Printer** did not suspend its caller. Instead of indefinitely delaying the **Monitor** task, we shall use a timed entry call so that **Monitor** can proceed if it is delayed too long. Thus, we can write:

```
with Calendar;
separate (Monitor_Temperatures)
task body Monitor is
  Seconds       : constant Duration := 1.0;
  Time_Interval : constant Duration := 60 * Seconds;
  Next_Time     : Calendar.Time := Calendar.Clock;
  The Value     : Natural;
  Out_Of_Limits : Boolean;
```

```
      procedure Print (Line : String) is
        Delay_Limit   : constant Duration := 1 * Seconds;
      begin
        select
          Printer.The_Printer.Put_Line(Line);
        or
          delay Delay_Limit;
          Alarm.The_Alarm.Report_Printer_Error;
        end select;
      end Print;
      use Calendar;
    begin  -- Monitor
      loop
        select
          accept Shut_Down;
          exit;
        or
          delay Next_Time - Calendar.Clock;
          Print ("");
          for Index in Sensor_Names
            loop
              The_Sensors(Index).Get_Status(The_Value, Out_Of_Limits);
              Print (Format (Index, The_Value, Out_Of_Limits));
            end loop;
          Next_Time := Next_Time + Time_Interval;.
        end select;
      end loop;
    end Monitor;
```

The body of Monitor could be fairly complex: a timed entry call, nested in a loop, nested in a selective wait statement with a delay alternative. We manage some of the complexity with a nested subprogram (Print). We use this procedure to modularize the error-handling capabilities of this task. Print thus separates the error-handling concern from the polling aspect of Monitor.

Referring back to the body of The_Printer, if the string-to-printer code were included in the accept statement, Monitor would be suspended in a rendezvous when the printer is off-line. Furthermore, if Monitor was suspended, it could not sound the alarm. Since Monitor is the only caller to The_Printer, the alarm would never be sounded and our solution would not be reliable.

The last remaining procedure is Process_Commands, which handles all the user interaction. Here, we allow the user a choice of commands: set the limits of a given sensor, display a status report, or quit. This procedure uses a basic loop, which we exit only when the user enters Quit.

```ada
with Text_IO;
separate (Monitor_Temperatures)
procedure Process_Commands is
  type Command is (Limit, Status, Quit);
  package Command_IO is new Text_IO.Enumeration_IO(Command);
  package Name_IO    is new Text_IO.Enumeration_IO(Sensor_Names);
  package Value_IO   is new Text_IO.Integer_IO(Value);
  The_Command  : Command;
  The_Name     : Sensor_Names;
  The_Value    : Value;
  Out_Of_Limits : Boolean;
  procedure Complain is
  begin
    Text_IO.Skip_Line;
    Text_IO.Put_Line ("... invalid command... try again");
  end Complain;
  procedure Get (The_Command : out Command) is
  begin  -- Get
    loop
      begin
        Text_IO.New_Line;
        Text_IO.Put("Enter a command (limit, status, quit): ");
        Command_IO.Get(The_Command);
        return;
      exception
        when Text_IO.Data_Error => Complain;
      end;
    end loop;
  end Get;
  procedure Get (The_Name : out Sensor_Names) is
  begin  -- Get
    loop
      begin
        Text_IO.Put_Line("Possible sensor names are:");
        for Index in Sensor_Names
          loop
            Text_IO.Put(' ');
            Name_IO.Put(Index);
            Text_IO.New_Line;
          end loop;
        Text_IO.Put("Enter a name: ");
```

```
          Name_IO.Get(The_Name);
          Text_IO.Skip_Line;
          return;
        exception
          when Text_IO.Data_Error => Complain;
        end;
      end loop;
    end Get;
    procedure Get (The_Value : out Value) is
    begin
      Text_IO.Put("Enter a value: ");
      Value_IO.Get(The_Value);
      Text_IO.Skip_Line;
    exception
      when Text_IO.Data_Error =>
        Complain;
        Get (The_Value);
    end Get;
  begin -- Process_Commands
    loop
      Get (The_Command);
      case The_Command is
        when Limit =>
          Get (The_Name);
          Get (The_Value);
          The_Sensors(The_Name).Set_Limit(The_Value);
        when Status =>
          for Index in Sensor_Names
            loop
              The_Sensors(Index).Get_Status(The_Value, Out_Of_Limits);
              Text_IO.Put_Line(Format(Index, The_Value, Out_Of_Limits));
            end loop;
        when Quit => exit;
      end case;
    end loop;
  end Process_Commands;
```

As an aside, notice that the first two Get procedures use iteration until the user enters valid data. The last Get routine uses recursion for the same purpose. Some programming experts consider the iterative technique unreadable, since the loop and block statements obscure the real purpose of the routine. Others contend that the run-time overhead of recursion is unnecessary, although some compilers will optimize this simple recursive loop into an iterative loop. Either technique will work perfectly well in this example solution. The recursive version is, however, neat, tidy, and in this case well worth the minimal overhead.

Exercises

1. Modify the solution so that the sample rate of the clean room and the terminal room are twice that of the other rooms. Do so without changing the Sensors package.

2. Modify the Sensors package so that each task object can have a different sense rate.

3. What would happen to the system if for some reason one of the sensor tasks aborted during execution?

4. What changes are necessary to support 100 sensors? What would the impact be if we had not declared Sensors as generic?

5. What is the recompilation cost if we alter the location of an I/O port?

6. Modify the Definitions package so that sensor ports can only be read, not written, and alarm ports can only be written, not read. Modify the alarm ports so that the only value that can be written is On (255).

7. Try implementing this problem without using tasks. Compare and contrast the two approaches.

8. Modify the system so that a user can enable and disable the activity of a given sensor.

PACKAGE

6

Systems Development

A complex system that works is invariably found to have evolved from a simple system that worked.

John Call
Systemantics: How Systems
Work and Especially How
They Fail [1]

Input/Output

File Management
Input/Output for Nontextual Data
Input/Output for Textual Data
Application
Low-Level Input/Output

Providing programming language facilities for input and output (I/O) has always been like going to the dentist for a toothache—it's something that language designers have to do, but they tend to put it off in the hope that it might go away. As a result, we find languages like ALGOL, which leave the choice of I/O facilities up to the particular implementation, and languages like Pascal, which provide only the most restricted forms of control. Ada does not treat I/O as a thorn in the side of the language. In fact, with the extensibility provided by Ada's packaging mechanism and generic facilities, we do not have to provide any special language features to accommodate I/O.

What we desire is the ability to build our own I/O routines for communication with unique devices. Furthermore, without adding any new language constructs, we want predefined units for I/O of common data types, such as characters, integers, and real numbers, which we can select as needed. In this chapter, we shall see that Ada provides all of these features and more.

18.1   File Management

Ada provides predefined packages for three kinds of I/O, namely:

- Sequential_IO   A generic package for sequential access to nontext files.

- Direct_IO   A generic package for random access to nontext files.

- Text_IO   A package for character (text) I/O.

In addition, the predefined package IO_Exceptions defines the exceptions needed by Sequential_IO, Direct_IO, and Text_IO. For reference, Appendix C provides the specifications for each of Ada's predefined I/O packages.

Keep in mind that this chapter introduces only Ada's predefined I/O facilities. Through the extensibility of the language, a given implementation is free to add its own I/O packages, and so the details of I/O processing may vary slightly from site to site. However, this does not mean that program portability is destroyed, since any such user-defined I/O packages must be expressed within the rules of the language itself. In other words, I/O packages do not produce a superset of the language; rather, they provide new facilities within the context of Ada's existing form.

The I/O procedures defined for all three I/O packages include:

- Close   Severs file object–external file association.
- Create   Establishes a new external file.
- Delete   Causes an external file to cease to exist.
- Open   Associates a file object with an existing external file.
- Reset   Restarts from the beginning.

The following functions are also included:

- End_Of_File   Returns True if no more can be read.
- Form   Returns the form string for external file.
- Is_Open   Returns True if the file is open.
- Mode   Returns In_File, Out_File, or InOut_File.
- Name   Returns string name of the external file.

More detail will be given about these I/O procedures and functions as we proceed through the chapter.

18.2   Input/Output for Nontextual Data

The generic packages Sequential_IO and Direct_IO provide all the primitive features needed for I/O of a specific element type. These packages are for nontext I/O. In other words, Sequential_IO and Direct_IO operate with machine-dependent data represented as bit streams exactly as the data is represented within any given system. Both packages provide virtually identical facilities, the difference being that Sequential_IO is suitable for sequential files and Direct_IO is suitable for random-access files. Text_IO, covered in a later section, provides I/O facilities for ASCII character data.

Both nontext I/O packages have Read and Write procedures, as opposed to Get and Put textual I/O. In addition, Direct_IO provides the procedure Set_Index and the functions Size and Index to allow a client to access a particular item directly.

Because both of these packages are generic, they must be instantiated for a given data type (through the generic formal parameter Element_Type). For example, we may wish to input or output several numeric types:

```
with Direct_IO, Sequential_IO;
procedure Main is
  type Dollar is delta 0.01 range 0.0..1_000.0;
  type Payroll is record
                  Name : String( 1..20 );
                  Ssn  : Long_Integer;
                  Pay  : Dollar;
                end record;
  type Part is record
                  Description  : String( 1..20 );
                  Stock_Number : Positive;
                  Quantity     : Integer;
                  Price        : Dollar;
                end record;
  package Payroll_IO is new Sequential_IO ( Element_Type => Payroll );
  use Payroll_IO;
  package Float_IO is new Sequential_IO ( Element_Type => Float );
  use Float_IO;
  package Part_IO is new Direct_IO ( Element_Type => Part );
  use Part_IO;
  Float_File : Float_IO.File_Type;
  Payroll_File : Payroll_IO.File_Type;
  My_Pay : Payroll;
  Average : Float;
begin
  Open ( File => Payroll_File, Mode => In_File, Name => "Company.Pay" );
  Open ( File => Float_File, Mode => In_File, Name => "Real_Stuff" );
  ...
  Read (File => Payroll_File, Item => My_Pay);
  Write(File => Float_File, Item => Average + 25.0);
  ...
end Main;
```

Since all three predefined I/O packages are library units, they must be imported using a `with` clause. We have used named parameter association to improve the readability of the instantiation. We can instantiate a new I/O package for predefined types (such as `Integer` and `Float`). Composite user-defined types (records and arrays, such as `Payroll` and `Part`) can be used for nontext files as long as they are constrained. In addition, an implementation can prohibit instantiations of the two nontext I/O packages for access types.

As a natural consequence of Ada's strong typing rules, a package must be instantiated for every data type that we want to input or output. Ada was designed with the understanding that we write code only once but read it many times. This is one case where writing Ada code can become lengthy, yet explicit. If a particular application uses a given set of I/O packages frequently, we recommend that you declare the typical instantiations as library units, or nest them in the specification of a library package. This approach minimizes any I/O overhead we may have in an embedded system by ensuring that we bind only those I/O routines actually needed. For example, the following declares two library units, which are instantiations of predefined I/O generic packages:

```
with Sequential_IO;
package Integer_IO is new Sequential_IO(Element_Type => Integer);
with Measures, Text_IO;
package Kg_IO is new Text_IO.Integer_IO(Measures.Kilograms);
```

Also note that all of the predefined I/O packages are sequential; that is, their semantics are guaranteed only in the presence of a single task. Thus, if multiple tasks must manipulate files, it is important that all operations be serialized, via some programmer-defined mechanism.

File Structure

All high-level I/O in Ada is associated with a file. A *file* is a finite sequence of elements. Every element of the file must be of the same type. Externally, a file is associated with a physical device such as a disk, terminal, or printer. Internally, all I/O is logically processed through a file object. Every file operation is defined upon objects of a certain `File_Type`. From the example of the `Main` program given previously, we can declare the following files:

```
with Text_IO; use Text_IO;
with Sequential_IO;
```

```
procedure Main is
   type Dollar is delta 0.01 range 0.0..1_000.0;
   package Integer_IO is new Integer_IO ( Num => Integer );
   package Float_IO is new Sequential_IO ( Element_Type => Float );
   package Dollar_IO is new Fixed_IO ( Num => Dollar );
   Integer_File : Text_IO.File_Type;
   Float_File   : Float_IO.File_Type;
   Dollar_File  : Text_IO.File_Type;
begin

   ...
end Main;
```

The *mode* of a file is established when the file is opened or created. The following three modes are defined:

- In_File

- Out_File

- Inout_File

The modes In_File and Out_File are available for all three predefined I/O packages. The mode Inout_File, however, is available only for Direct_IO files. The name of each mode indicates the direction of data flow, relative to the program. For example, a file with mode In_File can be used only to input data. The mode of a file can be changed at run-time, while it is open, using the procedure Reset. Not all environments support the use of Reset; thus its use reduces portability.

A Direct_IO file is viewed as a set of elements (all of the same type) occupying consecutive positions in a linear order. This is not unlike a one-dimensional array. We can transfer a value to or from an element of the file at any selected position. Every file has a current, finite size, indicating the number of elements in the file. File positions are indexed, starting with position 1 and continuing through the current size. Furthermore, Ada defines an integer value, called Current_Index, that represents the current read/write position; the function Index returns this value. We can explicitly set Current_Index using the procedure Set_Index.

Random access requires a certain amount of overhead. For those applications in which direct random access is not required, the Sequential_IO package provides a better abstraction. For Sequential_IO files, there is no concept of position selection, and so values are simply transferred in the order of their appearance. The procedure Reset, however, can change the position from anywhere within a sequential file back to the beginning of the file.

File Processing

For consistency, file-processing subprograms in Ada are independent of any physical limitations. As a result, some of the routines we will describe are not appropriate for all physical files—obviously we cannot write to a file that the operating system will not give us access to. If we try to apply any inappropriate operation to a file, the system will raise an exception.

The package IO_Exceptions defines the following exceptions appropriate to file processing. For convenience, these exceptions are renamed in the specifications of Sequential_IO, Direct_IO, and Text_IO.

- Data_Error   Raised if an input operation cannot yield a value of the appropriate type, such as when a program tries to read an integer value but instead receives character data from the environment, or when the value -23 is read from a file defined for only positive numbers.

- Device_Error   Raised if there is a malfunction in the underlying system.

- End_Error   Raised if we try to read beyond the end of a file.

- Mode_Error   Raised if we try to read an Out_File or write to an In_File.

- Name_Error   Raised if we try to create or open a file whose given name is prohibited or is not unique.

- Status_Error   Raised if we try to read or write a file that is not open, or if we try to open a file that is already open.

- Use_Error   Raised if we try to apply an operation that is not allowed for the identified physical file, for example, if we write to a file that the operating system does not give us access to, or write to a file on a disk that is full.

Note that checking the conditions for Data_Error is optional for Sequential_IO and Direct_IO; if it is deemed too difficult, an implementation need not do so. No such limitation exists, however, for Text_IO. In addition, there is the exception Layout_Error, which refers only to Text_IO processing.

Before any file processing can begin, a file object must be associated with a physical file. The subprograms Create and Open are used to make this association. In addition, these routines permit us to name the mode of a file. We use Create to establish a new file, while Open makes available an existing file. Calls to these routines are written as follows:

```
Create(File => Payroll_File,
       Mode => Out_File,
       Name => "SystemFile",
       Form => "Disk2");
Open (File => Part_File, Mode => In_File, Name => "BlackBoxFile");
```

Again, we have used named parameter association to improve the readability of the calls. The File parameter denotes the file object to be associated, while the Mode parameter identifies the mode of the logical file (In_File, Out_File, or Inout_File). The next parameter, Name, is a string that identifies an external physical file. External file names, of course, are implementation dependent and based on the naming conventions used by a given system. The last parameter, Form, is an optional string value and is also implementation dependent. Different systems use Form to allow users to identify various file properties, such as "save for 30 days."

Note that, for both Name and Form, we do not have to supply a literal string, but we can use a string object, such as:

```
with Text_IO; use Text_IO;
procedure Main is
  Float_File : File_Type;
  Last       : Natural;
  Title      : String(1..80);
begin
  Get_Line (Title, Last); -- read in a title from the user
  Create(File => Float_File, Name => Title(1..Last));
end Main;
```

Also note that for newly created sequential and text files, the default mode is Out_File; for new direct access files, the default is Inout_File. In addition, if the default value for the Name parameter of Create is a null string, the system creates a temporary file whose name we are not concerned with and whose existence will end when the program ends.

After we have finished processing a file, we must explicitly close the file in one of two ways:

```
Close(Part_File);
Delete(Float_File);
```

In the first example, we simply sever the association between the file object and the external system name, and the physical file is retained. In the second example, we sever the association, but the physical file is not retained.

Ada provides five primitive selectors to test the state of files. All of these functions require a single parameter: a file object. The functions are:

- `Name`   Returns a string that uniquely names the physical file.

- `Form`   Returns the current form string of a given file.

- `Is_Open`   Returns `True` if the file is open, else `False`.

- `End_Of_File`   Returns `True` if no more elements can be read from the file.

- `Mode`   Returns the current mode of a given file.

For `Direct_IO` files, Ada also defines the functions `Size` (which returns the current number of elements in the file) and `Index` (which returns the value of the current read/write position). For `Direct_IO` files only, we can explicitly set the current read/write position using `Set_Index`. For example:

```
Open( File => Part_File, Mode => Inout_File, Name => "Inventory.Prt" );
    ...
Set_Index(Part_File, To => 137);
```

At this point, the function `Index` would return 137. If we attempted to set the index to a position greater than the end of the file, no exception would be raised until we tried to read from that undefined position. When performing output, we can set the position beyond the end of the file and write new elements.

For both `Direct_IO` and `Sequential_IO` files, primitive file processing is achieved with the procedures `Read` and `Write`. By definition, we can read a file of mode `In_File` or `Inout_File`, and we can write a file of mode `Out_File` or `Inout_File`. Again, remember that only `Direct_IO` supports mode `Inout_File`. In any case, we must supply the logical file, plus a value or object of the appropriate element type:

```
Read (File => Payroll_File, Item => My_Pay);
Write(File => Float_File, Item => Average + 25.0);
```

Whenever we apply these subprograms, the effect is to input or output the given values in a binary form, reflecting the underlying internal machine representation. Thus, if we are communicating with a unique I/O device, we can use representation specifications to tailor the form of the values as they are transmitted to or received from the device. We should add that the `Direct_IO` package also exports a form of the `Read` and `Write` subprograms with an `Index` parameter that explicitly defines the read or write position. `Read` and `Write` for `Direct_IO` also automatically increment the file position after the I/O operation is complete. Lastly, note that the binary representation of a type may differ from system to system. If, on one system, we use the following Sequential_IO instance to write a file:

```
with Sequential_IO;
procedure Main is
  type Integer_16 is range -32_768..32_767;
  for Integer_16'Size use 16;
  package Integer_16_IO is new Sequential_IO(Integer_16);
begin
  ...
end Main;
```

and then use the same code to read the file on a different system, the numbers written may not be those read. For example, one system may represent the integer value 1 using the bits 0000000000000001, while another represents 1 as 1000000000000000.

To demonstrate the high-level I/O facilities that Ada provides, we apply some of these features to a simple problem. In the following example we read a sequence of integers from a file, calculate a running total, and then write the sum to a newly created file. The code can be written as follows:

```
with Sequential_IO;
procedure Simple_Example is
  package Integer_IO is new Sequential_IO (Element_Type => Integer);
  Input_Data  : Integer_IO.File_Type;
  Output_Data : Integer_IO.File_Type;
  Value       : Integer;
  Sum         : Integer := 0;
  use Integer_IO;
begin  -- Simple_Example
  Open ( Input_Data, In_File, "c:my-input.dat" );
  Create( Output_Data, Out_File, "a:my-output.dat" );
  loop
    exit when End_Of_File ( Input_Data );
    Read ( Input_Data, Value );
    Sum := Sum + Value;
  end loop;
  Write ( Output_Data, Sum );
  Close ( Input_Data );
  Close ( Output_Data );
end Simple_Example;
```

Since the size of the file is unknown, notice how the End_Of_File function is used to control the number of reads.

18.3   Input/Output for Textual Data

Using the facilities provided by the generic packages `Sequential_IO` and `Direct_IO`, we theoretically have all the primitive operations needed to perform I/O for any data type. Although we often interface with unique peripheral devices in the embedded computer system domain, input and output may still be required in human-readable form. We could instantiate the generic packages for `Character` elements, but we would have to build our own routines to provide numeric I/O in human-readable form. (This would be necessary because numeric values are not represented inside the machine in character form.) Since this is a common requirement, Ada defines a separate package (which is not generic) called `Text_IO`. This package provides functions similar to those of the generic packages, but additional subprograms are available for text layout.

File Structure

The package `Text_IO` provides I/O facilities where the input and output of data are composed only of ASCII characters. Just like the generic packages, all `Text_IO` processing is achieved through files. In addition, when the `Text_IO` package is used, standard input and output files are opened at the beginning of program execution. In an interactive environment, we would expect the default input file to be associated with a keyboard and the default output file to be associated with a display. Many systems allow users to define which files are associated with standard input and output when the program is executed. Remember also that `Text_IO` is not guaranteed to work in the presence of multiple tasks. Thus, if an application has one task that inputs data and another that outputs data, the behavior of this program may vary with the implementation.

Of course, we can open and create our own `Text_IO` file explicitly. For example:

```
with Text_IO;
procedure Main is
  My_Input,
  My_Output : Text_IO.File_Type;
begin
  Text_IO.Open(My_Input, Text_IO.In_File, "Data-set-i");
  Text_IO.Create(My_Output, Text_IO.Out_File, "output");
  ...
end Main;
```

Notice that since Text_IO is a library unit, it must be imported using a with clause. As is the case with Sequential_IO, only files of modes In_File and Out_File can be opened and created; text files of mode Inout_File are not supported. Like the generic I/O packages, Text_IO has all of the I/O procedures Close, Create, Delete, Open, and Reset, as mentioned earlier in section 18.1.

All Text_IO operations are defined on the given File_Type object. As a consequence of allowing default file objects, most of the routines in Text_IO have two parameter profile forms: One includes no file and therefore operates on a default file; the other requires an explicit file object. Initially, the default files are the standard files. Using the functions Standard_Input and Standard_Output, we can acquire the value of the standard files. In addition, the functions Set_Input and Set_Output permit us to reassociate the default files at execution time, while the functions Current_Input and Current_Output return the default files. For example:

```
with Text_IO;
procedure Redirection is
   Log       : Text_IO.File_Type;
   Log_Name  : String(1..100);
   Name_Last : Natural;
   use Text_IO;
begin
   Put ("Enter a log file name: ");
   Get_Line (Log_Name, Name_Last);
   Create (Log, Out_File, Log_Name (1..Name_Last));
   Set_Output(Log);
   Put_Line ("Hello...  This is a log.");
   Set_Output(Standard_Output);
   Close(Log);
   Put_Line("Done.");
end Redirection;
```

The call to Put writes to standard output, and the call to Get_Line reads from standard input. Then, after creating the log file, we make it the default output. That is, after the first call to Set_Output, Current_Output would return Log. Thus, the first call to Put_Line writes to the file we have created. Next we again make standard output the default before closing Log, and we output a final message to Standard_Output.

For Text_IO files, the functions Is_Open, End_Of_File, Mode, Name, and Form are also available (see section 18.1). These functions operate in the same manner as those described for the generic I/O packages.

File Layout

Text_IO provides line-oriented output, whether that output is to a human-readable device such as a printer or monitor display, or to a machine-readable device such as a disk. Ada provides facilities to help format the output. A text file, be it Standard_Output or a disk file, is dimensioned as pages x lines x characters. Each page consists of a list of lines that can be of variable or fixed length. Furthermore, each line consists of a variable or fixed number of columns (characters). Text_IO maintains the current page, line, and column position of a file.

The line length and page length of an Out_File can be established by using the procedures Set_Line_Length and Set_Page_Length. For example:

```
Set_Page_Length (My_Output, To => 66);
```

The detailed specifications of Set_Page_Length and the other subprograms discussed in this section are provided in Appendix C.

If we try to output more than 66 lines, a page terminator (sometimes called a "page break" or "form feed") will automatically be output after the 66th line. To establish an explicit line or page terminator, we do one of the following:

```
New_Line;        -- output a line terminator
New_Page;        -- output a page terminator
```

In the event that we want only explicitly output line or page terminators and no automatic line or page terminators, we can set the length to zero. To Text_IO, a length of zero means an unbounded length. We can inquire as to the current parameters with the functions Line_Length and Page_Length.

Apart from the procedures Put and Get, which implicitly affect the value of the current column, the column count can also be set explicitly. Text_IO defines two subprograms related to the column position:

- Col   Returns the current column value.

- Set_Col   Sets the current column.

If we try to set a column position beyond the current line length, the exception Layout_Error is raised.

Text_IO also provides several subprograms associated with the current line position:

- Line   Returns the current line value.

- Set_Line   Sets the current line.

To skip to the next line, Text_IO provides the following procedures:

- New_Line   Writes one or more line terminators.
- Skip_Line   Reads past one or more line terminators.

We also have the function End_Of_Line, which returns the value True if there are no more characters to be read on the current input line.

Text_IO also defines several operations that affect the current page number. These subprograms parallel the operations defined for the line number. In particular:

- Page   Returns the current page number.
- New_Page   Writes one or more page terminators.
- Skip_Page   Reads past one or more page terminators.
- End_Of_Page   Returns True if there are no more characters to be read on the current page (for In_File only).

Given these facilities, we can now provide a simple example that writes seven line terminators on the default output file and then sets the current position to the 26th column:

```
New_Line(Spacing => 7);
Set_Col (To      => 26);
```

The effect on the screen would be to move the cursor to the 26th position 7 lines down from the present line.

Note that the actual character or characters comprising a page or line terminator are device dependent. Indeed, this is why Ada abstracts them with the procedures New_Page, Skip_Page, New_Line and Skip_Line.

Text_IO for Character and String Types

All basic file processing for Text_IO is achieved with the overloaded subprograms Put and Get. For character and string types, Put will output the specified value, starting at the current page, line, and column. Get will input to a specified variable starting at the current page, line, and column. After a Put or Get operation, column, line, and page numbers will be updated to point to the next position beyond the values read or written.

We often combine Put and Get operations with the operations New_Line and Skip_Line. For example, assume a line length of 10 and a current column and line position of 1. Consider the following operations:

```
with Text_IO; use Text_IO;
procedure Main is
begin
  Set_Line_Length( 10 );
  Set_Col( 1 );
  Put("Now ");
  Put("is the time ");
  Put("for ");
  New_Line;
  Put("all people");
  New_Line;
end Main;
```

The following output will be displayed on the standard output device:

```
Now is the
 time for
all people
```

Even though we used only two explicit New_Line operations, three lines of output were displayed. We exceeded the current line length during the second Put operation, thus forcing an additional line terminator. Notice also that for string output (and input) the width of the value either written or read is equal to the length of the string.

Text_IO provides two additional reading and writing routines that are associated with the line terminator. Put_Line simply outputs a given string, followed by a line terminator. Get_Line begins reading characters from the current position on the line. Get_Line stops reading characters when a line terminator is met or when the string variable parameter is completely filled with characters. If a line terminator is met while reading, a Skip_Line is issued to read past the line terminator, and the current column position is set to 1. If the string variable parameter is filled before a line terminator is met, *no* Skip_Line is executed, and the current column position is set to the character after the last character that was read in. Get_Line returns a string and an index indicating the position of the last character read into the string variable.

Finally, note that the reading and writing of graphic characters is portable. Graphic characters are those you can see, such as letters, digits, punctuation, and so on. Reading and writing control characters (Ascii.Nul through Ascii.Us and Ascii.Del) is device dependent.

Text_IO **for Other Data Types**

For text files and interactive applications, there is a need to handle I/O values for numeric and enumeration types and not just character values. If we use the standard routines from Sequential_IO or Direct_IO, the results will be in nontext form and will not be human-readable. Again, Ada recognizes this as a common situation and includes within Text_IO the facilities for numeric and enumeration type I/O. The following four generic packages are exported by Text_IO:

- Integer_IO   Textual I/O for integer types.
- Float_IO   Textual I/O for floating-point types.
- Fixed_IO   Textual I/O for fixed-point types.
- Enumeration_IO Textual I/O for enumeration types.

These generic units are nested within Text_IO because they share File_Type and the basic operations (e.g., Open, Close, and New_Line) with Text_IO.

As before, the procedures Put and Get are used to achieve these forms of textual I/O. However, since numeric and enumeration types will be user-defined, an appropriate generic unit that is already part of Text_IO must be instantiated. For numeric types, any of the first three packages mentioned above can be instantiated, depending on the numeric type, that is, integer, floating-point, or fixed-point. The following are examples of instantiations of all four generic I/O packages:

```
with Text_IO;
procedure Main is
   type Index is range 0..100;
   package Index_IO is new Text_IO.Integer_IO(Index);
   type Mass is digits 10;
   package Mass_IO is new Text_IO.Float_IO (Mass);
   type Length is delta 0.125 range 0.0..10.0;
   package Length_IO is new Text_IO.Fixed_IO(Length);
   package Bool_IO is new Text_IO.Enumeration_IO(Boolean);
begin
   ...
end Main;
```

Text_IO provides an overloaded subprogram Get for each of these four generic packages. In each case, input is achieved in a free-field form. For each Get operation, Text_IO also defines a form that includes an explicit field Width (indicating the number of characters to be read). There are other forms of Get, but we refer you to Appendix C for details. In general, however, when we get a value, the operation first skips any terminators or blanks and then reads characters until the next character read would violate the syntax of the indicated type or until Width characters have been input. The exception Data_Error is raised if the input sequence does not have the required syntax (in particular, if no characters can be read or if characters not associated with numeric values are read when using any of the numeric I/O packages).

Because the textual representation of a numeric value can be of varying length, Text_IO defines the overloaded subprogram Put. Put includes parameters for specifying field Width, Base for integer values. Fore and Aft parts relative to the decimal point are specified as part of the Put for floating- and fixed-point numbers. Put also has Exp for the exponent of floating- and fixed-point numbers. The following examples illustrate the layout (ƀ indicates a blank):

```
with Text_IO;
procedure Main is
   type Index is range 0..100;
   package Index_IO is new Text_IO.Integer_IO(Index);
   type Mass is digits 10;
   package Mass_IO is new Text_IO.Float_IO (Mass);
   type Length is delta 0.125 range 0.0..10.0;
   package Length_IO is new Text_IO.Fixed_IO(Length);
   package Bool_IO is new Text_IO.Enumeration_IO(Boolean);
   use Text_IO;
begin
-- Operation                                            Display
   Index_IO.Put(26); New_Line;                          -- 26
   Index_IO.Put(26, Width => 5); New_Line;              -- ƀƀƀ26
   Index_IO.Put(26, Width => 6, Base => 8); New_Line;   -- ƀ8#32#
   Mass_IO.Put(3.14159, Fore => 1, Aft => 3, Exp => 1);
   New_Line;                                             -- 3.142E+0
   Length_IO.Put(2.78159, Fore => 5, Aft => 3);
   New_Line;                                             -- ƀƀƀƀ2.750
end Main;
```

Note that if the Put operation exceeds the Width provided, the explicit Width is ignored and the display expands to fit the value. Also consider the last Put operation; the value printed is not that given in the call to Put. This is because the value given is not a number that models a value of type Length, and so the value was rounded to the nearest delta increment (0.125) for that type.

Text_IO provides similar facilities for enumeration types. We must instantiate the generic package Enumeration_IO for the specific data type. Like input for numeric I/O, input for enumeration types is of free-field form, using the subprogram Get. However, the overloaded routine Put includes some additional layout parameters. For enumeration I/O, Get makes no distinction between lowercase and uppercase characters. With the following declarations, we can use these forms for Put:

```
with Text_IO;
procedure Main is
  type Status is (Normal, Warning, Alarm);
  package Status_IO is new Text_IO.Enumeration_IO (Enum => Status);
  use Status_IO;
  use Text_IO;
begin
-- Operation                                          Display
  Put(Normal);                                     -- NORMAL
  Put(Warning, Width => 10);                       -- WARNINGⱢⱢⱢ
  Put(Alarm, Width => 7, Set => Lower_Case);  -- alarmⱢⱢ
  New_Line;
end Main;
```

Each of the four generic packages within Text_IO also provides Get and Put operations that read from and write to strings, rather than files. For example, the following will display ⱢⱢ3.142E+0:

```
with Text_IO;
procedure Main is
  type Mass is digits 10;
  package Mass_IO is new Text_IO.Float_IO (Mass);
  Buffer : String (1.. 10);
begin
  Mass_IO.Put(To => Buffer, Item => 3.14159, Aft => 3, Exp => 1);
  Text_IO.Put_Line(Buffer);
end Main;
```

No Fore field width is needed, since the size of the string (Buffer), together with Aft and Exp, determines how much space to use.

Lastly, the following parameters have default values that can be changed by the programmer: Width and Base of Integer_IO; Fore, Aft, and Exp of Float and Fixed_IO; and Width and Setting of Enumeration_IO. These defaults are not explicit in the various subprogram specifications. Rather, the subprograms refer to variables declared in the various packages, and these variables can be changed. For example, Enumeration_IO includes the following:

```
Default_Width   : Field    := 0;
Default_Setting : Type_Set := Upper_Case;
procedure Put(Item  : in Fnum;
              Width : in Field    := Default_Width;
              Set   : in Type_Set := Default_Setting);
```

We can change the default setting as follows:

```
with Text_IO;
procedure Main is
   type Status is (Normal, Warning, Alarm);
   package Status_IO is new Text_IO.Enumeration_IO (Enum => Status);
begin
   Status_IO.Default_Setting := Text_IO.Lower_Case;
   Status_IO.Put(Warning);                          -- warning
   Text_IO.New_Line;
end Main;
```

The use of variables to set and change subprogram default parameters is a common and very useful technique. It provides more flexibility than does hard-coding defaults in subprograms.

18.4   Application

Now that we have examined the facilities provided by the package Text_IO, let us turn back to the problem we presented in Chapter 5 and consider the implementation of the package Document. Recall that Document served as an abstract-state machine: We use the package to open and close documents and extract one word at a time. Clearly, Text_IO is a reasonable facility for us to use to implement Document. However, there are some challenges here. As Document builds words, it encounters line, page, and file terminators, all of which act as word delimiters. Further, the line numbers used on our application are absolute line numbers from the beginning of the file, rather than line numbers relative to the current page used by Text_IO. Thus we must maintain our own absolute, current line number.

The following code embodies the framework of the Document package:

```
with Text_IO;
package body Document is
   The_File     : Text_IO.File_Type;
   Current_Line : Line_Numbers.Number := 1;
```

```
   procedure Open (The_Name : in String) is separate;
   procedure Close is separate;
   procedure Get (The_Word   : out Words.Word;
                  The_Number : out Line_Numbers.Number) is separate;
end Document;
```

Open and Close set the state of The_File object. Thus, we write:

```
separate (Document)
procedure Open (The_Name : in String) is
begin
  Text_IO.Open (The_File, Text_IO.In_File, The_Name);
exception
  when others => raise Open_Error;
end Open;

separate (Document)
procedure Close is
begin
  Text_IO.Close (The_File);
exception
  when others => raise Close_Error;
end Close;
```

Our Get procedure then reads from The_File, searching for word delimiters, composing the characters between delimiters, and maintaining our absolute line count (Current_Line). In addition to page and line terminators, any character other than a letter, digit, or underscore is a delimiter. As a result, a document word can contain the same characters as an Ada identifier, meaning that we could run this application on Ada programs. We can implement Get as follows:

```
separate (Document)
procedure Get (The_Word   : out Words.Word:
               The_Number : out Line_Numbers.Number) is
  Temporary_Character : Character;
  Temporary_Word      : String (1.. 80);
  Index               : Natural := 0;
  function Done return Boolean is
  begin
    if Index > 0 then
      Words.Create(The_Word, Temporary_Word(1..Index));
      The_Number := Current_Line;
      return True;
```

```
        else
          return False;
        end if;
      end Done;
      function "+" (Left, Right : in Line_Numbers.Number)
        return Line_Numbers.Number;
      use Text_IO;
    begin  -- Get
      loop
        if End_Of_Line(The_File) then
          exit when Done;
          Skip_Line(The_File);
          Current_Line := Current_Line + 1;
        elsif End_Of_Page(The_File) then
          exit when Done;
          Skip_Page(The_File);
        else
          Get(The_File, Temporary_Character);
          case Temporary_Character is
            when 'a'.. 'z' | 'A'.. 'Z' | '0'.. '9' | '_' =>
              if Index = Temporary_Word'Last then
                raise Word_Too_Long;
              else
                Index := Index + 1;
                Temporary_Word(Index) := Temporary_Character;
              end if;
            when others => exit when Done;
          end case;
        end if;
      end loop;
    exception
      when Text_IO.End_Error => raise End_Of_File;
    end Get;
```

Notice how we explicitly check for the Word_Too_Long condition, but
allow the End_Of_File condition to be reported as a lower-level exception.
We do this because encountering a word that is too long would implicitly
be reported by Constraint_Error, and Constraint_Error could be raised for
many reasons in this procedure. Thus, for reliability, we do not allow
Constraint_Error to be raised implicitly. Rather, we explicitly check for the
condition ourselves. Reaching the end of the file, on the other hand, is
reported by Text_IO.End_Error. This is the only reason Text_IO.End_Error is ever

raised, so we can be certain that raising End_Of_File is the appropriate response. Also, notice that we have used a renaming declaration (function "+") to make the addition operation for Current_Line directly visible; this declaration permits us to use the operation in a natural, infix notation.

We can complete the body of Document with the function Is_End_Of_File, which simply serves to hide the use of Text_IO.End_Of_File:

```
function Is_End_Of_File return Boolean is
begin
   return Text_IO.End_Of_File(The_File);
end Is_End_Of_File;
```

18.5   Low-Level Input/Output

In some situations, the facilities provided by Sequential_IO, Direct_IO, and Text_IO may be at too high a level for our purposes, especially if we need to manipulate a unique peripheral device. With Ada's packaging facilities, one solution is to build our own I/O routines, using representation specifications to reference hardware dependencies. In such situations, it is common practice to treat each peripheral device as a concurrent task, which we then embed inside a package. Another way is to use code procedures that contain explicit machine language statements.

For devices that require a primitive level of control, an implementation can provide a package called Low_Level_IO, which contains the procedures Send_Control and Receive_Control. Ada defines these procedures with two parameters that are highly implementation dependent. The first parameter in each routine specifies the name of the device, while the second parameter specifies the type of data to be sent or received.

As we have seen, Ada provides a number of facilities for I/O within the context of existing language constructs. In the next chapter we shall further study the impact of Ada's extensibility, and see how it relates to the construction of large software systems.

Summary

- Input and output in Ada are provided by several predefined packages, including Sequential_IO, Direct_IO, and Text_IO. Applications can extend these facilities by introducing other I/O packages.

- Sequential_IO and Direct_IO provide I/O of arbitrary types as bit streams. Text_IO provides I/O facilities destined for human consumption.

- All I/O is defined in terms of file objects. Operations such as Open, Close, Delete, and Create manipulate file objects. Corresponding to these constructs are selectors such as Is_Open and End_Of_File, via the procedures which return the current state of file objects.

- File objects are associated with physical files and devices via the procedures Open and Create. These procedures require the implementation-dependent parameters Name and Form.

- The mode of a file designates the direction of data flow relative to the program. The modes are In_File, Out_File, and Inout_File.

- Direct_IO and Sequential_IO files are treated as sequential lists of elements. Direct_IO files also permit direct access to a specific element.

- Text_IO files consist of a number of pages, each of which contains a number of lines. Each line consists of a number of characters. Text_IO maintains the current page, line, and column of a file, which can be altered with various constructors (such as Get, Put, and Set_Col) and retrieved by various selectors (such as Page and Line).

- Associated with every I/O package is a set of predefined exceptions (such as End_Error, Mode_Error, and Name_Error) that can be raised during an I/O operation.

- In addition to operations for character and string types, Text_IO exports a number of nested generic units to support I/O for arbitrary integer, floating-point, fixed-point, and enumeration types. These must be instantiated with appropriate types before any such operations are available.

- Standard and default input/output files are defined for Text_IO. Initially, the standard files are the defaults. The user can redirect the default files to any Text_IO file.

Exercises

1. Declare a type named Personnel_Record, which contains the components Name (a string of length 40), SSN (an integer of range 0 to 999_99_9999), and Address (a string of length 80). Instantiate a package for random-access I/O for the record and declare a file object named Company_Data.

2. Write a subprogram that reads every record from Company_Data (from Exercise 1) and places the record in an array. As parameters to the subprogram, return the array containing the records, plus a natural number that contains the number of records that were in the file.

*3. Write a subprogram that writes the contents of the array (from Exercise 2) to a physical file named Printer. Print the Name in the first 40 columns, skip 5 spaces, print the SSN as a three-digit field, a dash, a two-digit field, another dash, and a four-digit field. Then print the address on the next line. Skip two lines after each record, and print at most 10 records per page.

*4. Instantiate a Text_IO package for data of type Integer. Write a subprogram that takes as parameters Low, High, and Result. Low and High are mode in parameters that represent the bounds of the number desired for input, and Result is a mode out parameter whose value is within these bounds. Within the subprogram, try to Get a Result from the default input file. Use exception handling to recover from Data_Error. In addition, output an appropriate message if Result is not within the desired bounds, and make the user repeat the operation until a valid result is given.

5. Write a function that returns a string input from Standard_Input. The string should be the remainder of the current line when the function is called. Does your implementation work even when current input is redirected?

6. The procedures Set_Input and Set_Output are constructors on the hidden state of Text_IO, and have the corresponding selectors Current_Input and Current_Output. What does this tell us about the implementation of Text_IO.File_Type?

7. Using the criteria for evaluating objects presented in Chapters 10 and 13, evaluate Text_IO.

8. Text_IO does not provide such common operations as checking whether an external file exists before we try to open it, opening an Out_File so that all output is appended to the file, and reading from an In_File until a specific character is encountered. Implement a package called Text_IO_Utilities that provides at least these operations. Subprograms of the package should take Text_IO.File_Type objects as parameters, rather than building a higher-level abstraction on top of Text_IO.

CHAPTER 19

The Software Life Cycle with Ada

Analysis Phase
Requirements Definition Phase
Design Phase
Coding Phase
Testing Phase
Operation and Maintenance Phase

The life cycle of software extends from the conception of the software until its final use. Traditionally, software developers have taken a restricted view of this life cycle and treated each phase in the life cycle phase as an independent part. Thus, implementors might design a system using one technique, code in another language, and then test the entire system using a totally different set of tools. This approach leads to numerous problems, the least of which includes configuration-control nightmares and sets of software modules that do not function together. In the end, the developers might complete the system, although probably not on time and certainly not without much wailing and gnashing of teeth.

The software life cycle can be divided into six major phases. Various sources name each phase slightly differently, but for our purposes we will name them as follows:

- Analysis

- Requirements definition

- Design

- Coding

- Testing

- Operation and maintenance

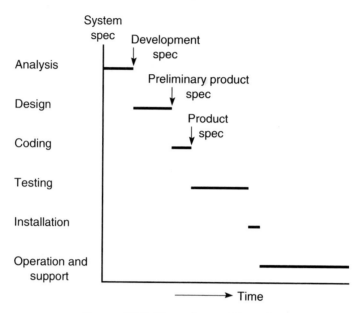

Figure 19.1 The software life cycle

Figure 19.1 represents these phases over time.

Large systems do not simply spring up overnight. They evolve from smaller ones. Ideally, such systems should be evolved using consistent tools and notations. In this sense, we should no longer just code with our languages, we should design with them also. In Ada, we now have a language that can be applied in a consistent manner across the entire life cycle of software. As we discussed in Chapter 3, Ada is a design language; in this chapter, we shall examine exactly what that statement means.

19.1   Analysis Phase

During the analysis phase of our system life cycle, we seek to better understand the nature of the problem and determine the extent to which a computerized solution is appropriate. Once the need to computerize is determined, we then allocate particular functions to the software, usually documented in the form of a system specification. During this phase, we also begin to identify the resources needed to complete the solution, such as the capabilities of the implementation hardware and the staffing levels of software personnel.

It would be inappropriate to even think of programming in the Ada language at this point in the life cycle. The reason is simple; the language is part of the solution, not part of the problem space, and the problem is what we are concerned with at this point. Analysis should be accomplished independently of any implementation language, and our use of Ada at this point would be premature. These statements may seem to contradict what was said two paragraphs earlier about using Ada across the life cycle. However, if we have a reasonable APSE (Ada Programming Support Environment) available, we should develop the system specifications using a documentation tool so that we can later track the requirements against the solution.

19.2   Requirements Definition Phase

This phase usually begins with the approval of the system specifications and terminates with the successful completion of a preliminary design review. The purpose of this phase is to take the allocated functions from the system specifications and determine the detailed requirements for the software. Actually, it is very difficult to refrain from trying to design a complete solution at this point, but we must stay at a higher level of design. The primary product of this phase is an approved development (functional) software specification.

At this point, we shall assume that we have chosen Ada as the design language. Since one product of this phase is an initial design, we can use Ada program unit specifications to document this highest level of our system, just as we did in each of the design problems earlier. We recommend at this point that a designer take a declarative view of the solution, not the imperative one that many other languages force us into. Wheeler notes that "the constraints on the system structure imposed by the use of the Ada language as the means for documenting the system's design not only cause the system's design and implementation to be easier, but also cause the resulting system to be more maintainable" [1].

This approach starts us on an integrated life cycle development, since we now have a consistent language of expression. As before, with the appropriate APSE tools, we can use configuration-management software to help us keep track of each iteration and increment of the design. In addition, we can continue to use the APSE to track system requirements against the functional allocation of each program unit.

19.3   Design Phase

The design phase of software development begins with the completion of a requirements definition and terminates with the successful completion of a final design review. The primary documentation product is a preliminary set of product specifications that reflect the design of the software. Basically, the purpose of this phase is to develop a detailed design for our software solution, including a definition of the relationships (interfaces) among units and a detailed procedural flow.

Since the user probably did not understand or recognize all of the software requirements during the previous phase, the design phase is usually an iterative process, involving changes in the development specification and corresponding changes in the design. Such changes, if they are not major, are a healthy sign that the user and developer are at least communicating. Perhaps the best management tool that can be employed during this phase is the structured walkthrough, which seeks to make the design process even more visible and hopefully leads to a more understandable product.

It is during this phase that we can begin to use Ada more directly. In the past, we would have documented our software designs with flowcharts or a different PDL. With Ada, the eventual implementation is an extension of our PDL. Actually, there are two approaches we can take with Ada as the PDL. The first approach, best illustrated by the approach used at IBM Federal Systems Division, uses a "design language" subset of Ada as the design language and is augmented by detailed documentation [2]. In the other approach, Hart proposes the use of a freer form of Ada/PDL that relaxes some of the syntactic rules [3].

The IBM approach stresses hierarchical decomposition, interface definition, and modularity; however, its use does require attention to the syntax and semantics of Ada. As such, it requires a more thorough training in Ada before it can be used successfully. The Hart approach relaxes all of the attention to Ada itself and therefore can be used with less training. Either method is appropriate, although we prefer the use of the syntactically correct subset of Ada as the design language.

With proper care taken in naming objects in our units, we have found that the Ada design becomes virtually self-documenting (see Appendix D) for even moderate-sized systems. As we move into the realm of large software solutions, internal documentation of design decisions becomes essential. No matter which design approach is employed, we still suggest the use of a declarative view of the solution, at least at the higher levels. We further recommend the employment of an object-oriented design method, at the higher declarative levels. Simple top-down decomposition techniques are sufficiently powerful at lower, purely functional levels.

As was illustrated in each of the previous design problems, we can create our software design using Ada unit specifications to formally define the interfaces among the objects in the solution space. At this point, we can provide stubs for the unit bodies, with appropriate comments indicating the design and requirements of the eventual implementation. The advantage of this approach is that, even at this early point, we can compile the system (using the IBM approach) and let the language check for logical inconsistencies. If we have the proper APSE tools, we can employ some configuration-management software to control versions of completed units. In addition, we can continue to track requirements and use the APSE to develop the rest of the external documentation.

Developers should realize that this approach does have its costs. Experience has shown that when Ada is used as a design language, more resources are expended during the design phase. However, experience also shows that this approach provides tremendous benefits that far outweigh the costs. In particular, using Ada as a design language can improve the quality of the design by highlighting interfaces and formally capturing many important design decisions. Additionally, if syntactically and semantically correct Ada is used as the design language, we can begin to compile our designs at this point and detect and correct interface problems early in the life cycle. Finally, it is common to have documentation tools that can traverse a collection of program units and extract important parts, including commented annotations. Thus, it is possible to generate design documentation semiautomatically, removing much of the tedium from the job of the developer.

19.4   Coding Phase

The coding phase traditionally begins after successful completion of the design phase and terminates . . . eventually. In a sense, the coding phase never really finishes until we abandon the corresponding piece of software. The primary documentation product from this phase is the completed product specification, which indicates the software "as built." The purpose of this phase is to implement the design generated from the previous phase.

With Ada chosen as the implementation language, the coding phase is relatively simple and is actually an extension of the process started during design. Before starting the coding phase, we should have a detailed design, represented by a collection of Ada program units with complete specifications. During the coding phase, we need only complete the implementation of our unit bodies. Of course, as we implement these bodies, we will find the need for further decomposition. In this regard, the phases of design/code/test are no longer distinct; rather, they should form an iterative process at each level of the solution.

If Ada is not the implementation language, as in the case where the target machine does not support it, we can take the Ada design and convert it into the target language. Actually, this is no different from using a foreign

PDL; we still have to do some form of conversion. However, note that it is much easier to go from a structured language such as Ada to an unstructured one such as an assembly language.

We can readily develop a paradigm to translate our Ada design to another high-order language such as FORTRAN or Pascal. We estimate that the conversion process can be automated by approximately 75% (depending on the application) when moving to a FORTRAN or Pascal implementation. As in the previous phases, we can use our APSE to maintain version control and assist in documentation preparation. Advanced APSE tools, such as syntax-directed editors, can make the design/coding phases even easier by letting us create only program units that are syntactically correct. In some cases, they may also be semantically correct.

19.5   Testing Phase

The purpose of the testing phase is to check the execution of the software against the requirements agreed upon in the development specifications. This phase should not wait until all the code is completed: A "design a little, code a little, test a little" approach is far superior. In this manner, we seek to correct design and coding errors in a much more timely fashion.

Developers usually divide the testing phase into two parts, unit testing and system testing. We can readily accomplish unit testing in an incremental design/code/test fashion. During each increment, more and more of the completed integrated system is progressively tested. Once we have completed unit testing, we proceed to system testing. We should test the system in an environment that matches the operational environment as closely as possible. In many cases, this means operating the system in parallel with an existing system during a live operation. The primary documentation products of this phase include the test reports and test certification.

We have already noted how Ada and the APSE can support an incremental design/code/test. During the testing phase, we may also employ other APSE tools such as symbolic debuggers. Traditionally, one of the biggest headaches of the testing phase is maintaining a baseline configuration of the system. In a large system, the problem is complicated as testing uncovers small changes that must be made to single program units. Again, an APSE configuration-control tool will help manage all the different versions of the software. Furthermore, since the language recognizes the existence of a program library, the APSE will indicate which units must be recompiled if a change is made in another unit. This may seem difficult, but in fact it is relatively easy, since it is a natural consequence of the Ada rule that unit dependencies are explicitly named in unit context clauses (see also Chapter 20).

19.6   Operation and Maintenance Phase

The operation and maintenance phase begins once final system testing has been successfully completed. In actuality, this situation is a bit idealistic since, in practice, developers often use a system operationally before it is completed or fully tested. If we have used a design/code/test iteration, this is not a problem, since we have confidence in the functions tested thus far. The maintenance phase is traditionally the most costly in terms of resources used. The maintenance phase usually never terminates but rather slowly fades away. In some cases, we may declare the underlying hardware to be obsolete and thus throw away the entire system, but in many cases, we evolve the smaller system into a larger system.

Since maintenance involves a design/code/test process, the points mentioned thus far with regard to Ada support still apply. Unlike other design processes, where the design is documented in a form different from the implementation language, once we change the Ada implementation, we have in principle updated the documentation. Furthermore, since Ada is a highly structured language, it is easy to maintain the original structure of the system while modifying pieces of it. As in all other phases, the APSE can help maintain control over the configuration of the program units.

Obviously, we have presented a simplified explanation of some of the activities in the software life cycle; a full description would demand several volumes of text. As we have seen, Ada can be applied throughout the software life cycle. Unlike other language systems, Ada gives us a consistent language of expression to provide stability during the development process.

Summary
- Software development usually follows the phases of analysis, requirements definition, design, coding, testing, installation, and operation and maintenance.

- Ada has very little impact on the analysis phase. In this phase we concentrate on building an abstraction of the problem.

- Requirements definition involves determining the characteristics of the automated system in terms of its functional behavior as well as its performance.

- Design involves engineering the structure of a system. Ada can be used as a design language, to capture the design decisions made during this phase. This approach implies a higher resource cost, but it also provides important benefits in terms of facilitating the creation of a quality design.

- Coding involves taking the design and transforming it into executable units. If Ada is used as a PDL, this transformation is relatively simple.

- Testing is usually done at the unit and system level. Because Ada is such a static language, simple compilation can detect many (but definitely not all) errors that other high-order languages would not detect until execution.

Programming in the Large

Managing the Name Space
Separate Compilation Issues
Large Systems Architecture

We have examined most of Ada's constructs at length and have illustrated their use through a number of small examples. However, Ada was designed to be applied not just to small problems but also to domains whose solutions might contain hundreds of thousands—even millions—of lines of code. Extending our experience of small problems to the domain of large solutions is not just a matter of simple extrapolation. Fortunately, as we shall see in this chapter, Ada provides a number of features to help deal with the complexity of large systems.

20.1   Managing the Name Space

In any nontrivial application, the solution will most certainly consist of several program units, including subprograms, packages, and tasks. If we are dealing with a large system containing many thousands of lines of code, we can decompose the solution into hundreds if not thousands of units. In addition, there will undoubtedly be more than a few programmers developing the software. Furthermore, in such large systems there may be hundreds of software objects that map to our abstractions of real-world objects; likewise, there may be many subprograms and tasks that name abstract actions. As a result, our software will contain many names for declared entities.

If we were using an early language, such as FORTRAN or COBOL, we would be forced by the topology of the language to make most of these names global to the entire system. Thus, in projects using such languages, we would find huge listings of data dictionaries, describing the use for each name. Before using or declaring a program entity, a programmer would have to consult the listings to make certain that he or she was using the name in the proper context or was not trying to declare an entity with a conflicting name. Because all these names would be global to the entire system, trying to determine the impact of changing one entity would require a consideration of virtually every component of the system. We call the domain of all names visible at one point the *name space*. Obviously, managing the name space in large FORTRAN or COBOL systems is not a simple task.

Using Ada in large software systems also involves hundreds of named entities in the solutions. However, Ada permits us to nest and package program units, making visible only those features that are important at a given level and hiding all unnecessary details. As we will see in the next section, Ada provides some relatively simple scope and visibility rules similar to the rules of ALGOL to help manage the name space. We have already considered most of these rules informally; these sections introduce the remaining details.

Scope and Visibility

In formal terms, the *scope* of an entity is the region of program text where its declaration has effect. On the other hand, the *visibility* of an entity defines where its name can be referenced. In all cases, an entity is visible only within its scope, and, in most cases, that entity is visible throughout its entire scope. In the next section, we shall examine entities whose names are overloaded or hidden and, hence, have restricted visibility. For the moment, however, let us concern ourselves only with a simple case.

The scope of an identifier starts at the point where the identifier is declared (first named) and extends to the end of the subprogram, package, task, or block that contains the declaration. Furthermore, for identifiers introduced in the specification of a subprogram, package, or task, the scope extends to the end of the corresponding unit body. However, the reverse is not true. The scope of an identifier introduced in a unit body is limited to the body and is not visible in the specification.

This formalism may seem confusing, so let us look at some examples in which brackets indicate the scope of entities within the program text:

```
procedure Main is
  Object_1 : Integer;
```

```
      procedure Inner_Procedure is
        Object_2 : Integer;
      begin
        -- body of Inner_Procedure
      end Inner_Procedure;
   begin  -- Main
     Inner_Block:
     declare
        Object_3 : Integer;
     begin
        -- body of Inner_Block
     end Inner_Block;
     -- remainder of Main body
   end Main;
```

In this example, Object_1 has a scope that extends from its point of declaration to the end of Main. Furthermore, Object_1 is visible for its entire scope, so we can refer to Object_1 just by its simple name. Object_2 has a scope and visibility that is limited to the Inner_Procedure. We can refer to Object_2 only inside Inner_Procedure. Similarly, Object_3 has a scope and visibility limited to the Inner_Block. Since Object_1 is visible to both the Inner_Procedure and the Inner_Block, it can be used in the body of either unit.

Formally, Object_1 is *nonlocal* to Inner_Procedure and Inner_Block, whereas Object_2 and Object_3 are *local* to the subprogram and block statement, respectively, in which they are declared. Ada permits reference to nonlocal objects as long as they are visible. However, at any given level, we may not reference entities that are declared in nested units—an entity cannot be referred to outside its scope.

If an entity is introduced in the declarative part of a given subprogram, task, package, named block, or named loop, we can always name the entity as a selected component, using the unit name as the prefix. Thus, throughout its scope we can refer to Object_1 as Main.Object_1. Correspondingly, we can use the names Inner_Procedure.Object_2 and Inner_Block.Object_3 within the scope of the respective objects. As will be seen in the next section, this facility is most useful when we are dealing with overloaded or hidden entities. We suggest the use of this notation whenever it improves the clarity of the code.

In the above example, we were able to refer to a given entity just by using its simple name; we say that each entity was directly visible. However, components of records, packages, and tasks are not directly visible, as we have already seen. For example:

```
procedure Main is
  type Node is (System_1, System_2, System_3);
  type Packet is
    record
      Source      : Node;
      Destination : Node;
      Message     : String (1..100);
    end record;
  My_Packet :  Packet;
begin
  -- body of Main
end Main;
```

Following the rules presented earlier, the entities Node, Packet, and My_Packet have a scope and visibility that extend from their point of introduction downward to the end of Main. Furthermore, the three enumeration literals System_1, System_2, and System_3 have the same scope as Node. However, the three components of Packet, namely Source, Destination, and Message, are not directly visible; that is, in the body of Main, Source cannot be referred to by its simple name. Instead, selected component notation must be used to gain direct visibility. Thus, inside Main, we can refer to My_Packet.Source, My_Packet.Destination, and My_Packet.Message.

A similar rule applies to packages and task components, as illustrated in the following example:

```
procedure Main is
  Object_1 : Integer;
  package My_Package is
    Object_2 : Integer;
    procedure Inner_Procedure;
  end My_Package;
  package body My_Package is
    Object_3 : Integer;
    procedure Inner_Procedure is
    begin
      -- remainder of Inner_Procedure
    end Inner_Procedure;
    -- remainder of My_Package body
  end My_Package;
  task My_Task is
    entry Path_1;
    entry Path_2;
  end My_Task;
```

```
    task body My_Task is
    begin
       -- remainder of My_Task
    end My_Task;
  begin
    -- body of Main
  end Main;
```

In this example, `Object_1` is visible throughout `Main` and can even be referenced inside `My_Package` or `My_Task`. Furthermore, the scope of `Object_2` extends throughout the body of `My_Package`, although `Object_3` is visible only to the body. Since `Object_2` and `Inner_Procedure` are introduced in the specification of `My_Package`, they can be used within the scope of the body of `My_Package`. However, like record components, package components (and task entries) are not directly visible, and so we must again use selected component notation to refer to these entities outside the package (or task) itself. Thus, in `Main`, we can refer to `My_Package.Object_2` and `My_Package.Inner_Procedure`. In addition we can reference `My_Task.Path_1` and `My_Task.Path_2`.

Since packages are frequently used in Ada systems, the names for package components can become rather lengthy, particularly if there are nested package specifications. One way to avoid these long names is through the **use** clause. In any declarative region in which `My_Package` is visible, or following a **with** clause naming `My_Package`, we can make a statement such as:

```
use My_Package;
```

From that point onward we no longer have to prepend the package name to components of the package unless there is an ambiguity.

Generally, the **use** clause should be applied carefully. The trade-off between shorter names, infix operator notation, and being able to tell where an entity is declared will affect readability. The **use** clause can lead to ambiguity by increasing the number of entities in the name space, and to unexpected side effects when code is modified [1, 2]. Others argue that it is these very ambiguities that make the **use** clause so valuable [3, 5]. If two packages both export a type named `Mass`, and a **use** clause is applied to both, neither becomes visible, since `Mass` is now ambiguous:

```
package Measures is
  type Mass is digits 6;
    ...
end Measures;
package Weights is
  type Mass is (Grams, Kilograms, Pounds);
    ...
end Weights;
```

```
with Measures, Weights;
procedure Mix_In is
  use Measures, Weights;
  Something : Mass;
begin  -- Mix_In
  ...
end Mix_In;
```

The declaration of Something is illegal since Mass does not become directly visible. Having two types at the same level of visibility, with the same name but different representations, often indicates a design problem. If any reference is made to an ambiguous name like the one in this example, the use clause detects this problem and reports it at compile time.

Note that the use clause cannot be used in association with tasks or records.

Overloading, Hiding, and Renaming

In any system, we do not want to have to worry about name clashes. Rather, for the sake of understandability, we would like to give each entity a name that implies its purpose or use. Especially in large systems, the same name may apply logically to two different entities. As we shall see, Ada provides some constructs to deal with such situations.

Whenever the same name or operator symbol is used for different entities whose scopes overlap, the name is said to be *overloaded*. For example:

```
declare
  type Color is (Red, Green, Blue);
  type Light is (Red, Yellow, Green);
  Pixel     : Color;
  Stoplight : Light;
begin
  ...
end;
```

In this case, the names Red and Green are overloaded since they are used in two different contexts. Ada permits us to use these names freely, as long as there is no ambiguity as to which Red or Green we are referring to. Thus, we can state:

```
Pixel := Green;
Stoplight := Green;
```

In both cases, the compiler can implicitly determine which Green is being referenced by examining the type of the left-hand side of the assignment statement. If we cannot use the context to remove the ambiguity, we can explicitly indicate the type with a qualified expression, as the following indicates:

```
Pixel := Color'(Red);
```

We can overload entities other than enumeration literals, such as aggregates, subprograms, and task entries. For example, we can define several overloaded subprograms called Put, each of which operates with different parameters:

```
procedure Put (Element : Integer);
procedure Put (Element : Float);
procedure Put (Element : Color);
procedure Put (Element : Light);
```

It is reasonable to use overloaded names for this purpose. As long as the object or operation is logically the same, it is appropriate to use the same name. However, note that overloading is to be used carefully, since it can lead to confusion for the reader.

In the above example, we can freely call each procedure, letting the rules of the language determine to which subprogram we are referring:

```
Put (367);          -- Put an Integer
Put (4.6);          -- Put a Float value
Put (Blue);         -- Put a Color value
Put (Light'(Green)); -- Put a Light value
```

Notice in the last example that we have to apply a qualified expression, since Put(Green) would be ambiguous. We can use other qualifiers, such as selected component notation or a unit name used as a prefix, in order to remove the ambiguity among overloaded entities.

A name is overloaded if it is being used to represent different entities. However, there are some classes of program entities, such as objects, that cannot be overloaded. If we use a name in a declaration in a nested structure, we effectively hide an outer entity with the same name. For example, consider the following code:

```
procedure Main is
  My_Object : Boolean;
begin
  Inner_Block:
    declare
      My_Block : Boolean;
```

```
begin
  -- body of Inner_Block
end Inner_Block;
-- remainder of Main body
end Main;
```

In this example, `Main.My_Object` has a scope that extends from its point of introduction to the end of `Main`, while the scope of `Inner_Block.My_Object` is limited to the block itself. The name `My_Object` has been used for two different entities, so if we use the simple name `My_Object` inside `Inner_Block`, the Ada visibility rules will state that we are referring to the local object (`Inner_Block.My_Object`). `Main.My_Object` is effectively hidden. If we need to refer to this nonlocal entity, we must use explicit component notation: `Main.My_Object`.

Normally, the hiding of program entities is not a problem, since it is uncommon to reference global entities. If we need to reference such objects, we should instead import the object through, perhaps, a subprogram parameter. For the most part, as solutions are decomposed to deeper and deeper levels, we do not care what names have been used in an outer context.

As we start nesting to deeper levels, however, we find that if we have to reference entities in a nested context, the names become rather long because of the selected component notation. To avoid this situation, Ada permits the renaming of packages. For example, consider the following nested package declaration:

```
package Math_Library is
  type Radians is ...
  package Trig_Functions is
    function Cos (Angle : Radians) return Float;
    ...
  end Trig_Functions;
  package Matrix is
    ...
  end Matrix;
end Math_Library;
```

In the absence of `use` clauses, which would increase the size of the name space, we would have to refer to the `Cos` function as:

```
Math_Library.Trig_Functions.Cos(Some_Angle)
```

However, we can rename this inner package as:

```
package Trig renames Math_Library.Trig_Functions;
```

Thus, we can refer to `Cos` as:

```
Trig.Cos(Some_Angle)
```

As we discussed in Chapter 11, renaming is a powerful mechanism for controlling the visibility of entities, especially those exported across package boundaries. Ada permits the renaming of objects, exceptions, task entries, and subprograms. We can therefore resolve name conflicts, achieve partial evaluation, and introduce synonyms for entities. For example, consider the following declarations:

```
My_Array : array (1..10) of Integer;
Alarm    : exception;
procedure Quick_Sort(Elements : in out List);
```

We can rename these entities as:

```
Your_Integer : Integer renames My_Array(3);
Water_Level  : exception renames Alarm;
procedure Sort(Things : in out List) renames Quick_Sort;
procedure Quick_Sort(Elements : in out List) is separate;
```

In each case we have introduced a new name for a previously declared entity. In the first case, we used the renaming declaration to evaluate the array index one time. Notice in the example of the subprogram renaming below that different names can be used for formal parameters. As an aside, notice that the body for the procedure Quick_Sort must come after its renaming. Renaming declarations are part of basic declarations, which must come before any bodies.

In addition, different default values, if any, can be applied to such parameters. For example:

```
function Append (E1, E2 : Element) return List;
function "&" (Left, Right : Element) return List renames Append;
function Center (The_Item     : String;
                 Within_Length : Positive;
                 Padding_With  : Character) return String;
function Pad (The_String    : String;
              Location      : Positive;
              Pad_Character  : Character := ´ ´)
   return String renames Center;
function Make_Title (The_Item : String;
                     Length   : Positive := 80;
                     Pad      : Character := ´*´)
   return String renames Center;
```

Renaming declarations can also be used to give simple names to record components and task entries. Although this often leads to less understandable code, it can be used with effect in small scopes:

```
Set_My_Packet:
declare
   Source  : Node renames My_Packet.Source;
   Message : String renames My_Packet.Message:
begin
   Message(1..2) := "Hi";
end Set_My_Packet;
Ping_System_1:
declare
   procedure Ping renames My_Task.Path_1;
begin
   Ping;
end Ping_System_1;
```

Notice that the renaming of Message does not require a range constraint, since the renaming does not declare a new object. Rather, we have created a new name for an existing object, and the existing object already has a range constraint. Also, task entries can be renamed as procedures. This use of entries is similar to using them as generic actual subprogram parameters, as we did in Chapter 17.

If we need to introduce an alternative name for a type, we may achieve the same effect as a renaming declaration by using a subtype, as the following example illustrates:

```
package Abstract.Type is
   type My_Type is ...
end Abstract_Type;
subtype Local_Type is Abstract_Type.My_Type;
```

As we continue to create nested program units, as is typical in a large system, we are actually increasing the number of elements in the name space. Renaming permits the use of shorter names, but it still does not help limit the number of names visible at one point. To help control the number of names that must be dealt with at a given level, and thereby reduce the complexity of the situation, we must turn to the features provided by separate compilation of program units.

20.2   Separate Compilation Issues

In any software system consisting of more than a handful of program units, it is not only good practice but it is also often necessary to make each unit relatively independent of the others. Different groups may be working on separate parts of the solution, and so each unit may be at a different point in its development. Testing is enhanced if individual units can be physically separated and then studied in controlled isolation. Furthermore, in a large system, it would be inefficient to have to recompile all the software just because some minor changes were made in low-level modules.

What is desired, then, is to be able to compile the different modules of the program separately. Of course, other languages already provide this feature, but, as we shall see in this section, Ada provides some additional tools for managing the complexity of independent modules.

Library Units

As we observed in Chapter 4, in Ada we do not have to compile an entire program at one time, although we can do so if desired. Rather, Ada permits us to submit the text a program in one or more compilations. A given compilation consists of one or more compilation units, including:

- Generic declaration
- Generic instantiation
- Subprogram declaration
- Subprogram body
- Package declaration
- Package body
- Subunit

Notice that a task is not a compilation unit. For that reason, it is common practice to embed a task inside a package so that we can achieve the effect of a library unit.

The compilation units of a program are said to belong to a *program library*. Formally, every compilation unit is called a *library unit* or a *secondary unit* (bodies of library units and subunits). We must provide a unique name for each unit. As we mentioned earlier, the main unit of any program must be a subprogram, which by definition will be a program library unit. The language rules do not specify how we identify a main unit; that selection is left up to the environment. Whenever program text is submitted for compilation, Ada treats those compilation units as if they were declared in the context of package Standard (see Appendix C). Think of it as if `with Standard; use Standard;` were attached to the beginning of each compilation unit. As a result, unless the names are hidden, we can use any of the entities introduced in `Standard`.

If we have some previously compiled library units, another unit can apply a `with` clause to gain the visibility of any given unit. Referring back to our first design example in Chapter 5, we can independently submit the units `Words`, `Lines`, `Document`, and `Concordance` for compilation. Another unit can reference these units in the context specification:

```
with Words, Lines;
package Concordance is...
```

From that point onward, selected component notation and renaming declarations can be used to achieve visibility of the package components, or a `use` clause can be applied to achieve direct visibility. In any case, the benefit of this approach is that we can selectively make visible only those units that we need to use. We can use a `with` clause for any library unit, including generic units. The reference to a library unit in a context clause identifies a dependency among program units that affects the order of compilation and recompilation.

The concept of separate compilation of units is not a new one, but, unlike some other languages, Ada requires that compilers enforce type rules as if the unit were not separated from its parent. In this manner, the protection that strong typing offers is preserved, even if programs are submitted in many separate compilations. Although this increases the complexity of Ada compilers, this rule is of great benefit in building large systems.

As shown in Figure 20.1, Ada compilers recognize the existence of a program library [4]. Whenever a compilation is submitted, various units can specify the use of a library unit in their context specification. As a result of the compilation, listings, reports, and perhaps object code are supplied. In addition, the compilation unit can then be added to the library if it is a unique one, or an older unit can be updated. In any case, if the compilation was successful, the compilation units submitted now become part of the library and are thus available for use by other units.

Subunits

Programs are built from existing lower-level modules using library units. With subunits, programs can be developed in a hierarchical fashion, from the top down. When decomposing a system, we can design the specification of a subprogram, package, or task, but we may wish to defer the implementation of the unit body. In Ada, we can create body stubs that can be compiled separately; these separately compiled bodies are called *subunits*.

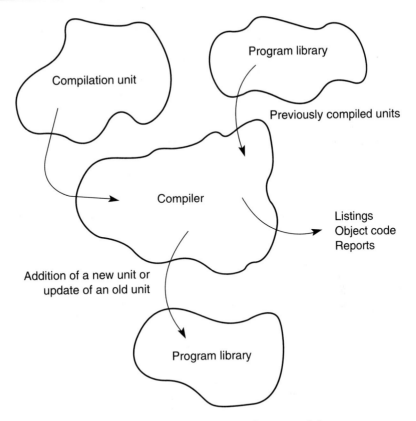

Figure 20.1 Ada compilation model

Consider the following main program, in which we have applied a functional decomposition:

```
procedure Main is
  task Black_Box is
    entry Receive (Message : out String);
    entry Send    (Message : in  String);
  end Black_Box;
  task body Black_Box is separate;
  package Transform is
    procedure Decypher (Message : in out String);
    procedure Encode   (Message : in out String);
  end Transform;
  package body Transform is separate;
  procedure Report (Message : in String) is separate;
begin  -- Main
  ...
end Main;
```

We can separately compile the task, package, and subprogram bodies using the following form:

```
separate (Main)
task body Black_Box is
begin
  ...
  accept Receive (Message : out String);
  ...
  accept Send    (Message : in  String);
  ...
end Black_Box;

separate (Main)
package body Transform is
  procedure Decypher (Message : in out String) is
  begin
    ...
  end Decypher;
  procedure Encode (Message : in out String) is
  begin
    ...
  end Encode;
end Transform;

separate (Main)
procedure Report (Message : in String) is
begin
  ...
end Report;
```

Each of these three bodies can be compiled separately; all the subunits of Main need not be compiled together. In this manner, we first provide minimal or null code for each subunit, replacing it later with the complete implementation. Notice that we must include a **separate** clause to identify the parent unit. Similar to the **with** clause, a **separate** clause defines a dependency among program units. In addition, a subunit can have its own context specification, identifying the library units it needs through a **with** clause. The names listed in these **with** clauses will be visible to the subunit, along with all other names that are visible at the point of the body stub in the parent.

If a subunit has a subunit (and so on), the **separate** clause must include the fully qualified parent name. For example, if Transform has a subunit, its clause is:

```
separate (Main.Transform)
```

It is a consequence of Ada's library rules that all subunits that have the same ancestor library unit must have unique names. On large systems this could be a problem if it isn't managed properly.

Order of Compilation and Recompilation

Whenever a system is built from several compilations, the dependencies explicitly defined among units require that they be compiled in a certain order. Basically, the role is that a given unit must be compiled before it can be visible to another unit. In particular, the specification of a subprogram, package, or task must be compiled before the corresponding body. In addition, a parent unit must be compiled before its subunits. Furthermore, if a given compilation unit names other library units in a `with` clause, those library unit specifications must be compiled first. As a result of Ada's visibility rules, this means that package bodies can be compiled in any order. In a good programming environment, tools will be provided to help us adhere to this order, although the Ada compiler will warn us if we try to compile a unit before any units that it depends upon are compiled.

During the development of a system, we will certainly be resubmitting modules for compilation, perhaps to correct an error or to change or complete an implementation. Ada's separate compilation facilities provide the system builder with a very powerful tool: A single program unit becomes the dimension of change. Because of the visibility rules, the body of a subprogram, package, task, or subunit can be recompiled without affecting any other unit (unless it is the parent of a subunit). Thus, as long as we do not change the specification of a program unit, we can freely alter the corresponding implementation. In this manner, we preserve the logical design structure of the system. If we make a change for the sake of efficiency or to correct an error, Ada permits us to localize the effects of the change.

If we do modify the parent of a subunit, that subunit must be recompiled; in fact, all subunits of the parent must be recompiled. In addition, if we modify the specification of a library unit, we must recompile the corresponding body, along with any other units that mention that library unit in a `with` clause.

Generic units and in-lined subprograms subtly alter these rules. In the case of `pragma Inline`, we introduce a dependency between a unit specification and its body. Specifically, we must compile the body before a client can reference the unit. Similarly, some implementations require that a generic specification and body be compiled before any instantiation.

Table 20.1:   Recompilation Rules

If you alter a(n):	You must recompile:
Specification	The specification, its body, its subunits, and transitively all units that depend upon this unit
Body	The body and its subunits
Subunit	The subunit and its subunits
Generic body	The body and all instantiations*
In-lined unit	The body and all using occurrences

*Implementation dependent

Table 20.1 summarizes Ada's compilation rules. Although Ada's separate compilation facilities help us to decompose a large system into manageable parts, recompilation can become a bottleneck for system development. For example, altering just one unit may force recompilation of hundreds of other units at a cost of hours—even days—of compilation time. Thus, as a system grows in size, it is essential that the design of all units be as simple as possible to avoid massive recompilations. The degree to which a change to a unit forces recompilation of other units is a good measure of the coupling of a design (as discussed in Chapters 2 and 10): Ada compilers and Ada development environments thus provide a means of evaluating coupling, since these tools must enforce a strict recompilation order.

20.3   Large Systems Architecture

As we discussed in Chapter 2, we cannot hope to successfully complete a large software system using an undisciplined design approach. Furthermore, large systems are never built all at once; they evolve from smaller systems. Ideally, the structure of a solution should parallel our evolving view of the real world. Using Ada's rich set of program units and separate compilation facilities, we can construct a solution so that its architecture matches the objects and operations in the problem space. As we shall see, Ada permits us to evolve our software from the top down or the bottom up.

Top-Down Development

Top-down design methodology involves starting at the highest levels of abstraction and then decomposing a system to more primitive levels. As we discussed in Chapter 2, the functional design approach by Yourdon follows this model.

In Ada, subunits can be used in support of this approach. For example, we can design the highest level of a program as follows:

```
procedure Main is
   type Data is ...
   procedure Input   (Item : out     Data) is separate;
   procedure Process (Item : in out Data) is separate;
   procedure Output  (Item : in      Data) is separate;
begin
   ...
end Main;
```

We have effectively declared stubs for each procedure, which can then be separately compiled as follows:

```
separate (Main)
procedure Input   (Item : out     Data) is
begin
   ...
end Input;

separate (Main)
procedure Process (Item : in out Data) is
begin
   ...
end Process;

separate (Main)
procedure Output  (Item : in      Data) is
begin
   ...
end Output;
```

As we further decompose each of these units, we may declare other subunits.

Top-down design is the traditional approach for most systems, and Ada does support this methodology. However, since each subunit must explicitly declare its parent, this approach is not suitable if several program units need to use the facilities of the same module.

Bottom-Up Development

A bottom-up approach permits the creation of units that many modules can share. In Ada, library units are used to implement this methodology. In this manner, we first create packages and subprograms that provide the primitive facilities we need, and then we build up from the tools they give us. For example, we can declare a package that exports the abstract data type Complex.Number as follows:

```
package Complex is
   type Number is ...
   ... -- abstract operations for Number objects
end Complex;
```

We can reference this module in a context specification and then use the facilities the package provides:

```
with Complex;
procedure Main is
   ...
   My_Number : Complex.Number;
   ...
begin
   ...
end Main;
```

In a large system, both a top-down and a bottom-up approach to development will normally be used. In the object-oriented design method we have suggested, we actually use both approaches: We identify and refine objects and operations from the top down, but we use their facilities from the bottom up.

Consider representing the compilation-unit dependencies of a system as a directed graph. If unit A depends on unit B, there will be an arrow from A to B. In a top-down approach, such dependency graphs form a tree, with the main program as the root, and subtrees (procedures and functions) forming wider and wider levels as they are decomposed. In an object-oriented method, such graphs often form a diamond shape. The main program is again at the top. At the bottom are a few highly reusable and well abstracted units such as Text_IO, Linked_Lists, and Trig_Functions. In the middle are the application-specific levels of abstraction.

Summary

- The scope of an entity is the region of program text where its declaration has effect.

- The visibility of an entity defines the region of text where its name can be referenced.

- An entity is directly visible if it can be designated by its simple name. If its simple name does not apply within its scope, we say that it is hidden.

- Certain entities (enumeration literals, aggregates, subprograms, and task entries) can be overloaded—that is, the same name can denote different things. Within a given context, each name must have a unique meaning or, in the case of overloaded names, must have a meaning that can be determined by its use.

- Renaming declarations are a versatile and powerful tool for controlling a name space.

- Ada systems are typically broken into separately compiled units. Compilation units include packages, subprograms, generic units, and subunits.

- Ada's compilation rules require that a unit specification be compiled before it is referenced. Conversely, if such a specification is altered, all using occurrences must be recompiled. As a result, recompilation can become a bottleneck in the development of massive systems.

Exercises   1. Refer back to the four design problems we have examined. Identify the design approach in each (top-down, bottom-up, or a combination of the two).

2. What would be the effect if Ada's separate compilation facility did not rigorously enforce type checking across program units?

3. An Ada entity is visible only within its scope. What language facility may affect processing beyond its scope?

4. Contrast the concepts of overloading and hiding.

5. If a package exports objects and constants, altering their value may force recompilation. How might we use subprograms to defer setting their value?

6. In terms of recompilation, what is the value of using incomplete types across package specifications and bodies?

7. What are the advantages and disadvantages of using separately compiled packages instead of subunits?

The Fifth Design Problem: Heads-Up Display

Define the Problem
Identify the Objects
Identify the Operations
Establish the Visibility
Establish the Interface

As we discussed in Chapter 2, one of the reasons for the software crisis is the fact that managing massive, software-intensive systems often exceeds our intellectual capacity. It is doubtful that a single computer programmer could comprehend all the details of a million-line system. For another individual to maintain such a program without destroying its structure is an even more difficult task.

In the last several chapters, we examined the characteristics of Ada and studied its constructs in detail. We emphasized how Ada embodies many modern programming principles, such as abstraction and information hiding. This support makes Ada more than just another programming language; Ada provides a set of coherent facilities that help developers manage complex solutions.

Although an individual may still not understand the detail of an extremely large program, Ada helps express such a solution in a clear, modular fashion. In this way, a developer can study the composite parts of a system, and then assemble the parts to form an integrated whole. Of course, these principles also apply to smaller programs. The point is that Ada helps us express the architecture of our solutions clearly while providing an efficient vehicle for execution. At this point, we have studied four design problems of increasing complexity. Since Ada is designed for use in massive systems, it is reasonable that we study how Ada is used in massive systems. Because of the probable size of the final solution—on the order of thousands of lines of code—we shall obviously not present the full system. Instead, we shall develop an overall architecture for our solution and study only the higher levels of abstraction.

21.1   Define the Problem

During target engagement by a high-performance aircraft, it is critical that the human/machine interface be kept very simple. There is simply no time to scan the cockpit for flight information; in close engagements, the pilot must watch the target at all times. A solution to this problem is to create a "heads-up" display (HUD) so that the pilot can observe both the target and critical flight parameters simultaneously. In most HUDs, the flight information is projected onto the windshield of the canopy so that the pilot can continually look outside the aircraft. The pilot will view a display similar to that shown in Figure 21.1.

The object of this display is to provide sufficient information with low complexity. The correct scenario is for the pilot to fly the aircraft so that the selected target falls within the target box; firing a weapon during that time yields a high probability for a hit. Assuming that the pilot has selected a trainable weapon (that is, one that can be aimed automatically within a few degrees), the cursor inside the box points to where the weapon is currently aimed. In addition, the target box, which indicates the effective radius of the weapon, will vary in size, depending upon the target range and type of armament selected. As the aircraft gets closer to the target, the box grows in size. The display also provides a presentation of critical flight parameters, such as altitude and angle of attack, plus a summary

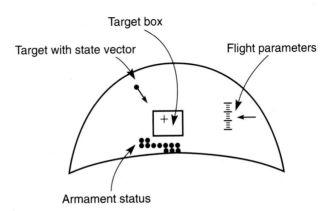

Figure 21.1 Pilot's view of a typical heads-up display (HUD)

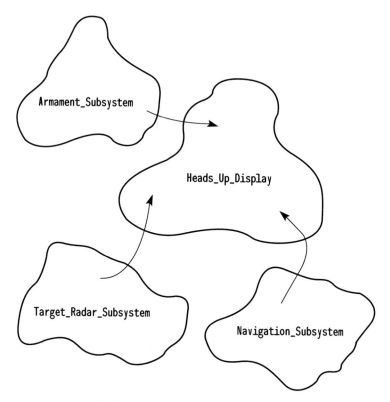

Figure 21.2 Subsystem allocation relative to the HUD

of the armament status. Furthermore, an arrow is superimposed on top of the selected target; the arrow assures the pilot that the correct target is being tracked and also presents the target's predicted direction of flight.

There are many embedded subsystems within a system as complex as an aircraft. When we design our HUD, there will certainly be physical constraints on the solution that are beyond our control; we simply cannot redesign the entire aircraft to meet our needs. Most likely, another design team has already made a functional allocation for each major aircraft subsystem, such as the avionics computer or radar subsystem, even before we start the design of our particular subsystem. As a result, our HUD will have to depend upon several predefined, usually static, interfaces. Even so, we can still apply our object-oriented design method to the problem.

Figure 21.2 illustrates the functional allocation of the aircraft systems from the perspective of the HUD. The other subsystems that the HUD must interface with include:

- **Armament_Subsystem**   Controls weapon resources and targeting.

- **Navigation_Subsystem**   Includes all flight avionics equipment for aircraft guidance and control.

- **Target_Radar_Subsystem**   Acquires and tracks target vehicles.

In a sense, the high-level design of our solution has been dictated to us; the objects and classes of objects at this level include the three subsystems and the HUD itself. At this point, we do not care about the implementation of any of these objects, but we do need a formal definition of the object interfaces that we can describe using Ada packages. In particular, we will assume that the following external objects and their corresponding operations are available to us:

- Armament_Subsystem.Armament_Interface

  Type: Armament

  Operation: Get

- Navigation_Subsystem.Navigation_Interface

  Type: Navigation

  Operation: Get

- Target_Radar_Subsystem.Radar_Interface

  Type: Radar

  Operation: Get

Each subsystem, such as the Navigation_Subsystem, will certainly consist of many compilation units. We do not need to see all the details of an entire subsystem, so in each case we use an interface package that exports only those entities relevant to the HUD. Since we might treat each interface as a package nested inside a larger system, we could use selected component notation to refer only to that part of the larger subsystem. Alternatively, we might have some support from the programming environment to keep these abstractions apart. Either way, these approaches control the configuration of the interface and explicitly define the responsibilities of each subsystem and HUD development team. These interfaces are represented in Figure 21.3.

Next we define these interfaces in Ada. For the purposes of this example, we omit the details of each type representation. In a complete solution, the details would be added at this level. If each object represented a record of data transmitted between two computer systems, we would use

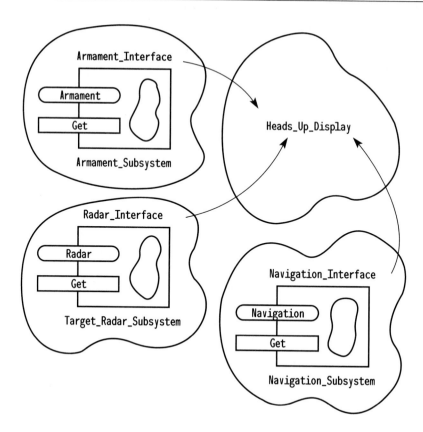

Figure 21.3 Design of the HUD interface

the Ada representation specifications to explicitly describe the layout of
each record component down to the bit level. Note that packaging these
interfaces in this manner directly supports the principles of modularity
and abstraction as presented in Chapter 2.

Within the Armament_Subsystem, the interface can be implemented as:

```
package Armament_Interface is
  type Armament is private;
  Procedure Get (The_Status : out Armament);
private
  type Armament is ...
end Armament_Interface;
```

Similar interfaces exist for the Navigation_Subsystem and the Target_Radar_
Subsystem:

```
package Navigation_Interface is
   type Navigation is private;
   procedure Get (The_Status : out Navigation);
private
   type Navigation is ...
end Navigation_Interface;

package Radar_Interface is
   type Radar is private;
   procedure Get (The_Status : out Radar);
private
   type Radar is ...
end Radar_Interface;
```

In all three cases we would not be concerned with the development of the package bodies; they would be the responsibility of each individual subsystem team.

We have completed the description of the relevant objects in the external world. Our next step is to examine the internal structure of the HUD subsystem.

21.2   Identify the Objects

Continuing with our object-oriented method, we focus on the heads-up display subsystem itself and consider the objects of interest in this problem space. For the sake of clarity and maintainability, it is critical that our solution map directly to the real world. At this level, our best view of the architecture of our solution is through the eyes of the pilot. Thus, we extract each entity in Figure 21.1 as an object. We might name these entities:

- Actual_Target
- Armament_Status
- Flight_Parameters
- Target_Box

In addition, we should include the physical display device itself, so we name the object Heads_Up_Display.

21.3   Identify the Operations

Our next step is to characterize the behavior of each abstraction by identifying the operations that each object can undergo. Before we do this, however, we must isolate one more important common abstraction. We must apply a uniform coordinate system to describe the state of each of these objects. For example, using different coordinate systems for the Actual_Target object and the aircraft itself would be foolhardy. For this reason, it is useful to include a package we shall call World_System, which provides this uniformity. This package acts like a collection of declarations, as we described in Chapter 11. We do not expect this entity to provide an encapsulated set of types; it is probably suitable to apply primitive types in describing the abstractions. However, at this point in our design, we might not have enough information to bind this interface; hence, we use something simple:

```
package World_System is
    type Latitude     is private;
    type Longitude    is private;
    type Altitude     is private;
    type State_Vector is private;
    type Dimension    is private;
private
    type Latitude     is new Float range -90.0..90.0;
    type Longitude    is new Float range 0.0..360.0;
    type Altitude     is new Long_Integer range 0..100_000;
    type State_Vector is array (1..10) of Boolean;
    type Dimension    is new Integer;
                      -- the above are only examples
                      -- of how these types might be described
end World_System;
```

A classical use of Ada as a design language is to provide a minimal (temporary) completion of each private type. We then use this package specification to capture the intent of our design, without binding any implementation decisions. Clearly, left alone, this is a useless package. However, it serves our purposes at this level. As our design evolves, we shall update this unit specification.

We shall apply a similar strategy to the identification of the operations of each object. At this level of design, we specify only the minimal outside view of each object to capture the intent of our design. Thus, for each object, we provide only simple types and a single operation to determine its status. Since each object in the real world can operate concurrently with the others, we shall capture this observation in our solution space and treat each as a task.

21.4   Establish the Visibility

We are now ready to describe the relationships among these abstractions. At this level of abstraction, we can treat each object as a complete independent entity. The only exception is the object `Heads_Up_Display` which, as viewed in the real world, depends on all the other objects we have identified. In other words, the `Heads_Up_Display` object must import all the other objects. This approach gives us the greatest degree of freedom in allocating the detailed design of each object. As we evolve the design of each entity, at the highest level we can assert that changes in one object do not affect any others.

Figure 21.4 provides a view of this design. The careful reader will realize that there is no main program. Indeed, as our problem description indicates, the heads-up display subsystem is not necessarily the root of our entire system; therefore, it is best to abstract the design only as packages. What happened to the various subsystem interfaces that we isolated earlier? They are not important at this level of abstraction. Rather, we expect that we need them to implement each of the objects we have described. Nonetheless, it

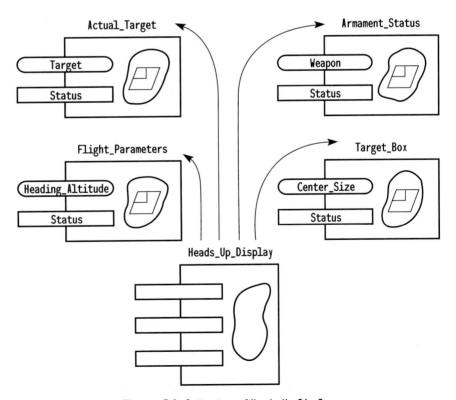

Figure 21.4 Design of `Heads_Up_Display`

was important for us to identify these interfaces early on so that we could bound our problem space.

21.5   Establish the Interface

We proceed with binding our design decisions in the form of Ada package specifications. Again, at this level of design, we have little detail to show. However, proceeding with this step is still useful, for it lets us capture for ourselves and other developers and managers our decisions about the architecture of our solution. Given the information we have, we capture the outside view of each abstraction as:

```
with World_System;
package Actual_Target is
  type Target is new World_System.State_Vector;
  task Coupler is
    entry Status (The_Target    : out Target);
  end Coupler;
end Actual_Target;

with World_System;
package Armament_Status is
  type Weapon is (Fixed_Gun, Missile);
  task Coupler is
    entry Status (The_Weapon    : out Weapon;
                  The_Quantity : out Natural);
  end Coupler;
end Armament_Status;

with World_System;
package Flight_Parameters is
  type Altitude is new World_System.Altitude;
  type Heading is new World_System.State_Vector;
  task Coupler is
    entry Status (The_Altitude  : out World_System.Altitude;
                  The_Heading   : out World_System.State_Vector);
  end Coupler;
end Flight_Parameters;

with World_System;
package Target_Box is
  type Center is new World_System.State_Vector;
  type Size    is new World_System.Dimension;
```

```
            task Coupler is
                entry Status (The_Center    : out World_System.State_Vector;
                                  The_Size   : out World_System.Dimension);
            end Coupler;
        end Target_Box;
        package Heads_Up_Display is
            task Coupler is
                entry Start;
            end Coupler;
        end Heads_Up_Display;
```

Notice that the specification of the package Heads_Up_Display does not import the other objects as Figure 21.3 indicated. Actually, these objects are not a part of the outside view of this abstraction; they are part of its inside view. Thus, we write:

```
        with Actual_Target, Armament_Status, Flight_Parameters, Target_Box;
        package body Heads_Up_Display is
            task body Coupler is
            begin
                accept Start;
            end Coupler;
        end Heads_Up_Display;
```

The next level of our solution introduces no new concepts, so we continue no further. However, consider what we have achieved. At this point, we have a compilable system whose architecture maps directly to our understanding of the problem space. Furthermore, we have seen how Ada can be used to approach a very large system: We explicitly identify intersubsystem interfaces using Ada's separately compiled units. In this manner, we not only decouple each subsystem to the maximum extent, but we also minimize the complexity of the outside view of each subsystem. In other words, we have taken Ada semantics for small units (specifically, single packages) and applied them to much larger abstractions (entire subsystems). Thus, we can conclude that Ada's concepts are appropriate for controlling the complexity of massive systems as well as small abstractions.

Exercises   1. What is the recompilation cost of introducing a new display item, such as a suggested flight path, on the heads-up display described in this chapter?

2. We have not fully considered task activation and termination. Modify the outside view of each object to apply the activation and termination technique we applied to the environment-monitoring problem in Chapter 17.

3. Why might it be dangerous to treat each object as a sequential entity, given that other subsystems may use the same abstractions?

*4. Suppose we make the hardware design decision to use a separate processor to handle each displayed item. How does this affect the design of our system at this level of abstraction?

Predefined
Language Attributes

The following appendix is taken, with permission of the Ada Joint Program Office (OUSDRE), U.S. Department of Defense, from the "Reference Manual for the Ada® Programming Language," (1983), Appendix A.

Attribute	Meaning
P'Address	*For a prefix P that denotes an object, a program unit, a label, or an entity:* Yields the address of the first of the storage units allocated to P. For a subprogram, package, task unit or label, this value refers to the machine code associated with the corresponding body or statement. For an entry for which an address clause has been given, the value refers to the corresponding hardware interrupt. The value of this attribute is of the type Address defined in the package System.
P'Aft	*For a prefix P that denotes a fixed-point subtype:* Yields the number of decimal digits needed after the point to accommodate the precision of the subtype P, unless the delta of the subtype P is greater than 0.1, in which case the attribute yields the value 1. (P'Aft is the smallest positive integer N for which (10**N) * P'Delta is greater than or equal to one.) The value of this attribute is of the type *universal_integer.*
P'Base	*For a prefix P that denotes a type or subtype:* This attribute denotes the base type of P. It is only allowed as the prefix of the name of an other attribute, for example P'Base'First.

P´Callable	*For a prefix* P *that is appropriate for a task type:*
	Yields the value False when the execution of the task P is either completed or terminated, or when the task is abnormal; yields the value True otherwise. The value of this attribute is of the type Boolean.
P´Constrained	*For a prefix* P *that denotes an object of a type with discriminants:*
	Yields the value True if a discriminant constraint applies to the object P, or if the object is a constant (including a formal parameter or generic formal parameter of mode in); yields the value False otherwise. If P is a generic formal parameter of mode in out, or if P is a formal parameter of mode in out or out and the type mark given in the corresponding parameter specification denotes an unconstrained type with discriminants, then the value of this attribute is obtained from that of the corresponding actual parameter. The value of this attribute is of the type Boolean.
P´Constrained	*For a prefix* P *that denotes a private type or subtype:*
	Yields the value False if P denotes an unconstrained non-formal private type with discriminants; also yields the value False if P denotes a generic formal private type and the associated actual subtype is either an unconstrained type with discriminants or an unconstrained array type; yields the value True otherwise. The value of this attribute is of the predefined type Boolean.
P´Count	*For a prefix* P *that denotes an entry of a task unit:*
	Yields the number of entry calls presently queued on the entry (if the attribute is evaluated within an accept statement for the entry P, the count does not include the calling task). The value of this attribute is of the type *universal_integer.*
P´Delta	*For a prefix* P *that denotes a fixed-point subtype:*
	Yields the value of the delta specified in the fixed accuracy definition for the subtype P. The value of this attribute is of the type *universal_real.*

P´Digits	*For a prefix* P *that denotes a floating-point subtype:* Yields the number of decimal digits in the decimal mantissa of model numbers of the subtype P. The value of this attribute is of the type *universal_integer.*
P´Emax	*For a prefix* P *that denotes a floating-point subtype:* Yields the largest exponent value in the binary canonical form of model numbers of the subtype P. (This attribute yields the product 4*B.) The value of this attribute is of the type *universal_integer.*
P´Epsilon	*For a prefix* P *that denotes a floating-point subtype:* Yields the absolute value of the difference between the model number 1.0 and the next model number above for the subtype P. The value of this attribute is of the type *universal_real.*
P´First	*For a prefix* P *that denotes a scalar subtype or a subtype of a scalar type:* Yields the lower bound of P. The value of this attribute has the same type as P.
P´First	*For a prefix* P *that is appropriate for an array type, or that denotes a constrained array subtype:* Yields the value of the lower bound of the first index range of P. The value of this attribute has the same type as this lower bound.
P´First(N)	*For a prefix* P *that is appropriate for an array type, or that denotes a constrained array subtype:* Yields the value of the lower bound of the Nth index range. The value of this attribute has the same type as this lower bound. The argument N must be a static expression of type *universal_integer.* The value of N must be positive (nonzero) and no greater than the dimensionality of the array.
P´First_Bit	*For a prefix* P *that denotes a component of a record object:* Yields the offset, from the start of the first of the storage units occupied by the component, of the first bit occupied by the component. This offset is measured in

bits. The value of this attribute is of the type *universal_integer*.

P′Fore | For a prefix P *that denotes a fixed-point subtype:*

Yields the minimum number of characters needed for the integer part of the decimal representation of any value of the subtype P, assuming that the representation does not include an exponent, but that it does include a one-character prefix that is either a minus sign or a space. (This number is no smaller than 2, and it does not include superfluous zeros or underlines.) The value of this attribute is of the type *universal_integer*.

P′Image | For a prefix P *that denotes a discrete type or subtype:*

This attribute is a function with a single parameter. The actual parameter X must be a value of the base type of P. The result type is of the predefined type String. The result is the *image* of the value of X, that is, a sequence of characters representing the value in display form. The image of an integer value is the corresponding decimal literal; without underlines, leading zeros, exponent, or trailing spaces, but with a one-character prefix that is either a minus sign or a space.

The image of an enumeration value is either the corresponding identifier in uppercase or the corresponding character literal (including the two apostrophes); neither leading nor trailing spaces are included. The image of a character other than a graphic character is implementation defined.

P′Large | For a prefix P *that denotes a real subtype:*

The attribute yields the largest positive model number of the subtype P. The value of this attribute is of the type *universal_real.*

P′Last | For a prefix P *that denotes a scalar subtype:*

Yields the upper bound of P. The value of this attribute has the same type as P.

P′Last | For a prefix P *that is appropriate for an array type, or that denotes a constrained array subtype:*

Yields the value of the upper bound of the first index range. The value of this attribute has the same type as this upper bound.

P´Last(N)　　　*For a prefix P that is appropriate for an array type or that denotes a constrained array subtype:*

This attribute yields the value of the upper bound of the Nth index range. The value of this attribute has the same type as this upper bound. The argument N must be a static expression of type *universal_integer*. The value of N must be positive (nonzero) and no greater than the dimensionality of the array.

P´Last_Bit　　　*For a prefix P that denotes a component of a record object:*

Yields the offset, from the start of the first of the storage units occupied by the component, of the last bit occupied by the component. This offset is measured in bits. The value of this attribute is of the type *universal_integer.*

P´Length　　　*For a prefix P that is appropriate for an array type or that denotes a constrained array subtype:*

Yields the number of values of the first index range (zero for a null range). The value of this attribute is of the type *universal_integer.*

P´Length(N)　　　*For a prefix P that is appropriate for an array type or that denotes a constrained array subtype:*

Yields the number of values in the Nth index range (zero for a null range). The value of this attribute is of the type *universal_integer.* The argument N must be a static expression of type *universal_integer.* The value of N must be positive (nonzero) and no greater than the dimensionality of the array.

P´Machine_Emax　　　*For a prefix P that denotes a floating-point type or subtype:*

Yields the largest value of *exponent* for the machine representation of the base type of P. The value of this attribute is of the type *universal_integer.*

`P´Machine_Emin`	*For a prefix* `P` *that denotes a floating-point type or subtype:*
	Yields the smallest (most negative) value of *exponent* for the machine representation of the base type of `P`. The value of this attribute is of the type *universal_integer.*
`P´Machine_Mantissa`	*For a prefix* `P` *that denotes a floating-point type or subtype:*
	Yields the number of digits in the *mantissa* for the machine representation of the base type of `P` (the digits are extended digits in the range 0 to `P´Machine_Radix - 1`). The value of this attribute is of the type *universal_integer.*
`P´Machine_Overflows`	*For a prefix* `P` *that denotes a real type or subtype:*
	Yields the value `True` if every predefined operation on values of the base type of `P` either provides a correct result or raises the exception `Numeric_Error` in overflow situations; yields the value `False` otherwise. The value of this attribute is of the type `Boolean`.
`P´Machine_Radix`	*For a prefix* `P` *that denotes a floating-point type or subtype:*
	Yields the value of the *radix* used by the machine representation of the base type of `P`. The value of this attribute is of the type *universal_integer.*
`P´Machine_Rounds`	*For a prefix* `P` *that denotes a real type or subtype:*
	Yields the value `True` if every predefined arithmetic operation on values of the base type of `P` either returns an exact result or performs rounding; yields the value `False` otherwise. The value of this attribute is of the type `Boolean`.
`P´Mantissa`	*For a prefix* `P` *that denotes a real subtype:*
	Yields the number of binary digits in the binary mantissa of model numbers of the subtype `P`. (This attribute yields the number `B` for a floating-point type or for a fixed-point type.) The value of this attribute is of the type *universal_integer.*

P´Pos

For a prefix P *that denotes a discrete type or subtype:*

This attribute is a function with a single parameter. The actual parameter X must be a value of the base type of P. The result is of the type *universal_integer;* it is the position number of the value of the actual parameter.

P´Position

For a prefix P *that denotes a component of a record object:*

Yields the offset, from the start of the first storage unit occupied by the record, of the first of the storage units occupied by the component. This offset is measured in storage units. The value of this attribute is of the type *universal_integer.*

P´Pred

For a prefix P *that denotes a discrete type or subtype:*

This attribute is a function with a single parameter. The actual parameter X must be a value of the base type of P. The result is of the base type of P; it is the value whose position number is one less than that of X. The exception Constraint_Error is raised if X equals P´Base´First.

P´Range

For a prefix P *that is appropriate for an array type or that denotes a constrained array subtype:*

Yields the first index range of P, that is, the range P´First . . P´Last.

P´Range(N)

For a prefix that is appropriate for an array type, or that denotes a constrained array subtype:

Yields the Nth index of P, that is, the range P´First(N) . . P´Last(N).

P´Safe_Emax

For a prefix P *that denotes a floating-point type or subtype:*

Yields the largest exponent value in the binary canonical form of safe numbers of the base type of P. (This attribute yields the number E.) The value of this attribute is of the type *universal_integer.*

P´Safe_Large

For a prefix P *that denotes a real type or subtype:*

Yields the largest positive safe number of the base type P. The value of this attribute is of the type *universal_real.*

P´Safe_Small   *For a prefix* P *that denotes a real type or subtype:*

Yields the smallest positive (nonzero) safe number of the base type of P. The value of this attribute is of the type *universal_real.*

P´Size   *For a prefix* P *that denotes an object:*

Yields the number of bits allocated to hold the object. The value of this attribute is of the type *universal_ integer.*

P´Size   *For a prefix* P *that denotes any type or subtype:*

Yields the minimum number of bits that are needed by the implementation to hold any possible object of the type or subtype P. The value of this attribute is of the type *universal_integer.*

P´Small   *For a prefix* P *that denotes a real subtype:*

Yields the smallest positive (nonzero) model number of the subtype P. The value of this attribute is of the type *universal_real.*

P´Storage_Size   *For a prefix* P *that denotes an access type or subtype:*

Yields the total number of storage units reserved for the collection associated with the base type of P. The value of this attribute is of the type *universal_integer.*

P´Storage_Size   *For a prefix* P *that denotes a task type or a task object:*

Yields the number of storage units reserved for each activation of a task of the type P or for the activation of the task P. The value of this attribute is of the type *universal_integer.*

P´Succ   *For a prefix* P *that denotes a discrete type or subtype:*

This attribute is a function with a single parameter. The actual parameter X must be a value of the base type of P. The resulting type is of the base type of P; it is the value whose position number is one greater than that of X. The exception Constraint_Error is raised if X equals P´Base´Last.

P´Terminated

For a prefix P *that denotes a task object:*

Yields the value True if the task P is terminated; yields the value False otherwise. The value of this attribute is of the type Boolean.

P´Val

For a prefix P *that denotes a discrete type or subtype:*

This attribute is a special function with a single parameter that can be of any integer type. The result is of the base type of P; it is the value whose position number is the *universal_integer* value corresponding to the actual parameter. The exception Constraint_Error is raised if the *universal_integer* value corresponding to X is not in the range P´Pos..(P´Base´First)..P´Pos (P´Base´Last).

P´Value

For a prefix P *that denotes a discrete type or subtype:*

This attribute is a function with a single parameter. The actual parameter X must be a value of the predefined type String. The resulting type is of the base type of P. Any leading and any trailing spaces of the sequence of characters that corresponds to X are ignored.

For an enumeration type, if the sequence of characters has the syntax of an enumeration literal, and if this literal exists for the base type of P, the result is the corresponding enumeration value. For an integer type, if the sequence of characters has the syntax of an integer literal with an optional single leading character that is a plus or minus sign, and if there is a corresponding value in the base type of P, the result is this value. In any other case, the exception Constraint_Error is raised.

P´Width

For a prefix P *that denotes a discrete subtype:*

Yields the maximum image length over all values of the subtype P (the image is the sequence of characters returned by the attribute Image). The value of this attribute is of the type *universal_integer.*

B

Predefined Language Pragmas

The following appendix is taken, with permission of the Ada Joint Program Office (OUSDRE), U.S. Department of Defense, from the "Reference Manual for the Ada® Programming Language" (1983), Appendix B.

Pragma	Meaning
Controlled	Takes the simple name of an access type as the single argument. This pragma is only allowed immediately within the declarative part or package specification that contains the declaration of the access type; the declaration must occur before the pragma. This pragma is not allowed for a derived type. This pragma specifies that automatic storage reclamation must not be performed for objects designated by values of the access type, except upon leaving the innermost block statement, subprogram body, or task body that encloses the access type declaration, or after leaving the main program.
Elaborate	Takes one or more simple names denoting library units as arguments. This pragma is only allowed immediately after the context clause of a compilation unit (before the subsequent library unit or secondary unit). Each argu-

ment must be the simple name of a library unit mentioned by the context clause. This pragma specifies that the corresponding library unit body must be elaborated before the given compilation unit. If the given compilation unit is a subunit, the library unit body must be elaborated before the body of the ancestor library unit of the subunit.

Inline
Takes one or more names as arguments; each name is either the name of a subprogram or the name of a generic subprogram. This pragma is only allowed at the place of a declarative item in a declarative part or package specification, or after a library unit in a compilation, but before any subsequent compilation unit. This pragma specifies that the subprogram bodies should be expanded inline at each call whichever possible; in the case of a generic subprogram, the pragma applies to calls of its instantiations.

Interface
Takes a language name and a subprogram name as arguments. This pragma is allowed at the place of a declarative item, and must apply in this case to a subprogram declared by an earlier declarative item of the same declarative part or package specification. This pragma is also allowed for a library unit; in this case the pragma must appear after the subprogram declaration, and before any subsequent compilation unit. This pragma specifies the other language (and thereby the calling conventions) and informs the compiler that an object module will be supplied for the corresponding subprogram.

List
Takes one of the identifiers On or Off as the single argument. This pragma is allowed anywhere a pragma is allowed. It specifies that listing of the compilation is to be continued or suspended until a List pragma with the opposite argument is given within the same compilation. The pragma itself is always listed if the compiler is producing a listing.

Memory_Size
Takes a numeric literal as the single argument. This pragma is only allowed at the start of a compilation, before the first compilation unit (if any) of the compilation. The effect of this pragma is to use the value of

the specified numeric literal for the definition of the named number Memory_Size.

Optimize   Takes one of the identifiers Time or Space as the single argument. This pragma is only allowed within a declarative part and it applies to the block or body enclosing the declarative part. It specifies whether time or space is the primary optimization criterion.

Pack   Takes the simple name of a record or array type as the single argument. The allowed positions for this pragma, and the restrictions on the named type, are governed by the same rules as for a representation clause. The pragma specifies that storage minimization should be the main criterion when selecting the representation of the given type.

Page   This pragma has no argument, and is allowed anywhere a pragma is allowed. It specifies that the program text which follows the pragma should start on a new page (if the compiler is currently producing a listing).

Priority   Takes a static expression of the predefined integer subtype Priority as the single argument. This pragma is only allowed within the specification of a task unit or immediately within the outermost declarative part of a main program. It specifies the priority of the task (or tasks of the task type) or the priority of the main program.

Shared   Takes the simple name of a variable as the single argument. This pragma is allowed only for a variable declared by an object declaration and whose type is a scalar or access type; the variable declaration and the pragma must both occur (in this order) immediately within the same declarative part or package specification. This pragma specifies that every read or update of the variable is a synchronization point for that variable. An implementation must restrict the objects for which this pragma is allowed to objects for which each of direct reading and direct updating is implemented as an indivisible operation.

Storage_Unit   Takes a numeric literal as the single argument. This pragma is only allowed at the start of a compilation, before the first compilation unit (if any) of the compilation. The effect of this pragma is to use the value of the specified numeric literal for the definition of the named number Storage_Unit.

Suppress

Takes as arguments the identifier of a check and optionally also the name of either an object, a type or subtype, a subprogram, a task unit, or a generic unit. This pragma is only allowed either immediately within a declarative part or immediately within a package specification. In the latter case, the only allowed form is with a name that denotes an entity (or several overloaded subprograms) declared immediately within the package specification. The permission to omit the given check extends from the place of the pragma to the end of the declarative region associated with the innermost enclosing block statement or program unit. For a pragma given in a package specification, the permission extends to the end of the scope of the named entity.

If the pragma includes a name, the permission to omit the given check is further restricted: it is given only for operations on the named object or on all objects of the base type of a named type or subtype; for calls of a named subprogram; for activations of tasks of the named task type; or for instantiations of the given generic unit.

System_Name

Takes an enumeration literal as the single argument. This pragma is only allowed at the start of a compilation, before the first compilation unit (if any) of the compilation. The effect of this pragma is to use the enumeration literal with the specified identifier for the definition of the constant System_Name. This pragma is only allowed if the specified identifier corresponds to one of the literals on the type Name declared in the package System.

APPENDIX C

Predefined Language Environment

The following appendix is taken, with permission of the Ada Joint Program Office (OUSDRE), U.S. Department of Defense, from the "Reference Manual for the Ada® Programming Language" (1983), Appendix C.

The definition of the Ada language includes several predefined library units. Among these are:

- Calendar
- Direct_IO
- IO_Exceptions
- Low_Level_IO
- Sequential_IO
- System
- Text_IO
- Unchecked_Conversion
- Unchecked_Deallocation

In addition, there exists a predefined package named Standard which contains all predefined objects and operations. When a library unit is translated, the compiler treats the unit as if it were declared at the end of the specification of Standard. Thus, all of these predefined identifiers are directly visible.

The specification of package Standard follows; the body is not included since it is implementation dependent. The symbol {. . .} indicates a value that is implementation defined. The specifications for the other predefined program units follow that of package Standard.

STANDARD

```
package STANDARD is

    type BOOLEAN is (FALSE, TRUE);
    function "="    (LEFT, RIGHT : BOOLEAN) return BOOLEAN;
    function "/="   (LEFT, RIGHT : BOOLEAN) return BOOLEAN;
    function "<"    (LEFT, RIGHT : BOOLEAN) return BOOLEAN;
    function "<="   (LEFT, RIGHT : BOOLEAN) return BOOLEAN;
    function ">"    (LEFT, RIGHT : BOOLEAN) return BOOLEAN;
    function ">="   (LEFT, RIGHT : BOOLEAN) return BOOLEAN;
    function "not"  (X          : BOOLEAN) return BOOLEAN;
    function "and"  (X, Y       : BOOLEAN) return BOOLEAN;
    function "or"   (X, Y       : BOOLEAN) return BOOLEAN;
    function "xor"  (X, Y       : BOOLEAN) return BOOLEAN;


    type INTEGER is {...};
    function "="    (LEFT, RIGHT : INTEGER) return BOOLEAN;
    function "/="   (LEFT, RIGHT : INTEGER) return BOOLEAN;
    function "<"    (LEFT, RIGHT : INTEGER) return BOOLEAN;
    function "<="   (LEFT, RIGHT : INTEGER) return BOOLEAN;
    function ">"    (LEFT, RIGHT : INTEGER) return BOOLEAN;
    function ">="   (LEFT, RIGHT : INTEGER) return BOOLEAN;
    function "+"    (X          : INTEGER) return INTEGER;
    function "-"    (X          : INTEGER) return INTEGER;
    function "abs"  (X          : INTEGER) return INTEGER;
    function "+"    (X, Y       : INTEGER) return INTEGER;
    function "-"    (X, Y       : INTEGER) return INTEGER;
    function "*"    (X, Y       : INTEGER) return INTEGER;
    function "/"    (X, Y       : INTEGER) return INTEGER;
    function "rem"  (X, Y       : INTEGER) return INTEGER;
    function "mod"  (X, Y       : INTEGER) return INTEGER;
    function "**"   (LEFT, RIGHT : INTEGER) return INTEGER;

    -- An implementation may provide additional predefined
    -- integer types. It is  recommended that the names of
    -- such additional types end with INTEGER as in
    -- SHORT_INTEGER or LONG_INTEGER

    type FLOAT    is digits {...} range {...};
    function "="    (LEFT, RIGHT : FLOAT)   return BOOLEAN;
    function "/="   (LEFT, RIGHT : FLOAT)   return BOOLEAN;
    function "<"    (LEFT, RIGHT : FLOAT)   return BOOLEAN;
    function "<="   (LEFT, RIGHT : FLOAT)   return BOOLEAN;
    function ">"    (LEFT, RIGHT : FLOAT)   return BOOLEAN;
    function ">="   (LEFT, RIGHT : FLOAT)   return BOOLEAN;
```

```
function "+"   (X          : FLOAT)    return FLOAT;
function "-"   (X          : FLOAT)    return FLOAT;
function "abs" (X          : FLOAT)    return FLOAT;
function "+"   (X,Y        : FLOAT)    return FLOAT;
function "-"   (X,Y        : FLOAT)    return FLOAT;
function "*"   (X,Y        : FLOAT)    return FLOAT;
function "/"   (X,Y        : FLOAT)    return FLOAT;
function "**"  (LEFT       : FLOAT
                RIGHT      : INTEGER) return FLOAT;
```

```
-- An implementation may provide
-- additional floating-point types.
-- It is  recommended that the
-- names of such additional
-- types end with FLOAT, as in
-- SHORT_FLOAT or LONG_FLOAT;
-- The types universal-integer,
-- universal-float, and
-- universal-fixed are predefined.
```

```
function "*" (LEFT : universal-integer; RIGHT : universal-real)
             return universal-real;
function "*" (LEFT : universal-real;    RIGHT : universal-integer)
             return universal-real;
function "/" (LEFT : universal-real;    RIGHT : universal-integer)
             return universal-real;
function "*" (LEFT : any-fixed-type;    RIGHT : any-fixed-type)
             return universal-fixed;
function "/" (LEFT : any-fixed-type;    RIGHT : any-fixed-type)
             return universal-fixed;
```

```
-- The following characters comprise the standard ASCII character
-- set. Character literals corresponding to control characters are
-- not identifiers; they are underlined in this example.
```

```
type CHARACTER is (
    nul,   soh,   stx,   etx,   eot,   enq,   ack,   bel,
    bs,    ht,    lf,    vt,    ff,    cr,    so,    si,
    dle,   dc1,   dc2,   dc3,   dc4,   nak,   syn,   etb
    can,   em,    sub,   esc,   fs,    gs,    rs,    us,
    ' ',   '!',   '"',   '#',   '$',   '%',   '&',   ''',
    '(',   ')',   '*',   '+',   ',',   '-',   '.',   '/',
    '0',   '1',   '2',   '3',   '4',   '5',   '6',   '7',
    '8',   '9',   ':',   ';',   '<',   '=',   '>',   '?',
    '@',   'A',   'B',   'C',   'D',   'E',   'F',   'G',
    'H',   'I',   'J',   'K',   'L',   'M',   'N',   'O',
```

```
'P',   'Q',   'R',   'S',   'T',   'U',   'V',   'W',
'X',   'Y',   'Z',   '[',   '\',   ']',   '^',   '_',
''',   'a',   'b',   'c',   'd',   'e',   'f',   'g',
'h',   'i',   'j',   'k',   'l',   'm',   'n',   'o',
'p',   'q',   'r',   's',   't',   'u',   'v',   'w',
'x',   'y',   'z',   '{',   '|',   '}',   '~',   del);

for CHARACTER use (0, 1, 2, ... 126, 127);
package ASCII is
   NUL : constant CHARACTER := nul;
   SOH : constant CHARACTER := soh;
   STX : constant CHARACTER := stx;
   ETX : constant CHARACTER := etx;
   EOT : constant CHARACTER := eot;
   ENQ : constant CHARACTER := enq;
   ACK : constant CHARACTER := ack;
   BEL : constant CHARACTER := bel;
   BS  : constant CHARACTER := bs;
   HT  : constant CHARACTER := ht;
   LF  : constant CHARACTER := lf;
   VT  : constant CHARACTER := vt;
   FF  : constant CHARACTER := ff;
   CR  : constant CHARACTER := cr;
   SO  : constant CHARACTER := so;
   SI  : constant CHARACTER := si;
   DLE : constant CHARACTER := dle;
   DC1 : constant CHARACTER := dc1;
   DC2 : constant CHARACTER := dc2;
   DC3 : constant CHARACTER := dc3;
   DC4 : constant CHARACTER := dc4;
   NAK : constant CHARACTER := nak;
   SYN : constant CHARACTER := syn;
   ETB : constant CHARACTER := etb;
   CAN : constant CHARACTER := can;
   EM  : constant CHARACTER := em;
   SUB : constant CHARACTER := sub;
   ESC : constant CHARACTER := esc;
   FS  : constant CHARACTER := fs;
   GS  : constant CHARACTER := gs;
   RS  : constant CHARACTER := rs;
   US  : constant CHARACTER := us;
   DEL : constant CHARACTER := del;

   EXCLAM  : constant CHARACTER := '!';
   SHARP   : constant CHARACTER := '#';
   DOLLAR  : constant CHARACTER := '$';
```

```
QUERY        : constant CHARACTER := '?';
AT_SIGN      : constant CHARACTER := '@';
L_BRACKET    : constant CHARACTER := '[';
BACK_SLASH   : constant CHARACTER := '\';
R_BRACKET    : constant CHARACTER := ']';
CIRCUMFLEX   : constant CHARACTER := '^';
GRAVE        : constant CHARACTER := '`';
L_BRACE      : constant CHARACTER := '{';
BAR          : constant CHARACTER := '|';
R_BRACE      : constant CHARACTER := '}';
TILDE        : constant CHARACTER := '~';
QUOTATION    : constant CHARACTER := '"';
COLON        : constant CHARACTER := ':';
SEMICOLON    : constant CHARACTER := ';';
PERCENT      : constant CHARACTER := '%';
AMPERSAND    : constant CHARACTER := '&';
UNDERLINE    : constant CHARACTER := '_';
LC_A         : constant CHARACTER := 'a';
...
LC_Z         : constant CHARACTER := 'z';
end ASCII;


-- predefined types and subtypes

subtype NATURAL  is INTEGER range 0..INTEGER'LAST;
subtype POSITIVE is INTEGER range 1..INTEGER'LAST;
type    STRING     is array (POSITIVE range <>) of CHARACTER;
function "="  (LEFT , RIGHT : STRING)                return BOOLEAN;
function "/=" (LEFT , RIGHT : STRING)                return BOOLEAN;
function "<"  (LEFT , RIGHT : STRING)                return BOOLEAN;
function "<=" (LEFT , RIGHT : STRING)                return BOOLEAN;
function ">"  (LEFT , RIGHT : STRING)                return BOOLEAN;
function ">=" (LEFT , RIGHT : STRING)                return BOOLEAN;
function "&"  (LEFT : STRING;    RIGHT : STRING)    return STRING;
function "&"  (LEFT : CHARACTER; RIGHT : STRING)    return STRING;
function "&"  (LEFT : STRING;    RIGHT : CHARACTER) return STRING;
function "&"  (LEFT : CHARACTER; RIGHT : CHARACTER) return STRING;

pragma PACK(STRING);

type DURATION is delta {...} range {...};

-- predefined exceptions

CONSTRAINT_ERROR : exception;
NUMERIC_ERROR    : exception;
```

```
                PROGRAM_ERROR      : exception;
                STORAGE_ERROR      : exception;
                TASKING_ERROR      : exception;

        end STANDARD;
```

CALENDAR

```
        package CALENDAR is;

            type TIME is private;

            subtype YEAR_NUMBER  is INTEGER  range 1901..2099;
            subtype MONTH_NUMBER is INTEGER  range 1..12;
            subtype DAY_NUMBER   is INTEGER  range 1..31;
            subtype DAY_DURATION is DURATION range 0.0..86_400.0;
            function CLOCK return TIME;

            function YEAR    (T : TIME) return YEAR_NUMBER;
            function MONTH   (T : TIME) return MONTH_NUMBER;
            function DAY     (T : TIME) return DAY_NUMBER;
            function SECONDS (T : TIME) return DAY_DURATION;

            procedure SPLIT  (DATE      : in  TIME;
                              YEAR      : out YEAR_NUMBER;
                              MONTH     : out MONTH_NUMBER;
                              DAY       : out DAY_NUMBER;
                              SECONDS   : out DAY_DURATION);
            function TIME_OF (YEAR      :     YEAR_NUMBER;
                              MONTH     :     MONTH_NUMBER;
                              DAY       :     DAY_NUMBER;
                              SECONDS   :     DAY_DURATION := 0.0) return
                                                                  TIME;

            TIME_ERROR : exception

            function "+" (X : TIME;      Y : DURATION) return TIME;
            function "+" (X : DURATION;  Y : TIME)     return TIME;
            function "-" (X : TIME;      Y : DURATION) return TIME;
            function "-" (X : TIME;      Y : TIME)     return DURATION;

            function "<"  (X, Y : TIME) return BOOLEAN;
            function "<=" (X, Y : TIME) return BOOLEAN;
            function ">"  (X, Y : TIME) return BOOLEAN;
            function ">=" (X, Y : TIME) return BOOLEAN;
```

```
private
   -- implementation defined
end CALENDAR;
```

IO_EXCEPTIONS

```
package IO_EXCEPTIONS is
   NAME_ERROR    : exception;
   USE_ERROR     : exception;
   STATUS_ERROR  : exception;
   MODE_ERROR    : exception;
   DEVICE_ERROR  : exception;
   END_ERROR     : exception;
   DATA_ERROR    : exception;
   LAYOUT_ERROR  : exception;
end IO_EXCEPTIONS;
```

DIRECT_IO

```
with IO_EXCEPTIONS;
generic
   type ELEMENT_TYPE is private;
package DIRECT_IO is

   type FILE_TYPE is limited private;

   type FILE_MODE          is (IN_FILE, INOUT_FILE, OUT_FILE);
   type COUNT              is range 0..implementation-defined;
   subtype POSITIVE_COUNT is COUNT range 1..COUNT'LAST;

   procedure CREATE (FILE : in out FILE_TYPE;
                     MODE : in      FILE_MODE := INOUT_FILE;
                     NAME : in      STRING    := "";
                     FORM : in      STRING    := "");
   procedure OPEN   (FILE : in out FILE_TYPE;
                     MODE : in      FILE_MODE;
                     NAME : in      STRING;
                     FORM : in      STRING    := "");
   procedure CLOSE  (FILE : in out FILE_TYPE);
   procedure DELETE (FILE : in out FILE_TYPE);
   procedure RESET  (FILE : in out FILE_TYPE;
                     MODE : in      FILE_MODE);
   procedure RESET  (FILE : in out FILE_TYPE;
```

```
function MODE      (FILE : in FILE_TYPE) return FILE_MODE;
function NAME      (FILE : in FILE_TYPE) return STRING;
function FORM      (FILE : in FILE_TYPE) return STRING;
function IS_OPEN (FILE : in FILE_TYPE) return BOOLEAN;

procedure READ   (FILE : in  FILE_TYPE;
                  ITEM : out ELEMENT_TYPE) ;
procedure READ   (FILE : in  FILE_TYPE;
                  ITEM : out ELEMENT_TYPE;
                  FROM : in  POSITIVE_COUNT) ;
procedure WRITE (FILE : in  FILE_TYPE;
                  ITEM : in  ELEMENT_TYPE) ;
procedure WRITE (FILE : in  FILE_TYPE;
                  ITEM : in  ELEMENT_TYPE;
                  TO   : in  POSITIVE_COUNT) ;

procedure SET_INDEX  (FILE : in FILE_TYPE;
                      TO   : in POSITIVE_COUNT) ;

function INDEX      (FILE : in FILE_TYPE) return POSITIVE_COUNT;
function SIZE       (FILE : in FILE_TYPE) return COUNT;

function END_OF_FILE (FILE : in FILE_TYPE) return BOOLEAN;

NAME_ERROR   : exception renames IO_EXCEPTIONS.NAME_ERROR;
USE_ERROR    : exception renames IO_EXCEPTIONS.USE_ERROR;
STATUS_ERROR : exception renames IO_EXCEPTIONS.STATUS_ERROR;
MODE_ERROR   : exception renames IO_EXCEPTIONS.MODE_ERROR;
DEVICE_ERROR : exception renames IO_EXCEPTIONS.DEVICE_ERROR;
END_ERROR    : exception renames IO_EXCEPTIONS.END_ERROR;
DATA_ERROR   : exception renames IO_EXCEPTIONS.DATA_ERROR;

private
  -- implementation_defined
end DIRECT_IO;
```

LOW_LEVEL_IO

```
package LOW_LEVEL_IO is
  -- declaration of the possible types for DEVICE and DATA
  -- declaration of overloaded procedures for these types
  procedure SEND_CONTROL    (DEVICE :          device_type;
                             DATA   : in out data_type);
  procedure RECEIVE_CONTROL (DEVICE :          device_type;
                             DATA   : in out data_type);
end LOW_LEVEL_IO;
```

SEQUENTIAL_IO

```
with IO_EXCEPTIONS;
generic
  type ELEMENT_TYPE is private;
package SEQUENTIAL_IO is

  type FILE_TYPE is limited private;

  type FILE_MODE is (IN_FILE, OUT_FILE);

  procedure CREATE (FILE : in out FILE_TYPE;
                    MODE : in      FILE_MODE := OUT_FILE;
                    NAME : in      STRING    := "";
                    FORM : in      STRING    := "");
  procedure OPEN   (FILE : in out FILE_TYPE;
                    MODE : in      FILE_MODE;
                    NAME : in      STRING;
                    FORM : in      STRING    := "");

  procedure CLOSE  (FILE : in out FILE_TYPE);
  procedure DELETE (FILE : in out FILE_TYPE);
  procedure RESET  (FILE : in out FILE_TYPE;
                    MODE : in      FILE_MODE);
  procedure RESET  (FILE : in out FILE_TYPE);

  function MODE    (FILE : in FILE_TYPE) return FILE_MODE;
  function NAME    (FILE : in FILE_TYPE) return STRING;
  function FORM    (FILE : in FILE_TYPE) return STRING;
  function IS_OPEN (FILE : in FILE_TYPE) return BOOLEAN;

  procedure READ  (FILE : in  FILE_TYPE;
                   ITEM : out ELEMENT_TYPE);
  procedure WRITE (FILE : in  FILE_TYPE;
                   ITEM : in  ELEMENT_TYPE);

  function END_OF_FILE (FILE : in FILE_TYPE) return BOOLEAN;

  NAME_ERROR   : exception renames IO_EXCEPTIONS.NAME_ERROR;
  USE_ERROR    : exception renames IO_EXCEPTIONS.USE_ERROR;
  STATUS_ERROR : exception renames IO_EXCEPTIONS.STATUS_ERROR;
  MODE_ERROR   : exception renames IO_EXCEPTIONS.MODE_ERROR;
  DEVICE_ERROR : exception renames IO_EXCEPTIONS.DEVICE_ERROR;
  END_ERROR    : exception renames IO_EXCEPTIONS.END_ERROR;
  DATA_ERROR   : exception renames IO_EXCEPTIONS.DATA_ERROR;
```

```
  private
    -- implementation defined
  end SEQUENTIAL_IO;
```

SYSTEM

```
package SYSTEM is

  type ADDRESS is implementation_defined;
  type NAME    is implementation_defined;

  SYSTEM_NAME   : constant NAME := implementation_defined;
  STORAGE_UNIT  : constant      := implementation_defined;
  MEMORY_SIZE   : constant      := implementation_defined;
  MIN_INT       : constant      := implementation_defined;
  MAX_INT       : constant      := implementation_defined;
  MAX_DIGITS    : constant      := implementation_defined;
  MAX_MANTISSA  : constant      := implementation_defined;
  FINE_DELTA    : constant      := implementation_defined;
  TICK          : constant      := implementation_defined;

  subtype PRIORITY is INTEGER range {...}
  ...
end SYSTEM;
```

TEXT_IO

```
with IO_EXCEPTIONS;
package TEXT_IO is

  type FILE_TYPE is limited private;

  type FILE_MODE is (IN_FILE, OUT_FILE);
  subtype FIELD         is INTEGER range 0..implementation-defined;
  subtype NUMBER_BASE   is INTEGER range 2..16;
  type COUNT            is range 0..implementation-defined;
  subtype POSITIVE_COUNT is COUNT range 1..COUNT'LAST;
  type TYPE_SET         is (LOWER_CASE, UPPER_CASE);

  UNBOUNDED : constant COUNT := 0;

  procedure CREATE (FILE : in out FILE_TYPE;
                    MODE : in     FILE_MODE := OUT_FILE;
                    NAME : in     STRING    := "";
                    FORM : in     STRING    := "");
```

```
procedure OPEN      (FILE :  in out FILE_TYPE;
                     MODE :  in      FILE_MODE;
                     NAME :  in      STRING;
                     FORM :  in      STRING     := "");
procedure CLOSE    (FILE :  in out FILE_TYPE);
procedure DELETE   (FILE :  in out FILE_TYPE);
procedure RESET    (FILE :  in out FILE_TYPE;
                     MODE :  in      FILE_MODE);
procedure RESET    (FILE :  in out FILE_TYPE);

function MODE      (FILE :  in FILE_TYPE) return FILE_MODE;
function NAME      (FILE :  in FILE_TYPE) return STRING;
function FORM      (FILE :  in FILE_TYPE) return STRING;
function IS_OPEN   (FILE :  in FILE_TYPE) return BOOLEAN;

procedure SET_INPUT   (FILE :  in FILE_TYPE);
procedure SET_OUTPUT  (FILE :  in FILE_TYPE);

function STANDARD_INPUT   return FILE_TYPE;
function STANDARD_OUTPUT  return FILE_TYPE;
function CURRENT_INPUT    return FILE_TYPE;
function CURRENT_OUTPUT   return FILE_TYPE;

procedure SET_LINE_LENGTH (FILE :  in FILE_TYPE;
                           TO   :  in COUNT);
procedure SET_LINE_LENGTH (TO   :  in COUNT);

procedure SET_PAGE_LENGTH (FILE :  in FILE_TYPE;
                           TO   :  in COUNT);
procedure SET_PAGE_LENGTH (TO   :  in COUNT);

function LINE_LENGTH (FILE :  in FILE_TYPE) return COUNT;
function LINE_LENGTH                         return COUNT;

function PAGE_LENGTH (FILE :  in FILE_TYPE) return COUNT;
function PAGE_LENGTH                         return COUNT;

procedure NEW_LINE (FILE    :  in FILE_TYPE;
                    SPACING :  in POSITIVE_COUNT := 1);
procedure NEW_LINE (SPACING :  in POSITIVE_COUNT := 1);

procedure SKIP_LINE (FILE    :  in FILE_TYPE;
                     SPACING :  in POSITIVE_COUNT := 1);
procedure SKIP_LINE (SPACING :  in POSITIVE_COUNT := 1);

function END_OF_LINE (FILE :  in FILE_TYPE) return BOOLEAN;
function END_OF_LINE                         return BOOLEAN;
```

```
procedure NEW_PAGE (FILE : in FILE_TYPE);
procedure NEW_PAGE;

procedure SKIP_PAGE (FILE : in FILE_TYPE);
procedure SKIP_PAGE;

function END_OF_PAGE (FILE : in FILE_TYPE) return BOOLEAN;
function END_OF_PAGE                        return BOOLEAN;

function END_OF_FILE (FILE : in FILE_TYPE) return BOOLEAN;
function END_OF_FILE                        return BOOLEAN;

procedure SET_COL (FILE : in FILE_TYPE;
                   TO   : in POSITIVE_COUNT);
procedure SET_COL (TO   : in POSITIVE_COUNT);

procedure SET_LINE (FILE : in FILE_TYPE;
                    TO   : in POSITIVE_COUNT);
procedure SET_LINE (TO   : in POSITIVE_COUNT);

function COL (FILE : in FILE_TYPE) return POSITIVE_COUNT;
function COL                       return POSITIVE_COUNT;

function LINE (FILE : in FILE_TYPE) return POSITIVE_COUNT;
function LINE                       return POSITIVE_COUNT;

function PAGE (FILE : in FILE_TYPE) return POSITIVE_COUNT;
function PAGE                       return POSITIVE_COUNT;

procedure GET (FILE : in  FILE_TYPE;
               ITEM : out CHARACTER);
procedure GET (ITEM : out CHARACTER);
procedure PUT (FILE : in  FILE_TYPE;
               ITEM : in  CHARACTER);
procedure PUT (ITEM : in  CHARACTER);

procedure GET (FILE : in  FILE_TYPE;
               ITEM : out STRING);
procedure GET (ITEM : out STRING);
procedure PUT (FILE : in  FILE_TYPE;
               ITEM : in  STRING);
procedure PUT (FILE : in  STRING);

procedure GET_LINE (FILE : in  FILE_TYPE;
                    ITEM : out STRING;
                    LAST : out NATURAL);
```

```
           procedure GET_LINE (ITEM : out STRING;
                               LAST : out NATURAL);
           procedure PUT_LINE (FILE : in  FILE_TYPE;
                               ITEM : in  STRING);
           procedure PUT_LINE (ITEM : in  STRING);

  generic
     type NUM is range <>;
  package INTEGER_IO is
     DEFAULT_WIDTH : FIELD := NUM'WIDTH;
     DEFAULT_BASE  : NUMBER_BASE := 10;
     procedure GET (FILE  : in  FILE_TYPE;
                    ITEM  : out NUM;
                    WIDTH : in  FIELD := 0);
     procedure GET (ITEM  : out NUM;
                    WIDTH : in  FIELD := 0);
     procedure PUT (FILE  : in  FILE_TYPE;
                    ITEM  : in  NUM;
                    WIDTH : in  FIELD := DEFAULT_WIDTH;
                    BASE  : in  NUMBER_BASE := DEFAULT_BASE);
     procedure PUT (ITEM  : in  NUM;
                    WIDTH : in  FIELD := DEFAULT_WIDTH;
                    BASE  : in  NUMBER_BASE := DEFAULT_BASE);
     procedure GET (FROM  : in  STRING;
                    ITEM  : out NUM;
                    LAST  : out POSITIVE);
     procedure PUT (TO    : out STRING;
                    ITEM  : in  NUM;
                    BASE  : in  NUMBER_BASE := DEFAULT_BASE);
  end INTEGER_IO;

  generic
     type NUM is digits <>;
  package FLOAT_IO is
     DEFAULT_FORE : FIELD := 2;
     DEFAULT_AFT  : FIELD := NUM'DIGITS - 1;
     DEFAULT_EXP  : FIELD := 3;
     procedure GET (FILE  : in  FILE_TYPE;
                    ITEM  : out NUM;
                    WIDTH : in  FIELD := 0);
     procedure GET (ITEM  : out NUM;
                    WIDTH : in  FIELD := 0);
     procedure PUT (FILE  : in  FILE_TYPE;
                    ITEM  : in  NUM;
                    FORE  : in  FIELD := DEFAULT_FORE;
                    AFT   : in  FIELD := DEFAULT_AFT;
                    EXP   : in  FIELD := DEFAULT_EXP);
```

```
                procedure PUT (ITEM   :  in   NUM;
                               FORE   :  in   FIELD := DEFAULT_FORE;
                               AFT    :  in   FIELD := DEFAULT_AFT;
                               EXP    :  in   FIELD := DEFAULT_EXP);
             procedure GET (FROM   :  in   STRING;
                            ITEM   :  out  NUM;
                            LAST   :  out  POSITIVE);
             procedure PUT (TO     :  out  STRING;
                            ITEM   :  in   NUM;
                            AFT    :  in   FIELD := DEFAULT_AFT;
                            EXP    :  in   FIELD := DEFAULT_EXP);
   end FLOAT_IO;


   generic
      type NUM is delta <>;
   package FIXED_IO is
      DEFAULT_FORE  :  FIELD := NUM'FORE;
      DEFAULT_AFT   :  FIELD := NUM'AFT;
      DEFAULT_EXP   :  FIELD := 0;
      procedure GET (FILE   :  in   FILE_TYPE;
                     ITEM   :  out  NUM;
                     WIDTH  :  in   FIELD := 0);
      procedure GET (ITEM   :  out  NUM;
                     WIDTH  :  in   FIELD := 0;
      procedure PUT (FILE   :  in   FILE_TYPE;
                     ITEM   :  in   NUM;
                     FORE   :  in   FIELD := DEFAULT_FORE;
                     AFT    :  in   FIELD := DEFAULT_AFT;
                     EXP    :  in   FIELD := DEFAULT_EXP);
      procedure PUT (ITEM   :  in   NUM;
                     FORE   :  in   FIELD := DEFAULT_FORE;
                     AFT    :  in   FIELD := DEFAULT_AFT;
                     EXP    :  in   FIELD := DEFAULT_EXP);
      procedure GET (FROM   :  in   STRING;
                     ITEM   :  out  NUM;
                     LAST   :  out  POSITIVE);
      procedure PUT (TO     :  out  STRING;
                     ITEM   :  in   NUM;
                     AFT    :  in   FIELD := DEFAULT_AFT;
                     EXP    :  in   FIELD := DEFAULT_EXP);
   end FIXED_IO;


   generic
      type ENUM is (<>);
   package ENUMERATION_IO is
      DEFAULT_WIDTH   :  FIELD    := 0;
      DEFAULT_SETTING :  TYPE_SET := UPPER_CASE;
```

```
      procedure GET (FILE  :  in   FILE_TYPE;
                     ITEM  :  out  ENUM);
      procedure GET (ITEM  :  out  ENUM);
      procedure PUT (FILE  :  in   FILE_TYPE;
                     ITEM  :  in   ENUM;
                     WIDTH :  in   FIELD      := DEFAULT_WIDTH;
                     SET   :  in   TYPE_SET := DEFAULT_SETTING);
      procedure PUT (ITEM  :  in   ENUM;
                     WIDTH :  in   FIELD      := DEFAULT_WIDTH;
                     SET   :  in   TYPE_SET := DEFAULT_SETTING);
      procedure GET (FROM  :  in   STRING;
                     ITEM  :  out  ENUM;
                     LAST  :  out  POSITIVE);
      procedure PUT (TO    :  out  STRING;
                     ITEM  :  in   ENUM;
                     SET   :  in   TYPE_SET := DEFAULT_SETTING);
  end ENUMERATION_IO;

    NAME_ERROR    :  exception renames IO_EXCEPTIONS.NAME_ERROR;
    USE_ERROR     :  exception renames IO_EXCEPTIONS.USE_ERROR;
    STATUS_ERROR  :  exception renames IO_EXCEPTIONS.STATUS_ERROR;
    MODE_ERROR    :  exception renames IO_EXCEPTIONS.MODE_ERROR;
    DEVICE_ERROR  :  exception renames IO_EXCEPTIONS.DEVICE_ERROR;
    END_ERROR     :  exception renames IO_EXCEPTIONS.END_ERROR;
    DATA_ERROR    :  exception renames IO_EXCEPTIONS.DATA_ERROR;
    LAYOUT_ERROR  :  exception renames IO_EXCEPTIONS.LAYOUT_ERROR;

private
    -- implementation_defined
end TEXT_IO;
```

UNCHECKED_CONVERSION

```
generic
   type SOURCE is limited private;
   type TARGET is limited private;
function UNCHECKED_CONVERSION(S : in SOURCE) return TARGET;
```

UNCHECKED_DEALLOCATION

```
generic
   type OBJECT is limited private;
   type NAME   is access OBJECT;
procedure UNCHECKED_DEALLOCATION(X : in out NAME);
```

APPENDIX

D

Ada Style Guide

Programming style is a topic that is often hotly debated but still poorly understood. Nevertheless, the style with which a system is developed will greatly affect that system's understandability, maintainability, and efficiency. Throughout our examples and discussions, we have tried to demonstrate a programming style that meets these goals and at the same time exploits the power of the Ada language. In this appendix, we discuss the three levels of programming style, summarizing the suggestions made throughout the book.

When we speak of programming style, most people think of standards such as "Thou shalt use no GOTOs!" or "Each module must fit on one page!" Such rules are not only artificial, but they also force a programmer to worry about microefficiency issues, as opposed to the macro design philosophy that is needed in any system. On the other hand, following a programming style that sculpts the overall structure of a system to directly reflect the view of the real world is a far superior approach.

Such a style can only be described in the form of guidelines—since Ada is a large language, designed for the solution of complex problems, it is impossible to describe a rule for every possible application. Furthermore, adding style rules to a language forces the programmer to learn even more about the language, often blinding or even prohibiting the programmer from using a language feature that would clearly be more efficient or readable.

From this perspective, we break the scope of guidelines for programming style into three major areas, namely:

- Style of design.

- Style of applying the language.

- Style of presentation.

Style of Design

A group of professional programmers were once asked how they designed their systems. The only replies were blank stares. After a few probing questions, the reason for their nonresponse became evident: These programmers did not design their solutions, they simply wrote code.

To create reliable solutions to complex problems, we must design consistent, logical structures for them. It is purposeful structure that makes a solution comprehensible and maintainable. Even if the best possible tools were used in developing a solution, the most expressive programming language in the world could not make a poor design better.

As we have mentioned many times, we think of real-world problems in terms of nouns and verbs. The Ada programming language parallels our real-world solutions by providing a means of clearly expressing objects and operations in a balanced manner. To support this view of the world, we have used an object-oriented design method in this book (see Chapter 5) This design style seems to work well for a large domain of problems. Furthermore, this style is well supported by Ada.

The essence of this design method is that a user can abstract the data and algorithms at a particular level, while at the same time hiding details unnecessary to that level of abstraction (the Parnas decomposition criterion). Unlike purely functional design techniques, however, this method recognizes the importance of both objects and operations in solutions. In its most basic sense, it provides a tool for managing the complexity of solutions.

We offer the following guidelines for design style:

- Use an object-oriented style to abstract both data and control structures.

- At any given level of abstraction, keep in mind the number of entities a programmer can manage at one time.

- Program units should exhibit strong cohesion and weak coupling (see Chapter 4).

You may say to yourself that applying such a style is inefficient, especially for real-time systems, because of all the overhead associated with so many units. To reduce this overhead, we may always use the pragma Inline, which eliminates parameter passing and related linkage while at the same time maintaining the clarity of the high-order language (see Chapter 20).

Furthermore, we suggest that a system is inherently more reliable if it directly reflects the real world—it is those parts of the solution that do not match the real world that are most likely to exhibit errant behavior. Besides, the 90-10 rule applies, namely, that 90% of a system's resources are spent on 10% of the code. If an efficiency bottleneck is found, don't tear the whole fabric of the solution to resolve the problem. A better approach is to identify that 10% and apply constructs for local efficiency (such as a redesign of that section of code or the use of Ada's representation specifications). From the perspective of a system's life cycle, designing a system with a good style will have large payoffs. On the other hand, a poor design structure will never be forgiven.

Style of Applying the Language

No one can claim to know all there is to know about the English language, but we all get by with what we do know. Generally, we use only a simple subset of the English language, but sometimes we resort to more complex constructs (such as "referential disambiguation") when we need to express a more precise shade of meaning. The same concept is true of programming languages. Most of the time, we apply just a subset of the language's constructs; sometimes we apply a more complex structure because it solves our problems more efficiently or more clearly. When we refer to a style of applying our tools, we mean to encourage the use of certain language constructs, while discouraging (but not necessarily banning) the use of others.

In our examples, we have noted language constructs that are sometimes dangerous or lack clarity. No matter what the language facility, there are proper and improper ways to apply any structure. Since these guidelines are too numerous to list here, we instead provide the following metaguidelines. In particular, for the listed Ada features, the following applications are suggested:

- *Subprograms*

  Main program units

  Definition of functional control

  Definition of type operations

- *Packages*

  Named collection of declarations

  Groups of related program units

  Abstract data types

  Abstract-state machines

- *Tasks*

  Concurrent actions

  Routing messages

  Controlling resources

  Interrupts

- *Generic program units*

  Reusable software components

  Controlling visibility

- *Exceptions*

  Detecting and recovering from error conditions

  Detecting and correcting expected but exceptional conditions

The programmer should also pay attention to how he or she names entities in the language. With even simple language features, such as the underscore within identifiers or the use of named parameter association, very readable code can be produced. We offer the following guidelines for naming program entities:

- Subprograms should be named with verb phrases; functions that return a boolean value should be named with phrases that use forms of the verb *to be*.

  `Start_Mixing_Process, Sort_List, Is_Not_Empty`

- Packages should be named with noun phrases.

  `Math_Functions, Earth_Constants`

- Tasks should be named with noun phrases (usually denoting some action)

  `Timer, Message_Router, List_Searcher`

- Types should be named as common noun phrases.

  `Tree, Linked_List, Index`

- Objects should be named as proper noun phrases.

  `My_Tree, Personnel_Linked_List, Data_Base_Index`

No matter how the language is applied, we suggest the following primary guideline: *If a choice among two or more constructs exists, choose the one that offers the greatest clarity.*

Style of Presentation

This is the area of style that is usually given the most attention, since it is the easiest to describe and automatically enforce. As opposed to the style of applying the language, which recommends the use of certain constructs, style of presentation refers to the physical layout of source code. This level of style is entirely for the benefit of the human reader; it has no effect upon the runtime environment.

Most of the guidelines associated with presentation include suggestions for indentation, use of comments, and textual layout. Throughout this book, the code has been written using the recommended manner of indentation. In terms of commenting style, Ada code can be largely self-documenting (at least at a local level) through the use of such features as named parameter association. Finally, if the separate compilation facility of the language is exploited (as it should be), textual layout will be important only at a low level. The overall textual organization need not exist in the linear fashion of most languages. Rather, the language supports a multidimensional topology.

Given this philosophy, the guidelines for presentation may be stated as follows:

- Follow the recommended style of indentation.
- Judicious use of white space in a program improves clarity.
- Localize all logically related entities
- Simple techniques such as lining up all colons or alphabetizing a list of declarations can greatly improve readability.

In the last guideline, note that even a program should have an esthetic appeal. A program should look pleasing to the eye and, upon closer examination, should be comprehensible. Finally, keep in mind the fact that code may be written only once but will be read many times. Program with the reader in mind, not the writer.

APPENDIX E

Ada Syntax Charts

There exist several ways to formally define the syntax of a programming language, with Bachus-Naur Form (BNF) being the most popular due to its conciseness. However, BNF productions are not very readable to the uninitiated; so we instead present Ada's form with syntax charts, which are essentially graphic representations of the BNF.

Syntax charts are read from left to right, following the direction of the arrows. The directed lines may loop back on themselves, indicating that a construct may be repeated. A rectangle surrounds a construct that is defined in another syntax chart (a nonterminal). A circle or ellipse denotes a literal string that appears exactly as stated. If a syntactic category is prefixed by an italicized word, it is equivalent to the unprefixed corresponding category name; the prefix simply conveys some semantic information.

We present the syntax charts in alphabetical order. Every construct is included, except for `upper_case_character`, `digit`, `lower_case_character`, and `graphic_character`, since their form is obvious. In addition, we have drawn the syntax charts in a style that indicates the recommended indentation style for each production.

ABORT_STATEMENT

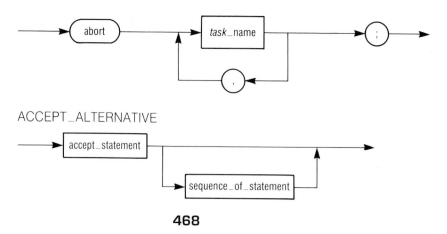

ACCEPT_ALTERNATIVE

ACCEPT_STATEMENT

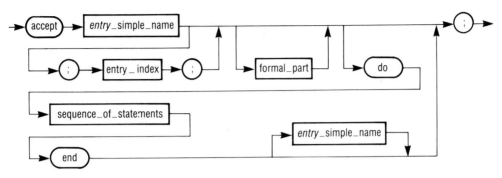

ACCESS_TYPE_DEFINITION

ACTUAL_PARAMETER

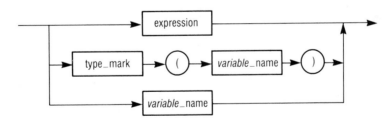

ACTUAL_PARAMETER_PART

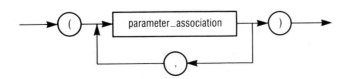

ADDRESS_CLAUSE

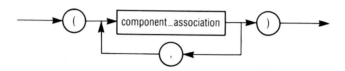

AGGREGATE

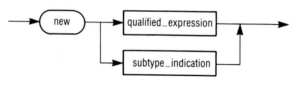

ALIGNMENT_CLAUSE

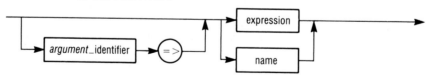

ALLOCATOR

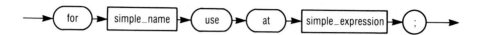

ARGUMENT_ASSOCIATION

ARRAY_TYPE_DEFINITION

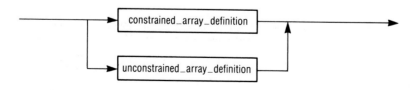

ASSIGNMENT_STATEMENT

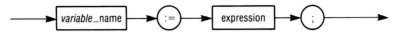

ATTRIBUTE

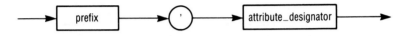

ATTRIBUTE_DESIGNATOR

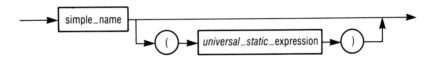

BASE

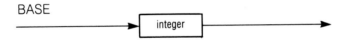

BASED_INTEGER

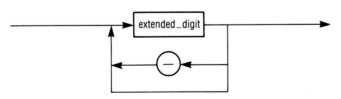

BASED_LITERAL

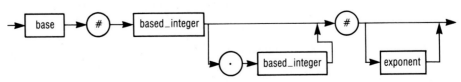

BASIC_DECLARATION

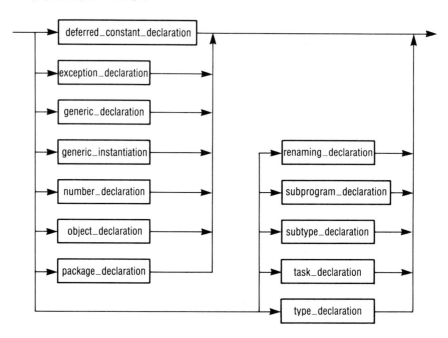

BASIC_DECLARATIVE_ITEM

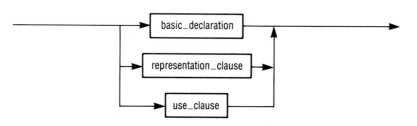

BINARY_ADDING_OPERATOR

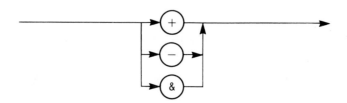

BLOCK_STATEMENT

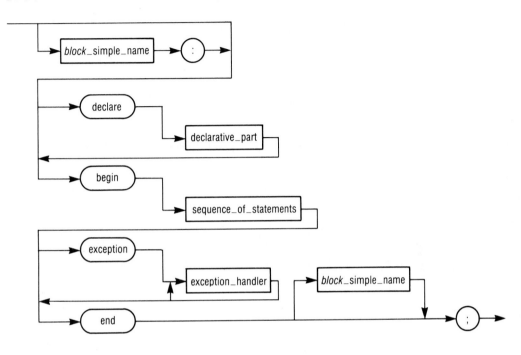

BODY

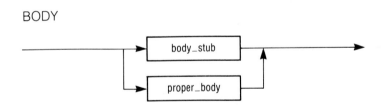

BODY_STUB

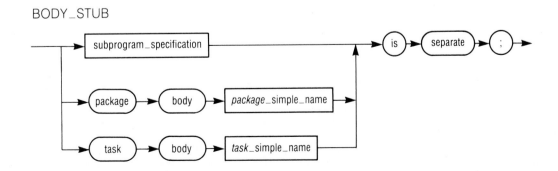

CASE_STATEMENT

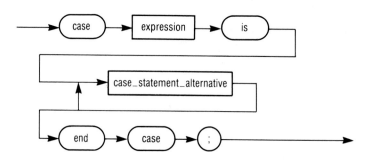

CASE_STATEMENT_ALTERNATIVE

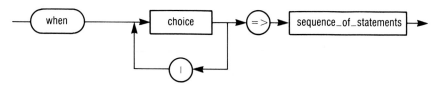

CHARACTER_LITERAL

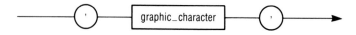

CHOICE

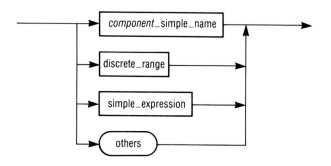

CODE_STATEMENT

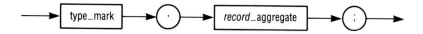

COMPILATION

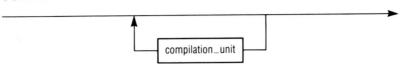

COMPILATION_UNIT

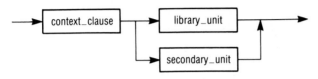

COMPONENT_ASSOCIATION

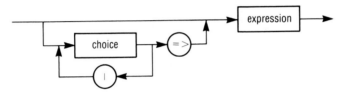

COMPONENT_CLAUSE

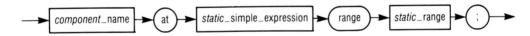

COMPONENT_DECLARATION

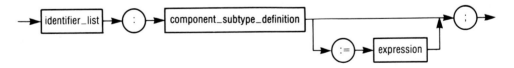

COMPONENT_LIST

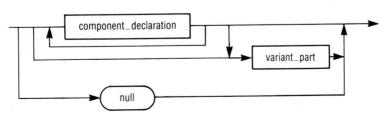

COMPONENT_SUBTYPE_DEFINITION

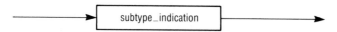

COMPOUND_STATEMENT

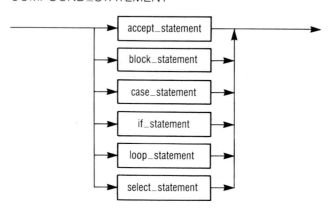

CONDITION

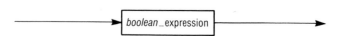

CONDITIONAL_ENTRY_CALL

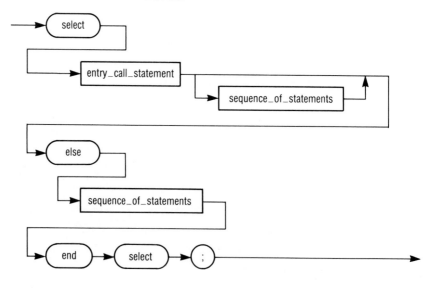

CONSTRAINED_ARRAY_DEFINITION

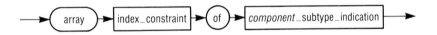

CONSTRAINT

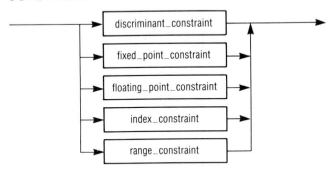

CONTEXT_CLAUSE

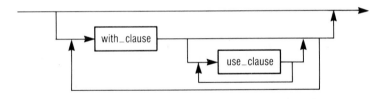

DECIMAL_LITERAL

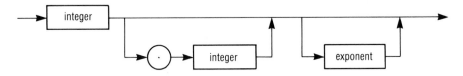

DECLARATIVE_PART

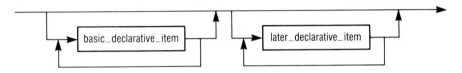

DEFERRED_CONSTANT_DECLARATION

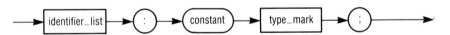

DELAY_ALTERNATIVE

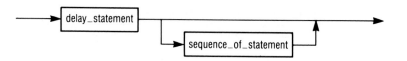

DELAY_STATEMENT

DERIVED_TYPE_DEFINITION

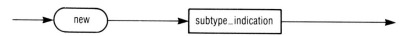

DESIGNATOR

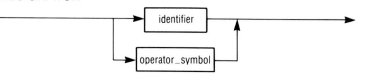

DISCRETE_RANGE

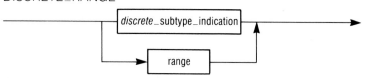

DISCRIMINANT_ASSOCIATION

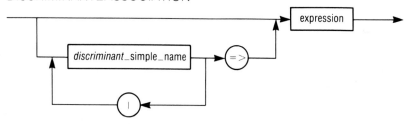

DISCRIMINANT_CONSTRAINT

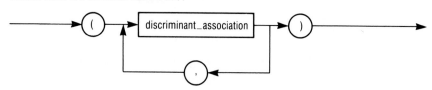

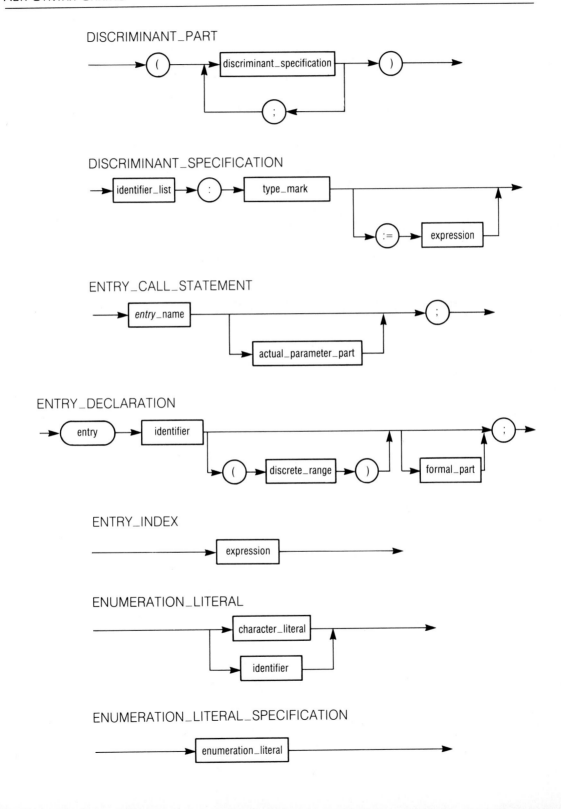

DISCRIMINANT_PART

DISCRIMINANT_SPECIFICATION

ENTRY_CALL_STATEMENT

ENTRY_DECLARATION

ENTRY_INDEX

ENUMERATION_LITERAL

ENUMERATION_LITERAL_SPECIFICATION

ENUMERATION_REPRESENTATION_CLAUSE

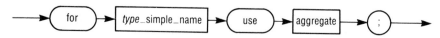

ENUMERATION_TYPE_DEFINITION

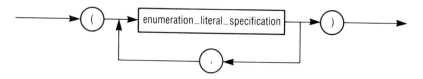

EXCEPTION_CHOICE

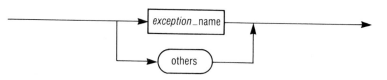

EXCEPTION_DECLARATION

EXCEPTION_HANDLER

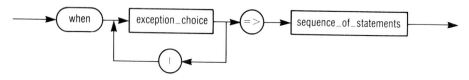

EXIT_STATEMENT

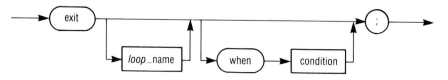

EXPONENT

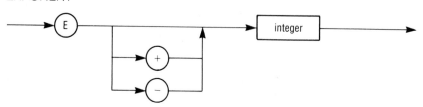

EXPRESSION

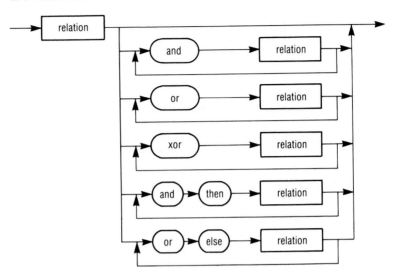

EXTENDED_DIGIT

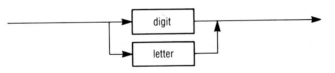

FACTOR

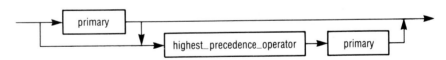

FIXED_ACCURACY_DEFINITION

FIXED_POINT_CONSTRAINT

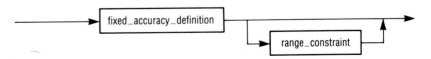

FLOATING_ACCURACY_DEFINITION

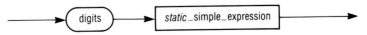

FLOATING_POINT_CONSTRAINT

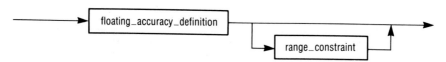

FORMAL_PARAMETER

FORMAL_PART

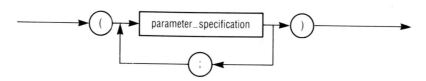

FULL_TYPE_DECLARATION

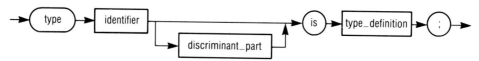

FUNCTION_CALL

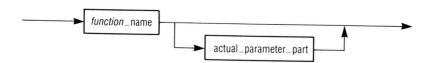

GENERIC_ACTUAL_PARAMETER

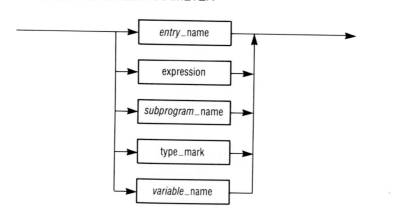

GENERIC_ACTUAL_PART

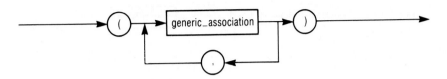

GENERIC_ASSOCIATION

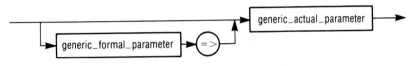

GENERIC_DECLARATION

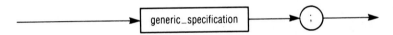

GENERIC_FORMAL_PARAMETER

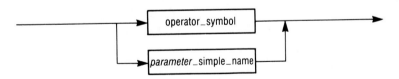

GENERIC_FORMAL_PART

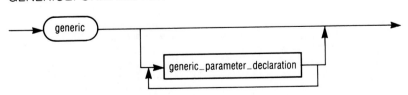

GENERIC_INSTANTIATION

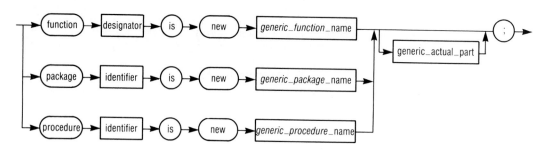

GENERIC_PARAMETER_DECLARATION

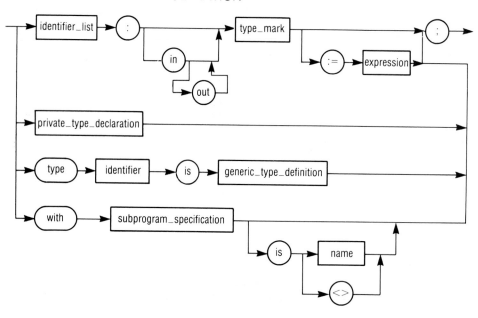

GENERIC_SPECIFICATION

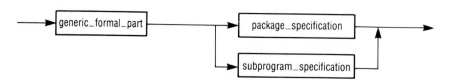

GENERIC_TYPE_DEFINITION

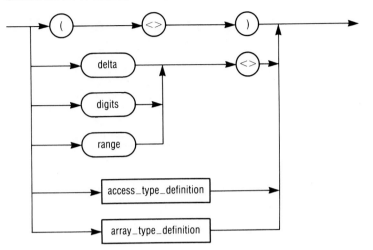

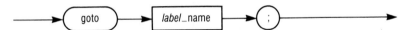

GOTO_STATEMENT

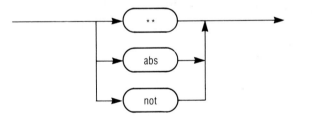

HIGHEST_PRECEDENCE_OPERATOR

IDENTIFIER

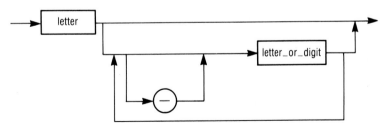

IDENTIFIER_LIST

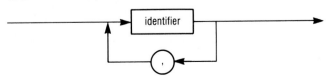

IF_STATEMENT

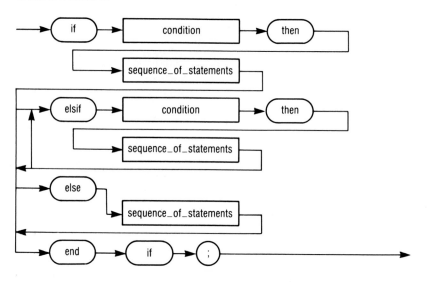

INCOMPLETE_TYPE_DECLARATION

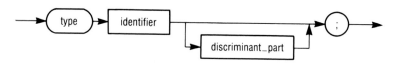

INDEX_CONSTRAINT

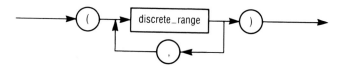

INDEX_SUBTYPE_DEFINITION

INDEXED_COMPONENT

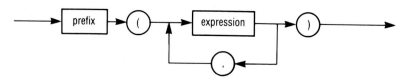

INTEGER

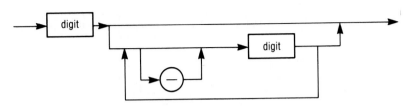

INTEGER_TYPE_DEFINITION

ITERATION_SCHEME

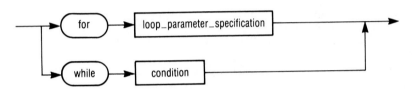

LABEL

LATER_DECLARATIVE_ITEM

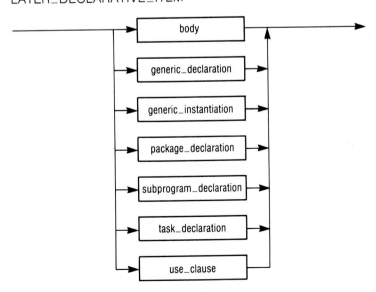

LENGTH_CLAUSE

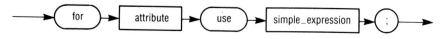

LETTER

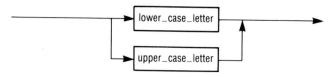

LETTER_OR_DIGIT

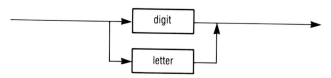

LIBRARY_UNIT

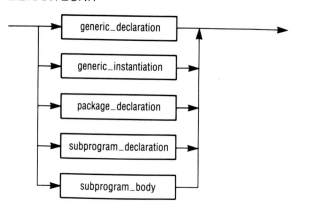

LIBRARY_UNIT_BODY

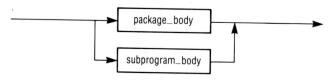

LOGICAL_OPERATOR

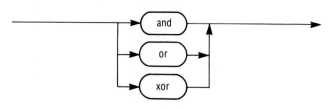

LOOP_PARAMETER_SPECIFICATION

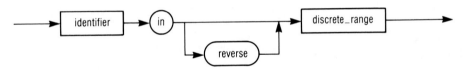

LOOP_STATEMENT

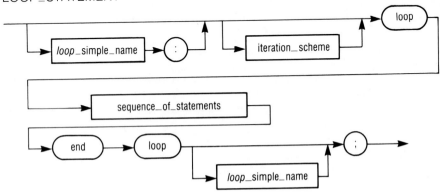

MODE

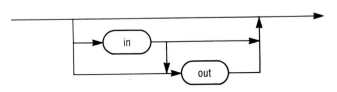

MULTIPLYING_OPERATOR

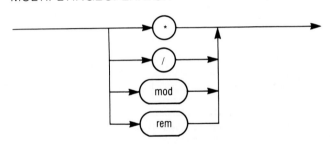

NAME

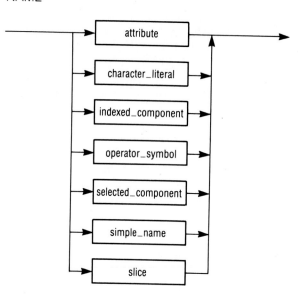

NULL_STATEMENT

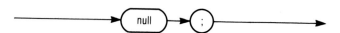

NUMBER_DECLARATION

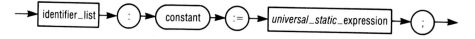

NUMERIC_LITERAL

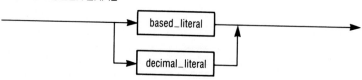

OBJECT_DECLARATION

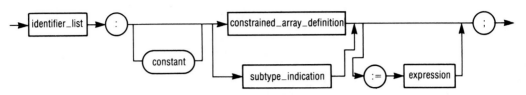

OPERATOR_SYMBOL

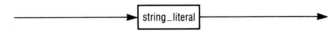

PACKAGE_BODY

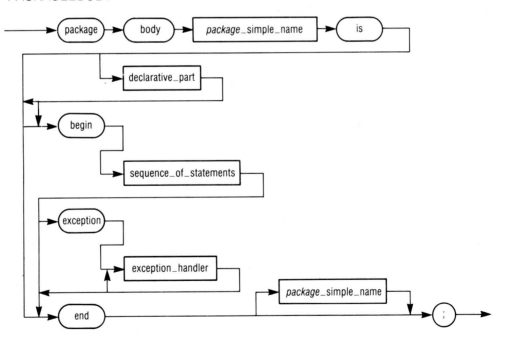

PACKAGE_DECLARATION

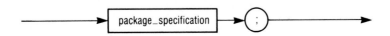

PACKAGE_SPECIFICATION

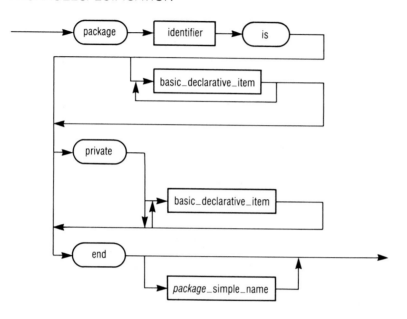

PARAMETER_ASSOCIATION

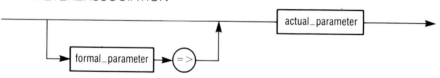

PARAMETER_SPECIFICATION

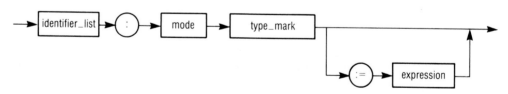

PRAGMA

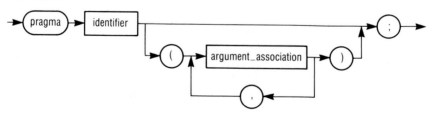

PREFIX

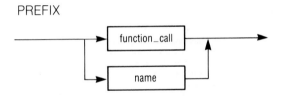

PRIMARY

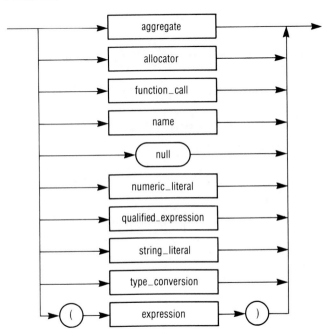

PRIVATE_TYPE_DECLARATION

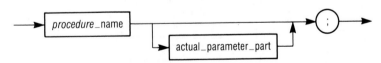

PROCEDURE_CALL_STATEMENT

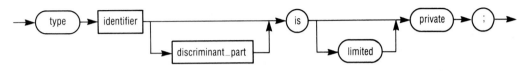

PROPER_BODY

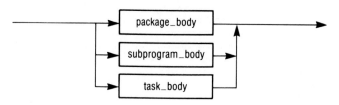

QUALIFIED_EXPRESSION

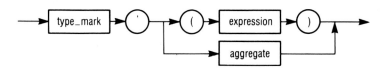

RAISE_STATEMENT

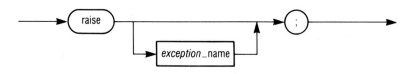

RANGE

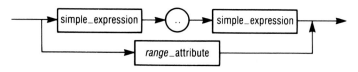

RANGE_CONSTRAINT

REAL_TYPE_DEFINITION

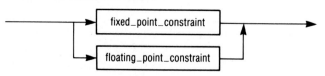

RECORD_REPRESENTATION_CLAUSE

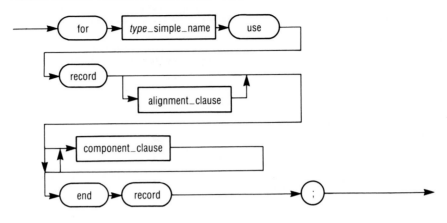

RECORD_TYPE_DEFINITION

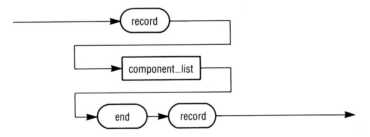

RELATION

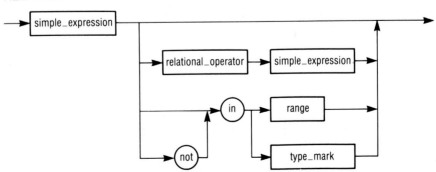

RELATIONAL_OPERATOR

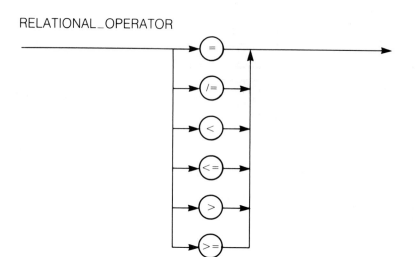

RENAMING_DECLARATION

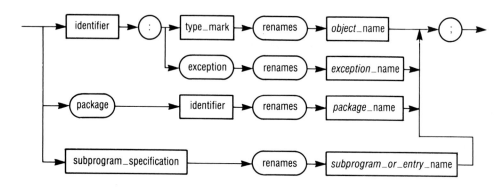

REPRESENTATION_CLAUSE

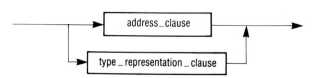

RETURN_STATEMENT

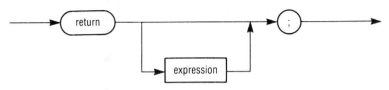

SECONDARY_UNIT

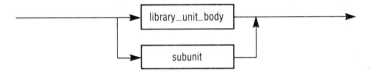

SELECT_ALTERNATIVE

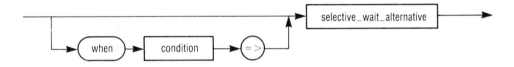

SELECT_STATEMENT

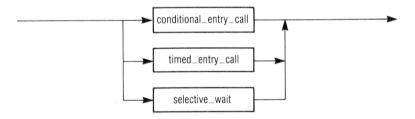

SELECTED_COMPONENT

SELECTIVE_WAIT_ALTERNATIVE

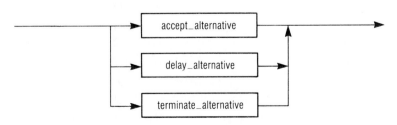

SELECTIVE_WAIT

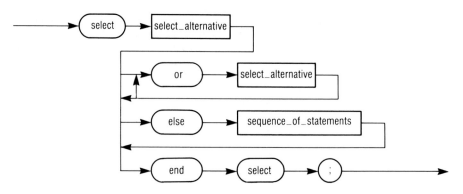

SELECTOR

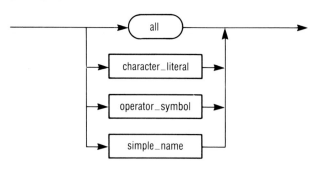

SEQUENCE_OF_STATEMENTS

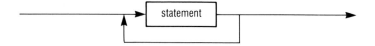

SIMPLE_EXPRESSION

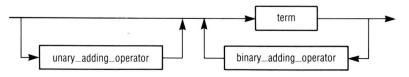

SIMPLE_NAME

SIMPLE_STATEMENT

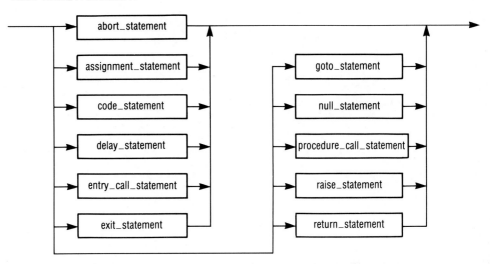

SLICE

STATEMENT

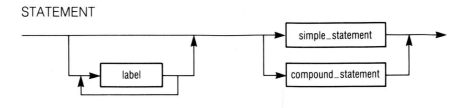

STRING_LITERAL

SUBPROGRAM_BODY

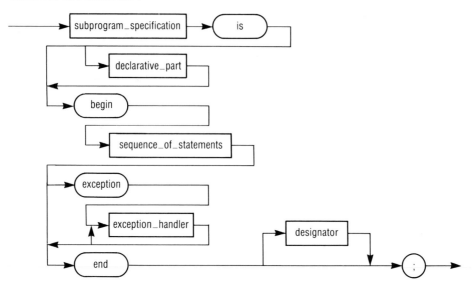

SUBPROGRAM_DECLARATION

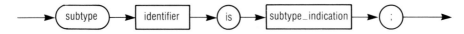

SUBPROGRAM_SPECIFICATION

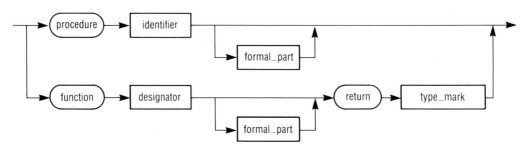

SUBTYPE_DECLARATION

SUBTYPE_INDICATION

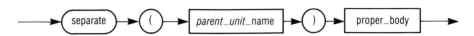

SUBUNIT

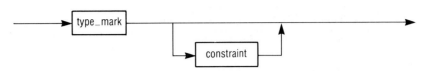

TASK_BODY

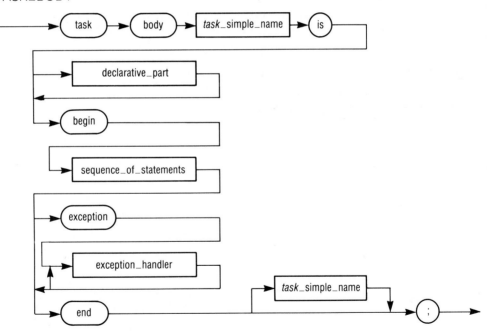

TASK_DECLARATION

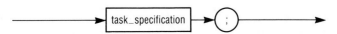

TASK_SPECIFICATION

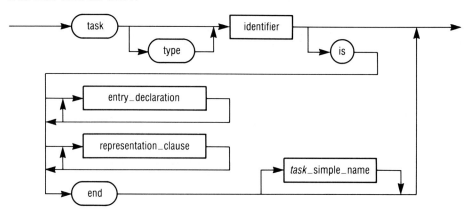

TERM

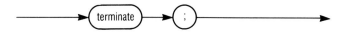

TERMINATE_ALTERNATIVE

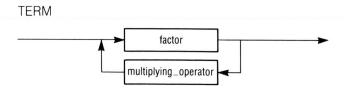

TIMED_ENTRY_CALL

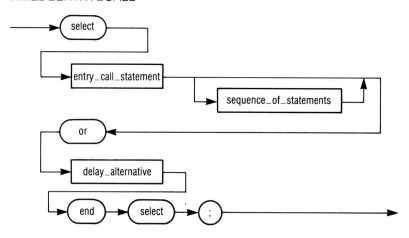

TYPE_CONVERSION

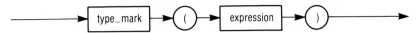

TYPE_DECLARATION

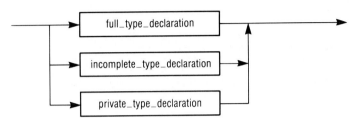

TYPE_DEFINITION

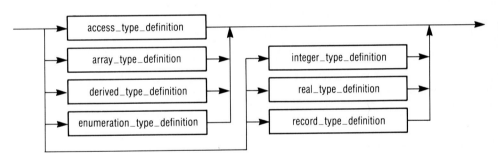

TYPE_MARK

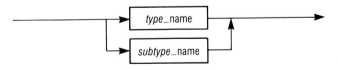

TYPE_REPRESENTATION_CLAUSE

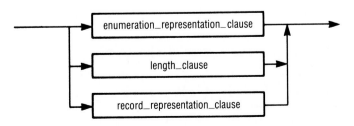

UNARY_ADDING_OPERATOR

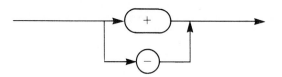

UNCONSTRAINED_ARRAY_DEFINITION

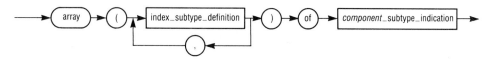

USE_CLAUSE

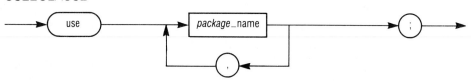

VARIANT

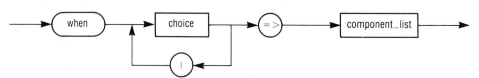

VARIANT_PART

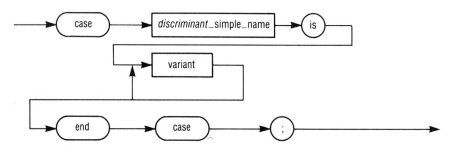

WITH_CLAUSE

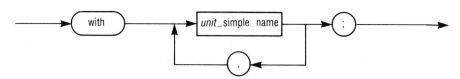

Ada 9X

Background

The first standard for the Ada Programming Language was established in 1983 (Ada 83). The standard was published by the United States Department of Defense (DoD) on February 17, 1983, in a document titled "Reference Manual for the Ada® Programming Language." (Many people refer to this document as simply the *Language Reference Manual* (LRM).) The standard is a military standard (MIL), and it was also approved by the American National Standards Institute, Inc. (ANSI). The standard's official reference is ANSI/MIL-STD-1815A-1983. The 1815 number was assigned because it was the birth date of the namesake of the language, Augusta Ada Lovelace. Following the 1815 is the initial "A" indicating that this is the first standard to be established for the Ada programming language.

Ada 9X Project

Although the standard was rigidly enforced through the trademark owned by the DoD and validation tests for Ada 83 compilers, it was intended from the start that Ada 83 would eventually be revised after experience had been gained with the new language. The Ada 9X Project was established in 1988 to investigate suggested changes to Ada (Ada 9X). The "9X" part of the title was intended to indicate the year (199?) in which the project would be completed. At the time of this writing, the official publication date of the new standard has not been announced, but it is expected to be December 1993, with the final ISO standard voting to be complete within a year.

Even though the new standard has not been completed, the Ada 9X Project has published information [1,2,3,12] about Ada 9X, and several of the experts in the field [4,5,6,7,8] and the technical director of the Ada 9X

Mapping/Revision Team [9] have written articles about Ada 9X. This appendix is based on the published information, but since it predates the official publication date of the standard it is subject to some minor errors.

Some of the changes in the language will be small improvements, while others will have a major impact on the use of the language. An example of a small change is that type `Character` will be expanded from 128 to 256 literals; major changes include the addition of object-oriented programming capabilities.

Incompatibilities

There will be some incompatibilities between Ada 83 and Ada 9X. Some of these will make Ada 83 programs illegal, while others, albeit a small number, will change their meaning. The new compilers will be required to identify Ada 83 incompatibilities, rejecting illegal programs and issuing warnings about any changes in meaning. Ploedereder [10] provides guidelines along with explanations to help avoid these incompatibility problems when writing Ada 83 programs today. The following is a list of those guidelines taken from that article:

The guidelines for Ada 83 programs:

1. Do not use the following Ada 9X keywords (reserved words) as Ada 83 identifiers in your program: `aliased`, `protected`, `requeue`, `tagged`, `until`.

2. Do not declare the identifiers `Wide_String` and `Wide_Character` in package specifications.

3. Do not apply `use` clauses to package `System`.

4. Do not declare the identifier `Append_File` in a package specification. Alternately, do not apply `use` clauses to package `Text_IO` and instantiations of `Sequential_IO`.

5. For type `Character`, be prepared that the enumeration will comprise 256, rather than 128, literals. Similarly, for type `File_Mode`, be prepared for the added literal `Append_File`.

6. Do not use accuracy constraints in subtype declarations.

7. Put representation clauses for real types immediately after the type declaration.

8. All library unit packages must have bodies, even if the bodies are empty.

9. Do not derive from a type declared in the same package. Or, if you do, derive the new types before redefining any predefined operations on the parent type.

10. Add a distinctive comment to all generic formal private types that can be legally instantiated with unconstrained types.

11. Do not assume "too much" about the state of the computation when exceptions are implicitly raised. Do not cause implicit exceptions knowingly. Be prepared for the elimination of the exception `Numeric_Error`.

12. Be prepared for the attribute values of real types to more closely reflect the actual hardware. Be aware that accuracy requirements for operations combining fixed-point types with differently based `'Small` may be lessened.

Ploedereder [10] also provides a complete explanation of all of these guidelines.

If we think of the above as reflecting small or minor changes, the large or major changes come in three areas: object-oriented programming, programming in the large, and real-time and parallel programming.

Object-Oriented Programming

As discussed in Chapter 3, Ada 83 has complete support for object-oriented development. Because of these capabilities, Ada 83 is often referred to as an object-based language. This term implies that Ada 83 falls short of being a fully implemented object-oriented programming language. There are several things that mark a language as object-oriented [11]:

Major features, such as:
- Abstraction
- Encapsulation
- Modularity
- Hierarchy

Minor features, such as:
- Typing
- Concurrency
- Persistence

Ada 9X is not a "pure" object-oriented language; it is a hybrid language that has object-oriented features such as fully implemented single inheritance and run-time polymorphism (dynamic or late binding). Single inheritance gets its name from the fact that things can be inherited from only a single parent. Multiple inheritance, in contrast, allows inheritance from any number of parents.

There is no consensus regarding the benefits of multiple inheritance over single inheritance. For example, Smalltalk uses single inheritance while C++ allows multiple inheritance. Both Ada 83 and Ada 9X provide for inheritance through derived types. A derived type inherits all of the primitive operations of the parent type. Ada 9X, through a simple extension of the language, allows the new derived type to contain additional components of its own. The extension adds no new reserved words; it simply gives expanded meaning to the existing reserved word `with`. For example:

```
subtype Name_Type is String(1..20);
type Employee is
  record
    Name           : Name_Type;
    Identification : Social_Security_Number;
  end record;
type Hourly is new Employee with
  record
    Pay_Rate     : Dollar;
    Hours_Worked : Hour;
  end record;
type Salaried is new Employee with
  record
    Monthly_Pay : Dollar;
  end record;
```

Both `Hourly` and `Salaried` workers inherit all of the operations of `Employee`, and these operations act on components that are common to `Employee`, `Hourly`, and `Salaried`: (`Name` and `Identification`). If there are any operations with parameter type or a return type `Employee`, those operations can serve as a signature for the derived types. To accomplish this the references to `Employee` in the operation specification must be marked as being available class-wide, that is, available to all types that are derived, directly or indirectly, from `Employee`. To mark the parameter type or return type as class-wide, a new attribute named `'Class` has been added to the language. For example:

```
procedure Put ( A_Person : in Employee'Class ) is
begin
  Text_IO.Put_Line ( A_Person.Name );
end Put;
```

Then all we have to do is replace all references to Employee types with references to things of type Hourly or Salaried.

```
Assembly_Person : Hourly;
  ...
Put ( Assembly_Person );
```

Inherited operations can also be overridden by declaring the operation for the child type (Hourly and/or Salaried).

The concept of a class-wide type is nothing new to Ada, it existed in Ada 83 where *universal_integer* and *universal_real* types were class-wide types for any integer or real literal. The extension that Ada 9X provides is to allow this same capability for user-defined types.

All employees expect to get pay for their services, so it is reasonable to assume that one of the operations associated with the type Employee might be:

```
function Pay ( A_Person : Employee ) return Dollar;
```

However, we know that the computation for pay is different for Hourly and Salaried employees, so we need separate function implementations for each of the two types. When computing a person's pay, we would like to choose the proper implementation implicitly based on the type of person passed as a parameter to the function Pay. This can be accomplished in Ada 9X using the concept of run-time polymorphism.

To implement run-time polymorphism, Ada 9X has the added reserved word tagged. A tagged type in Ada 9X is marked as follows:

```
type Employee is tagged
  record
    Name           : Name_Type;
    Identification : Social_Security_Number;
  end record;
```

All types derived, directly or indirectly, from a tagged type are also considered to be tagged types. With this addition the functions for computing pay for Hourly and Salaried types can be added:

```
function Pay ( A_Person : Hourly ) return Dollar;
function Pay ( A_Person : Salaried ) return Dollar;
```

With the implementation of these functions, we could, on pay day, go down the lists of employees (Hourly and Salaried) and be assured that the correct pay would be computed for each person.

Real-Time and Parallel Programming

Protected Record

The concept of shared variables presented in Ada 83 required a managing task to provide mutual exclusion. This has been a controversial approach. Ada 9X introduces the concept of a "protected" record to provide synchronized access to shared data objects. A protected record type is limited private and it contains not only a private section for component declaration but also protected operations. The operations take the form of a subprogram or an entry declaration. A protected record also has a body that contains the bodies of the protected operations. Protected operations have an implicit parameter, the protected record object itself, with **in** mode for functions and **in out** mode for procedures and entries. The following is an example of a generic queue package that serves as a buffer implemented using a protected record type.

```
generic
   type Element_Type is private;
package Protected_Queue_Package is
   type Buffer_Array is array(Positive range <>) of Element_Type;
   protected type Buffer (Maximum_Size : Natural ) is
     function Number_Held return Natural;
     procedure Initialize;
     entry Insert ( Item : in Element_Type );
     entry Remove ( Item : out Element_Type );
   private record
     Element : Buffer_Array( 1..Maximum_Size );
     Count,
     Front,
     Rear : Natural;
   end Buffer;
end Protected_Queue_Package;
package body Protected_Queue_Package is
   protected body Buffer is
     function Number_Held return Natural is
```

```
      begin
        return Count;
      end Number_Held;
      procedure Initialize is
      begin
        Front := 1;
        Rear := 1;
        Count := 0;
      end Initialize;
      entry Insert ( Item : in Element_Type )
        when Count < Maximum_Size is
      begin
        Front := Front mod Maximum_Size + 1;
        Element( Front ) := Item;
        Count := Count + 1;
      end Insert;
      entry Remove ( Item : out Element_Type )
        when Count > 0 is
      begin
        Rear := Rear mod Maximum_Size + 1;
        Item := Element( Rear );
        Count := Count - 1;
      end Remove;
    end Buffer;
  end Protected_Queue_Package;
```

Note that the code for the entry is not in an **accept** statement as is the case of a task body. The **entry** operation in a protected record uses the word **entry** and looks very much like a **procedure** operation except that it *must* have a barrier condition specified in the when.

Entry calls will be queued if the barrier condition is **False** or if a previous entry call to any of the entry's operations has not been completed. The barrier condition is rechecked for every entry call in the queue.

Requeue

The purpose of the **requeue** facility within the language is to provide a single statement that allows the programmer to write control algorithms for various specific control applications such as availability and race controls.

The `requeue` statement appears only with an entry body or an `accept` statement, and it allows the redirection of the present entry call to a new entry. The statement's form is:

```
requeue new_entry_name
```

or

```
requeue new_entry_name with abort
```

Once the entry call has been redirected to another entry queue, the entry body or `accept` statement that issued the requeue is exited.

There are some additional restrictions: (1) `requeue` must be within the body proper of an entry or an accept statement and not within any nested program unit; (2) if the requeue is within an entry body, it can only be requeued to a protected record entry; the `accept` can be requeued to either a task or a protected record entry.

If the `with abort` option is chosen, the abort is not deferred while the task is waiting on the new entry queue.

Delay

The `delay` statement has been enhanced to optionally include the new reserved word `until`. If the `until` option is used, the task is delayed until a specific time based on the type `Calendar.Time`. These options allow the programmer to specify the delay to be until a given point in time or to specify how long the delay is to last. The duration expression of the latter form must be of type `Standard.Duration`.

Programming in the Large

The separate compilation features of Ada 83 enhance the ability to break large projects into smaller separate units. Once the interfaces are established and the subprogram or task bodies can be marked as `is separate`, the parent unit can be compiled. The bodies can be developed and compiled one at a time or concurrently by different teams. The bodies are simply marked as `separate`, and the bodies' ancestors are listed. If there are no changes in the parent unit, it never needs to be recompiled, although the separate child can be compiled many times during development and testing; we need only to relink after each child compilation.

Although this system has worked well for many large programming projects, there is one problem that reduces the developer's freedom of naming the children. The name space for separately compiled units within a given Ada 83 library is flat. The following example skeleton program demonstrates the problem.

```
procedure S is
  procedure E is separate;
  procedure P is separate;
begin
  ...
end S;
```

At this point S is placed in the library name space.

```
separate (S)
procedure E is
begin
  ...
end E;
```

The library name space now has two names: S and E.

```
separate (S)
procedure P is
  procedure E is separate;
begin
  ...
end P;
```

P is added to the library name space, giving us S, E, and P.

```
separate (S.P)
procedure E is
begin
  ...
end E;
```

Since the Ada 83 name space is flat, when we go to add the second E to the library we run into a conflict that cannot be resolved without giving one of the Es a new name.

The obvious solution to the problem is to have the name space in the library reflect the full name of a separately compiled subprogram. Within a given library, Ada 9X has dropped the requirement that subunits have distinct simple identifiers. The new system requires only that the fully expanded name of each subunit be unique.

While this expanded name space is an improvement, the combination of overloaded subprogram names and the use of separate compilation is still not possible, as shown in the following example:

```
procedure Main is
  procedure Get ( An_Item : out Integer ) is separate;
```

```
    procedure Get ( An_Item : out Float ) is separate;
begin
    ...
end Main;
```

Even though there is no apparent ambiguity in this example, the hierarchical name space in the library can't solve this problem, because the names do not reflect the difference in the types of the parameters.

In addition, this same naming convention is possible for package library units. Thus, a package library unit can have child units. It is possible to create entire hierarchies of library units. The package name of the child unit simply reflects its ancestry in a manner similar to but not the same as subprogram units. For example:

```
package Grandparent is
    ...
end Grandparent;
package Grandparent.Parent is
    ...
end Grandparent.Parent;
package Grandparent.Parent.Child_1 is
    ...
end Grandparent.Parent.Child_1;
package Grandparent.Parent.Child_2 is
    ...
end Grandparent.Parent.Child_2;
```

Context clauses can be expanded using the same naming convention, as in:

```
with Grandparent.Parent;
```

This context clause implies the inclusion of the `Grandparent` and `Parent` packages, but not any of the child units.

Thus, Ada 9X allows the library name space to be made up of hierarchies, a forest of trees reflecting the parent-child relationships.

A program in Ada 83 consisted of all library units that were loaded and elaborated together. The library name space in Ada 9X is further enhanced by allowing programs to be "partitioned" into separate units but still preserve the safety afforded by strong typing. Partitioned programs will be able to communicate with one another using special shared packages. Each partition can be separately and incrementally developed, updated, and loaded. A program in Ada 9X is thus defined as one or more separately elaborated partitions.

Specialized Needs Annex

The designers of Ada 9X have recognized that there are special, specific needs for various applications. Instead of cluttering up the language with all these application specifics, Ada 9X allows annexes to the system. The "core" language, as it has been dubbed, defines all syntax of the language and the minimum semantics. Optional annexes are allowed in seven specific applications areas: Systems Programming, Real-Time Systems, Distributed Systems, Language Interfaces, Information Systems, Safety and Security, and Numerics. None of these annexes introduces any new syntax; instead they include pragmas and packages that address the special needs of each individual group.

Systems Programming

The rationale for a systems programming and embedded computer applications annex is to allow software to interface directly with hardware devices. This does introduce nonportability, but that is unavoidable when one is dealing directly with a specific machine. The annex introduces standard package specifications for `Interrupt_Management`, user-defined finalization through `Finalization_Support`, named unsigned integer types, plus operations including treatment as a sequence of bits, and `Task_Identification`. Also included are pragmas for shared variable control.

Real-Time Systems

Any implementation of the real-time systems annex must conform to the systems programming annex. As the annex name implies, this section is intended for real-time system software. One of the major thrusts of this annex is the handling of task entry call-queuing priorities. It also includes a package specification called `Cpu_Time_Accounting` and one for `Monotomic_Time`. The latter of these was, at the time of this writing, incomplete and still subject to major changes. Also included is a pragma to suppress all run-time checks.

Distributed Systems

Since Ada 9X will allow a program to be partitioned, it seems only natural that the partitions should be allowed to run on a distributed system. These partitions can be elaborated independently, can communicate, and can then eventually terminate. The purpose of this annex is to establish a standard, portable approach to distributed system execution. The package `Communication_Support` serves as a standard interface to the user-provided communications subsystem.

Language Interfaces

The language interfaces annex is intended to help interface with external system, files, and database system. In recognition of the fact that many of these applications are written in COBOL or C, help is provided to interface specifically with these two languages.

Information Systems

The information systems annex has several subsections:
- Decimal arithmetic and representation

- Character manipulation

- String handling

- Input-output

Decimal types are defined in the "core" language as part of the fixed-point types. Decimal types can be distinguished from general fixed-point types because they include not only a delta specification but also a digits specification. For example:

```
type Money is delta 0.01 digits 8 range 0.0..99_999.99;
```

Unlike general fixed-point types whose computational results are approximations, decimal computations must be exact.

Safety and Security

At the time of this writing, this section merely addresses issues of concern to two communities: safety-critical and trusted systems. The annex notes three classes of safety-critical usage: untrusted, trusted, and trusted applications programs. Furthermore, all issues may not be addressed in the final draft of this annex.

Numerics

At the time of this writing, the section on numerics is not in its final form. Two major sections are identified: semantics of floating- and fixed-point arithmetic and functions both elementary and primitive. Addressed are such issues as floating-point machine and model numbers and their attributes and accuracy of operations. In the section on fixed-point, arithmetic issues concerning type declarations, accuracy of operations, and attributes are covered. The section on elementary functions includes the specifications for the generic package Generic_Elementary_Functions. A list of required attributes is provided in the section on primitive functions.

Glossary

The following glossary is taken, with permission of the Ada Joint Program Office (OUSDRE), U.S. Department of Defense, from the "Reference Manual for the Ada® Programming Language," (1983), Appendix A and includes additional items, which are marked with an asterisk.

Abstraction* Our view of an entity in the problem space; in fact, everything we know is an abstraction. All abstractions are part of a ladder of abstraction in which given levels are implemented at a lower level.

Accept statement See *entry.*

Access type A value of an access type (an access value) is either a null value or a value that designates an object created by an allocator. The designated object can be read and updated via the access value. The definition of an access type specifies the type of the objects designated by values of the access type. See also *collection.*

Actual parameter See *parameter.*

Aggregate The evaluation of an aggregate yields a value of a composite type. The value is specified by giving the value of each of the components. Either positional association or named association may be used to indicate which value is associated with which component.

Allocator The evaluation of an allocator creates an object and returns a new access value, which designates the object.

Array type A value of an array type consists of components that are all of the same subtype (and hence, of the same type). Each component is uniquely distinguished by an index (for a one-dimensional array) or by a sequence of indices (for a multidimensional array). Each index must be a value of a discrete type and must lie in the correct index range.

Assignment Assignment is the operation that replaces the current value of a variable by a new value. On the left, an assignment statement specifies a variable; on the right, it specifies an expression whose value is the new value of the variable.

Attribute   The evaluation of an attribute yields a predefined characteristic of a named entity. Some attributes are functions.

Block statement   A block statement is a single statement that may contain a sequence of statements. It may also include a declarative part and exception handlers whose effects are local to the block statement.

Body   A body defines the execution of a subprogram, package, or task. A body stub is a form of body that indicates that this execution is defined in a separately compiled subunit.

Character*   Any of the ASCII symbols that are used to form source Ada programs or are used as data. *Graph characters* have a visible (humanly readable) representation; *control characters* have visible attributes that are implementation defined. Source programs are built from the graphic character set plus control characters, which indicate passage to a new line.

Collection   A collection is the entire set of objects created by evaluation of allocators for an access type.

Compatible*   In regard to constraints, a declaration is compatible if its constraints satisfy (are within the limits of) the parent or base type.

Compilation unit   A compilation unit is the declaration or the body of a program unit, which is presented for compilation as an independent text. It may be preceded by a context clause, which names other compilation units upon which it depends by means of one or more `with` clauses.

Component   A component is a value that is a part of a larger value or an object that is part of a larger object.

Composite type   A composite type is one whose values have components. There are two kinds of composite types: array types and record types.

Constant   See *object*.

Constraint   A constraint determines a subset of the values of a type. A value in that subset satisfies the constraint.

Context clause   See *compilation unit*.

Conversion*   The process of translating one type to another.

Declaration   A declaration associates an identifier (or some other notation) with an entity. This association is, in effect, within a region of text called the *scope of the declaration*. Within the scope of a declaration, there are places where it is possible to use the identifier to refer to the associated declared entity. At such places the identifier is a *simple name of the entity;* the name denotes the associated entity.

Declarative part   A declarative part is a sequence of declarations. It may also contain related information such as subprogram bodies and representation clauses.

Denote   See *declaration.*

Derived type   A derived type is a type whose operations and values are replicas of those of an existing type. The existing type is the *parent type* of the derived type.

Designate   See *access type,* and *task.*

Direct visibility   See *visibility.*

Disambiguation*   The process of selecting one named entity from any number of overloaded names.

Discrete type   A discrete type is a type that has an ordered set of distinct values. The discrete types are *enumeration* and *integer* types. Discrete types are used for indexing and iteration and for choices in `case` statements and record variants.

Discriminant   A discriminant is a distinguished component of an object or value of a record type. The subtypes of other components, or even their presence or absence, may depend on the value of the discriminant.

Discriminant constraint   A discriminant constraint on a record type or private type specifies a value for each discriminant of the type.

Elaboration   The elaboration of a declaration is the process by which the declaration achieves its effect (such as creating an object); execution.

Entry   An entry is used for communication between tasks. Externally, an entry is called just as a subprogram is called; its internal behavior is defined by one or more `accept` statements specifying the actions to be performed when the entry is called.

Enumeration type   An enumeration type is a discrete type whose values are represented by enumeration literals, which are given explicitly in the type declaration. These enumeration literals are either identifiers or character literals.

Error*   A condition that violates some syntactic or semantic rule or a logical condition. Errors may be classified into three categories: those that must be detected at compilation time (a violation of a language rule), those that must be detected at execution time (by raising an exception), and violations of language rules that must be obeyed by all Ada programs but which need not be checked by an Ada compiler. A program that violates such rules is considered *erroneous,* and the effect of the program is unpredictable.

Evaluation   The evaluation of an expression is the process by which the value of the expression is computed. This process occurs during program execution.

Exception   An exception is an error situation that may arise during program execution. To raise an exception is to abandon normal program execution to signal that the error has taken place. An exception handler is a portion of program text specifying a response to the exception. Execution of such a program text is called handling the exception.

Expanded name   An expanded name denotes an entity that is declared immediately within some construct. An expanded name has the form of a selected component. The prefix denotes the construct (a program unit or a `block`, `loop`, or `accept` statement), and the selector is the simple name of the entity.

Expression   An expression defines the computation of a value.

Fixed-point type   See *real type.*

Floating-point type   See *real type.*

Formal parameter   See *parameter.*

Function   See *subprogram.*

Generic unit   A generic unit is a template for a set of subprograms or for a set of packages. A subprogram or package created using the template is called an instance of the generic unit. A generic instantiation is the kind of declaration that creates an instance. A generic unit is written as a subprogram or package with the specification prefixed by a generic formal part which may declare generic formal parameters. A generic formal parameter is either a type, a subprogram, or an object. A generic unit is one of the kinds of program unit.

Handler   See *exception.*

Identifier*   One of the basic lexical elements of the language. An identifier is used as the name of an entity or as a reserved word.

Index   See *array type.*

Index constraint   An index constraint for an array type specifies the lower and upper bounds for each index range of the array type.

Indexed component   An indexed component denotes a component in an array. It is a form of name that contains expressions that specify the values of the indices of the array component. An indexed component may also denote an entry in a family of entries.

Instance   See *generic unit.*

Integer type   An integer type is a discrete type whose values represent all integer numbers within a specific range.

Lexical element   A lexical element is an identifier, a literal, a delimiter, or a comment.

Library unit*   A compilation unit that is not a subunit of another unit. Library units belong to a program library.

Limited type   A limited type is a type for which neither assignment nor the predefined comparison for equality is implicitly declared. All task types are limited. A private type can be defined as limited. An equality operator can be explicitly declared for a limited type.

Literal   A literal represents a value literally, that is, by means of letters and other characters. A literal is either a numeric literal, an enumeration literal, a character literal, or a string literal.

Mode   See *parameter.*

Model number   A model number is an exactly representable value of a real type. Operations of a real type are defined in terms of operations on the model numbers of the type. The properties of the model numbers and of their operations are the minimal properties preserved by all implementations of the real type.

Name   A name is a construct that stands for an entity. It is said that the name denotes the entity, and that the entity is the meaning of the name. See also *declaration* and *prefix.*

Named association   A named association specifies the association of an item with one or more positions in a list by naming the positions.

Number*   A literal of the type *universal_integer* or *universal_real.* A *named number* is a constant number to which the identifier given in the number declaration may refer.

Object   An object contains a value. A program creates an object either by elaborating an object declaration or by evaluating an allocator. The declaration or allocator specifies a type for the object; the object can only contain values of that type.

Operation   An operation is an elementary action associated with one or more types. It is either implicitly declared by the declaration of the type, or it is a subprogram that has a parameter or result of the type.

Operator   An operator is an operation with one or two operands. A unary operator is written before an operand; a binary operator is written between two operands. This notation is a special kind of function call. An operator can be declared as a function. Many operators are implicitly declared by the declaration of a type. For example, most type declarations imply the declaration of the equality operator for values of the type.

Overloading   An identifier can have several alternative meanings at a given point in the program text; this property is called overloading. For example, an overloaded enumeration literal can be an identifier that appears in the definitions of two or more enumeration types. The effective meaning of an overloaded identifier is determined by the context. Subprograms, aggregates, allocators, and string literals can also be overloaded.

Package   A package specifies a group of logically related entities, such as types, objects of those types, and subprograms with parameters of those types. It is written as a package declaration and a package body. The package declaration has a visible part, which contains the declarations of all entities that can be explicitly used outside the package. It may also have a private part, which contains structural details that complete the specification of the visible entities but are irrelevant to the user of the package. The package body contains implementations of subprograms (and possibly tasks as other packages) that have been specified in the package declaration. A package is one of the kinds of program unit.

Parameter   A parameter is one of the named entities associated with a subprogram, entry, or generic unit, and used to communicate with the corresponding subprogram body, accept statement, or generic body. A formal parameter is an identifier that denotes the named entity within the body. An actual parameter is the particular entity associated with the corresponding formal parameter by a subprogram call, entry call, or generic instantiation. The mode of a formal parameter specifies whether the associated actual parameter supplies a value for the formal parameter, or the formal supplies a value for the actual parameter, or both. The association of actual parameters with formal parameters can be specified by named associations, by positional associations, or by a combination of these.

Parent type   See *derived type*.

Positional association   A positional association specifies the association of an item with a position in a list by using the same position in the text to specify the item.

Pragma   A pragma conveys information to the compiler.

Prefix   A prefix is used as the first part of certain kinds of names. A prefix is either a function call or a name.

Private part   See *package.*

Private type   A private type is a type whose structure and set of values are clearly defined but not directly available to the user of the type. A private type is known only by its discriminants (if any) and by the set of operations defined for it. A private type and its applicable operations are defined in the visible part of a package or in a generic formal part. Assignment, equality, and inequality are also defined for private types, unless the private type is limited.

Procedure   See *subprogram.*

Program   A program is composed of a number of compilation units, one of which is a subprogram called the main program. Execution of the program consists of execution of the main program, which may invoke subprograms declared in the other compilation units of the program.

Program library*   Part of the APSE recognized by an Ada compiler and which serves as a collection of compilation units.

Program unit   A program unit is a generic unit, package, subprogram, or task unit.

Qualified expression   A qualified expression is an expression preceded by an indication of type or subtype. Such qualification is used when its absence causes the expression to be ambiguous. A program developer may have to qualify an expression as a consequence of overloading, for example.

Raising an exception   See *exception.*

Range   A range is a contiguous set of values of a scalar type. A range is specified by giving the lower and upper bounds for the values. A value in the range is said to belong to the range.

Range constraint   A range constraint of a type specifies a range and thereby determines values of the type that belong to the range.

Real type   A real type is a type whose values represent approximations to the real numbers. There are two kinds of real types: fixed-point types are specified by absolute error bound, and floating-point types are specified by a relative error bound expressed as a number of significant decimal digits.

Record type   A value of a record type consists of components that are usually of different types or subtypes. For each component of a record value or record object, the definition of the record type specifies an identifier that uniquely determines the component within the record.

Renaming declaration   A renaming declaration declares another name for an entity.

Rendezvous   A rendezvous is the interaction that occurs between two parallel tasks when one task has called an entry of the other task, and a corresponding `accept` statement is being executed by the other task on behalf of the calling task.

Representation clause   A representation clause directs the compiler in the selection of the mapping of a type, an object, or a task onto features of the underlying machine that executes a program. In some cases, representation clauses completely specify the mapping; in other cases, they provide criteria for choosing a mapping.

Satisfy   See *constraint* and *subtype*.

Scalar type   An object or value of a scalar type does not have components. A scalar type is either a discrete type or a real type. The values of a scalar type are ordered.

Scope   See *declaration*.

Selected component   A selected component is a name consisting of a prefix and an identifier called the selector. Selected components are used to denote record components, entries, and objects designated by access value. They are also used as expanded names.

Selector   See *selected component*.

Semantics*   The meaning of a given structure of entity.

Simple name   See *declaration* and *name*.

Statement   A statement specifies one or more actions to be performed during the execution of a program.

Subcomponent   A subcomponent is either a component or a component of another subcomponent.

Subprogram   A subprogram is either a procedure or a function. A procedure specifies a sequence of actions and is invoked by a procedure call statement. A function specifies a sequence of actions and also returns a value called the result; therefore, a function call is an expression. A subprogram is written as a subprogram declaration—which specifies its name, formal parameters, and the result if it is a function—and a subprogram body, which specifies the sequence of actions. The subprogram call specifies the actual parameters that are to be associated with the formal parameters. A subprogram is one of the kinds of program units.

Subtype   A subtype of a type characterizes a subset of the values of the type. The subset is determined by a constraint on the type. Each value in the set of values of a subtype belongs to the subtype and satisfies the constraint determining the subtype.

Subunit   See *body*.

Syntax*   The rules of the language (the grammar) that defines how strings are put together to produce well-formed source programs. Appendix E provides the syntax charts for the language; syntax charts provide a graphic representation of these rules.

Task   A task operates in parallel with other parts of the program. It is written as a task specification—which specifies the name of the task and the names and formal parameters of its entries—and a task body, which defines its execution. A task unit is one of the kinds of program unit. A task type is a type that permits the subsequent declaration of any number of similar tasks of the type. A value of a task type designates a task.

Type   A type characterizes both a set of values and a set of operations applicable to those values. A type definition is a language construct that defines a type. A particular type is either an access type, or array type, a private type, a record type, a scalar type, or a task type.

use clause   A **use** clause achieves direct visibility of declarations that appear in the visible parts of named packages.

Variable   See *object*.

Variant part   A variant part of a record specifies alternative record components, depending on a discriminant of the record. Each value of the discriminant establishes a particular alternative of the variant part.

Visibility   At a given point in a program text, the declaration of an entity with a certain identifier is visible if the entity is an acceptable meaning for an occurrence at that point of the identifier. The declaration is visible by selection at the place of the selector in a selected component or at the place of the name in a named association. Otherwise, if the identifier alone has that meaning, the declaration is directly visible.

Visible part   See *package*.

with clause   See *compilation unit*.

Notes

Package 1: Introducing Software Engineering with Ada

Chapter 1: Introduction

[1] Dijkstra, E. W. October 1972. The Humble Programmer (Turing Award Lecture). *Communications of the ACM* 15(10):861. Copyright 1972, Association for Computing Machinery, Inc. Reprinted by permission.

[2] Fisher, D. A. June 1976. *A Common Programming Language for the Department of Defense—Background and Technical Requirements.* Institute for Defense Analysis, Report P-1191.

[3] *See also* Hoare, C. A. R. Professionalism (Invited talk given at BCS—81, British Computing Society, July 1, 1981).

[4] Wulf, W. A. 1977. Languages and Structured Programs. In R. Yeh, ed. *Current Trends in Computer Programming* Vol. 1, p. 33. Englewood Cliffs, NJ: Prentice-Hall, Inc. Reprinted by permission of Prentice-Hall, Inc., Englewood Cliffs, NJ, and W. A. Wulf, Tartan Laboratories, Pittsburgh, PA.

[5] Dijkstra, op. cit., p. 863.

[6] Fisher, op. cit., p. 2.

[7] Ibid., pp. 2–3.

[8] Devlin, M. T. 1980. *Introducing Ada: Problems and Potentials.* USAF Satellite Control Facility (unpublished report). p. 2.

[9] Ibid., p. 2.

[10] Wulf, op. cit., p. 34.

[11] *See also* Dijkstra, E. W. September 1965. Programming Considered as a Human Activity (Paper presented to the International Federation of Information Processing Conference, New York). p. 6.

[12] Brooks, F. 1975. *The Mythical Man Month.* Reading, MA: Addison-Wesley. p. 94. Reprinted with permission.

[13] Pyle, I. C. 1985. *The Ada Programming Language: A Guide For Programmers.* 2nd ed, p. ix. Englewood Cliffs, NJ: Prentice-Hall, Inc. Reprinted by permission of Prentice-Hall, Inc., Englewood Cliffs, NJ.

[14] Wulf, op. cit., p. 60.

[15] Fisher, op. cit., p. 5.

[16] Ibid., p. 3.

[17] W. A. Whitaker, private communication.

[18] Fisher, op. cit., p.6.

[19] Whitaker, W. A. February 1978. The U. S. Department of Defense Common High Order Language Effort. *SIGPLAN Notices* 13(2):2.

[20] Fisher, op. cit., pp. 21–23.

[21] Whitaker, High Order Language Effort, p. 4.

[22] Department of Defense. July 29, 1975. *Department of Defense Requirements for High Order Programming Languages—"STRAWMAN."* Washington, D.C.: Government Printing Office.

[23] Department of Defense. August 1975. *Department of Defense Requirements for High Order Programming Languages—"WOODENMAN."* Washington, D.C.: Government Printing Office.

[24] Department of Defense. June 1976. *Department of Defense Requirements for High Order Programming Languages—"TINMAN."* Washington, D.C.: Government Printing Office.

[25] *See also* Amoroso, S.; Wegner, P.; Morris, D.; and White, D. January 14, 1977. Language Evaluation Coordinating Committee Report to the High Order Language Working Group. High Order Language Working Group. Washington, D.C.: Government Printing Office.

[26] Whitaker, High Order Language Effort, pp. 7–8.

[27] Department of Defense. January 14, 1977. *Department of Defense Requirements for High Order Programming Languages—"IRONMAN."* Washington, D.C.: Government Printing Office.

[28] Carlson, W. E.; Druffel, L. E.; Fisher, D. A.; and Whitaker, W. A. October 1980. Introducing Ada (Paper presented at ACM-80). p. 264. Copyright 1972, Association for Computing Machinery, Inc. Reprinted by permission.

[29] Carlson, W. E. March 1980. Ada: A Standard Language for Defense Systems. *Signal.* p. 25. Reprinted by permission from SIGNAL, the official journal of the Armed Forces Communications and Electronics Association, Copyright 1980.

[30] Department of Defense. July 1977. *Department of Defense Requirements for High Order Programming Languages—Revised "IRONMAN."* Washington, D.C.: Government Printing Office.

[31] Buxton, J. N.; Druffel, L. E.; and Standish, T. A. July/August 1981. Recollections on the History of Ada Environments. *Ada Letters.* 1(1):I-1.16. With permission from *Ada Letters,* publication of Ada Tech.

[32] Department of Defense. July 1978. *Department of Defense Requirements for the Programming Environment for the Common High Order Language—"SANDMAN."* Washington, D.C.: Government Printing Office.

[33] Department of Defense. July 1978. *Department of Defense Requirements for the Programming Environment for the Common High Order Language—"PEBBLEMAN."* Washington, D.C.: Government Printing Office.

[34] Department of Defense. June 1978. *Department of Defense Requirements for High Order Programming Languages—"STEELMAN."* Washington, D.C.: Government Printing Office.

[35] *See also* Moore, D. L. 1977. *Ada, Countess of Lovelace, Byron's Legitimate Daughter.* New York: Harper & Row.

[36] Carlson, Druffel, Fisher, and Whitaker, op. cit., p. 265.

[37] Cohen, P. M. July/August 1981. From HOLWG to AJPO-Ada in Transition. *Ada Letters* 1(1):I-1.23. With permission from *Ada Letters,* a publication of Ada Tech.

[38] Foss, D. J., and Hakes, D. T. 1978. *Psycholinguistics: An Introduction to the Psychology of Language.* Englewood Cliffs, NJ: Prentice-Hall, Inc. p. 385. Reprinted by permission of Prentice-Hall, Inc., Engle wood Cliffs, NJ.

[39] Fisher, op. cit., p. 8.

[40] Reifer, D. December 1987. Ada's Impact: A Quantitative Assessment. *Proceedings of ACM SIGADA International Conference.* New York: Association of Computing Machinery Press.

[41] Reifer, D. December 1990. Softcost-Ada: User Experiences and Lessons Learned at the Age of Three. *Proceedings of TRI-ADA '90 Conference.* New York: Association of Computing Machinery Press.

[42] *Foundation for Competitiveness and Profitability: FS2000 System, Rational, and Ada.* 1992. Santa Clara, CA: Rational.

[43] McGarry, F,; and Waligora, S. December 1991. Experiments in Software Engineering Technology. *Proceedings of the 16th Annual Software Engineering Workshop.* Baltimore: University Park Press.

[44] Tanaka, K. 1991. Using Ada at NTT. *Ada Letters* 11(1).

[45] Doscher, H. 1990. An Ada Case Study in Cellular Telephone Testing Tools. In B. Lynch, ed. *Ada Experiences and Prospects, Proceedings of Ada-Europe '90.* New York: Cambridge University Press.

[46] Hines, K. December 1990. Ada Impact on a Second Generation Project. *Proceedings of TRI-ADA '90 Conference.* New York: Association of Computing Machinery Press.

[47] Loesh, R.; Conover, R.A.; and Malhotra, S. November 1990. JPL's Real-Time Weather Processor Project (RWP): Metrics and Observations at System Completion Build3. *Proceedings of the 16th Annual Software Engineering Workshop.* Baltimore: University Park Press.

Chapter 2: Software Engineering

[1] Ross, D. T.; Goodenough, J. B.; and Irvine, C. A. May 1975. Software Engineering: Process, Principles, and Goals. *Computer* 8(5):65.

[2] Ibid.

[3] Ibid.

[4] Ibid., p. 66.

[5] Ibid.

[6] Ibid.

[7] Devlin, op, cit., p. 5.

[8] Ross, Goodenough, and Irvine, op. cit., p. 67.

[9] Ibid.

[10] Ibid.

[11] Ibid., p. 66.

[12] Ibid., p. 67

[13] Yourdon, E., and Constantine, L. 1979. *Structured Design: Fundamentals of a Discipline of Computer Program and System Design.* Englewood Cliffs, NJ: Prentice-Hall, Inc. p. 85. Reprinted by permission of Prentice-Hall, Inc., Englewood Cliffs, NJ.

[14] Ibid., p. 106.

[15] Ross, Goodenough, and Irvine, op. cit., p. 67.

[16] Ibid.

[17] Ibid.

[18] *See also* Miller, G. A. March 1956. The Magical Number Seven, Plus or Minus Two. *The Psychological Review* 63(2).

[19] Yourdon and Constantine, op. cit., p. 69.

[20] Ibid. *See also* Department of Defense, Ada Joint Program Office. 1982. "METHODMAN."

[21] Sommerville, I. 1992. *Software Engineering,* 4th ed. Reading, MA: Addison-Wesley. p. 69.

[22] Yourdon and Constantine, op. cit., p. 246.

[23] *See also* Jackson, M. 1975. *Principles of Program Design.* New York: Academic Press.

[24] *See also* Parnas, D. December 1972. On the Criteria to Be Used in Decomposing Systems into Modules. *Communications of the ACM* 15(12).

[25] *See also* Ross, D. T., and Schoman, J. R. January 1977. Structured Analysis for Requirements Definition. *IEEE Transactions on Software Engineering* SE-3(1).

[26] *See also* Gane, C. 1979. *Structured System Analysis: Tools and Techniques.* Englewood Cliffs, NJ: Prentice-Hall, Inc.

[27] *See also* LaBudde, K. P. 1987. *Structured Programming Concepts.* New York: McGraw-Hill.

[28] Yourdon, E. 1979. *Structured Walkthroughs,* 2nd ed. Englewood Cliffs, NJ: Prentice-Hall.

[29] Wegner, P. April 1980. The Ada Programming Language and Environment. *SIGSOFT Software Engineering Notes.*

[30] *See also* Pyle, I. C. May 1991. Real-World Software Engineering. *Software Engineering Journal* 6(3).

[31] *See also* Orr, K.; Gane, C.; and Yourdon, E. April 1989. Methodology: The Experts Speak. *Byte* 14(4).

[32] *See also* King, D. 1988. *Creating Effective Software: Computer Program Design Using the Jackson Methodology.* Englewood Cliffs, NJ: Yourdon Press.

[33] *See also* King, M. J. 1985. *Program Design Using JSP: A Practical Introduction.* New York: Wiley.

[34] *See also* Downs, E. 1988. *Structured System Analysis and Design Method: Application and Context.* New York: Prentice-Hall, Inc.

Chapter 3: Object-Oriented Design

[1] Ledgard, H., and Marcotty, M. 1981. *The Programming Language Landscape.* Chicago: Science Research Associates. p. 166.

[2] Abbott, R. November 1983. Program Design by Informal English Descriptions. *Communications of the ACM* 26(11).

[3] Gane, C., and T. Sarson. July 1977. Structured Systems Analysis: Tools and Techniques. *Computer* 10(7).

[4] *See also* Booch, G. March 1986. Object-Oriented Development. *IEEE Transactions on Software Engineering* 12(3).

[5] *See also* Booch, G. 1990. On the Concepts of Objected-Oriented Design. In P. A. Ng and R. T. Yeh, eds. *Modern Software Engineering: Foundations and Current Prospectives.* New York: Van Nostrand Reinhold Co. pp. 165–204.

[6] *See also* Booch, G. September 1992. The Booch Method Notation, Part I. *Computer Language* 9(9).

[7] *See also* Booch, G. October 1992. The Booch Method Notation, Part II. *Computer Language* 9(10).

[8] *See also* Gane, C. 1979. *Structured System Analysis: Tools and Techniques.* Englewood Cliffs, NJ: Prentice-Hall.

Chapter 4: An Overview of the Language

[1] Department of Defense, Ada Joint Program Office. 1983. *Reference Manual for the Ada Programming Language (ANSI/MIL-STD-1815A).* Washington, D.C.: Government Printing Office.

[2] Booch, G. March/April 1982. Object-Oriented Design. *Ada Letters* 1(3):64.

[3] Booch, G. September 1981. Describing Software Design with Ada. *SIGPLAN Notices* 16(9).

[4] *See also* Booch, G. September 1992. The Booch Method Notation, Part I. op. cit.

[5] *See also* Booch, G. October 1992. The Booch Method Notation, Part II. op. cit.

Package 2: Data Structures

[1] With permission from Hoare, C. A. R. Notes on Data Structuring. 1972. In Dahl, O. J.; Dijkstra, E. W.; and Hoare, C. A. R. *Structured Programming.* London: Academic Press. p. 83. Copyright Academic Press Inc. (London).

Chapter 6: Data Abstraction and Ada's Types

[1] Ichbiah, J.; Barnes, J.; and Firth, R. 1980. *Ada Programming Course.* La Cella Saint Cloud, France: ALSYS. p. 38.

[2] Ibid., p. 131.

Package 3: Algorithms and Control

[1] Shakespeare, W. *Hamlet,* act 3, sc. 2, line 17.

Chapter 9: Expressions and Statements

[1] Fisher, op. cit.

[2] Boehm, C., and Jocopini, G. May 1966. Flow Diagrams, Turing Machines, and Languages with Only Two Formation Rules. *Communications of the ACM.* pp. 366–371. Copyright 1966, Association for Computing Machinery, Inc. Reprinted by permission.

Package 4: Packaging Concepts

[1] Hofstadter, D. R. *Godel, Escher, Bach: An Eternal Golden Braid.* New York: Basic Books, Inc. Copyright 1979. By permission of Basic Books, Inc., Publishers, New York.

Package 5: Concurrent Real-Time Processing

[1] Shakespeare, W. *Macbeth,* act 1, sc. 7, line 1.

Chapter 14: Tasks

[1] Hoare, C. A. R. 1989. Communicating Sequential Processes. In C. B. Jones, ed. *Essays in Computing Science.* New York: Prentice Hall. pp. 259–288.

Package 6: Systems Development

[1] Gall, J. *Systemantics: How Systems Work and Especially How They Fail.* New York: TIMES BOOKS. Copyright 1975. Reprinted by permission of TIMES BOOKS, a division of Quadrangle/The New York Times Book Co., Inc.

Chapter 19: The Software Life Cycle with Ada

[1] Wheeler, T. J. 1982. *Embedded Systems Design with Ada as the System Design Language.* Ft. Monmouth, NJ: Army CORADCOM.

[2] *PDL/ADA: DSM Project's Ada-Program Design Language Reference Manual.* April 22, 1981. IBM Federal Systems Division.

[3] Hart, H. July/August 1982. Ada for Design: An Approach for Transitioning Industry Software Developers. *Ada Letters* 2(1):50.

Chapter 20: Programming in the Large

[1] Bryan, D. January/February 1987. Dear Ada. *Ada Letters* 7(1).

[2] Mendal, G. O. January/February 1988. Three Reasons to Avoid the Use Clause. *Ada Letters* 8(1).

[3] Rosen, J. P. November/December 1987. In Defense of the "use" clause. *Ada Letters* 7(7).

[4] Ichbiah, Barnes, and Firth, op. cit., p. 212.

[5] Racine, R. May/June 1988. Why the Use Clause is Beneficial. *Ada Letters* 8(3).

Appendix F: Ada 9X

[1] United States Department of Defense. March 1992. *Ada 9X Project Report/Ada 9X Mapping Document, Volume I, Mapping Rationale.* Washington D.C.: Office of the Under Secretary of Defense for Acquisition. Copyright 1993, Intermetrics, Inc. Reprinted by permission.

[2] United States Department of Defense. December 1991. *Ada 9X Project Report/Ada 9X Mapping Document, Volume II, Mapping Specifications.* Washington D.C.: Office of the Under Secretary of Defense for Acquisition. Copyright 1993, Intermetrics, Inc. Reprinted by permission.

[3] United States Department of Defense. March 1992. *Ada 9X Project Report/Ada 9X Mapping Document, Volume II, Mapping Specifications, Annexes.* Washington D.C.: Office of the Under Secretary of Defense for Acquisition. Copyright 1993, Intermetrics, Inc. Reprinted by permission.

[4] Burns, A., and Davies, G. L. November/December 1992. Ada 9X Protected Types in Pascal-FC. *ACM Ada Letters* XII(6).

[5] Wrege, D. E. November/December 1992. Protected Kernels and Ada 9X Real-Time Facilities. *ACM Ada Letters* XII(6).

[6] Burns, A., and Wellings, A. J. November/December 1992. In Support of the Ada 9X Real-Time Facilities. *ACM Ada Letters* XII(6).

[7] Rosen, J. P. November 1992. What Orientation Should Ada Objects Take? *Communications of the ACM* 35(11).

[8] Anderson, C. November 1992. *Ada 9X Project Management. Communications of the ACM* 35(11).

[9]   Taft, S. T. November 1992. Ada 9X: A Technical Summary. *Communications of the ACM* 35(11).

[10] Ploedereder, E. November/December 1992. How to Program in Ada 9X, Using Ada 83. *ACM Ada Letters* XII(6).

[11] Booch, G. 1991. *Object-Oriented Design with Applications.* Redwood City, CA: Benjamin/Cummings Publishing Company, Inc.

[12] United States Department of Defense. February 1993. *Introducing Ada 9X.* Washington D.C.: Office of the Under Secretary of Defense for Acquisition.

Bibliography

General References

A Common Language for Computers. March 23, 1981. *Business Week.* pp. 84B–84E.

Ada Course Notes. 1980. Atlanta: Georgia Institute of Technology.

Ada—A Report to the Department of Industry. May 1979. United Kingdom: Department of Industry.

General Trends in the DoD. January 1981. Briefing to Automatic Data Processing Single Managers Conference. Colorado Springs, Colorado: USAF Academy.

Proceedings of the ACM-SIGPLAN Symposium on the Ada Programming Language. December 1980. New York: Association of Computing Machinery Press.

Proceedings of the Ada Debut. Defense Advanced Research Projects Agency. September 1980. Report AD-A095 569/0. Washington, DC: Government Printing Office.

Barnes, J. 1980. An Overview of Ada. *Software Practices and Experience* 10.

Barnes, J. 1989. *Programming in Ada.* 3rd ed. Reading, MA: Addison-Wesley.

Booch, G. January 7, 1981. Ada Promotes Software Reliability with Pascal-like Simplicity. *EDN.*

Booch, G. November 1981. Software Engineering with Ada. *Proceedings 15th IEEE Conference on Circuits, Systems, and Computers.* New York: The Institute of Electrical and Electronics Engineers, Inc.

Booch, G. November 1981. Introducing Ada. *Proceedings of American Institute of Aeronautics and Astronautics Conference.* Dayton, Ohio.

Booch, G., and Bolz, D. 1981. *Software Engineering with Ada* (course notes). Colorado Springs, Colorado: Department of Computer Science, USAF Academy.

Bowles, K. L. June 1982. The Impact of Ada on Software Engineering. Paper presented at National Computer Conference. New York: Association of Computing Machinery Press.

Braun, C. L. June 1981. Ada: Programming in the 80's. *Computer* 14(6).

Brender, R. F., and Nassi, I. R. June 1981. What is Ada? *Computer* 14(6).

Carlson, W. E. March 1980. Ada: A Standard Language for Defense Systems. *Signal.*

Carlson, W. E. June 1981. Ada: A Promising Beginning. *Computer* 14(6).

Carlson, W. E.; Druffel, L. E.; Fisher, D. A.; and Whitaker, W. A. October 1980. Introducing Ada. *Proceedings of ACM-80.* New York: Associa-tion of Computing Machinery Press.

Cohen, P. M. July/August 1981. From HOLWG to AJPO-Ada in Transition. *Ada Letters* 1(1).

Cornhill, D., and Gordon, M. E. September 1, 1980. Ada—The Latest Words in Process Control. *Electronic Design.*

Devlin, M. T. 1980. *Introducing Ada: Problems and Potentials.* Sunnyvale, CA: USAF Satellite Control Facility.

Estell, R. G. March 1978. A Chapter in the History of DoD-1. *SIGPLAN Notices* 13(3).

Filipski, G. L.; Moore, D. R.; and Newton, J. E. November 1980. Ada as a Software Transition Tool. *SIGPLAN Notices* 15(11).

Fisher, D. A. October 31, 1977. The Common Programming Language Effort in the Department of Defense. Paper presented at Computers in Aerospace Conference.

Fisher, D. A. March 1978. DoD's Common Programming Language Effort. *Computer* 11(3).

Glass, R. L. July 1979. From Pascal to Pebbleman...and Beyond. *Datamation* 25(8).

Gross, S. September 22, 1980. Ada Language Finds Wide Acceptance. *Electronic News.*

Halloran, R. November 30, 1980. Pentagon Pins Its Hopes on Ada. *New York Times.*

Hibbard, P.; Hisgen, A.; Rosenberg, J.; and Sherman, M. October 1980. *Programming in Ada: Examples.* Report CMU-CS-80-149. Pittsburgh, PA: Department of Computer Science, Carnegie-Mellon University.

Hibbard, P.; Hisgen, A.; Rosenberg, J.; Shaw, M.; and Sherman, M. 1983. *Studies in Ada Style,* 2nd ed. New York: Springer-Verlag.

Ichbiah, J.; Barnes, J.; and Firth, R. December 1980. *Ada Programming Course.* La Cella Saint Cloud, France: ALSYS.

Johnson, R. C. February 10, 1981. Ada: The Ultimate Language? *Electronics.*

Kamijo, F. 1978. *A New Programming Language—HOL Project of DoD.* Tokyo: Information Processing Society of Japan.

Kling, R., and Scacchi, W. February 1979. The DoD Common High Order Programming Language Effort (DoD-1): What Will the Impacts Be? *SIGPLAN Notices* 14(2).

Kunits, J. K. December 1992. Evaluating Software Costs. *Clavier* 31(10).

LeBlanc, R. J., and Goda, J. J. April 1981. The Impact of Ada on Software Development. *Proceedings of SOUTHEASTCON 81.*

Ledgard, H. 1981. *Ada—An Introduction.* New York: Springer-Verlag.

Lomuto, N. June 1982. Early Experiences with Ada Tasks. Paper presented to National Computer Conference. New York: Association of Computing Machinery Press.

Loveman, D. May 1981. Ada: How Big a Difference Will It Make in Software? *Military Electronic/Countermeasures.*

Mathis, R. F. March/April 1981. Names for Programming Languages: A Dubious Analysis. *Ada Letters* 1(2).

Mayoh, B. 1981. *Problem Solving with Ada.* New York: Wiley.

Moore, D. 1981. *Ada Course Notes.* Los Angeles: Integrated Computer Systems.

Morrison, D. C. January 14, 1989. Software Crisis. *National Journal* 21(2).

Pyle, I. C. 1985. *The Ada Programming Language: A Guide For Programmers.* 2nd ed. Englewood Cliffs, NJ: Prentice-Hall, Inc.

Rymer, J. October 1980. An Ada Tutorial. *IBM Software Engineering Exchange.* Bethesda, MD: IBM Federal Systems Division.

Schwartz, L. 1981. *Ada Course Notes.* Bethesda, MD: IBM Federal Systems Division.

Waugh, D. W. October, 1980. Ada as a Design Language. *IBM Software Engineering Exchange.* Bethesda, MD: IBM Federal Systems Division.

Wegner, P. W. December 1979. Programming with Ada—An Introduction by Means of Graduated Examples. *SIGPLAN Notices* 14(12).

Wegner, P. W. 1980. *Programming with Ada—An Introduction by Means of Graduated Examples.* Englewood Cliffs, NJ: Prentice-Hall.

Wegner, P. W. April 1980. The Ada Language and Environment. *SIGSOFT Software Engineering Notes.*

Wegner, P. W. October 1981. An Ada Self-Assessment. *Communications of the ACM* 24(10).

Werner, F. October 5, 1981. Is Ada the Programming Language for the '80's? *Computerworld.*

Wheeler, T. J. 1982. *Embedded Systems Design with Ada as the System Design Language.* Ft. Monmouth, NJ: Army CORADCOM.

Whitaker, W. A. February 1978. The U.S. Department of Defense Common High Order Language Effort. *SIGPLAN Notices* 14(2).

Whitaker, W. A. 1979. Ada—The DoD Common High Order Language. National Aerospace and Electronics Conference.

Whitaker, W. A. July 1979. Ada—The New Standard High DoD Order Language. 1979 Summer Computer Simulation Conference.

Wolf, M. I.; Babich, W.; Simpson, R.; Tholl, R.; and Weissman, L. June 1981. The Ada Language System. *Computer* 14(6).

Language Technical Issues

Ada Compiler Validation Capability. February 1980. Report 1067-1.1. Waltham, Mass: SofTech, Inc.

Ada Language Reference Card. March 1981. Cambridge, MA: Intermetrics Inc.

Ada Test and Evaluation. February 1981. Report IR-663. Cambridge, MA: Intermetrics Inc.

Computer Experts Discuss Merits of Defense Dept. Software Plan. April 1990. *Aviation Week and Space Technology* 132(16).

Defense Advanced Research Projects. October 23–26, 1979. *Ada Test and Evaluation Workshop.* Washington, D.C.: United States Department of Defense.

Defense Advanced Research Projects Agency. January 1980. *DoD Common High Order Language, Phase II Reports and Analyses.* Report ADA-80-1-M. Washington, D.C.: United States Department of Defense.

Department of Industry. April 1979. *Red/Green Evaluation Report.* Washington, D.C.: United States Department of Defense.

Diana Reference Manual. March 1981. Report 1/81. Institut fur Informatik II, Universitat Karlsruhe. Pittsburgh, PA: Department of Computer Science, Carnegie-Mellon University.

Engineering Specifications of the iAPX 432 Extensions to Ada. January 1981. Manual 171871-001. Aloha, OR: Intel Corp.

Foundation for Competitiveness and Profitability: FS2000 System, Rational, and Ada. 1992. Santa Clara, CA: Rational.

High Order Language Working Group. June 1978. *DoD Common High Order Language, Phase I Reports and Analyses.* Washington, D.C.: United States Department of Defense.

iAPX 432 Object Primer. 1980. Manual 171858-001 Rev. B. Aloha, OR: Intel Corp.

IBM PDL/ADA Language Reference Card. May 1981. Bethesda, MD: IBM Federal Systems Division.

Pentagon DP Battle. November 30, 1992. *Informationweek* 402.

PDL/ADA: DSM Project's Ada—Program Design Language Reference Manual. April 1981. Bethesda, MD: IBM Federal Systems Division.

PDL/Ada. October 1980. *IBM Software Engineering Exchange* 2(1).

Software Technology Development Division. 1981. *Using Selected Features of Ada: A Collection of Papers.* Ft. Monmouth, NJ: CENTACS Center for Tactical Computer Systems, U.S. Army, Communications Electronics Command.

United States Department of Defense. March 1992. *Ada Project Report/Ada 9X Mapping Document, Volume I, Mapping Rationale.* Washington D.C.: Office of the Under Secretary of Defense for Acquisition. Copyright 1993, Intermetrics, Inc.

United States Department of Defense. December 1991. *Ada Project Report/Ada 9X Mapping Document, Volume II, Mapping Specifications.* Washington D.C.: Office of the Under Secretary of Defense for Acquisition. Copyright 1993, Intermetrics, Inc.

United States Department of Defense. December 1991. *Ada Project Report/-Ada 9X Mapping Document, Volume II, Mapping Specifications, Annexes.* Washington DC: Office of the Under Secretary of Defense for Acquisition. Copyright 1993, Intermetrics, Inc.

Abbott, R. December 1980. *Report on Teaching Ada.* Report SAI-81-312-WA. Los Angeles: Science Applications, Inc.

Amoroso, S.; Wegner, P.; Morris, D.; and White, D. January 14, 1977. Language Evaluation Coordinating Committee Report to the High Order Language Working Group. High Order Language Working Group. Washington D.C.: Government Printing Office.

Anderson, C. November 1992. Ada 9X Project Management. *Communications of the ACM* 35(11).

Arnold, R. D. May/June 1981. The Nebula Architecture: Ada Issues. *Ada Letters* 1(3).

Bjorner, D., and Oest, O. N., eds. 1980. *Towards a Formal Description of Ada.* New York: Springer-Verlag.

Boehm, B., and Jocopini, G. May 1966. Flow Diagrams, Turing Machines, and Languages with Only Two Formation Rules. *Communications of the ACM* 6(5).

Booch, G. September 1981. Describing Software Design in Ada. *SIGPLAN Notices* 16(9).

Booch, G. 1991. *Object Oriented Design with Applications.* Redwood City, CA: Benjamin/Cummings Publishing Company, Inc.

Bryan, D. January/February 1987. Dear Ada. *Ada Letters* VII(1).

Burns, A., and Davies, G. L. November/December 1992. Ada 9X Protected Types in Pascal-FC. *ACM Ada Letters* XII(6).

Burns, A., and Wellings, A. J. November/December 1992. In Support of the Ada 9X Real-Time Facilities. *ACM Ada Letters* XII(6).

Clapp, J. A.; Loebenstein, E.; and Rhymer, P. September 1977. *A Cost/Benefit Analysis of High Order Language Standardization.* Report P 78-206. Washington, D.C.: Mitre Corp.

Cole, S. N. March 1981. Ada Syntax Cross Reference. *SIGPLAN Notices* 16(3).

Dahl, F.; Dijkstra, E. W.; and Hoare, C. A. R. 1972. *Structured Programming.* New York: Academic Press.

Dijkstra, E. W. July 1978. DoD-1: The Summing Up. *SIGPLAN Notices* 13(7).

Doscher, H. 1990. An Ada Case Study in Cellular Telephone Testing Tools. In B. Lynch, ed. *Ada Experiences and Prospects, Proceedings of Ada-Europe '90.* New York: Cambridge University Press.

Druffel, L. E. September 1979. Ada—How Will It Affect College Offerings? *Interface.*

Duncan, A. G., and Hutchinson, J. S. November 1980. Using Ada for Industrial Embedded Microprocessor Applications. *SIGPLAN Notices* 15(11).

Galkowski, J. T. June 1980. A Critique of the DoD Common Language Effort. *SIGPLAN Notices* 15(6).

Giese, C., and Mitchell, J. February 1981. *Ada—A Suitable Replacement for COBOL?* Ft. Monmouth, NJ: U.S. Army Institute for Research.

Good, D. I.; Young, W. D.; and Tripathi, A. R. September 1980. *An Evaluation of the Verifiability of Ada.* Unpublished report.

Goodenough, J. B. June 1981. The Ada Compiler Validation Capability. *Computer* 14(6).

Goos, G., and Hartmanis, J., eds. 1977. *Design and Implementation of Programming Languages. DoD Sponsored Workshop. Ithaca 1976.* New York: Springer-Verlag.

Groves, L. J., and Roger, W. J. November 1980. The Design of a Virtual Machine for Ada. *SIGPLAN Notices* 15(11).

Hart, H. July/August 1982. Ada for Design: An Approach for Transitioning Industry Software Developers. Ada Letters II(1).

Hines, K. December 1990. Ada Impact on a Second Generation Project. *Proceedings of TRI-ADA '90 Conference.* New York: Association of Computing Machinery Press.

Hoare, C. A. R. 1989. Communication Sequential Processes. In C. B. Jones, *Essays in Computing Science.* pp. 259–288. New York: Prentice Hall.

Hoare, C. A. R. 1989. The Emperor's New Clothes. In C. B. Jones, *Essays in Computing Science.* pp. 1–18. New York: Prentice Hall.

Ichbiah, J. D. September 1979. Ada and the Development of Software Components. *Proceedings of the 4th International Conference on Software Engineering.*

Knobe, B. January/February 1981. Flight Languages: Ada vs HAL/S. *Journal for Guidance and Control.*

Loesh, R.; Conover, R.A.; and Malhotra, S. November 1990. JPL's Real-Time Weather Processor Project (RWP): Metrics and Observations at System Completion Build. *Proceedings of the 16th Annual Software Engineering Workshop.* Baltimore, MD: University Park Press.

Loveman, D. September 27, 1980. Ada Defines Reliability as a Basic Feature. *Electronic Design.*

Loveman, D. October 25, 1980. Subprograms and Types Boost Ada Versatility. *Electronic Design.*

Loveman, D. December 6, 1980. Ada Knack for Multitasking Benefits Process Control. *Electronic Design.*

Loveman, D. January 22, 1981. Ada Resolves the Unusual with "Exceptional" Handling. *Electronic Design.*

Luckum, D. C.; Larsen, H. J.; Stevenson, D. R.; and von Henke, F. W. December 7, 1980. *Ada-M: An Ada-based Medium-level Language for Multiprocessing.* Palo Alto, CA: Stanford University.

Mendal, G. O. January/February 1988. Three Reasons to Avoid the Use Clause. *Ada Letters* 8(1).

McGarry, F., and Waligora, S. December 1991. Experiments in Software Engineering Technology. *Proceedings of the 16th Annual Software Engineering Workshop.* Baltimore, MD: University Park Press.

Ploedereder, E. November/December 1992. How to Program in Ada 9X, Using Ada 83. *ACM Ada Letters* XII(6).

Racine, R. May/June 1988. Why the Use Clause is Beneficial. *Ada Letters* VIII(3).

Rattner, J., and Lattin, W. W. February 24, 1981. Ada Determines Architecture of 32-bit Microprocessor. *Electronics.*

Reifer, D. December 1987. Ada's Impact: A Quantitative Assessment. *Proceedings of ACM SIGADA International Conference.* New York: Association of Computing Machinery Press.

Reifer, D. December 1990. Softcost-Ada: User Experiences and Lessons Learned at the Age of Three. *Proceedings of TRI-ADA '90 Conference.* New York: Association of Computing Machinery Press.

Rosen, J. P. November/December 1987. In Defense of the "use" Clause. *Ada Letters* VIII(7).

Rosen, J. P. November 1992. What Orientation Should Ada Objects Take? *Communications of the ACM* 35(11).

Scheer, L., and McClimers, M. 1980. *DoD's Ada Compared to Present Military Standard HOLs: A Look at New Capabilities.* Dayton, OH: Systems Consultants, Inc.

Taft, S. T. November 1992. Ada 9X: A Technical Summary. *Communications of the ACM* 35(11).

Tanaka, K. 1991. Using Ada at NTT. *Ada Letters* XI(1).

Walters, N. May 1991. Requirements Specification for Ada Software Under Dod-Std-2176A. *The Journal of Systems and Software* 15(2).

Wrege, D. E. November/December 1992. Protected Kernels and Ada 9X Real-Time Facilities. *ACM Ada Letters* XII(6).

Whitaker, W. A. October 26, 1978. *Professor Dijkstra's SIGPLAN Letter.* Defense Advance Research Projects Agency Memorandum for the Record. Washington, D.C.: Government Printing Office.

Winterstein, G.; Peusih, G.; Drossopoulous, S.; and Dausmann. September 1981. *Ada Documentation and Programming Guidelines.* Universitat Karlsruhe: Institu fur Informatik II.

Zeigler, S.; Allegre, N.; Johnson, R.; Morris, J.; and Burns, G. June 1981. Ada for the Intel 432 Microcomputer. *Computer* 14(6).

Programming Environment Issues

Buxton, J. N.; and Druffel, L. E. October 1980. Requirements for an Ada Programming Support Environment; Rationale for Stoneman. *Proceedings of COMPSAC.*

Buxton, J. N., Druffel, L. E.; and Standish, T. A. July/August 1981. Recollections on the History of Ada Environments. *Ada Letters* I(1).

DoD High Order Language Working Group. November 27, 1979. *Ada Environment Workshop.* Washington, D.C.: United States Department of Defense.

Elzer, P. F. May 1979. *Some Observations Concerning Existing Software Environments.* DORNIER Systems. Unpublished DoD Report.

Fisher, D. A. October 1980. *Design Issues for Ada Program Support Environments: A Catalog of Issues.* Report SAI-81-289-WA. Washington, D.C.: Science Applications Inc.

Loveman, D. March/April, 1981. The Ada Integrated Environment: An Introduction to the Problem. *Ada Letters* I(3).

Standish, T. A. June 1978. *Proceedings of the Irvine Workshop on Alternatives for the Environment, Certification, and Control of the DoD Common High Order Language.* Report UCI-ICS-78-83. Irvine, CA: Department of Information and Computer Science, University of California.

Standish, T. A. June 1982. The Importance of Ada Programming Support Environments. Paper presented at National Computer Conference. New York: Association of Computing Machinery Press.

Stenning, V.; Froggatt, T.; Gilbert, R.; and Thomas, E. June 1981. The Ada Environment: A Perspective. *Computer* 14(6).

Requirements and Specifications

Ada Compiler Validation Implementer's Guide. October 1, 1980. Report 1067-2.3. Waltham, MA: SofTech Inc.

Booch, G. September 1981. Describing Software Design with Ada. *SIGPLAN Notices* 16(9).

Booch, G. March/April 1982. Object-Oriented Design. *Ada Letters* 1(3):64.

Booch, G. September 1992. The Booch Method Notation, Part I. *Computer Language* 9(9).

See also Booch, G. October 1992. The Booch Method Notation, Part II. *Computer Language* 9(10).

Defense Advanced Research Projects Agency. July 1975. *Department of Defense Requirements for High Order Programming Language— "STRAWMAN."* Washington, D.C.: Government Printing Office.

Defense Advanced Research Projects Agency. August 1975. *Department of Defense Requirements for High Order Programming Languages— "WOODENMAN."* Washington, D.C.: Government Printing Office.

Defense Advanced Research Projects Agency. June 1976. *Department of Defense Requirements for High Order Programming Languages—"TINMAN."* Washington, D.C.: Government Printing Office.

Defense Advanced Research Projects Agency. January 1977. *Department of Defense Requirements for High Order Programming Languages—"IRONMAN."* Washington, D.C.: Government Printing Office.

Defense Advanced Research Projects Agency. July 1977. *Department of Defense Requirements for High Order Programming Languages— Revised "IRONMAN."* Washington, D.C.: Government Printing Office.

Defense Advanced Research Projects Agency. June 1978. *Department of Defense Requirements for High Order Programming Languages— "STEELMAN."* Washington, D.C.: Government Printing Office.

Defense Advanced Research Projects Agency. July 1978. *Department of Defense Requirements for the Programming Environment for the Common High Order Language—"PEBBLEMAN."* Washington, D..C: Government Printing Office.

Defense Advanced Research Projects Agency. July 1978. *Department of Defense Requirements for the Programming Environment for the Common High Order Language—"SANDMAN."* Washington, D.C.: Government Printing Office.

Defense Advanced Research Projects Agency. January 1979. *Department of Defense Requirements for the Programming Environment for the Common High Order Language—Revised "PEBBLEMAN."* Washington, D.C.: Government Printing Office.

Defense Advanced Research Projects Agency. November 1979. *Department of Defense Requirements for the Programming Environment for the Common High Order Language—Preliminary "STONEMAN."* Washington, D.C.: Government Printing Office.

Defense Advanced Research Projects Agency. February 1980. *Department of Defense Requirements for the Programming Environment for the Common High Order Language—"STONEMAN."* Washington, D.C.: Government Printing Office.

Department of Defense. October 30, 1968. *Specifications Practices.* MIL-STD-490 (USAF). Washington, D.C.: Government Printing Office.

Department of Defense. March 21, 1979. *Configuration Management Practices for Systems, Equipment, Munitions, and Computer Programs, Note 2.* MIL-STD-483 (USAF). Washington, D.C.: Government Printing Office.

Department of Defense, Ada Joint Program Office. 1983. *Reference Manual for the Ada Programming Language (ANSI/MIL-STD-1815A).* Washington, D.C.: Government Printing Office.

Fisher, D. A. June 1976. *A Common Programming Language for the Department of Defense—Background and Technical Issues.* Report P-1191. Arlington, VA: Institute for Defense Analysis.

Formal Definition of the Ada Programming Language. November 1980. Cii, France: Honeywell Inc. Honeywell-Bull and India.

Informal Language Specification (Red). March 1979. Cambridge, MA: Intermetrics Inc.

Preliminary Ada Reference Manual. June 1979. *SIGPLAN Notices* 14(6).

Rationale for the Design of the Green Programming Language. February 15, 1978. Cii, France: Honeywell and Cii Honeywell-Bull.

Red Language Design Rationale. March 1979. Report IR-382. Cambridge, MA: Intermetrics Inc.

Red Language Reference Manual. March 1979. Report IR-310.2. Cambridge, MA: Intermetrics Inc.

Reference Manual for the Green Programming Language. March 15, 1979. Cii, France: Honeywell and Cii Honeywell-Bull.

Software Methods

Abbott, R. J. November 1983. Program Design by Informal Descriptions. *Communications of the ACM* 26(11).

Balzer, R.; Goldman, N.; and Wile, D. March 1978. Informality in Program Specification. *IEEE Transactions on Software Engineering* SE-4(2).

Boehm, B. W., and Ross, R. July 1989. Theory-W Software Project Management: Principles and Examples. *IEEE Transactions on Software Engineering* 15(7).

Boehm, C., and Jocopini, G. May 1966. Flow Diagrams, Turing Machines, and Languages with Only Two Formation Rules. *Communications of the ACM.* p. 366–371.

Booch, G. September 1981. Describing Software Design with Ada. *SIGPLAN Notices* 16(9).

Booch, G. March/April 1982. Object Oriented Design. *Ada Letters* II(3).

Booch, G. March 1986. Object-Oriented Development. *IEEE Transactions on Software Engineering* 12(3).

Booch, G. 1990. On the Concepts of Objected-Oriented Design. In P.A. Ng., R. T. Yeh, eds. *Modern Software Engineering, Foundations and Current Prospectives.* New York: Van Nostrand Reinhold Co. p. 165–204.

Booch, G. 1991. *Object-Oriented Design with Applications.* Reading, MA: Addison-Wesley Publishing Co.

Booch, G. September 1992. The Booch Method Notation, Part I. Computer Method Notation, Part I. *Computer Language* 9(9).

Booch, G. October 1992. The Booch Method Notation, Part II. *Computer Language* 9(10).

Borger, M. W., and Goodenough, J. B. Fall 1990. Real-Time Ada Issues: Proceeding of 4th International Workshop. *Ada Letters* X (9):65–69.

Collard, P. September/October 1989. Object-Oriented Programming Techniques with Ada. *Ada Letters* IX(6):119–126.

Connell, J. L. 1989. *Structured Rapid Prototyping: An Evolutionary Approach to Software Development.* Englewood Cliffs, NJ: Yourdon Press.

Dijkstra, E. W. September 1965. Programming Considered as a Human Activity. Paper presented to the International Federation of Information Processing Conference, New York. p. 6.

Dijkstra, E. W. October 1972. The Humble Programmer. *Communications of the ACM* 15(10).

Downs, E. 1988. *Structured System Analysis and Design Method: Application and Context.* Englewood Cliffs, NJ: Prentice-Hall.

Gane, C. 1979. *Structured System Analysis: Tools and Techniques.* Englewood Cliffs, NJ: Prentice-Hall.

Graham, I. 1991. *Object-Oriented Methods.* Reading, MA: Addison-Wesley Publishing Co.

Hart, H. October 14, 1981. Ada for Design: An Approach for Transitioning Industry Software Developers. *NSIA Software Group Conference.*

Hoare, C. A. R. 1972. Notes on Data Structuring. In Dahl, O. J.; Dijkstra, E. W.; and Hoare, C. A. R. *Structured Programming.* New York: Academic Press.

Hoare, C. A. R. December 1989. Formal Methods in Computer System Design. *Computer Physics Communications* 57(1/3).

Jackson, M. 1975. *Principles of Program Design.* New York: Academic Press.

Jackson, M. 1978. The Jackson Design Methodology. Infotec State of the Art Report, Structured Programming.

Jackson, M. A. 1983. *System Development.* Englewood Cliffs, NJ: Prentice-Hall.

Jensen, R. W. March 1981. Structured Programs. *Computer* 14(3).

King, D. 1988. *Creating Effective Software: Computer Program Design Using the Jackson Methodology.* Englewood Cliffs, NJ: Yourdon Press.

King, M. J. 1985. *Program Design Using JSP : A Practical Introduction.* New York: Wiley.

LaBudde, K. P. 1987. *Structured Programming Concepts.* New York: McGraw-Hill.

Ledgard, H., and Marcotty, M. 1981. *The Programming Language Landscape.* Chicago: Science Research Associates.

Orr, K.; Gane, C.; and Yourdon, E. April 1989. Methodology: The Experts Speak. *Byte* 14(4).

Overmyer, S. P. October, 1990. DoD-Std-2167A and Methodologies. *SIGSOFT Software Engineering Notes* 15(5).

Parnas, D. L. February 1971. *Information Distribution Aspects of Design Methodology.* Pittsburgh, PA: Computer Science Department, Carnegie-Mellon University.

Parnas, D. L. March 1971. *A Paradigm for Software Module Specification with Examples.* Pittsburgh, PA: Computer Science Department, Carnegie-Mellon University.

Parnas, D. L. December 1972. On the Criteria to Be Used in Decomposing Systems into Modules. *Communications of the ACM* 15(12).

Perkins, J. 1989. Programming Practices: Analysis of Ada Source Developed for the Air Force, Army, and Navy. *Ada Technology in Context: Application, Development, and Deployment. TriAda '89 Proceedings.* New York: Association of Computing Machinery Press.

Polack, D. L. January 1990. Practical CASE Tools for DoD Projects. *SIGSOFT Software Engineering Notes* 15(1).

Pyle, I. C. May 1991. Real-World Software Engineering. *Software Engineering Journal* 6(3).

Ross, D. T., and Brackett, J. W. September 1976. An Approach to Structured Analysis. *Computer Decisions.*

Ross, D. T., Goodenough, J. B.; and Irvine, C. A. May 1975. Software Engineering: Process, Principles, and Goals. *Computer.*

Ross, D. T.; and Schoman, K. E. January 1977. Structured Analysis for Requirements Definition. *IEEE Transactions on Software Engineering* SE-3(1).

Sommerville, I. 1992. *Software Engineering,* 4th ed. Reading, MA: Addison-Wesley.

Sommerville, I., and Morrison, R. 1987. *Software Development with Ada.* Reading, MA: Addison-Wesley.

Springman, M. 1989. Incremental Software Test Approach for Dod-STD-2167A Ada Projects. *Ada Technology in Context: Application, Development, and Deployment. TriAda '89 Proceedings.* New York: Association of Computing Machinery Press.

Springman, M. 1989. Software Design Documentation Approach for a Dod-STD-2167A Ada Project. *Ada Technology in Context: Application, Development, and Deployment. TriAda '89 Proceedings.* New York: Association of Computing Machinery Press.

Thayer, R. H.; Pyster, A.; and Wood, R. August 1980. The Challenge of Software Engineering Project Management. *Computer.*

Urban, J. March 1989. Advances in Software Engineering for Ada Technology. *IEEE Transactions on Software Engineering* 15(3): 233-234.

Whitcomb, M; and Clark, B. 1989. Pragmatic Definition of an Object-Oriented Development Process for Ada. *Ada Technology in Context: Application, Development, and Deployment. TriAda '89 Proceedings.* New York: Association of Computing Machinery Press.

Wirth, N. December 1974. On the Composition of Well-Structured Programs. *Computing Surveys* 6(4).

Wulf, W. A. 1977. Languages and Structured Programs. In R. Yeh, ed. *Current Trends in Computer Programming,* Vol. 1. Englewood Cliffs, NJ: Prentice-Hall, Inc.

Yeung, W. L., and Topping, G. July 1990. Implementing JSD Designs in Ada: A Tutorial. *Software Engineering Notes* 15(3).

Yourdon, E. 1979. *Structured Walkthroughs,* 2nd ed. Englewood Cliffs, NJ: Prentice-Hall.

Yourdon, E., and Constantine, L. 1979. *Structured Design: Fundamentals of a Discipline of Computer Program and System Design.* Englewood Cliffs, NJ: Prentice-Hall.

Zelkowitz, M. V. June 1978. Perspectives on Software Engineering. *Computer Surveys* 10(2).

Special References

Caglayan, M. U.; van Wigen, J. W.; and Huskey, V. R. August 1981. On the Poetic Connection of Ada. *Communications of the ACM* 24(8).

Foss, D. J., and Hakes, D. T. 1978. *Psycholinguistics: An Introduction to the Psychology of Language.* Englewood Cliffs, NJ: Prentice-Hall.

Gall, J. 1977. *Systemantics: How Systems Work and Especially How They Fail.* New York: Times Books.

Hoare, C. A. R. July 1981. Professionalism. Paper presented to British Computing Society, London.

Hofstadter, D. R. 1979. *Godel, Escher, Bach: An Eternal Golden Braid.* New York: Basic Books.

Miller, G. A. March 1956. The Magical Number Seven, Plus or Minus Two. *Psychological Review* 63(2).

Moore, D. L. 1977. *Ada, Countess of Lovelace: Byron's Legitimate Daughter.* New York: Harper & Row.

Wegner, P. May 1981. Ada—The Poetic Connection. *Communications of the ACM* 24(5).

Weinberg, G. M. 1971. *The Psychology of Computer Programming.* New York: Von Nostrand Reinhold.

Index

Symbols

& (catenation operator), 176, 178
** (exponentiation operator), 175
* (multiplication operator), 176, 177–178
* (operator symbol), overload and, 154
+ (addition operator), 176, 178
+ (unary identity operator), 176, 178
- (subtraction operator), 176, 178
- (unary negation operator), 176, 178
— (double hyphen), as comment indicator, 52
. (dot notation), for designated object, 169
.. (double dot), as range bound indicator, 97
/ (division operator), 176, 177, 178
/= (inequality operator), 176, 178–179
   overload and, 154, 174
   visibility and, 221

:= (compound symbol), in assignment statements, 181
; (semicolon), statements terminated by, 181
< (generic formal subprogram parameter), 255
< (less than operator), 176, 178–179
<= (less than or equal to operator), 176, 178–179
<> (compound symbol), in generic subprogram parameters, 252
= (equality operator), 176, 178–179, 221
> (greater than operator), 176, 178–179
>= (greater than or equal operator), 176, 178–179
| (vertical bar), record structure and, 49, 52, 114

abort statement, 301
abs (absolute values operator), 176, 178
abstract data types
   data base system and, 145, 146, 206, 211
   multiple objects as, 77
   operations for, 164
   operator (overload) symbols and, 57
   package applications, 227, 232–236
   private types for creating, 55, 121–124
   subprograms and, 164
abstract-state machines
   generic units as templates for, 255–256
   initialization and, 80
   interface and, 84, 85
   local objects and, 201
   objects declared inside package, 201
   package applications, 227, 237–240
   single objects as, 76–77
abstraction, 73
   See also data abstraction
   completeness and, 24
   concept of, 21–23, 89–90
   data types and, 55, 56, 94
   derived types and, 127
   enforcing, 83

   information hiding and, 22
   integer range constraints and, 97–98
   interface as, 39–40, 83
   ladder of, 21, 77, 90, 94
   levels of, exception handling and, 325
   object declarations and, 129–131
   in object-oriented design, 40
   packages as support for, 60–61, 217, 224–226
   primitive operations and, 139
   private types and, 55, 121–124, 224–226, 233
   representation specifications and, 338
   as software engineering principle, 21–23
   subprograms for creating, 59
accept statements
   in environment monitoring, 360–364
   exception handling with, 328–329
   role of, 62
   in task body, 291, 292
   task communication and, 295
access objects, 115–116, 117
access types, 53, 55, 94, 115–121, 122
accuracy
   in fixed-point type, 101
   in subtypes, 125
actor/server tasks, 287